Great Lakes Books

A complete listing of the books in this series can be found online at wsupress.wayne.edu

United States District Court for the Eastern District of Michigan

People, Law, and Politics

David Gardner Chardavoyne

Wayne State University Press, Detroit

16 15 14 13 12   5 4 3 2 1

Library of Congress Cataloging-in-Publication Data
Chardavoyne, David G.
United states District Court for the Eastern District of Michigan : people, law, and politics / David Gardner Chardavoyne.
p. cm.
Includes bibliographical references and index.
ISBN 978-0-8143-3461-4 (cloth : alk. paper) — ISBN 978-0-8143-3720-2 (e-book)
1. United States. District Court (Michigan : Eastern District) 2. Justice, Administration—Michigan—History. 3. Judges—Michigan—History. I. United States. District Court (Michigan : Eastern District) II. Title.
KF8755.M52C48 2012
347.73'2209774—dc23   2011042966

∞

Designed by BookComp, Inc.
Typeset by BookComp, Inc.
Composed in ITC Bookman and Avenir

Dedicated to the memories of my parents,
Seward Reeve Chardavoyne and Miriam Gardner Chardavoyne,
and of my sister Susan Bates Chardavoyne.

Grateful acknowledgment is made to the following, whose financial support has made this volume possible:

United States District Court for the Eastern District of Michigan
Ralph M. and Emmalyn E. Freeman Fund
Theodore Levin Memorial Fund
Michigan State Bar Foundation
Knudsen Family Fund

Funding for this publication does not constitute an endorsement of any content or opinion expressed in it.

Contents

List of Illustrations

Foreword

Why write a history of the United States District Court for the Eastern District of Michigan? The best answer is found in the words of the Judicial Conference of the United States, the manager of the federal court system, to Congress in 1988, when it urged that the Federal Judicial Center, the educational and research arm of the federal court, be given the authority to establish a history program. The Conference said:

> Knowing how things came to be the way they are contributes substantially to any assessment of current effectiveness and to appreciating the promise of proposals for change.

Congress said yes to establishing such a program on November 19, 1998, with the enactment of Public Law 100-72, the Judicial Improvements and Access to Justice Act.

Stimulated by the Federal Judicial Center's establishment of its History Office, Chief Judge Julian Abele Cook, Jr., in 1991, appointed a Court History Committee for the district court, the first members of which were Professor Philip P. Mason of Wayne State University; attorney Dennis J. LeVasseur; David R. Sherwood, then chief of court operations; and Judith K. Christie, administrative manager.

The committee, early in 1992, sponsored the incorporation of The Historical Society for the Eastern District of Michigan. The first members of its Board of Trustees were Dores McGree, Stanley J.Winkelman, Dennis J. LeVasseur, Professor Harold Norris of the Detroit College of Law, and Joe H. Stroud. Professor Mason was appointed advisor to the board.

One of the purposes of the society, stated in its Articles of Incorporation was, "to increase the public knowledge of the United States District Court for the Eastern District of Michigan and its place in American history." Over the years, the society has engaged in multiple activities in fulfillment of its purposes, including regularly publishing a newsletter, *The Court Legacy*, maintaining a portrait fund for refurbishing portraits of the judges displayed in the courthouse, opening a historical museum in the courthouse, maintaining a website, sponsoring a speaker at a yearly luncheon in cooperation with the Eastern District of Michigan chapter of the Federal Bar Association, and sponsoring oral histories of senior and retired judges.

The first board early on adopted a five-year plan for the operation of the society, which included "sponsor[ing] the research and writing of the definitive history of the Court." It took a bit longer than five years to achieve that goal. The realization of the goal is David Chardavoyne's *The United States District Court for the Eastern District of Michigan 1837–2010: People, Law, and Politics.*

This history of the court, initially known as the Court for the District of Michigan, begins with its establishment by Congress simultaneously with admission of the state of Michigan to the Union and the appointment of Ross Wilkins as district judge by President Andrew Jackson.

In 2007, Michael Lavoie, president of the society, established a committee to consider the advisability of publishing a history of the district court with the encouragement of Chief Judge Bernard A. Friedman. A year later, David Chardavoyne was selected as the author of the history; I. W. Winsten and Ross Parker were designated to oversee the writing of the history and its publication by Wayne State University Press.

Thanks to the financial assistance of the Ralph and Emmalyn E. Freeman Fund, the Knudsen Family Foundation, the Theodore Levin Memorial Foundation, the State Bar of Michigan Foundation, and the United States District Court for the Eastern District of Michigan, the history of the court is a reality. Obviously, funding does not constitute an endorsement of the contents of the history or any opinions expressed in it. Content and opinion are solely those of the author, to whom much thanks is due for assuring, in the words of the late Joe Stroud, former chair of the Newsletter Committee of the society, in the first issue of *The Court Legacy*, "[Assuring] that the Court's role in the history of Michigan and the nation is recorded, preserved and celebrated." Thanks are also expressed to Chief Judge Gerald E. Rosen, on whose watch the book will become, in judge-speak, "part of the record."

Avern L. Cohn
United States District Judge
Eastern District of Michigan

Introduction

Tute rien turnë en declin,
tut chiet, tut moert, tut trait a fin;
tur funt, mur chiet, rose flaistrist,
cheval trebuche, drap viescist,
huem muert, fer use, fust purrist,
tute rien faite od mein perist.
Bien entendu e cunuis e sai
que tuit murrunt e clerc e lai,
e que mult ad curte duree
enprés la mort lur renumee,
si par clerc nen est mis en livre;
ne poet par el durer ne vivre.

All things decline,
All fall, all die, all draw to an end;
A tower tumbles, a wall falls, a rose withers,
A horse stumbles, clothes wear out,
A man dies, iron rusts, wood rots,
Everything made by hand perishes.
I understand well and know
That all men die, both clerk and lay,
And so will, only a short time
After death, their renown,
If a scribe does not put it in a book;
In no other way can it last or live.[1]

This is a history of the United States District Court for the Eastern District of Michigan, a federal court that came into existence in 1863. It is also, by necessity, a history of three extinct federal courts: the United States Circuit Court for the Eastern District of Michigan (1863–1912) and the United States District and Circuit Courts for the District of Michigan (1837–1863). Together these four courts have provided a federal forum and presence in the state of Michigan for a century and three quarters. All of them were

1

and are essentially trial courts, or "courts of original jurisdiction," places where masses of new cases are filed and litigated, where judges and juries see the parties and hear witnesses testify, where criminal defendants are convicted or acquitted, and where civil judgments are granted or denied. Although individual decisions on federal law by the U.S. Courts of Appeals and the U.S. Supreme Court obviously carry greater authority, district courts render an enormously greater number of such decisions, very few of which are appealed, and most of those that are appealed are affirmed; district courts are also where most citizens make contact with federal courts.[2] Judge Charles S. Simons of the Eastern District and later of the U.S. Circuit Court of Appeals for the Sixth Circuit often said that a United States district judge held more sheer power over the lives and property of litigants than any other member of the judiciary.

The subtitle of this book begins with "people" because its stories are about people. My experience with the district court for the Eastern District of Michigan began in 1976 when District Judge James Harvey hired me straight out of Wayne State University Law School in Detroit to be one of his three law clerks. Judge Harvey was, I believe, the only U.S. district judge authorized at that time to hire more than the standard two clerks at one time, a consequence of the burden he bore in his assignment to preside alone over proceedings in two courthouses, the district court's outposts in Flint and Bay City. I learned many things from Judge Harvey, not the least being that I was not as smart or wise as I thought I was. He also taught me the importance of preparation[3] and precision, and the value of mercy and discretion, particularly for young offenders who came before him. The most important lesson I learned during my two years with Judge Harvey was that cases, decisions, and opinions are not just words in books I read in law school; they are about real people with real problems who make real mistakes that have real consequences.

For me, people and their stories are the main reason to write about a court or about any other subject for that matter. Memorializing people who played some part in the life of the court is also a goal of the project's sponsor, the Historical Society for the United States District Court for the Eastern District of Michigan. Consequently, the book is principally a chronicle of people and events placed and judged in their historical context.[4]

The second word of the subtitle, "law," is a natural part of the history of any court, the "rules of decision" in their relentless increase in number and complexity. For a U.S. district court, law comes in two main categories: federal laws (the United States Constitution, the statute laws enacted by Congress, the regulations developed by administrative bodies, and certain unwritten laws such as those controlling admiralty and maritime cases) and state laws (state statutes and the vast realm of the unwritten common law), which control, for example, suits between citizens of different states or between an American citizen and a citizen of a foreign country. Although they can be very different in subject matter and scope, federal and state laws do have at least one common denominator: unless a law contains some constitutional defect, judges have very little if anything to say about what Congress and state legislatures enact. We all want justice, and judges hope to do justice, but because justice is an amorphous and subjective concept, judges are bound to decide cases according to the law.

Applying the law can be difficult, even painful, but time after time judges of the courts described here have set aside their personal feelings and decided cases in accordance with the law. Not that the law leaves them with no discretion: law is not mathematics. To the contrary, most laws leave some room for a judge to exercise discretion, and as Justice Sandra Day O'Connor has noted, "Each of us brings to our job, whatever it is, our lifetime of experience and values." This is especially so in those cases in which a trial judge determines the facts without a jury. Two judges from the same court can listen to the same testimony and read the same exhibits, yet come to categorically different conclusions about the facts. The reality, though, is that usually only one judge determines the facts in those cases, deciding which testimony to believe and which to reject, in what is often a heated and hostile environment.

This brings us to why the third titular word is "politics." When I asked myself *why* something in the court's history occurred, the answer was always law and/or politics. By politics, I mean not only partisan competition between Whigs and Jeffersonians or between Republicans and Democrats, although there is a goodly amount of that, but in the broader sense of the adjustment of competing interests.[5] Federal courts, including our courts, were born in political compromise and they live and operate in political compromise. Congress, that bastion of politics, determines what the laws are, which cases the court can decide and which it cannot, who gets to be a judge and how many there are, how many courthouses there are and where they are situated, what geographical areas each courthouse draws its cases from, and a host of other decisions relating to the jurisdiction and operations of the court. In making those decisions, Congress is strongly influenced by state, local, and personal interests. The value of the role politics plays in such decisions may be negative at times, but not always. As we shall see, some of the best judges ever to serve on the district's courts might never have been appointed if it were not for politics.

I must emphasize also what I do not mean by politics. I am not suggesting that federal judges, and particularly judges whose work is discussed in this history, used their decisions to obtain political ends, or that they were for sale, or that they are influenced by the needs and desires of any political party. Absolutely not. I have been observing the district court for 35 years, first as a law clerk, then as a practicing attorney, and now as a writer, and I am convinced that every judge has tried to judge every case fairly and sincerely. Perhaps the greatest invention of the drafters of the

Constitution was the provision in Article III that insulates federal judges from outside influence by granting them tenure for life and the assurance that Congress cannot punish them by reducing their pay.

For sources of references to population, case numbers, trials, or other numbers relating to the business of the courts, please refer to the Bibliographical Notes for sources and words of caution. Those who find legal citation form confusing should also consult the Bibliographical Notes.

Acknowledgments

I could not have written this book without the help of many other people and organizations. First and foremost, I am indebted to United States District Judge Avern L. Cohn, who conceived of a court history many years before I became involved with the project and whose characteristic energy and persistence kept the idea alive. I also thank the Historical Society for the U.S. District Court for the Eastern District of Michigan for selecting me to write this book, for generous financial assistance, and for years of support and encouragement. I am especially thankful to Judith Christie, Geneva Halliday, Magistrate Judge Charles Binder, and Ross Parker for providing incisive comments and assistance as the book progressed.

My research took me to several archives and libraries which patiently provided badly needed assistance and experience. These included the depositories of the U.S. National Archives and Records Administration at Chicago, Illinois, and College Park, Maryland; the Prints and Photographs Division of the Library of Congress in Washington, D.C.; the Library of Michigan at Lansing; the Bentley Historical Library on the North Campus of the University of Michigan, Ann Arbor; the Clarence M. Burton Historical Collection of the Detroit Public Library (with special thanks to Mark Bowden); the Arthur Neef Law Library and the Walter P. Reuther Library, both at Wayne State University, Detroit; the Genesee Historical Collections Center at the University of Michigan's Flint Campus; and the photographic archives of the *Midland Daily News*. During most of the years during which I worked on this book, I was a visiting professor at the University of Detroit-Mercy School of Law, and I very much appreciate the assistance provided by the staff of the school's Kresge Law Library. Finally, thanks to Professor Ellen White of Michigan State University for allowing me to use her maps of the changing borders of the court.

One of the most important developments for researchers over the last decade has been the enormous amounts of information and materials posted on-line. I used too many of those databases to acknowledge each one, but three were particularly helpful: the Law Libraries Microform Consortium (www.llmc.com), the Library of Congress' American Memory Collection (memory.loc.gov/ammem), and the Hathi Trust Digital Library (www.hathitrust.org/).

Notes

1. Wace, *Le Roman de Rou* (*The Tale of Rollo*), Part III, lines 131–142. Wace (ca. 1115–ca. 1183), an Anglo-Norman cleric, was born on the Island of Jersey and was at his death the Canon of Bayeux.

2. See generally, Kevin L. Lyles, *The Gatekeepers: Federal District Courts in the Political Process* (Westport, CN: Praeger, 1997).

3. On most days, the law clerks ate lunch with Judge Harvey. During one lunch, he recalled that after one of his first trials as a young attorney, in which his boss, the redoubtable Carl Smith, Sr., watched him lose to an experienced attorney, he remarked, "Well, I guess you can't beat experience," whereupon Smith gave him a stony stare and replied, "Jim, preparation beats experience."

4. As Thomas Macaulay wrote long ago in his *History of England*, "If we would study with profit the history of our ancestors, we must never forget that the country of which we read was a very different country from that in which we live." Or as a modern historian, Chris Wickham put it, "[E]very period in history has its own identity and legitimacy, which must be seen without hindsight." Chris Wickham, *The Inheritance of Rome: A History of Europe from 400 to 1000* (New York: Viking Penguin, 2009), 6. Another warning by Professor Wickham is also pertinent, "[A]ll our written accounts from the past are bound by narrative conventions, which have to be understood properly before the accounts can be used by historians at all." Idem., 8. Writers in the 19th century tended either to exaggerate praise of their subjects or to hateful vituperation.

5. "The Adjustment of Conflicting Interests" is the title of one of four figures on the ceiling of the Minnesota Supreme Court, this figure representing Raimon VI, Count of Toulouse (1156–1222). On that ceiling, Raimon, a wily medieval survivor, incongruously finds himself in the company of Moses, Confucius, and Socrates.

PART I
The Wilkins Years, 1837–1870

The law is the last result of human wisdom acting upon human experience for the benefit of the public.

—Dr. Samuel Johnson[1]

The first 33 years of the courts of the United States in Michigan were dominated by a single judge, Ross Wilkins. Those years saw Michigan progressing from a lightly populated frontier territory, relying on subsistence farming and a declining market for furs to support its economy, to an established state with burgeoning agricultural and industrial sectors. Throughout this period, Judge Wilkins spent most of his judicial time and energy dealing with collection cases on the civil side and prosecutions of the violators of federal customs and postal laws on the criminal side. Michigan's position on the border with Canada also brought him into contact with key issues of his day, including neutrality and slavery. The Civil War brought tremendous changes to his docket as Congress enacted new federal laws in support of the war effort, including a multitude of new taxes, that he was called on to enforce. Through it all, Judge Wilkins remained the steadfast face of federal law and presence in Michigan.

CHAPTER 1

The Courts of the United States and the District of Michigan in 1837

The Birth and Growth of the Courts of the United States, 1788–1837

At the beginning of the 21st century, Americans take for granted the existence of separate judicial systems, one for each state and one for the federal government, although few other federal countries have federal trial courts. During the first years of the nation, it was not a given that our federal government would have its own courts or that there would be parallel state and federal judiciaries. Logically, the federal government could have taken authority over all courts, but that option was a political impossibility that was never given serious consideration. Alternatively, the enforcement of federal laws and the protection of the federal government's interests could have been delegated entirely to the courts established by the states. That was, in fact, the solution in place from 1781 to 1789, under the first national compact, the Articles of Confederation, which provided for neither a federal supreme court nor federal trial courts. With a few specific exceptions, disputes involving the articles or federal laws were resolved by state and local courts.[2] To supporters, that system not only avoided the expense of a federal court system, it also ensured that federal laws would be interpreted and executed by local judges instead of by officials of a distant and, they feared, tyrannical federal government.

Just a few years' experience proved that the articles were unsatisfactory as a whole and regarding courts in particular. The articles relied on state officers to enforce decisions made under federal law, both by state courts and by the few federal tribunals, but too often they did not.[3] In 1789, delegates from every state gathered in Philadelphia to replace them. Improvement of the judicial system was a source of debate among the delegates. A

9

majority of states agreed on the necessity for a federal court of last resort to provide uniform interpretations of federal law, but a proposal to create a system of "inferior" courts to try cases involving federal laws divided the convention. Some delegates who represented commercial and mercantile interests noted the refusal of state courts to enforce contracts and collect debts during the economic depression that plagued the new nation. They argued that only federal trial courts, immune to local pressure, could ensure national unity and protect the interests of out-of-state litigants. Opponents were more concerned about federal tyranny than unity. George Mason of Virginia spoke for many Americans when he complained that a federal judicial system would "absorb and destroy the judiciaries of the several states, thereby rendering laws as tedious, intricate, and expensive, and justice as unattainable, by a great part of the community, as in England; and enabling the rich to oppress and ruin the poor."[4] Elbridge Gerry, one of the signers of both the Declaration of Independence and the Articles of Confederation, refused to sign the Constitution that emerged from the convention because it did not include a bill of rights and because of his belief "that the judicial department will be oppressive."[5] The provisions on a federal judiciary that emerged from the convention in Article III of the Constitution did mandate a federal supreme court, but did not create a federal court system. Instead, the convention delegates passed the buck to Congress by authorizing the legislative branch to decide whether and when to create federal "inferior courts."[6]

The first Congress convened under the Constitution accepted the drafters' invitation. On September 24, 1789, after months of sometimes bitter debate, it passed a law, now called the Judiciary Act of 1789,[7] which established a federal judiciary still recognizable in the federal courts of the 21st century. The act divided the United States into 13 judicial districts, one for each of the 11 states that had already ratified the Constitution and a second each for Massachusetts and Virginia, known as the districts of Maine and Kentucky, that included remote areas which Congress assumed would eventually become states. When North Carolina and Rhode Island finally ratified the Constitution (in November 1789 and May 1790), Congress added two new judicial districts[8] and did so again as each new state joined the Union. The judiciary act then created, for each district, "a court called a District Court," to consist of one judge "to be called a District Judge," who would "reside in the district for which he is appointed" and hold four district court terms each year.

Thus, district judges were permanent representatives of the federal judiciary in their districts and were the most visible evidence of the entire federal government in many districts. However, the judiciary act also provided for another federal court that brought the justices of the U.S. Supreme Court to the districts for a number of terms every year. The act grouped the district courts, except those of Maine and Kentucky, into three circuits and provided for a circuit court to be held twice annually in each district, presided over by the district's own district judge and two justices of the U.S. Supreme Court, known in this role as circuit justices. Although Congress gradually relieved the circuit justices of parts of that burden, the basic concept of a justice of the Supreme Court spending a substantial portion of his life riding circuit from one district to another continued until the creation of the U.S. Circuit Courts of Appeal in 1891, although justices rarely rode circuit after the Civil War. From the beginning, justices resented attending circuit courts, which required thousands of miles of travel each year over terrible roads, where there were any roads at all.[9]

In addition to creating the Supreme Court and authorizing inferior courts, Article III also affords the justices and judges of those courts, thus known as Article III judges, a degree of job security unknown to most of the rest of the populace, providing the federal judiciary with a shield against political influence and popular pressure. Article III judges are appointed, like many other federal office holders, after being nominated by the president and confirmed by the Senate,[10] but, unlike other federal officers, they hold their offices during good behavior, meaning, in practice, for life unless impeached by the House and convicted by the Senate for serious criminal offenses ("treason, bribery, and other high crimes and misdemeanors"), and their pay "shall not be diminished during their Continuance in Office."[11]

Article III defines "the judicial power of the United States," the outer limits of the types of cases that federal courts have the power (or "subject-matter jurisdiction") to entertain. The judicial power of the United States includes "all cases, in law and equity, arising under this Constitution, the Laws of the United States, and Treaties," cases involving foreign diplomats, cases of admiralty and maritime law, cases involving the United States or between two or more states and what we now call diversity jurisdiction, cases between citizens of different states or between a state and citizens of another state or country, and citizens of the same state claiming land under grants issued by different states. From the beginning, though, Congress assumed that, as the creator of inferior courts, it had the power to withhold some parts of that jurisdiction from them, although not from the Supreme Court. The choices Congress made in allocating this judicial power between circuit and district courts evidence the compromises needed to pass the act. The district courts, which were held by a single district judge, received cases that were either minor (petty crimes against the United States, "cases where no other punishment than whipping, not to exceed thirty stripes, a fine not exceeding one hundred dollars, or a term of imprisonment not exceeding six months is to be inflicted") or clearly national in interest (admiralty cases, seizures of property by the United States, or suits against foreign diplomats). The circuit courts, where the presence of Supreme Court justices on the bench added authority to decisions and moderated any tendency toward excess by a single judge, were allocated all other violations of federal criminal laws. In other areas, Congress provided for federal courts to share jurisdiction with state courts. For example, district courts had concurrent jurisdiction over suits at common law in which the United States was a plaintiff and the amount in controversy exceeded $100. By implication, the federal government could bring smaller cases only in state courts, likely to be closer to the defendant's home. The circuit courts had concurrent jurisdiction, where the amount in controversy exceeded $500, over diversity cases and cases brought by the United States as plaintiff.

The substantial piece of the judicial power of the United States that Congress did not grant to either the circuit or district courts is further evidence of the compromises necessary to pass the 1789 judiciary act. Until 1875, federal trial courts did not have jurisdiction over the first type of case listed in Article III: "all Cases, in Law and Equity, arising under this Constitution, the Laws of the United States." So, unless there was some other basis for asserting jurisdiction, such as diversity of citizenship or a specific grant of jurisdiction in a statute, the inferior federal courts were excluded from enforcing or interpreting the Constitution and the laws passed by Congress. Instead, those tasks were performed by state courts. Today, this "general federal question" jurisdiction constitutes a large and arguably the most important part of a district court's docket, so the obvious question is why Congress kept federal trial courts from deciding such cases for more than 85 years. In part, opponents of federal power feared that federal judges would interpret "laws of the United States" to include the laws of each of the states, and so take power over purely state-law matters. Besides, keeping the interpretation of federal laws in state courts was a further limit on federal power welcomed by many. Other protections won by antifederalists in negotiating the 1789 judiciary act included defining districts by state boundaries and requiring that district judges reside in their district.

Those not welcoming limits on federal courts included President John Adams and a lame-duck Federalist Congress, which passed a new judiciary act[12] on February 13, 1801, just days before the inauguration of President Thomas Jefferson. The 1801 judiciary act granted federal question jurisdiction to district and circuit courts, doubled the number of circuits from three to six, created the position of circuit judge and allocated three of them to each circuit, and created ten new districts. Among these was a "District of Ohio" the which covered the modern states of Ohio, Michigan, Indiana, Illinois, and Wisconsin. The 1801 act was also known derisively as the Midnight Judges Act, because President Adams worked up to the eve of Jefferson's inauguration to fill all new judge positions with his Federalist allies. When the new Jeffersonian Congress convened in April 1802, it passed its own judiciary act, which undid much, but not all, of what Adams had wrought. The 1802 judiciary act[13] kept the six circuits, but did away with the circuit judges, federal question jurisdiction, and the new districts, including the District of Ohio, which was dissolved before its district court ever opened for business. In a gesture to Supreme Court justices who hated riding through the country holding circuit courts, the 1802 act reduced the number of justices required to hold a circuit court to one. If the circuit justice and district judge could not agree on a question of law, the act allowed them to certify the issue to the Supreme Court. As a further sop to the justices, the 1802 act allowed district judges in Maine, Kentucky, and Tennessee to hold circuit courts without a justice, so that no justice had to endure the rigors of travel through the wilderness. There were other changes in the federal courts between 1802 and 1836, but they were mere tinkering, and the 1789 and 1802 judiciary acts were the basis for Michigan's U.S. district court.

The District Judge's Staff

In addition to creating inferior courts and their judges, the 1789 judiciary act provided each district court with four kinds of court officers to assist judges in carrying out their judicial business. These officers included a clerk of the court, a marshal, commissioners, and a district attorney.

The Clerk of the Court.   The act authorized each district judge to appoint a clerk to "enter and record all the orders, decrees, judgments, and pro-ceedings" of the district and circuit courts and to summon jurors.[14] Con-gress was not more specific about the clerk's duties, but the position was well known in colonial America and most of the first federal clerks were borrowed from local courts, so they knew how to go about their business. The federal clerk became the judge's factotum, doing whatever had to be done to keep the court running, from issuing arrest warrants to fixing the courthouse roof.[15] Until 1919, federal court clerks were compensated by fees paid by litigants for the clerk's services [16] and by a per diem sti-pend and reimbursement for expenses if the court traveled.[17] The amount a clerk earned, therefore, depended on the amount of business that par-ticular court attracted. Originally, the clerk was responsible for both the district and circuit courts, but, in 1839, Congress directed the judges of the circuit court (i.e., the district judge and the circuit justice) to appoint a separate clerk for the circuit court,[18] although often the same person held both clerkships until the district's judicial business generated enough in fees, per diem, and travel expenses to support two clerks and their fami-lies. If a court's business grew sufficiently, a federal clerk could employ one or more deputies, but the clerk had to pay them from his fee income, so that most clerks kept deputies to a minimum or hired their children or their relatives as deputy clerks.

The United States Marshal.   The act also provided that "a marshal shall be appointed in and for each district for the term of four years, but shall be removable from office at pleasure, whose duty it shall be to attend the district and circuit courts when sitting therein . . . . And to execute throughout the district, all legal precepts [orders, writs, warrants, attachments, etc.] directed to him and issued under the authority of the United States."[19] Although the act did not specify who was to appoint the marshal, presidents seized the opportunity for political patronage. In addition to providing security for the court, marshals paid the court's expenses, including "fuel, candles, and other contingencies," the fees and traveling expenses of witnesses, jurors, district attorneys, and clerks of court, funds paid for housing federal prisoners in local jails, salaries of the bailiffs and court criers, and rented space for courtrooms.[20] Marshals were paid through fees earned for serving court papers, executing arrest warrants, and summoning jurors.

The District Attorney.   The act mandated that, for each judicial district, the president was to nominate and the Senate confirm "a meet person learned in the law to act as attorney for the United States" in both criminal and civil cases. These meet persons came to be called district attorneys, a name kept until 1948 when the official title of United States attorney was granted. Until 1861, district attorneys acted with considerable independence from Washington, although, theoretically, they answered to the secretary of state. Like clerks and marshals, district attorneys were paid by fees taxed by the court against opposing parties in each case filed. This arrangement led to a common complaint that district attorneys had an incentive, which they too often gave in to, to file a large number of cases of questionable merit and to perform other tasks of doubtful usefulness simply to generate fees.

The Court Crier.   The act did not authorize employment of a court crier, but the Supreme Court quickly appointed one for itself. In 1799, Congress gave in and required district and circuit courts to appoint a crier, although the statute was silent as to a crier's duties.[21] Like federal clerks, criers in federal courts usually had experience in state courts and performed the same duties in the federal courts, "crying" any vocal announcement or direction needed and keeping order during court sessions.

Commissioners.   In addition to the administrative assistance of the clerk of the court, the federal trial courts have always had quasi-judicial officers who relieved them of minor courtroom chores. The 1789 act provided that, in the absence of a federal judge, certain duties, such as setting bail or taking depositions, might be performed by state magistrates or justices of the peace,[22] but events like the Whiskey Rebellion of 1791 demonstrated that court officials who were elected and paid locally could not always be relied upon to enforce unpopular federal laws. In 1793, Congress authorized the circuit courts to appoint "discreet persons learned in the law" (as contrasted to district attorneys who had to be "meet persons learned in the law") to set and collect bail in federal criminal proceedings in remote areas,[23] and, in 1812, to take affidavits and acknowledgments of bail in civil cases.[24] In 1817, Congress gave those "discreet persons" a title, "commissioners," and authorized them to take the depositions of witnesses who were unable to appear in federal court.[25] Throughout the remainder of the 19th century, Congress added to the commissioners' duties, assigning them to perform judicial tasks, without a judge's involvement, such as arresting runaway slaves and returning them to their masters, under the Fugitive Slave Act of 1850, enforcing, ironically, the rights of former slaves under the Civil Rights Act of 1866, and ordering the deportation of illegal immigrants from China, under the Chinese Exclusion Acts.

The Territory of Michigan Becomes the State of Michigan

What is now the state of Michigan became part of the United States in 1783, at the end of the Revolutionary War, although British armed forces did not relinquish control until 1796. In 1787, the Continental Congress enacted what has come to be called the Northwest Ordinance, which organized the form of government for the former British lands located northwest of the Ohio River.[26] Among other provisions, the ordinance promised that portions of the Northwest Territory that achieved a population of 60,000 residents would be admitted into the Union as states. Ohio became a state in 1802, followed by Indiana in 1816 and Illinois in 1818, but the population of the Michigan Territory, established in 1805,[27] lagged behind that of its neighbors until 1825, when the Erie Canal opened and families from New York and New England began to swarm to Michigan, looking for farmland.[28] Consequently, Michigan did not apply for statehood until December 1833 and did not become a state until January 1837 because of a boundary dispute with its politically powerful neighbor to the south, Ohio. The bone of contention was known as the Toledo Strip, an area containing a noisome swamp and few people, but also Maumee (then called Miami) Bay, the gateway from the eastern Great Lakes to the Mississippi River. Both Michigan and Ohio claimed the strip, and until Michigan agreed to renounce its claim, Ohio blocked Michigan's application for statehood. [29]

Throughout 1833 and 1834, Ohio's congressional delegation kept the issue from coming to a vote, and threatened to keep doing so unless Michigan agreed to give up its claim to Maumee Bay. The political odds were against Michigan—Ohio had 19 U.S. representatives and two U.S. senators, while Michigan had no voting representation in either house. Consequently, Ohio had 21 votes in the Electoral College and Michigan had none. Michigan also fell afoul of national politics, as senators and representatives from Southern states stalled until Arkansas was ready for admission, so that a slave and a non-slave state could be admitted simultaneously. Meanwhile, the militia of both jurisdictions were marching and posturing in the fatality-less comedy that has come to be called the Toledo War.[30] Finally, the Michigan Territory decided it could wait on Congress no longer. In the spring of May 1835, 91 elected delegates convened in Detroit to draft a constitution for the state to consist of the Lower Peninsula and the eastern quarter of the Upper Peninsula. They completed the document in 45 days. In October, the electorate overwhelmingly adopted it and elected a state governor and legislature. The legislature met in November 1835 and then adjourned to see what Congress would do. On June 15, 1836, Congress called Michigan's bluff by ratifying the proposed constitution and declaring Michigan "to be one of the United States of America," but effective only when and if a new convention met and voted to accept Ohio's version of the border location, known as the Harris Line, for its surveyor.[31]

As weeks and months passed, Michiganders could look forward with some hope to statehood, but also with considerable resentment toward Ohio and apprehension about how long they still had to wait. In September 1836, the legislature convened a ratification convention in Ann Arbor, but delegates refused to give up the Toledo Strip. The political fight and the cost of keeping the militia in arms to protect against any armed incursion from Ohio were straining Michigan's finances, and several leading citizens organized a second convention in Ann Arbor in December 1836, without the consent of the legislature. Those delegates passed a resolution accepting the federal government's terms, and Congress formally admitted Michigan into the Union as the 26th state on January 26, 1837.[32]

The District of Michigan and Its First U.S. District Judge

The significance of the border conflict for the federal courts was that Congress rarely included a territory in the Article III court system. The Michigan Territory did have a supreme court with three judges, nominated by the president and confirmed by the Senate, whose jurisdiction included suits filed by (but not against) the United States, but this was not an Article III court and its judges were not Article III judges. The judges spent most of their judicial efforts on local matters and tended to think of themselves as local officials, to the detriment of their U.S. cases such that Canadian vegetables or meat seized for violating customs laws in one year might not come before the court until the next year, long after they had rotted away.[33] Despite efforts by local attorneys beginning in 1818 to obtain a true district court for the Michigan Territory, no changes took place until statehood loomed.

While Congress waited for Michigan to decide whether to accept Ohio's line, it established the basis of federal judicial power in the putative state.

1836

District of Michigan

• Place of Holding Court

Detroit

Fig. 1.   The District of Michigan, 1836. (Ellen White)

On July 1, 1836, Congress created the District of Michigan and, on the next day, President Jackson nominated and the Senate confirmed territorial Judge Ross Wilkins as the first U.S. district judge for the District of Michigan, although the district and the judicial appointment were not to take effect until Michigan became a state.[34]

Ross Wilkins was an easy choice for President Jackson for more than one reason. Not only was he a fervent supporter of both Jackson and the president's Republican-Democratic (later Democratic) Party, he was also the son of a former quartermaster general of the U.S. Army and nephew of William Wilkins, a prominent Republican-Democrat who had been a U.S. district judge as well as U.S. senator and had recently been appointed by Jackson as U.S. minister to Russia and would serve as secretary of war for President John Tyler.[35] Strong support for Ross Wilkins as district judge also came from John Maugeridge Snowden, a Pittsburgh publisher and Jackson's confidant who wrote to the president in November 1835 praising Judge Wilkins and reminding him of the Wilkins family's service to the party.[36]

Judge Wilkins did have other professional options in 1836. On July 12, 1836, ten days after the Senate confirmed his appointment to the federal bench, he declined an offer from Michigan governor Stevens T. Mason to be appointed to the new state supreme court.[37] The state position had serious disadvantages. The annual salary of a state justice, $1,500 per year,[38] was no more than he was to receive as a district judge,[39] and he would have faced re-election every seven years.[40] Additionally, the legislature passed a law dividing the state into three judicial circuits, requiring that one justice live in each—Detroit, Monroe, and Pontiac—with the Detroit justice also required to attend court in the Upper Peninsula.[41] It is not surprising that Wilkins chose a federal district judge's lifetime tenure and the District of Michigan's single venue.

U.S. District Judge Ross Wilkins

Born: February 19, 1799 (Pittsburgh, Pennsylvania) to Catherine Stevenson
    Wilkins and John Wilkins, Jr.
Education: Dickinson College (A.B. 1816); read law
Nominated/Confirmed: July 2, 1836 (Andrew Jackson)
Left Court: February 18, 1870 (Retired)
Death: May 17, 1872 (Detroit, Michigan)

Born into a wealthy frontier family, Ross Wilkins began his public service as Pittsburgh's prosecuting attorney (1821–1823). He married 18-year-old Maria Duncan, a native of Ireland, on May 13, 1823, in Pittsburgh. They raised seven children, three of whom were alive at the time of the judge's death in 1872. After a term in the Pennsylvania House of Representatives (1829–1830), he accepted President Jackson's appointment to the Supreme Court of the Territory of Michigan. On June 17, 1832, he arrived with his family in Detroit, where he would serve as a judge for the next 40 years.

Ross Wilkins was a firm opponent of wealth and privilege. Writing to William Seward in 1851, he remembered that: "In early life I became a politician from a conviction that the monied corporate power of the Bank of the United States was oppressive to the masses and perilous to civil liberty."[42] In his later years, he warned that corporations, particularly railroads, posed the same menace. In addition to his other activities, Judge

Fig. 2.   Judge Ross Wilkins.
Portrait by Alvah Bradish.
(Historical Society for the United
States District Court for the
Eastern District of Michigan)

Wilkins was a Methodist lay preacher and a confirmed opponent of alcohol.[43] In 1835, U.S. district attorney George C. Bates described the judge as "[a]bout five feet ten inches in height, he was well proportioned, lithe and graceful, with fine features, long hair [and beard] and expressive eyes, magnificent teeth and a facial resemblance to Lord Byron and was one of the handsomest men of his day. His motions and intellect were both quick, and his reasoning was clear and lucid. While reading and studying the papers and evidence in the cases before him he was always moving restlessly in his chair, and when he was finished, he would rise and, going to the back of the courtroom, fill and light his long pipe and smoked as he walked around, always paying the keenest attention to the proceedings."[44] Bates also noted that Judge Wilkins had a "splendid, majestic head, an eye like Mars, full of brilliancy, and as restless as the eagle's."[45] At the time of his retirement, another Detroit lawyer described Wilkins as "[f]rank and impulsive, without cautious and calculating policy," and praised "the honesty of his heart and the sincerity of his convictions."[46] As for his approach to the law, one commentator described him as a jurist rather than a casuist, a believer in rules and laws, applied without regard to the facts or the circumstances.[47]

Wilkins worried constantly about his finances. His federal pay remained insufficient throughout his tenure on the bench.[48] Although his annual salary would increase in steps to a peak of $3,500 in 1867, three years before he retired,[49] finding enough money to support his large extended family, including children, grandchildren, and servants,[50] was Judge Wilkins's chief concern throughout his tenure as district judge, and his papers include a steady flow of pleas to his family and friends for loans.

Fig. 3.   Court Clerk John Winder.
(Burton Historical Collection,
Detroit Public Library)

Clerk of the District Court John Winder

Judge Wilkins did not have to look far to find his clerk of the district court.
During the 13 years since his arrival Michigan, John Winder had made
himself indispensable as clerk of the Supreme Court of the Territory of
Michigan, Wayne County and the Wayne County Circuit Court, Detroit's
Board of Aldermen, and most other agencies of government in the territory. Winder was born in Uniontown, Pennsylvania in 1804, and moved to
Detroit in 1824, then a frontier village of about 1,500 residents. At the
suggestion of the Michigan Territory's U.S. marshal, Thomas Rowland, a
friend of his father, he became Wayne County clerk. Winder was appointed
clerk of Michigan's supreme court in 1826, a post he held until 1843, while
also serving as clerk of the federal courts in Detroit. He married Elizabeth
Williams, the daughter of prominent merchant John R. Williams, but lost
his wife and infant son in the cholera epidemic of 1834. From 1837 to
1839, his appointment as clerk of the district court also made him responsible for the circuit court, and when Congress authorized a circuit court
clerk in 1839,[51] Wilkins and Circuit Justice John McLean appointed him
to that position as well, a common practice then.[52] He kept both clerkships
until 1848, and served as clerk of one or both of the federal courts until he
followed Judge Wilkins into retirement in April 1870.

U.S. Marshal Conrad ten Eyck

Accompanying Judge Wilkins's commission as district judge was another
presidential commission appointing Conrad ten Eyck as the district's U.S.

marshal.[53] "Coon" ten Eyck was, in fact, Michigan's fourth U.S. marshal, replacing Peter Desnoyers, who had served in the position since 1831. Ten Eyck was "a Democrat of undoubted orthodoxy, . . . a man of energy and purpose, of decided character, and by reason of these traits of marked influence during his active life."[54] He was, in fact, one of those headstrong, colorful characters who thrived on the frontier. Born in Albany, New York, in 1782, he emigrated to Detroit in 1801 and opened a store. In 1823, he opened a tavern on what is now Michigan Avenue in Dearborn, which became a popular stop for thousands of weary settlers traveling west.[55] Active in politics, he served as Wayne County treasurer from 1817 to 1825, was a delegate to the state constitutional convention in 1835, and was elected state senator. Although he was gregarious, he had enemies. One of them remarked of him that: "A man so utterly selfish cannot be expected to hold on to anything without being paid for it. He would sell his Saviour for a half worn Indian blanket."[56] His term as U.S. marshal ended in March 1841, when Whig president William Henry Harrison was inaugurated. Conrad ten Eyck died on August 21, 1847.

District Attorney Daniel Goodwin

As district attorney for the District of Michigan, President Jackson appointed Daniel Goodwin, who had represented the interests of the United States in Michigan since 1834.[57] Born in Geneva, New York, in 1799, Goodwin graduated from Grand Union College in 1819 and studied law in Canandaigua, New York. After a brief stay in Indiana, he moved to Detroit in 1825, established a successful private practice, and became involved in politics. Like Judge Wilkins and Conrad ten Eyck, he was a delegate to the conventions of 1835 and 1836. In 1834, President Jackson appointed him to replace Daniel LeRoy, a supporter of John Quincy Adams, as the federal government's attorney in the Michigan Territory. Until 1853, district attorney was a part-time position, and Goodwin continued his private practice while representing the United States. He lost his federal position following the Whig electoral victory in 1840. In 1843, Michigan governor John S. Barry appointed Goodwin to the Michigan Supreme Court, but circuit riding wore him out and he resigned in 1846 and moved to the Upper Peninsula where he served as a circuit court judge for 33 years. He died in 1886.

Crier John Gibson

The district court's first crier, John Gibson, originally a coach maker, was appointed crier of the territorial supreme court in June 1835.[58] At the time of his appointment to the federal courts, he was also crier for Wayne County Circuit Court.[59]

The First Sessions of the District Court

For most of the 19th century, American federal and state courts were not in session continuously throughout the year. Instead, courts sat in "terms," which began on a certain date, usually set by the appropriate legislature, and ran until the judges adjourned court. Depending on the business of the court, a term might last for days or months. Congress directed the District Court for the District of Michigan to hold two regular terms each year, beginning on the first Mondays of May and October,[60] but Judge Wilkins was not about to wait three months after he received his commission to open his new court. Federal judges had the power to hold "special terms" at any time as circumstances required, so he scheduled a special term of the district court to begin on Thursday, February 23, 1837. Before that could take place, though, he and ten Eyck had to find an appropriate space in which to hold court because, despite citizen petitions to Congress in 1836 praying for a federal "court-house and penitentiary in Detroit," there had been no response.[61] As District Judge Alfred Conkling of the Northern District of New York pointed out in 1831, the federal courts relied "upon the liberality of the local governments for the accommodation of the federal courts. . . . The circuit and district courts are generally held in public buildings belonging to the state, county or city where they sit, with the consent, either express or implied of the proprietors," although the judge thought that, in the absence of an offer of free space, "it would doubtless be competent for the marshal, under the direction of the court, to provide a suitable room at the expense of the United States."[62]

For his first session, Judge Wilkins was allowed to use Detroit's handsome new city hall, located in the middle of what is now Cadillac Square.[63] This two-story brick, Greek Revival-style structure was 50 feet wide by 100 feet long, topped by an octagonal belfry that lacked a bell.[64] The spacious lower floor was 16 feet high, while the total height from base to cornice was 36 feet. This stately building, designed by Alpheus White, a local architect who had trained in New Orleans, stood out in a town full of modest, single-story wooden construction. The project began in December 1833 as a new municipal market on the northern outskirts of town. By February 1835, it had evolved into "the new market and Council House," with space on the upper floor for Detroit's Common Council. By the time of the building's official inauguration, on November 18, 1835, it was officially known as the city hall, although the lower floor was given over to the town's butchers. In October 1835, the Common Council allowed the territorial courts, which had been evicted from the territorial capitol by the new legislature, to use the city hall's upper floor.[65] The territorial courts remained at city hall until their last sessions in June 1836, and their state successors continued on there for a time.[66]

Fig. 4.   Detroit City Hall, 1835–1871. (Burton Historical Collection, Detroit Public Library)

The first business of the district court's first session was swearing in John Winder as clerk of the court and John Gibson as court crier. After Winder took his oath of office and posted a bond "for the faithful performance of the duties of his office," he read aloud Judge Wilkins's commission as well as those of District Attorney Goodwin and Marshal ten Eyck, and then both Goodwin and ten Eyck took their oaths of office. Wilkins directed Gibson to call the court's first case, a customs "libel," *The United States of America v. One piece ingrain carpeting and 13 yards grey cloth.* Goodwin made his appearance for the United States and, nobody appearing to claim the goods, Judge Wilkins ordered that notice of the matter be posted in a Detroit newspaper, and he adjourned the matter to March 15. After five other cases were dealt with similarly, Winder swore in the first nine members of the bar of the court: Daniel Goodwin, George E. Hand, Charles Cleland, Samuel Pitts, Henry N. Walker, Henry T. Backus, William

Hale, Samuel G. Watson, and Asher B. Bates. The court adopted its first set of 39 rules, ordered the naturalization of an immigrant, John McReynolds, and adjourned until March 15.[67] On that day, the court made its first ruling. As nobody had appeared to claim the ingrain carpet and cloth, and "it appearing the goods were illegally imported from Upper Canada," Judge Wilkins ordered them forfeited to the United States. He then made the same ruling as to a case involving the smuggling of a bay horse and shortly thereafter adjourned the special term.

At 10:00 a.m. on May 1, 1837, the first Monday in May, Crier Gibson called the district court to order on the second floor of the city hall for its first regular term. Marshal ten Eyck swore in 22 grand jurors, many of them prominent men whose surnames would be given to Detroit streets, including Benjamin Kercheval, John R. Williams, John Griswold, Antoine Dequindre, Charles C. Trowbridge, and Joseph Campau.[68] In all, the district court was open for 24 days in 1837, although some days were very short and on at least one day, November 9, the court convened but conducted no business at all.[69]

The First Sessions of the Circuit Court

The law creating the District of Michigan gave its district judge "the same jurisdiction and powers which were by law given to the judge of the Kentucky district" by the 1789 judiciary act. That meant that Judge Wilkins was allowed to hold circuit courts alone, and during the special term and the first few sessions of the regular term he handled both district court and circuit court cases. However, a week after the first special session in Detroit, Congress deleted that provision and assigned the District of Michigan to a new seventh judicial circuit.[70] When he learned of the new law during the district court's May term, Judge Wilkins had no choice but to open a second docket for circuit court cases[71] and to wait for the arrival of the circuit justice, John McLean, to hold the circuit court's inaugural term.

Circuit Justice John McLean

Born: March 11, 1785 (Morris County, New Jersey) to Fergus and Sophia Blackford McLean
Education: Read law
Nominated/Confirmed, U.S. Supreme Court: March 6/7, 1829 (Andrew Jackson)
Vacancy: Justice Robert Trimble (Died)
Left Supreme Court: April 4, 1861 (Died at Cincinnati, Ohio)

John McLean's family moved to Virginia and Kentucky before settling in Ridgeville, Ohio. He was admitted to the bar in 1807, established a

Fig. 5.   Justice John McLean.
(Library of Congress)

Democratic-Republican newspaper in Lebanon, Ohio, and worked in the U.S. land office in Cincinnati. In 1812, he was elected to Congress as a Democratic-Republican and was re-elected in 1814, but left before the end of his term because he had been elected to the Ohio Supreme Court. In 1822, he returned to Washington when President James Monroe appointed him commissioner of the general land office and then postmaster general.

After his appointment to the U.S. Supreme Court, he began to display both his ambition for the presidency and his independence. He associated himself with every party on the political spectrum, always moving further away from his Democratic-Republican beginnings. Although he owed his seat on the Court to Jackson, he split with the president over the treatment of Native Americans and slavery, flirted with the anti-Masons, Whigs, and Free-Soilers, and finally joined the Republican Party. Even as he sat on the Supreme Court, he often sought the presidential nomination of each of those parties, always unsuccessfully. Justice McLean's most famous opinion, his fierce dissent in *Dred Scott v.Sandford*,[72] increased his popularity nationally among abolitionists, so much so that a columnist for the *New York Times*, writing in April 1860, considered him to be the frontrunner for the Republican presidential nomination.[73] Abraham Lincoln, not even mentioned in that *Times* article, won the nomination, of course, but McLean, despite his 75 years, received 12 votes at the Republican convention. In addition to his judicial service, Justice McLean is remembered for performing a vital service to the law and to historians by publishing six volumes of circuit court opinions, both his and those of the district judges with whom he presided.[74]

Justice McLean joined Judge Wilkins on the bench for the circuit court's first term on Monday, June 27, 1837.[75] The relative unimportance of the federal courts at that time can be seen from the fact that Detroiters other than litigants and attorneys barely noticed the opening sessions of either court. In a town that organized lucullan feasts for every public event of note, there is no evidence of any for either court's first term. Although McLean missed the June term in 1838, he did attend the November term that year,[76] and he returned for at least one term each year for the next two decades until July 1860, after which age and failing health precluded him from traveling.[77]

With the District of Michigan and its courts in place, the business of federal jurisprudence in Michigan was ready to begin in earnest. From small beginnings, only 73 cases filed in 1837, the district would grow to almost 300 cases filed in 1863, the year it split into Eastern and Western Districts, and that Eastern District would swell to a peak of 9,763 civil and criminal cases filed in 1998. During those years, the court would evolve from a single district judge in a single court room, hearing principally customs seizures and debt collection cases, to a colossus of 15 district judges, a dozen senior district judges, five courthouses with almost three dozen courtrooms hearing an ever increasing range of cases. Judge Wilkins could not have imagined all of that change, nor was the court's future of much concern to him as he struggled to keep his cases moving during his first decades on the federal bench.

Notes

1. As a lawyer writing about history (rather than a historian writing about the law), I am conscious of the warning in another of the Doctor's aphorisms: "What a mass of confusion should we have, if every Bishop, every Judge, every Lawyer, Physician and Divine, were to write books."

2. The articles did provide for arbitration of boundary disputes and conflicting land claims, and appeals of admiralty, maritime, and prize decisions by temporary arbitration boards.

3. Erwin C. Surrency, *History of the Federal Courts* (New York: Oceana Publications, 1987), 9.

4. W. B. Allen and Gordon Lloyd, *The Essential Antifederalist* (Lanham, MD: University Press of America, 1985), 11–12.

5. Russell R. Wheeler and Cynthia Harrison, *Creating the Federal Judicial System*, 2nd ed. (Washington, D.C.: Federal Judicial Center, 1994), 2.

6. U.S. Const. art. III, § 1: "The judicial Power of the United States, shall be vested in one supreme Court, and in such inferior Courts as the Congress may from time to time ordain and establish."

7. 1 Stat. 73.

8. 1 Stat. 126 (North Carolina); *id.*, 128 (Rhode Island).

9. In 1838, the second year that the District of Michigan held circuit courts, Justice John McLean traveled 2,500 miles circuit-riding through Illinois, Ohio, In-

diana, and Michigan. His colleague, John McKinley, covered 10,000 miles circuit-riding through the Deep South that year.

10. U.S. Const. art. II, § 2.

11. The drafters recognized the importance of lifetime tenure, which had become the norm for judges in the new states, in isolating judges from politics. See Surrency, 14.

12. 2 Stat. 89.

13. 2 Stat. 156.

14. 1 Stat. 73, 88.

15. I. Scott Messinger, *Order in the Courts: A History of the Federal Clerk's Office* (Washington, D.C: Federal Judicial Center, 2002), 1.

16. 1 Stat. 73, 76.

17. 1 Stat. 217.

18. 5 Stat. 321, 322.

19. 1 Stat. 73, 87.

20. 1 Stat. 275, 277.

21. 1 Stat. 626.

22. 1 Stat. 73.

23. 1 Stat. 334.

24. 2 Stat. 680, 681.

25. 3 Stat. 350.

26. 1 Stat. 50. The evolution of the Northwest Ordinance (or ordinances) began with the Land Ordinance of 1784, drafted by Thomas Jefferson, that called for the portion of the United States northwest of the Ohio River (what are now the States of Ohio, Indiana, Illinois, Wisconsin, and the portion of Minnesota east of the Mississippi River) to be divided into ten states. The Land Ordinance of 1785, also drafted by Jefferson, provided the method for surveying, platting, and selling the land to settlers. Although the Continental Congress adopted both ordinances, they were never put into action. In 1787, the Continental Congress passed a new law, known as the Northwest Ordinance, which established the political foundation for the creation of between three and five states in the northwest and the establishment of territorial governments pending statehood. In August 1789, after the ratification of the Constitution, the new U.S. Congress re-enacted the Northwest Ordinance with only a few changes.

27. 2 Stat. 309. The territory consisted of "all that part of the Indiana Territory, which lies North of a line drawn east from the southerly bend or extreme of lake Michigan, until it shall intersect lake Erie, and East of a line drawn from the said southerly bend through the middle of said lake to its northern extremity, and thence due north to the northern boundary of the United States."

28. Very few of them settled farther north than the Saginaw Valley. The glacier that crawled over northern North America 10,000 years ago not only carved out the Great Lakes, it also scraped up the topsoil from the Upper Peninsula and the northern Lower Peninsula and then deposited it south of a line from Saginaw Bay to the Grand River, creating a land of rich agricultural potential. North of that line, though, bedrock was left close to the surface and the remaining soil was sandy, resulting in land that was good for pines and other evergreens, but poor for crops. Temperature was also a factor in Michigan's migration and crop patterns. For example, the monthly mean temperature from March to October at Ann Arbor (42.2 degrees north)

is six degrees higher than at Oscoda (44.4 degrees north), and Ann Arbor is frost-free about two more months of the year than Oscoda. The result was that Michigan's early American population filled in the southern counties and left the north sparsely populated.

29. See T. C. Mendenhall and A. A. Graham, "Boundary Line between Ohio and Indiana, and between Ohio and Michigan," *Ohio Archaeological and Historical Quarterly* 4 (1896): 127. The problem was a discrepancy between the law passed by Congress in 1802, authorizing the Ohio Territory to prepare for statehood and the constitution subsequently adopted by Ohio. Congress adopted language from the Northwest Ordinance, enacted in 1787, that called for a future state consisting of "that part of the said territory which lies north of an east-west line drawn through the southerly bend or extreme of Lake Michigan." Ohio feared that this description would exclude Maumee Bay, now the site of the city of Toledo, because nobody really knew the exact latitude of the "southerly bend" of Lake Michigan. So Ohio's constitution specified that if the statutory boundary line reached Lake Erie east of the mouth of the Maumee, then the boundary would be adjusted to include Maumee Bay in Ohio. When a special congressional committee accepted Ohio's constitution in 1803, it dodged the boundary issue because the committee "thought it unnecessary to take [the location of the border], at the time, into consideration. " Subsequent surveys confirmed that a line due east from the southerly extreme of Lake Michigan did, indeed, meet Lake Erie several miles east and south of the mouth of the Maumee.

30. See Don Faber, *The Toledo War: The First Michigan-Ohio Rivalry* (Ann Arbor, MI: University of Michigan Press, 2008); Sister Mary Carl George, *The Rise and Fall of Toledo, Michigan: The Toledo War!* (Lansing, MI: Michigan Historical Commission, 1971).

31. 5 Stat. 49, 50. Congress did award Michigan a consolation prize. By 1835, the Territory of Michigan included what is now Wisconsin, Iowa, Minnesota, and parts of North Dakota, but it was understood during all of this turmoil that the state's northern and western boundaries would be those set out in the law creating the territory: the Lower Peninsula and that small part of the Upper Peninsula east of Mackinac. To replace Toledo, Congress offered Michigan the rest of the Upper Peninsula, a trackless wilderness that did not console many residents of the Lower Peninsula in 1836, but that became crucial to the state's development over the next century.

32. 5 Stat. 144.

33. For a broader explanation of the Michigan Territory's government, see David G. Chardavoyne, "The Northwest Ordinance and Michigan's Territorial Heritage," *The History of Michigan Law*, Paul Finkelman and Martin J. Hershock, eds. (Athens, OH: Ohio University Press, 2006).

34. 5 Stat. 61.

35. Although some sources identify Senator Wilkins as Judge Wilkins's brother, he was, in fact, the youngest brother of General Wilkins. Ross Wilkins's appointment to the Michigan Supreme Court in 1832 was Jackson's attempt to influence then-Senator William Wilkins to vote against the Second Bank of the United States.

36. John Snowden to Andrew Jackson, November 5, 1835, Record Group 59 (State Department Records), National Archives and Records Administration.

37. Stevens T. Mason to Ross Wilkins, July 12, 1836, 1830–1837 Folder, Wilkins Papers.

38. *Acts of the Legislature of the State of Michigan passed at the first and extra sessions of 1835 and 1836*, 30–34.

39. 5 Stat. 61.

40. Michigan Const. of 1835, art. VI, § 2.

41. *Acts of the Legislature of the State of Michigan passed at the first and extra sessions of 1835 and 1836*, 30–34.

42. Ross Wilkins to William Seward, October 2, 1851, 1850–1851 Folder, Wilkins Papers.

43. He was an early member of the Washingtonian Movement, which sought out drinkers and tried to bring them to abstinence by counseling and discussion, much like today's Alcoholics Anonymous.

44. Robert Budd Ross, *Early Bench and Bar of Detroit* (Detroit: 1907), 217.

45. Idem., 13.

46. Alexander D. Frazer, quoted in *Detroit Free Press*, December 3, 1869.

47. George I. Reed, *Bench and Bar of Michigan: A Volume of History and Biography* (Chicago: Century Publishing and Engraving Co., 1897), 160.

48. Even before he was sworn in as district judge, he wrote to John Norvell, Michigan's first U.S. senator, asking for his help in getting a raise in pay, but Norvell had to report that Congress would not agree. John Norvell to Ross Wilkins, January 30, 1837, 1830–1837 Folder, Wilkins Papers.

49. 14 Stat. 471.

50. The 1860 Census, for example, records a Wilkins household of 11 people, including two daughters, four grandchildren, and four servants, one of whom, 12-year-old Louis Parker, was reported as "Black."

51. 5 Stat. 321, sec. 2, at 322.

52. Surrency, 374.

53. Assistant secretary of state to Ross Wilkins, January 28, 1837, 1837 Folder, Wilkins Papers. Note on verso of letter states it was received on February 6, 1837.

54. *Michigan Biographies*, vol. 2.

55. According to one legend, his tavern was also the source of calling Michigan residents wolverines. When he told one settler that he had fed her wolf steaks, she replied that she must then be a wolverine, the obly animal that eats wolves. Friend Palmer, *Early Days in Detroit* (Detroit: Hunt and June, 1906), 906.

56. Palmer, 325–326.

57. Parker, 29–36.

58. William W. Blume, *Transactions of the Supreme Court of Michigan, 1805–1836*, 6 vols. (Ann Arbor: University of Michigan Press, 1935–1940), vol. 6, 374.

59. Profile of John Gibson, George B. Catlin Papers, Burton Historical Collection, Detroit Public Library.

60. 5 Stat. 62.

61. U.S. Senate Journal, 24th Cong., 1st sess., 236 (March 22, 1836); U.S. House Journal, 24th Cong., 1st sess., 427 (March 1, 1836). Indeed, the petitioners could not seriously have expected a positive response because, at that time, there was only one federal courthouse in the country, in New Orleans.

62. Alfred Conkling, *Treatise on the Organization, Jurisdiction and Practice of the Courts of the United States* (Albany, NY: William A. Gould and Co., 1831), 107.

63. U.S. District Court, Eastern District of Michigan, Journal A (hereafter, "Journal A"), February 23, 1837, RG21, National Archives and Records Administration, Great Lakes Division (hereafter RG21); *Detroit Daily Advertiser*, February 21–24, 1837.

64. W. Hawkins Ferry, *The Buildings of Detroit: A History* (Detroit, MI: Wayne State University Press, 1968), 32.

65. Blume, vol. 6, 385.

66. Blume, vol. 6, 385, 411.

67. See "The First Session and First Local Rules," *The Court Legacy*, vol. 11, no. 1 (February 2003), 10.

68. The first grand jurors called were James Abbott, Garry Spencer, John Griswold, John Norton, Jr., Charles Moran, Francis Cicotte, John Brunson, John Martin, Cullen Brown, William Russell, Abraham Cook, Antoine Dequindre, Benjamin B. Kercheval, Peter Desnoyers, John Largy, Benjamin Woodworth, N. P. Thayer, James Harmer, John C. McDowell, Ellis Doty, John R. Williams, and Charles C. Trowbridge, Joseph Campau, and Nathan B. Carpenter. Campau and Carpenter were excused.

69. Journal A. In 1837, the district court sat on February 23, March 15, May 1–6 and 7–13, June 22, July 6, October 2–5 and 10, and November 9–11.

70. 5 Stat. 176.

71. Journal A, May 5, 1837.

72. *Dred Scott v. Sandford*, 60 U.S. 393 (1857).

73. *New York Times*, April 18, 1860.

74. John McLean, *Reports of Cases Argued and Decided in the Circuit Court of the United States for the Seventh Circuit*, 6 vols. (1840–1856).

75. *Detroit Free Press*, June 27, 1837. Congress set the court's regular term for the first Monday in June. 5 Stat. 176. In March 1838, Congress added a second circuit court term, with the terms to begin on the third Monday in June and the first Monday in November. 5 Stat. 215. A year later, in March 1839, Congress changed the terms again, this time directing that the autumn term for both the district court and the circuit court begin on the second Monday in October. 5 Stat. 337.

76. John McLean to Ross Wilkins, June 10, 1838, 1938–1939 Folder, Wilkins Papers. McLean explained that: "Should any indictments grow out of the Canada insurrection, I presume the defendants will not be ready until the fall term."

77. Originally, justices were required to sit as circuit judges for two terms per year in each district. In 1838, Congress reduced the justice's annual duties from two terms to one in the districts of Illinois, Indiana, and Michigan. 5 Stat. 215. In 1844, one term became the rule nationwide. 5 Stat. 676. Justice McLean sat in Detroit in October from 1837 to 1844, then in June until 1858, in December 1859, and in July 1860.

CHAPTER 2

Establishing the Federal Presence, 1837–1850

Michigan and the Great Panic of 1837

The District of Michigan's first years coincided with one of the great financial crashes in the history of the United States, the Great Panic of 1837. As Michigan became a state, it was in the midst of a great migration sparked by the opening of the Erie Canal and sustained by cheap land and cheap credit. The state's population boomed from 29,000 non-Indian residents in 1830 to 175,000 in 1837. This growth continued during the state's first 14 years, to 212,000 in 1840 and to 400,000 in 1850. Wayne was the most populous county, but by 1850 southeast Michigan (Wayne, Oakland, Monroe, and Macomb Counties) held only a quarter of the total population, while other counties such as Jackson, Hillsdale, and Calhoun were becoming population centers. A majority of residents were farmers, most of them still in the subsistence stage, although exports of wheat, corn, and other produce were increasing each year. Sales of public lands in Michigan by the federal government at the fixed price of $1.25 per acre grew from 147,000 acres in 1830 to 4,190,000 acres in 1836.[1] Although a great deal of this land was purchased by speculators, most of it ended up in the hands of families from New York and New England who carved out farms from the forests and prairies of Michigan's lower tiers of counties. Those settlers were encouraged to begin new lives in the West by 15 years of unprecedented economic growth and by the availability of cheap credit in the form of banknotes issued by unregulated local and state banks. Technically, those banknotes were only as good as the ability of the issuing bank to redeem them in "specie," gold and silver, but during the boom few were, in fact, redeemed because of the great demand for currency and because the federal government supported the banknotes by accepting them at face value for the purchase of public land.

31

This increase in the money supply fueled inflation and speculation, especially in the prices for the resale of public land. Alarmed, in July 1836, President Andrew Jackson issued a "specie circular," an executive order which required all purchasers of public land from the United States to pay in gold or silver. Economists and historians still debate whether what happened next was the fault of the specie circular or the inevitable result of unsustainable speculation. If causation is unclear, what happened was not. Confidence in the value of private banknotes plunged, accelerating inflation and causing both banks and their customers to hoard gold and silver. On May 10, 1837, just nine days after the district court opened its first regular term in Detroit, every bank in New York City stopped payment in specie. The result was a national panic, which, as it spread, wiped out banks, businesses, jobs, and life savings.[2] Sales of real estate disappeared because "a man would no more buy a parcel of unproductive real estate, subject to taxes, than he would fondle a rattlesnake."[3] Private creditors also required payment in specie, but there was none.

The District and Circuit Courts, 1837–1850

During the District of Michigan's first 14 years, from 1837 to 1850, U.S. district attorneys filed 528 civil cases, most of which involved customs seizures and suits to collect debts owed to the United States, and 196 criminal cases charging violations of a variety of federal crimes, particularly counterfeiting, postal theft, and the cutting of timber on federal land. Some years brought clusters of other charges as well, such as six indictments for violations of the neutrality laws during the Canadian uprisings in 1838 and 14 for bankruptcy fraud in 1844, in the wake of the short-lived Bankruptcy Act of 1841. The great majority of cases filed during those years, though, were diversity suits filed in the circuit court between private parties to collect on notes, mortgages, or other debt, an average of 162 per year between 1838 and 1850. During the panic's worst years, from 1838 to 1841, they averaged 278 per year as debt defaults became an epidemic.

Courts in Search of a Home

The district's courts continued to sit in Detroit's city hall during 1837 and 1838, and might have stayed longer but for a dispute over rent between Judge Wilkins and the Common Council. The council did not raise the issue of compensation when it first allowed the territorial courts to use its second-story hall in October 1835,[4] but in January 1837, the council resolved that "the several courts which in turn occupy the City Hall as a court room be charged with rent."[5] The council decided that local courts would be charged between $150 and $300 per year and federal courts $150 per year.

Because of his civic-mindedness, Judge Wilkins found himself in a delicate situation. In April 1837, the council appointed him city recorder,[6] essentially a member of the council. On May 2, 1837, one day after the district court began its first regular term at city hall, Wilkins expressed his doubts that the city could legally demand that courts, including his, pay rent. He successfully moved to have the city council's Committee on Ways and Means "inquire into the propriety of taking measures to secure an appropriate rent for the use of the City Hall by the State and United States Courts, and report as soon as possible."[7] Wilkins resigned as recorder in October 1837,[8] and there is no evidence in the council's minutes of any report, but on February 2, 1838, the council directed the city clerk "to present to the proper authorities accounts for the use of the City Hall by the several courts since the same has been used by said courts."[9] Nothing more seems to have occurred until the morning of June 24, 1839, a week into the district court's term, when Judge Wilkins and his staff arrived at city hall to find that "the Courtroom is occupied by the Mayor's Court of the City, to whom the building belongs, and in consequence thereof that the Court cannot further hold its sessions there, the Court is now adjourned to meet again at the Capitol in the City of Detroit at half past ten on the forenoon of this day."[10] The next day, the council directed the clerk "to make out a bill against the United States for the use of the City Hall for the sessions of the District Court of the United States for the term it has been so used at the rates prescribed by a resolution of the Common Council in 1836 [sic]."[11] A bill for $300 accordingly went to Court Clerk John Winder, who certified that the amount was correct, but Judge Wilkins marked it "rejected and disallowed" and explained that the city "must apply to Congress" for payment.[12] When the federal courts returned to the city hall to conduct the October term without paying the bill,[13] the council vented its frustration by resolving to raise the rate charged to the courts to $500 per year for the U.S. courts, and to notify the courts that "the hall can be had on these terms and no other."[14]

For whatever reason, the federal courts began their June 1840 term on June 15 in the "long room" on the third floor of the Williams Building, located at the southeast corner of Jefferson Avenue and Bates Street.[15] Built in 1833 by John R. Williams, a wealthy investor who was several times mayor of Detroit and for whom Detroit's John R Street is named, this was Detroit's first four-story brick building.[16] Its lower floor was rented out to retail and wholesale stores while the upper floors housed other businesses, including the Michigan Supreme Court, which had transformed the long room into a court.[17]

The district and circuit courts were held in the Williams Building for three years, but an increase in the number of federal agencies and employees in Detroit made it apparent that there was a need for a building dedicated solely to the federal government. Rather than build a new structure,

Fig. 6.   The Williams Building. (Burton Historical Collection, Detroit Public Library)

though, the government took advantage of the demise of a local bank, the Bank of Michigan, which failed owing the United States $33,415.70. In December 1842, the United States obtained the building at auction for that amount and spent another $1,000 in remodeling costs.[18] Congress directed the secretary of the treasury to take charge of the building and "set apart the said premises for the use of the courts of the United States, the officers of such courts, and the post-office in the said City of Detroit."[19] In early June 1843, the federal courts and most of Detroit's other federal agencies moved to the bank's former home on the southwest corner of Jefferson Avenue and Griswold Street.

The Bank of Michigan building, designed by local architect Charles Lum and completed in 1836, was a two-story, flat-roofed building, "in the chaste Grecian style," notable as the first dressed-stone building in Detroit. Its shell limestone contained "many beautiful petrifactions [fossils]; in olden times the building was oiled yearly, and they were very noticeable."[20][21] The basement, which had a separate entrance, became a post office; the first floor, which had a lavishly-decorated 17-foot-high ceiling, became the courtroom; and the second floor became court offices and a

Fig. 7.   The Bank of Michigan Building. (Burton Historical Collection, Detroit Public Library)

jury room. On June 20, 1843, Judge Wilkins held the district court's first session in the bank building and continued to hold court there until 1855.[22]

Clerk William D. Wilkins

John Winder served as clerk for both the district and circuit courts for eleven years until Judge Wilkins gave the district court clerk position to William Duncan Wilkins, the judge's twenty-one-year-old son who had recently returned from serving in the Mexican War.[23] Winder probably agreed to the change as the district clerk's fees were very low at that time, with only twenty-five cases filed there from 1845 to 1848. Wilkins and Winder would switch jobs in 1857 after district attorneys began to file all non-capital criminal cases in the district court and the number of admiralty cases increased tremendously, so that the number of filings was almost equal.

The Patriot War

The Great Panic of 1837 also bears some responsibility for the involvement of Judge Wilkins and his courts with a raid in December 1838 by armed civilians across the river into Canada, intended to overthrow the British government and install a republic. Many of the raider's leaders were prominent, middle-class citizens inspired by the idea of exporting republican ideals to Canada, but the rank and file included men who had lost their farms or jobs and who hoped for land in a republican Canada, or at least food and shelter until the shooting started. These bands, which were active along the northern frontier from Maine to Michigan, called themselves Lodges of the Patriot Hunters, and their raids across the border, principally at Niagara and Detroit, came to be called the Patriot War. The Patriot movement in the United States was inspired by uprisings by Canadians in 1837 caused by real grievances against the ruling class, grievances that had been put down with force. Canadians fleeing to the United States convinced many Americans that the people of Canada would welcome an American invasion.

In December 1837, a few hundred Patriots seized a Canadian island in the Niagara River, about three miles above the falls. The lieutenant governor of Canada sent thousands of militia to eject them, but the island's steep banks, the river's swift current, and the threat of the falls made a direct invasion tricky. Instead, the officer in charge sent a party to capture or destroy the steamship *Caroline*, which the Patriots used to carry supplies to Navy Island. The raiding party found the *Caroline* docked on the American shore, boarded her, set her on fire, cut her loose into the current, and retired, leaving behind a dead American, shot through the head at close range. Eventually the Patriots withdrew from Navy Island, but the *Caroline* became the first of several international incidents that roiled British-American relations.

The Patriot War came to Michigan in late 1837, when a few hundred men and boys calling themselves the Patriot Army of the Northwest set up a camp downriver from Detroit, conducted close-order drill, and waited. They were welcomed by many (maybe most) Detroit residents. Public meetings were held to raise funds for their support, Michigan governor Stevens T. Mason and other local officers did little to hinder them, and even Judge Wilkins was rumored to have accepted a secret commission as a Patriot general.[24] Only General Hugh Brady, a flinty veteran of the War of 1812 and commander of the handful of regular soldiers in Michigan, seemed to be whole-heartedly trying to stop the Patriots.

On January 8, 1838, several Patriots led by a Detroit grocer and Patriot "general," Edward A. Theller, tried to maneuver a schooner, the *Anne*, in position to fire its cannon at Fort Malden, near Amherstburg, Canada. The crew was not very handy and managed to run the schooner aground on the Canadian side of the Detroit River, whereupon Canadian militia boarded her, killed several of her crew, and captured others, including Theller.[25] On February 24, about 200 Patriots crossed the frozen Detroit River to Fighting Island, on the Canadian side of the Detroit River, but when Canadian militia attacked, the Patriots ran back to Michigan where they were disarmed by Brady and a company of volunteer infantry known as the Brady Guards. On March 3, 1838, another Patriot force crossed Lake Erie on the ice from Sandusky, Ohio, to Pelee Island, where they exchanged volleys of musketry with British regulars. Both sides suffered casualties and then returned to their respective shores. The next day, John Prince, the commander of the Canadian militia opposite Detroit, caught a leader of the Patriots, Thomas Jefferson Sutherland, on the ice near Amherstburg.[26] With Theller and Sutherland in Canadian jails, the Patriots near Detroit were quiet for several months.

Although he did his best to stop Patriot incursions, General Brady was hindered by the lack of a federal law that prohibited armed civilians from gathering or from invading a foreign country. The Neutrality Act of 1818 did make it a high misdemeanor for an American "to accept and exercise a commission to serve a foreign prince, state, colony, district, or people," against another foreign prince, etc., with which the United States was at peace,[27] but it was questionable whether that law authorized federal officials to seize ships, guns, or armed men suspected of preparing to invade another country as private citizens. Faced with saber rattling by the British government, President Martin Van Buren did his best to avoid a real war. He sent General Winfield Scott to the border to intimidate both Americans and Canadians with his imperious arrogance, and in March 1838, he pushed through a stronger neutrality law that authorized federal officers "to seize and detain any vessel, or any arms, or munitions of war which may be provided or prepared for any military expedition" against a foreign state with which the United States was at peace.[28] In June 1838, using this act, District Attorney Daniel Goodwin obtained indictments against six Patriot leaders, including Theller and Sutherland, although all of them were in jail in Canada.[29]

During that summer, federal officials seemed to be in control of the situation. The United States filed suit to condemn the sloop *Texas*, seized with "16 guns, one pair of pistols and a sword,"[30] and customs officers seized three cannon destined for the Patriots. As winter approached, many Patriots who had summered in Detroit packed up and went home. The end of the troubles seemed to be sealed in the early morning of December 3, 1838, when General Brady and the Brady Guards seized what they believed to be the Patriots' entire arsenal of muskets, bayonets, and ammunition. Then, toward 11:00 p.m. on that same day, the current Patriot "general," Lucius Verus Bierce, a lawyer and politician from Akron, Ohio, gathered his remaining men (estimated at fewer than 200) in the woods outside Detroit, distributed a new supply of arms, probably stolen from a militia arsenal, and marched the men through town to the river bank where other Patriots had taken control of the paddle steamer *Champlain*. The *Champlain* slowly left the dock and steamed through icebergs to a point on the Canadian shore opposite Belle Isle where the men, many of them now very reluctant, were forced to go ashore. In the dark of an overcast night sky, the Patriots marched to Windsor, then a hamlet with a few houses, a tavern, and a ferry dock. They surprised a detachment of militia sleeping in a barrack, killed two in a firefight, and captured others, although a few Canadians escaped to warn their main body at Sandwich.

While the Patriots then milled around aimlessly, burned the barracks and a steamboat, looted a tavern, and shot an escaped slave in his home, Canadian militia was on the march. Two companies fired volleys at a Patriot detachment, killing and wounding a score, while those who were still standing ran for the woods, as did Bierce and the rest of the Patriots. After the shooting ended, John Prince arrived on the scene and ordered the militia back to Sandwich because of rumors that more Patriots were closing in. People in Detroit, watching from rooftops, were puzzled to see both forces retreating, but a few hours later, British regulars from Fort Malden and Native Americans from a local band pursued the remaining Patriots up the river, followed some time later by Prince and his militia. The *Champlain* had returned to its berth in Detroit, so the surviving Patriot leaders abandoned their troops and escaped back to Belle Isle by canoe, while other Patriots sneaked back to Detroit over the next several days. In total, the Patriots lost about 25 killed, including five prisoners shot on John Prince's orders after they had surrendered. Canadian losses were five or six killed, including a surgeon who rode up to the Patriots in the dark thinking they were militia. Another 45 Patriots were captured and, after trials by court-martial, all except one were convicted and sentenced to hang. Six death sentences were carried out, 25 Patriots were transported to a prison colony on Tasmania, and the rest, most of them very young, were eventually returned to the United States.

The reaction of Judge Wilkins to this flouting of federal law and authority was, to say the least, ineffectual. On December 5, the collector of customs, John McDonnell, did seize the *Champlain*, but the ship's owners, Julius Eldred, John Drew, and Lewis Godard, petitioned to recover it on the grounds that neither they nor any person acting in privity with them had been involved in the raid. On January 2, 1839, Judge Wilkins, after a hearing in which over 40 witnesses testified, exonerated the owners and returned their ship, although he added that "there are strong grounds of suspicion still resting on the captain and the crew."[31] In fact, the evidence against the ship's crew was very strong, and Judge Wilkins's decision reinforced the rumors that he was a secret Patriot.

After John Prince boasted of summarily executing five captured Patriots,[32] the public was more sympathetic than ever to the Patriot cause.

Edward Theller escaped from his Canadian prison, arrived in Detroit during the fighting on December 4, and was arrested two days later by the U.S. marshal on the pending indictment. Daniel Goodwin postponed the trial until the June 1839 term, hoping that passions would cool by then. They had not, and, following four days of testimony, a jury found Theller not guilty after barely a half hour of deliberation.[33] A few days later, the grand jury of the circuit court, after listening to dozens of witnesses, reported that it could not identify any living man as having participated in the December raid and so returned no indictments despite a "pointed" charge by Justice McLean.[34] Discouraged, Goodwin dismissed the other indictments relating to the *Anne.* Despite the continued high emotion in Detroit, though, the debacle at Windsor was the last gasp of the Patriot War in the West.

The Bankruptcy Act of 1841

The number of civil and criminal cases filed in the district court does not accurately reflect the burdens imposed on Judge Wilkins early in his federal career because it does not include cases filed under a bankruptcy statute enacted in 1841 and repealed in 1843. The U.S. Constitution grants Congress the power to enact "uniform laws on the subject of bankruptcies throughout the United States,"[35] but Congress was hesitant to use this power during most of the 19th century. Congress passed its first bankruptcy statute in 1800, during one of the nation's first recessions, but repealed it in 1803 as the economy improved.[36] In August 1841, largely in reaction to the Panic of 1837, Congress tried again, voting into law "an Act to establish a uniform system of bankruptcy throughout the United States."[37] Although this act offered bankrupts a discharge of debts, its major purpose was to assist creditors in marshaling and liquidating the bankrupt's property. Before it was repealed in March 1843,[38] less than two years later, 685 cases had been filed in the District of Michigan.[39] Although the law authorized district judges to hire commissioners to receive proof of debts and to carry out other administrative duties, jury trials on disputed facts and substantive orders remained the responsibility of the judges, and bankruptcy cases including 16 criminal cases alleging bankruptcy fraud, seriously disrupted the court's operations until the law was repealed.

The District of Michigan and the U.S. Supreme Court

Although some decisions of Michigan's three-judge territorial court could have been appealed to the U.S. Supreme Court, none were, and the Supreme Court did not hear an appeal from a federal court in Michigan until 1845, eight years after the District of Michigan was created. *Carroll v. Safford*[40] was an action filed in the circuit court to determine a point of law that, although somewhat technical, was of great interest to Michigan residents. In 1836, Charles H. Carroll, a resident of New York, purchased from the United States 3,550 acres of land in Michigan's Genesee County. When Carroll paid the purchase price, the federal land agent, following standard procedures, executed a "final certificate" and forwarded it to Washington where, in August 1837, the government issued its patent granting the land to Carroll. Meanwhile, the Genesee County treasurer, Orrin Safford, began to assess county taxes against Carroll's land from the date of purchase in 1836. When the taxes went unpaid, Safford foreclosed on the land and sold it. Rather than redeem the property by paying the tax, in 1842, Carroll sued the treasurer in the circuit court for the District of Michigan, alleging that the county had no right to tax the land until the United States issued the patent declaring him the owner. Carroll argued that, until then, he had no guarantee that the United States would issue a patent and the land remained the property of the federal government and, thus, exempt from state and local taxation.

Judge Wilkins and Justice McLean could not agree on the law, so they certified the question to the Supreme Court for decision. Oral argument took place in the old Supreme Court chamber on the first level of the U.S. Capitol's north wing. U.S. attorney general John Nelson represented Safford and the county while Carroll was represented by John Norvell, who had served as Michigan's first U.S. senator (1837–1841) and would shortly be appointed U.S. district attorney for the District of Michigan. In an opinion written by none other than Justice McLean, the Supreme Court ruled in favor of the county on the basis that, long before a purchaser had a federal patent in hand, he had had enjoyment of the land. More importantly, having paid the purchase price, Carroll had a right to receive the patent, resulting in an equitable title which was a sufficient basis for the county to impose the tax.

Carroll was the first of only ten cases from the District of Michigan that were reviewed by the Supreme Court during the district's first 25 years, from 1837 to 1862, and most of the others were of little interest except to the parties.[41] An exception is *Pease v. Peck*,[42] decided in 1855, involving an intriguing question of law: how to interpret a statute when the official printer omitted a crucial clause from the law as enacted. In 1820, Michigan's territorial legislature, composed of the governor and the three judges of the territorial supreme court, enacted a law providing that creditors had to file suits to collect on a judgment within eight years after the judgment was rendered. The first draft of the law excepted creditors "beyond seas" and that was how the law was printed in the compiled territorial statutes in 1827 and reprinted in 1833. Much later, it was discovered that the official, hand-written law, signed by the governor and judges in 1820, did not include the words "beyond seas." In 1836, John Peck received a judgment in a territorial court against William Pease and, more than eight years later, he sued Pease in the U.S. Circuit Court to collect on the judgment. Pease raised the defense of the statute of limitations, Peck replied that he was a person "beyond seas" (i.e., from New York) allowed to sue whenever he chose to, and Pease asserted that the exception was void because it was not included in the law signed in 1820. Judge Wilkins and Justice McLean siting as the circuit court ruled in favor of Peck, and the Supreme Court affirmed, holding that, although the law as enacted would usually prevail over a subsequently printed version, where the world had relied upon the incorrect version for more than thirty years, it would be wrong to upset that reliance.

Judge Wilkins v. the Michigan Senate

Relations between state and federal governments have not always run smoothly. The primacy of one over the other in any given situation has not always been clear, particularly during the first half of the 19th century, when the concept of states' rights and the nature of the Union were the subject of fierce debate throughout the country. In March 1845, Judge Wilkins found himself enmeshed in such a dispute, arrested by the sergeant-at-arms of the Michigan Senate and arraigned before that body on a charge of contempt.[43] It all began innocently enough when Alexander Davidson, the attorney for a judgment creditor, came to Clerk John Winder in his office in the bank building and asked that the court arrest his judgment debtor for failing to obey a writ of attachment. As was the custom, Winder signed a warrant for the arrest of the judgment debtor, one Gardiner D. Williams, and handed it to U.S. marshal Levi S. Humphrey. The marshal handed it to one of his deputies, Reynolds Gillet, who arrested Williams and brought him before Judge Wilkins. The judge advised Williams "to consider himself in custody of said deputy marshal until discharged by said court"[44] and then released him. An ordinary case on an ordinary day, except for one complication: Williams was a member of the Michigan Senate, which was then in session, and according to the Michigan Constitution all senators were immune from civil or criminal arrest during a session.[45]

Even though Judge Wilkins and Marshal Humphrey did not actually imprison Williams, the arrest aroused his fellow legislators to a fury of activity. On March 8, on the motion of Senator Flavius Littlejohn of Allegan County, the Senate went into private session to consider this "direct violation of the Michigan Constitution, and a breach of fundamental privilege."[46] At the Senate's direction, Sergeant-at-arms Moses Hawks arrested Gillet and brought him to the Senate chamber in the old territorial capitol. When Gillet stated that he had merely executed a warrant issued by John Winder, the Senate directed Hawks to arrest Winder, Davidson, and Judge

Wilkins.[47] On Monday, March 10, Hawks reported that he had arrested all three, "and that they were still in his custody," whereupon the Senate arraigned all three, "charged with a violation of the constitutional rights, and a breach of the fundamental privilege of the Senate, in high contempt of the dignity and authority of the same."[48]

Judge Wilkins was more than annoyed by this turn of events, which he described as "severely reflecting upon my personal and judicial character,"[49] but he reined in his temper in front of the senators, most of whom he knew personally. Called upon to plead, he declared that "he was in custody of the Sergeant-at-arms of the Senate, and present upon compulsion; that he declined to respond to the charges against him; that the Senate had no jurisdiction over him; that the situation he occupied forbade his making any answer to the charges; and that, with great respect for the Senate he declined responding either by himself or by counsel"[50] Winder and Davidson entered similar pleas, and the three defendants were discharged from custody on their promise to return when notified. Davidson promptly fled the state.[51]

The tumult and uproar in the Senate continued during the next two weeks during which there were dozens of roll-call votes on the matter (55 during the entire affair). A committee peppered Wilkins with interrogatories, conducted depositions of witnesses, and even interviewed the judge at his home. Charges against Gillet and Winder were dropped because they had acted as required by their positions, but the senators persisted in pursuing the charges against Judge Wilkins. He, in a stern but conciliatory message, explained that he had no intent to violate the senator's privilege but that he was "alone amenable to the Senate of the United States," and that the Michigan Senate had no jurisdiction over him.[52] The Michigan Senate, conversely, resolved that Wilkins had no jurisdiction over Gardiner Williams, but the drama had lasted long enough, and the Senate decided that "as the communication of said Wilkins purges him from all intent on his part, no further proceedings are necessary in the case."[53] And thus ended this particular comedy in the Michigan Senate, full of sound and fury, signifying little except the preservation of Judge Wilkins's claim of federal supremacy.

Enforcing the Fugitive Slave Act

Located just across narrow rivers from Canada, Detroit and Port Huron were favorite destinations of slaves fleeing bondage, as were communities of Quaker and free black families in western Michigan, which gave fugitives haven. Yet the Constitution and federal statutes required the courts to assist slave-owners in recovering fugitives. Inevitably, Michigan's federal courts were dragged into the contest of law versus justice that dominated the American political landscape during the first half of the 19th century.

Until the Civil War, Article IV of the U.S. Constitution included the words: "No person held to service or labour in one state, under the laws thereof, escaping into another, shall, in consequence of any law or regulation therein, be discharged from such service or labour, but shall be delivered up on claim of the party to whom such service or labour may be due." Although Congress passed a law in 1793 to enforce that provision, until the U.S. Supreme Court's 1842 decision in *Prigg v. Pennsylvania*,[54] suits to force the return of fugitive slaves tended to be filed in state courts. Although the Court's decision in *Prigg* struck down a state law barring slave owners from recovering fugitives, the Court also suggested that states could prohibit their judicial officers from hearing such cases. This left the federal court system as the main enforcer of slavery in non-slave states.

The number of slaves that Michigan's federal courts returned to their masters must have been large, but even an estimate is not possible because practically all such cases were heard by federal commissioners around the state who issued summary orders and whose records are lost. The cases we do know about tend to be those in which civilians, black or white, tried to prevent an escaped slave's capture and return to the slave states. In 1847, for example, a Missouri slave catcher captured Robert Cromwell, a former slave who had lived in Michigan since 1840. The slaver tricked Cromwell into entering the federal courtroom in the bank building, hoping to have Cromwell arrested quietly and then quickly returned south. Cromwell broke loose, ran to a courtroom window, and shouted for help. Several men, black and white, entered the bank building, rescued Cromwell, and escorted him across the river. The slaver was jailed on a state kidnaping charge, refused to post bail, and remained in the county jail for several months.[55]

When rescuers succeeded, they still faced the possibility of civil suits for damages brought by the slave owner. The most famous Michigan slave rescue, known as the Crosswhite Incident, began in the small town of Marshall, in Calhoun County, a stronghold of anti-slavery activity, where former slaves Adam and Sarah Crosswhite found refuge.[56] Their master, Francis Giltner, hired his nephew, Kentucky lawyer Francis Troutman, to track down the Crosswhite family and return them. Troutman followed their trail to Marshall where he posed as a schoolteacher to gather information. At dawn on Wednesday, January 26, 1847, Troutman, Francis Giltner's son David, and two other Kentuckians broke into the Crosswhite home. Neighbors reacted quickly, and before the raiders could leave they were surrounded by dozens of black men. Within a short time the crowd outside the Crosswhite home had grown to between 150 and 300 people, both black and white. After fruitless negotiations, Mr. Crosswhite charged Troutman and his associates with assault, battery, and housebreaking. Deputy Sheriff Dixon, who had accompanied the Kentuckians to the Crosswhite home, arrested the four raiders and took them before Justice of the Peace Randall Hobart. During the next two days, Justice Hobart kept the Kentuckians busy in court while the Crosswhite family was rushed to Detroit and then across the river to freedom (Mr. Crosswhite insisted on paying the rail fares for the whole group). With the Crosswhite family safe, Hobart fined Troutman $100 for housebreaking, charged one of his associates with assault, and sent the party packing and empty-handed.[57] The *Marshall Statesman* exulted that: "The time has passed when the slaveholder can, in the face and eyes of freemen, carry off human beings into Slavery, after they have once gained the protection of laws, which guarantee to every one living under them 'the enjoyment of life, liberty, and the pursuit of happiness.'"

Seven months later, in August 1847, another party of Kentucky slave hunters decided to raid another well-known haven for free and fugitive black families.[58] On August 16, they rode into Cass County, heavily armed and with a wagon to carry away their captives. Two groups were to strike simultaneously at the farms of Stephen Bogue and Zachariah Shugart, Quakers known to be "conductors" for the Underground Railroad. They would then join a third squad in attacking the farm of Quaker Josiah Osborn and make their escape to Indiana before anybody could raise the alarm.

At first, the raid seemed to be going according to the raiders' plan as they seized ten former slaves, but their operation was already unraveling. Some of their prey managed to avoid capture and raise the alarm. One posse of white and black residents discovered the raiders' wagon and sank it in a lake, while another surprised and captured one of the raiding parties. At dawn, the rest of the raiders found themselves surrounded by between 200 and 300 armed residents, black and white. Quakers in the crowd, hoping to avoid violence, convinced the raiders to surrender themselves and their captives to the court in Cassopolis, the county seat. Because the federal circuit court commissioner for Cass County was out of town, the raiders and their captives were brought before the commissioner for nearby Berrien County, Ebenezer McIlvain, who, unknown to the men from Kentucky, was an agent for the Underground Railroad. McIlvain ruled against the raiders on the technicality that they had failed to present a certified copy of the Kentucky statutes on slavery. He ordered the release of the ten fugitives whom Zachariah Shugart immediately escorted to Canada.

The incidents in Calhoun and Cass Counties created a furor in Kentucky, and the slave owners involved were urged to teach Michigan a lesson. In December 1847, Francis Troutman and David Giltner filed a civil suit in the U.S. Circuit Court for the District of Michigan for $2,752, the alleged value of the Crosswhite family as slaves. Represented by Abner

Pratt, a future judge of the Michigan Supreme Court, and John Norvell, who was the current U.S. district attorney, Giltner sued 12 residents of Marshall, although that number shrank to seven by the time trial began: three white men who led the "town-hall meeting" outside the Crosswhite home (Charles T. Gorham, Dr. Oliver Cromwell Comstock, Jr., and Jarvis Hurd) and four black men who prevented the raiders from leaving before help could arrive (Charles Bergen, Planter Morse, James Smith, and William Parker).[59] The defendants retained a team of equally redoubtable Michigan attorneys led by future U.S. Circuit Judge Halmer H. Emmons and including Calhoun County prosecutor Hovey K. Clarke and prominent Detroit attorneys Theodore Romeyn, James F. Joy, and Henry H. Wells.

Trial began on June 1, 1848, in the courtroom of the Bank of Michigan Building with Justice McLean presiding. McLean had dissented in *Prigg*, arguing for the constitutionality of the state law, but he also believed that he had a duty to uphold the law as written, whatever his own beliefs, just as the people had a duty to obey the law, whatever their beliefs. In 1843, in a charge to a jury trying a similar case, he warned the jury not to decide based on "the laws of nature, of conscience, and the rights of conscience."[60] Justice McLean reiterated the sense of that admonition in *Giltner v. Gorham*: "In no supposable case, has a juror a right to substitute his own views, and disregard established principles of law. A well instructed conscience is a proper guide for individual action; but [not] when we are called upon to act upon the interests of others."[61] However, at least one juror refused to follow McLean's admonition, and as the justice later reported: "The jury, after being out all night, returned at the opening of the court next morning, and declared they could not agree, and they were discharged."

Marshall erupted in joy, but Troutman and the Giltners were persistent. In November 1848, the parties reconvened in Detroit for a second trial, this time before Judge Wilkins. Proceedings began shortly after the close presidential election between Michigan's Lewis Cass and General Zachary Taylor. Local loyalty to Cass, who supported slave owners' rights, and anger at the new Free Soil Party, whose diversion of 300,000 votes to their candidate probably cost Cass the election, may explain why the second jury awarded Frank Giltner $1,926 in damages plus costs. Wealthy Detroit wholesale merchant Zachariah Chandler, a future U.S. senator and secretary of the interior, began a subscription to pay most of the judgment,[62] but Giltner's successful use of the Fugitive Slave Act encouraged imitation.

In January 1849, the Cass County raiders filed suits for damages in the circuit court in Detroit, and the trial of *Timberlake v. Osborn* began on December 18, 1850, in the same courtroom and before Judge Wilkins. Slave owner and raider Thornton Timberlake sued Josiah Osborn and his sons: Jefferson and Ellison Osborn; David T. Nicholson; Ishmael Lee; William Jones; and Commissioner Ebenezer McIlvain. Timberlake, like Francis

Giltner, was represented by Abner Pratt, while defendants' counsel included Detroit attorney Jacob Merritt Howard, an abolitionist and former member of Congress (1841–1843). In 1854, Howard would help found the Republican Party, and as a U.S. senator during the Civil War, he would draft the Thirteenth Amendment, abolishing slavery.

Timberlake sought $2,000 for the loss of five slaves: Jonathon, Nancy, Mary, Robert, and Gabriel. The jury heard depositions given by witnesses from Kentucky and testimony from about thirty witnesses. On January 7, 1851, Judge Wilkins instructed the jury. According to E. S. Smith, who represented the slaves in court in Cassopolis, Wilkins told the jury that the people of Cass County did not act as a mob, did not riot, did not violate the Constitution, and did not endanger the Union.[63] Judge Wilkins also impressed on the jurors that Timberlake had acted within the law, even if he used force to recover his slaves. In his trial notes, Howard quoted Wilkins's admonition that "The master cannot commit an assault in the recapture of his slaves," and Howard complained that "This savage remark is repeated with emphasis."[64] Although no verbatim record remains of Judge Wilkins's charge in this case, Howard's notes indicate that it was in the same spirit as his charge to a grand jury in May 1851, in which he warned that the fugitive slave laws "WILL be enforced in this Judicial District," and explained that "Our government is based upon public opinion. Its legal enactments are the expressed will of the people. If experience proves the justice, or the inexpediency of legislation, the will which ordained can also repeal; but until that repeal occurs, the law must be regarded as supreme, binding upon the conscience of all and commanding the support of all who know that the civil power is *ordained of God*, and that they who resist, resisteth His ordinance, and will receive His condemnation. The obligation to support the Constitution is THE AMERICAN OATH OF ALLEGIANCE and coextensive with American citizenship."[65]

The *Timberlake* jury retired to consider its verdict; on January 8, the jurors reported that they could not agree, and Judge Wilkins declared a mistrial.[66] Later that day, one juror told Howard that the jurors were split on believing the plaintiff's evidence, but that they had difficulty accepting the defendants' explanations as well.[67] Like Francis Troutman, Thornton Timberlake pursued a retrial which was scheduled to begin in December 1851. The defendants had incurred heavy attorney fees, about $2,200 in total, during the first trial[68] and faced similar fees for the second trial, in addition to the possibility of an unfavorable judgment. Although their chances of success were increased by the indictment of plaintiff's chief witness, Jonathon Crews, for perjury, many of the defendants decided not to present a defense in a second trial. Faced with the possibility of bearing the cost of a second trial alone, David T. Nicholson and Ishmael Lee decided to settle by paying Abner Pratt $1,000 plus costs, estimated at $300 to $500, in return for a dismissal of the case as to all of the defendants.[69]

Local legend in Cass County insists that the defendants all contributed to the settlement, at a great financial sacrifice. In February 1852, however, a Kentucky newspaper published a letter by Nicholson (possibly reprinted from a Michigan paper) complaining that only he and Lee had paid while the other defendants had refused to contribute.[70]

The 1851 grand jury matter referred to above involved a claim by a Tennessee slave owner, John Chester, that a U.S. marshal had telegraphed a warning to the Underground Railroad and then delayed serving a warrant to allow Chester's slaves to flee to Canada. Despite an aggressive effort by District Attorney George C. Bates, the grand jury refused to indict, finding that any telegram had been sent by a free black man and had, in any case, arrived after Chester's slaves were already in Canada.[71] Although Judge Wilkins's charge did not result in an indictment, Lewis Cass wrote to congratulate Wilkins on his words, noting that they "cannot but be highly appreciated by every lover of the Union and the Constitution."[72]

Judge Wilkins's attitude toward the legality of slavery and the court's duty to return fugitive slaves did not mean that he approved of slavery morally or lacked sympathy for blacks. Rather, he seems to have believed sincerely, with a great many of his contemporaries, that anti-slavery agitation would tear the nation apart and that only a united Democratic Party, deferring to its Southern adherents on slavery, could prevent a rupture.[73] Wilkins was a financial supporter of Detroit's African Methodist Episcopal Church, where he often acted as lay preacher and conducted Sunday school.[74] In a letter to abolitionist Rev. Charles Avery of Pittsburgh in 1851, Judge Wilkins described the anguish that he felt in enforcing the fugitive slave laws: "I have long sympathized with the persecutions to which our coloured brethren have been subjected—& the Lord has made me instrumental in this section of the country in contributing to their elevation by teaching the Sabbath School & preaching in the Pulpit. I will still continue, my Master supporting & sustaining me. Altho' our Sabbath School has measurably been broken up by—and our efforts here frustrated, by the alarm occasioned by the Fugitive Slave Bill. . . . Oh, how my soul longs for a . . . word of grace & more vital faith! I cannot resign the situation I hold for I have no other means of gaining a livelihood—but I have trembled in prospect of being called on to execute the Law to which you refer—Yet my Master—who has sustained me in wonderful trials & afflictions—& given me wisdom in cases of great moment & exigency–will not forsake me—come what may."[75]

Notes

1. Willis F. Dunbar and George May, *Michigan: A History of the Wolverine State,* 196.

2. Dunbar, 271 ff.; Ted Widmer, *Martin Van Buren* (New York: Henry Holt and Co., 2005), 93–107.

3. Silas Farmer, *History of Detroit and Wayne County and Early Michigan*, 3rd ed. (Detroit, MI: Silas Farmer and Co., 1890), 850.

4. *Journal of the Proceedings of the Common Council of the City of Detroit: From the Time of its First Organization, September 21, A.D. 1824* (n.p., n.d.), 349 (October 22, 1835).

5. *Journal of the Proceedings*, 414 (January 23, 1837).

6. *Journal of the Proceedings*, 429 (April 7, 1837).

7. *Journal of the Proceedings*, 436 (May 2, 1837).

8. *Journal of the Proceedings*, 470 (October 14, 1837).

9. *Journal of the Proceedings*, 485 (February 17, 1838).

10. Journal A, June 24, 1839.

11. *Journal of the Proceedings*, 563 (June 25, 1839).

12. In August 1839, Clerk John Winder certified that the U.S. district and circuit courts used the city hall in 1837 and 1838. John Winder to Ross Wilkins, August 9, 1839, 1838–1839 Folder, Ross Wilkins Papers. Invoice for $300, marked as refused by Ross Wilkins, August 9, 1839, 1838–1839 Folder, Ross Wilkins Papers.

13. According to Journal A, proceedings on October 14, 1839, took place at the "Courthouse," and from October 16 to 31 at "City Hall." Beginning on December 2, 1839, and continuing through the 19th century, the journal referred to the place the court occurred as the "District Court Room" whichever building the court occupied.

14. *Journal of the Proceedings*, 580 (October 22, 1839).

15. Farmer, 175; Clarence Burton, *1819–72 Court and Other Records Copied from Original Files* (Detroit: Burton Historical Collection, 1910–1911), 99.

16. Farmer, 458.

17. Burton, *Court and Other Records*, 187.

18. U.S. Senate Committee Report 89, "Statement of Appropriations and Expenditures for Public Buildings from March 4, 1789 to March 4, 1885, 49th Cong., 1st Sess." (February 8, 1886), 40.

19. 5 Stat. 649.

20. Farmer, 859.

21. 5 Stat. 649.

22. *Detroit Daily Advertiser*, June 20, 1843.

23. Le Roy Barnett and Roger Rosentreter, *Michigan's Early Military Forces: A Roster and History of Troops Activated Prior to the American Civil War* (Detroit, MI: Wayne State University Press, 2003), 500–501. William Wilkins was cited for "gallant and meritorious conduct" fighting Mexican guerillas near Veracruz.

24. Robert Budd Ross, *Early Bench and Bar of Detroit: From 1805 to the End of 1850* (Detroit, 1907), 70.

25. Theller's account of the incident, his arrest, death sentence, and eventual escape back to Detroit must be taken with a huge grain of salt. Edward A. Theller, *Canada in 1837–38: by Historical Facts, the Causes of the Late Attempted Revolution and Its Failure; the Present Condition of the People, Their Future Prospects, Together with the Personal Adventures of the Author*, 2 vols. (Philadelphia, PA: Henry F. Anners, 1841).

26. Sutherland, who had been charged in New York with violating the neutrality laws, had been surrendered to Judge Wilkins on March 2, 1838, by his bondsman who feared Sutherland was about to invade Canada again. Affidavit of Daniel Cole,

March 2, 1838; Order, March 2, 1838, United States v. Sutherland, Circuit Court Criminal Files, RG 21. The jail must have had a revolving door for Sutherland to be on the ice on March 4.

27. 3 Stat. 447.

28. 5 Stat. 212.

29. Robert B. Ross, *The Patriot War* (Detroit, MI: The Detroit News, 1890), 74.

30. Journal A.

31. *Detroit Free Press*, January 2, 1839.

32. *Detroit Free Press*, December 8, 1838.

33. *Detroit Free Press*, July 1, 1839.

34. Lucius Verus Bierce, *Historical Reminiscences of Summit County* (Akron, OH: T. and H. G. Canfield Publishers, 1854), 7.

35. U.S. Const., Art. I, § 8, cl. 4.

36. Bankruptcy Act of 1800, enacted 2 Stat. 19, repealed 2 Stat. 248.

37. 5 Stat. 440.

38. 5 Stat. 614.

39. NARA Great Lakes, Finding Aids, ED Mich. District Court Detroit.

40. 44 U.S. 441 (1845).

41. Another case was argued before the Supreme Court but was dismissed because the circuit court did not certify what issue was in dispute. *Nesmith v. Sheldon*, 47 U.S. 41 (1848).

42. 59 U.S. 595 (1855).

43. *Journal of the Senate of the State of Michigan (1845)*, "Breach of Privilege," 415–470.

44. Idem., 419.

45. The Michigan Constitution of 1836 provided that legislators were, during a session, "privileged from arrest, nor shall they be subject to any civil process." Mich. Const. (1836), Art. 4, § 9.

46. *Journal of the Senate (1845)*, 417.

47. *Journal of the Senate (1845)*, 420.

48. *Journal of the Senate (1845)*, 422.

49. Ross Wilkins to Edwin M. Cust, March 17, 1845, 1845 Folder, Ross Wilkins Papers.

50. *Journal of the Senate (1845)*, 424–425.

51. *Journal of the Senate (1845)*, 453.

52. *Journal of the Senate (1845)*, 468.

53. *Journal of the Senate (1845)*, 469.

54. *Prigg v. Commonwealth of Pennsylvania*, 41 U.S. 539 (1842).

55. *Detroit Tribune*, January 17, 1886.

56. Except as noted, this account is derived from John H. Yzenbaard, "The Crosswhite Case," *Michigan History* 53 (No. 2, Summer 1969): 131; John C. Sherwood, "One Flame in the Inferno: The Legend of Marshall's 'Crosswhite Affair,'" *Michigan History* 73 (March/April 1989): 40; and Justice John McLean's charge to the jury in *Giltner v. Gorham*, 10 F. Cas. 424 (C.C. Mich., 1848).

57. *Marshall (Michigan) Statesman*, February 1, 1847.

58. Cass County's Quakers had established a bi-racial society, which included both free-born and escaped African Americans living among whites.

59. Because Gorham was first on the list of defendants, the case is known as *Giltner v. Gorham.*

60. *Jones v. Vanzandt,* 13 F. Cas. 1040 (C.C. Ohio, 1843), *aff'd sub nom., Jones v. Van Zandt,* 46 U.S. 215 (1847).

61. *Giltner v. Gorham,* 10 F. Cas. 424 (C.C. Mich., 1848).

62. Rogers, *supra.*

63. E. S. Smith to Jacob M. Howard, August 23, 1851, Folder, "Kentucky Slaveowners v. Michigan Quakers," Box 7, Jacob Howard Papers, Burton Historical Collection, Detroit Public Library.

64. "Charge of the court," January 7, 1851, Folder, "Kentucky Slaveowners v. Michigan Quakers," Box 7, Jacob Howard Papers.

65. *Detroit Free Press,* May 31, 1851.

66. Docket, *Thornton Timberlake v. Josiah Osborn,* Case No. 2077, Record Group 21.

67. "Memo," January 8, 1851, Folder, "Kentucky Slaveowners v. Michigan Quakers," Box 7, Jacob Howard Papers.

68. *Covington (Kentucky) Journal,* February 22, 1852.

69. Stipulation to Dismiss, December 3, 1851, Folder, "Kentucky Slaveowners v. Michigan Quakers," Box 7, Jacob Howard Papers; *Covington (Kentucky) Journal,* February 22, 1852. The stipulation does not state the settlement amount; the figure given here is from Nicholson's letter in the *Journal.*

70. *Covington (Kentucky) Journal,* February 22, 1852.

71. *Detroit Free Press,* June 5, 1851.

72. Lewis Cass to Ross Wilkins, June 5, 1851, Lewis Cass Papers, Burton Historical Collection, Detroit Public Library.

73. In 1858, Wilkins was even willing to support the fraudulent pro-slavery Lecompton constitution for Kansas as a "settlement" of the Kansas question. Ross Wilkins to James Buchanan, March 30, 1858, *Records Group 60, Unit 350, Records Relating to the Appointment of Federal Judges, Marshals, and Attorneys, 1853–1901; Michigan (East),* Box 362, Folder 1857–1861, NARA, College Park, MD.

74. See receipts and letters, 1847 Files, Wilkins Papers.

75. Ross Wilkins to Charles Avery, 10/2201851, 1851 File, Wilkins Papers.

CHAPTER 3

Calm before the Storm, 1851–1861

Michigan and the Nation, 1851–1861

Nationally, the decade of the 1850s was tempestuous, as the question of the extension of slavery to the territories was debated ever more intractably and then fought out in blood. The Kansas-Nebraska Act of 1854,[1] which was meant to achieve a new and lasting compromise, led only to inflamed tempers on both sides of the slavery issue, to the merciless violence that became known as Bloody Kansas, and to the birth and rise of the Republican Party. As each year passed, a civil war seemed less avoidable. In the meantime, Michigan continued to enjoy a population boom. The great migration of settlers from New York and New England to Michigan continued in full force between 1850 and 1860, as the population nearly doubled again, from 397,654 to 749,113. As had been the case in the 1840s, most of the immigrants settled in Wayne County and the southeast, but several south-central counties were popular destinations as well. By 1860, while Wayne was the most populous county (75,547), six counties further west (Calhoun, Hillsdale, Jackson, Kent, Lenawee, and Washtenaw) each had more than 25,000 residents. Wayne County also remained the center of the state's burgeoning manufacturing sector, while business in other counties focused on farming, commercial lumbering, and fishing. A survey conducted in 1854 highlighted the commercial and industrial development of the city of Detroit, including 348 stores, 17 breweries, 21 bakeries, 47 schools, 264 mechanic shops, 13 iron and brass foundries, 11 iron machine shops, four boiler manufacturers, and 49 stationary steam engines.[2]

The District of Michigan

The business of the courts of the District of Michigan proceeded as before. The average number of new civil and criminal cases filed each year in the district and circuit courts grew more slowly than did the population, increasing from 230 between 1840 and 1850 to 285 between 1850 and 1860, including a peak of 509 new cases filed in 1858. The civil docket of the circuit court remained very active, averaging 160 civil cases per year, but from 1851, the district attorneys, beginning with George C. Bates, adopted a new federal law that gave them the discretion to file all criminal cases, except for those carrying the death penalty, in the district court. This change was not earth-shaking because an average of only 28 criminal cases were filed each year between 1851 and 1861, including the two cases Bates filed in 1852. In addition to a larger criminal docket, during the 1850s, the district court also gained its first substantial body of private civil litigation in the form of admiralty cases.

The King of Beaver Island

Although most of the criminal cases filed in the District of Michigan during the 1850s were matters of local interest, among the 37 criminal indictments returned by the grand jury in 1851 were 14 charging attacks on a postman and cutting government-owned timber. These relatively mundane charges drew attention from around the state and the nation because of the identity of the principal defendant. James Jesse Strang was the leader of a Mormon community that rejected the leadership of Brigham Young when Joseph Smith was killed and so refused to follow Young to Utah. Strang's faction settled first in Voree, Wisconsin, and then on Beaver Island in northern Lake Michigan, northwest of Charlevoix, Michigan. Over the next few years, Strang expanded his control over the island and enforced strict rules of conduct on the residents of the island, Mormon and "gentile" alike. He was also becoming a power in Democratic politics in northwestern Michigan, had himself proclaimed king of the community in 1850, and practiced polygamy. This combination of violence, politics, religion, and sex was as irresistible to the public and media in 1851 as it would be today.[3]

On May 21, 1851, George C. Bates, recently appointed to his second term as district attorney by President Franklin Pierce, boarded the U.S.S. *Michigan*, the navy's first iron-hulled warship, and raced to Beaver Island. There, the *Michigan's* powerful cannon convinced Strang and his armed militia not to resist arrest and transport back to Detroit. On June 3, the grand jury for the District of Michigan returned 14 indictments, including charges of interfering with the mails, counterfeiting, and trespassing on federal lands to steal timber, although the grand jury refused to indict Strang and his followers for treason.

On Thursday June 26, 1851, six months after the end of the Timberlake trial, Judge Wilkins was on the bench in the bank building again to try Strang and 23 of his followers on an indictment charging obstruction of the U.S. mail. George Bates chose to try the mail interference charge first,

Fig. 8. James Jesse Strang.
(Historical Society for the United
States District Court for the
Eastern District of Michigan)

even though the timber theft charges were sounder factually and even
though prosecuting timber cases had always been a priority for Bates. The
mail-theft indictment was based on an incident in February 1851, in which
a posse made up of Strangites tried to arrest Ari (or Eri) James Moore, a
former official in Strang's church, whom Strang had expelled, on a charge
that Moore sold whiskey to local American Indians. Moore claimed that the
"arrest" was an attempt to murder him for opposing the church.[4] The Mormons came upon Moore as he was crossing the ice near Garden Island, in
the Beaver Island chain. Moore and his wife were traveling with Augustus
Gould (who was commonly called Leblanc) and John Dorry who were taking a bag containing U.S. mail from Beaver Island to Mackinac Island by
dog sled. As the posse approached, Moore ran away to the protection of an
Indian village on Garden Island. According to Gould and Dorry, the posse
chased them as well to the Indian village, and they returned the mail to
the postmaster on Beaver Island because they were afraid to deliver it to
Mackinac.

At trial, the defendants were represented by Andrew Thomas McReynolds,
a popular and flamboyant hero of the Mexican War who was also active in
local Democratic politics.[5] He was not considered a particularly skilled
trial lawyer, however, and the short, pockmarked, charismatic Strang, who
had practiced law in his early days, directed the defense. On the opposite
side, George Bates may have lacked McReynolds's war record, but he was
a skilled advocate who radiated energy and ambition.[6] The first order of
business on June 26, seating a jury, was quickly disposed of as Bates and
McReynolds selected 12 men from eight counties across lower Michigan
(Livingston, Branch, Ottawa, Lenawee, Kalamazoo, Berrien, Wayne, and
Kent). After opening statements, Bates began to present the government's

case by reading depositions to the jury, a tactic that tends to put a jury to sleep. On June 27, the prosecution presented the live testimony of Mrs. Julia Moore, Micajah Drown, and George J. Adams. Drown testified that he had often heard Strang and other Mormons say that they intended to stop the mail to prevent outsiders learning what was going on at Beaver Island. Adams had once been Strang's chief lieutenant, but he, like Moore, had fallen out with King James. Adams testified that Strang had told him of his plans to take total control of the community, in order to drive out the gentiles, and to stop the mail to make sure there was no interference with those plans.

On Saturday June 28, before the trial resumed, Strang moved for a separate trial. At that time, the district court still adhered to the rule that a criminal defendant was incompetent to testify at his own trial, and Strang apparently wanted to use the testimony of some of his co-defendants to prove his innocence. Judge Wilkins denied the motion, and the trial continued without the defendants' testimony, although one of them, William Townsend, did testify for the defense after he was acquitted at the close of the prosecution's case. The cross-examination of Adams continued for most of Saturday. Although Adams stuck to his story, McReynolds was able to bring out Adams's extreme hatred of Strang. On Monday June 30, the prosecution closed with the testimony of Ari Moore. After Moore's testimony, the prosecution rested, and the jury promptly found two of the 24 defendants, William Townsend and William Chambers, not guilty.

Strang made an impressive opening statement for the defense in which he warned the jurors against religious bias, denied that his church claimed to be above the law, and asserted that Adams was not worthy of belief. The defense chose not to use the depositions but instead presented the live testimony of 15 Strangites from Monday June 30 to Thursday July 3. The gist of their testimony was that the posse had no designs on the mail and was only interested in arresting Moore, that the Mormons were not obliged to lie for Strang, and that Moore and Adams were liars. On Monday July 7, after the prosecution and defense presented rebuttal and sur-rebuttal witnesses, George Bates gave his closing argument. On July 8, McReynolds argued for the defense, and Judge Wilkins instructed the jury on the law, emphasizing that the defendants' religion was irrelevant to their deliberations. The jurors withdrew to the jury room that evening, but returned after a brief deliberation and delivered to the clerk a sealed verdict. When court reconvened the next day, Judge Wilkins unsealed the verdict which was found to be an acquittal of all of the remaining defendants.

James J. Strang and his followers returned triumphantly to Beaver Island, and in September, Bates quietly dismissed the other indictments against them. Why Bates chose to try the questionable charge of mail obstruction instead of the timber theft remains a mystery. Although he won the trial, and he also won two terms on the Michigan legislature, Strang did not live to expand his "kingdom." His flock eventually reached some 12,000 adherents, but on June 16, 1856, he was ambushed and shot on Beaver Island by two former followers. The killers surrendered to the captain of the U.S.S. *Michigan*, which was docked at the island. The captain delivered them to the sheriff of Mackinaw County, who eventually set them free.

Admiralty and Maritime Jurisdiction

Admiralty and maritime cases (usually referred to collectively as "admiralty") include sailors seeking pay or compensation for injuries, owners suing each other over collisions between ships, passengers injured by boiler explosions, and parties suing over contracts for carrying freight or repairing a ship. The drafters of the Constitution included admiralty cases within the federal "judicial power" because admiralty operates under internationally recognized rules that require a consistent interpretation across the nation and between nations. In 1789, Congress allocated all admiralty cases to the district courts, and no other trial court, federal or state, could hear an admiralty case.

That first Congress intended admiralty to be the primary business of district courts, and district judges in land-locked courts without admiralty cases were not very busy. Looking at a map, one might assume that the District of Michigan should have been, from its creation, a hotbed of admiralty litigation arising on the Great Lakes and the state's navigable rivers that were the primary transportation routes for goods and passengers. In fact, no admiralty complaints (called libels) between private parties were filed in the District of Michigan until 1846, not because of a lack of disputes subject to admiralty law, but rather because of an 1825 ruling by the U.S. Supreme Court in *The Steam-boat Thomas Jefferson*,[7] that claims arising on bodies of water not subject to ocean tides, such as the Great Lakes and other inland waters, were not part of a district court's admiralty jurisdiction. So, when the District of Michigan came into operation a dozen years later, it had no cases relying solely on admiralty for their jurisdiction.[8]

Maritime interests on the Great Lakes hated this ruling, not least because admiralty cases are brought against a ship rather than its owners who might live in another state or nation, and so outside of the forum court's jurisdiction. In admiralty, on the other hand, what mattered was the location of the ship, which, if found in the court's jurisdiction, would be seized by the U.S. marshal and held to satisfy any judgment. Congressional delegations from the states around the Great Lakes clamored for a change, but they had no success until 1845, when Congress voted to create a partial form of admiralty jurisdiction that authorized district courts to apply admiralty law to contract and tort matters involving "vessels of twenty tons burden and upwards" which were engaged in interstate commerce "upon the lakes and navigable waters connecting such lakes."[9] Many scholars of the time doubted that this law was constitutional, and few "statutory admiralty" cases were filed in the District of Michigan. Any constitutional controversy was rendered moot in 1852, when the Supreme Court changed its mind in *The Propeller Genesee Chief v. Fitzhugh*[10] and held that the constitutional grant of admiralty jurisdiction to the federal courts be applied to all navigable waters, including lakes and rivers, regardless of whether they were subject to tides.

The District of Michigan's first admiralty case, based on the 1845 statute, was *Thomas L. Parker v. The Schooner Congress & Chester Kimball & Gordon Kimball*, filed in 1846.[11] From that beginning, Michigan's District Court attracted about 40 admiralty cases per year until 1855, when they increased to just over 100 for each year from 1855 to 1858, and then returned to under 50 for another decade or so. The years 1876 to 1895 were the golden age for admiralty litigation in what was then the Eastern District of Michigan, averaging 133 new cases per year. In 1896, though, admiralty filings collapsed to 49 and have never since exceeded 100 despite the tremendous increase in the overall number of cases filed each year.[12]

Although he had no experience as a sailor or as an admiralty attorney, Judge Wilkins quickly established a reputation as an expert in the intricacies of admiralty law. John Stoughton Newberry, a Detroit attorney, published in 1857 a book of "the most important admiralty decisions, of seven Districts of the United States, bordering upon the great northern lakes and the Mississippi river and its tributaries, for the last ten years" which he dedicated to Judge Wilkins and which included 22 of Wilkins's opinions dating from 1852 to 1857.[13] Several of them, such as *The Pacific and the Brig Fashion*,[14] demonstrate the judge's mastery of the nautical rules of the road, particularly as to collisions between steamboats and sailing vessels. Other Wilkins opinions deal with the rights of creditors of a ship, such as in *Riggs v. The Schooner John Richards*,[15] which required Wilkins to decide a constitutional question, a rare event at a time when the U.S. courts lacked a general federal question jurisdiction. In that case, competing creditors each claimed to have title to the schooner based on in rem proceedings against the schooner instead of against the owners. One creditor had a bill of sale from the U.S. marshal based on proceedings in the district court, while the other had a bill of sale from the Wayne County sheriff based on proceedings in Wayne County circuit court under a Michigan statute creating a maritime lien under state law. Wilkins held that actions in rem involving ships were within the exclusive admiralty jurisdiction of the district court and, thus, the state statute was unconstitutional to the extent it authorized such an action. On appeal to the circuit court, Justice McLean affirmed the decision.[16] The collected decisions also include one that has a decidedly modern flavor. In *Sageman v. The Schooner Brandywine*,[17] a woman who served as a cook aboard the *Brandywine*,

Emily Sageman, filed an admiralty libel to recover her wages. Counsel for the ship apparently argued that a cook, and particularly a female cook, was not a seaman and so not entitled to avail herself of admiralty jurisdiction. Judge Wilkins rejected both arguments and directed the clerk to determine how much Ms. Sageman was owed.

Moving to Young Men's Hall

Not long after the courts and the post office moved to the bank building in 1843, Detroit's citizens began a campaign for the construction of a larger building designed specifically for the needs of the federal agencies in the city. Increasing populations brought an increase in the volume of mail, and in 1852 the post office had to move from its quarters in the bank building to the basement of the Mariners' Church.[18] That space, although larger, was not designed for efficient collection and distribution of the mail, and would soon become too small itself, while the number of employees of other federal agencies spread through town in rented spaces was growing as well. By 1855, the collector of customs had fourteen employees in the city and the post office had sixteen.[19] At the same time, prominent Detroiters argued that their city deserved the dignity of an imposing, purpose-built federal building.

If there was to be a new federal building, Congress wanted the bank building sold to defray the cost. The purchaser, the Michigan Insurance Company Bank, allowed Judge Wilkins and his staff to remain in their second-story offices until a new building could be completed, but insurance operations took over the first story, including the courtroom, after the fall term of 1855.[20] Expecting to have to wait only a short time for the new building, Judge Wilkins decided to hold court sessions during 1856 in Young Men's Hall on the north side of Jefferson Avenue, between Bates and Randolph Streets.

The Detroit Young Men's Society was organized in 1833, "to devise means for greater intellectual improvement." Members met weekly and "engaged in debates and literary exercises; in fact, most of our older and leading lawyers and politicians, living and dead, made their first speeches before this society."[21] In 1850, the society built a 48 by 95 foot, three story, brick building. The first story was "occupied by two fine stores, between which is the entrance to the Hall" on the second floor, seating 500 spectators, while the third floor had committee rooms and space for the society's large library.[22] Detroit historian Silas Farmer gushed that the Young Men's Hall was "the wonder and pride of the city for many years," and the *Detroit Daily Advertiser*, in its 1850 city gazetteer, lauded the new building: "The front is handsomely ornamented with bracketed caps to the windows and a fine bracketed cornice to correspond. The Hall of the Society, to be used for lectures and debates, is 43 feet wide by 70 in length and 22 feet in

Fig. 9. Young Men's Hall. (Burton Historical Collection, Detroit Public Library)

height, lighted by large windows in the rear, and by a dome from above. It is to be finished handsomely, with pilasters with ornamented capitals, and with a handsome cornice. It will be splendidly lighted with gas. The library is of large size, on the third story front."[23]

The first court term in Young Men's Hall began on June 16, 1856, when Judge Wilkins called the circuit court to order. Because Justice McLean had not yet arrived in Detroit, Wilkins quickly adjourned proceedings for the day.[24] On June 17, with McLean still absent, Wilkins did nothing of substance except to accept and hang in the hall a portrait of himself by Alvah Bradish, professor of the theory and practice of the fine arts at the University of Michigan.[25] This portrait now hangs in a courtroom on the seventh story of the Theodore Levin Federal Courthouse. On June 18, still alone on the bench, Wilkins swore in the grand jury which included men from 15 counties.[26] The circuit court finally began trying the first cases in Young Men's Hall after Justice McLean arrived in Detroit on Saturday, June 21.

United States v. William H. Tyler, Deputy U.S. Marshal

In 1858 and 1859, while most Americans concentrated their attention on the possibility of secession and a civil war, Michiganders found diversion in what began as an ordinary admiralty case, but grew into an international incident, morphed into a confrontation between the state and federal governments, and ended with the murder conviction of a deputy U.S. marshal. The admiralty case began, like many others, with a collision between two ships. On November 12, 1858, in a heavy fog near Lake Superior's Whitefish Point, the *Concord*, a two-masted, square-rigged sailing ship, collided with the propeller-driven steamship *General Taylor*. Although the *General Taylor* was almost twice the size of the *Concord*,[27] the *Taylor* "was badly damaged and was with much difficulty kept afloat and brought back to the Sault."[28] She limped down to Detroit where it was estimated that repairs would cost $3,000, the rough equivalent of $70,000 today.[29] On November 19, her owner, Sheldon McKnight, had his proctor in admiralty (i.e., his admiralty lawyer), Henry N. Walker, a former Michigan attorney general, file a libel in the district court in Detroit seeking $5,000 in damages from "the Brig Concord and her anchors, chains, boats, sails, tackle, apparel, and furniture."[30] As the libel indicates, admiralty actions are brought against the ship, not the owner, and as was usual in such cases, John Winder, acting for the court, issued a writ of attachment directing Marshal John S. Bagg to seize the *Concord* pending the outcome of the action.

The *Concord*, although slightly damaged, managed to reach Sarnia, Ontario, with its load of pig iron.[31] Perhaps warned of the writ, Captain Henry L. Jones did not continue down to Detroit. Instead, he tied up on the Canadian side of the St. Clair River expecting British sovereignty to protect his ship from any American writ. Bagg assigned Deputy Marshal William H. Tyler to secure the *Concord*. Both men were new on their jobs, having been sworn in only five months earlier,[32] neither man was a lawyer, and their understanding of international law was sketchy at best. They seem to have understood that so long as the *Concord* was actually connected to the Canadian shore they could not touch her, but Tyler, at least, seems to have believed that once her physical connection to Canadian soil was cut, she was fair game, even if still in Canadian waters. Based on that belief, Tyler set off for Port Huron with a posse to 'cut out' the *Concord* and return her to Detroit. At some point, he hired a Canadian to sneak up to the *Concord* just after midnight on the morning of November 29 and cut the Concord's mooring lines just as Tyler and his men came alongside the *Concord* on the steam tug *Cliff Belden*. Then Tyler and the posse would leap onto the *Concord's* deck, overpower any resistance, and sail or tow their prize to Port Huron.

Unfortunately, for all concerned, Tyler's plan went wrong from the beginning. First, Tyler's Canadian conspirator severed only one of the *Concord's* two mooring lines, leaving her securely attached to Canadian soil. Second, despite the hour, two of her crew were on watch on her deck as the *Cliff Belden* steamed up. According to one of those crewmen, Quinton Morgan, somebody on the tug asked if they could "hold on to us a little while." Morgan said no, as did Captain Jones who came up from below deck at that moment. When a voice from the *Belden* said they were going to throw over a line, Jones picked up an axe that Morgan had been using and stated that he would cut any such line. As the tug came alongside, Tyler jumped across onto the *Concord's* railing, a pistol in his right hand and holding onto the rigging with his left.

Historian Clarence Burton, who knew Tyler two decades later, insisted that the deputy was a small man, not aggressive or quarrelsome,[33] but he likely looked menacing to Jones and his crew. Tyler announced that he was an officer of the United States, but, according to Morgan, Captain Jones, still holding the axe, told Tyler "to get ashore—that he was Captain of that brig—and that she was moored in British . . . ." Before Jones could finish, Tyler's pistol, which he had trained on the Captain, fired. The bullet struck Jones under his left temple and he collapsed to the deck unconscious. Morgan and another crewman, David Brown, carried Jones to the *Belden* where Morgan held him in his arms as the tug steamed across the river to Port Huron. Jones was taken to a tavern and placed on a quilt on the floor where he died at about 3:00 a.m. Later that day, Morgan obtained a coffin and took the body to Detroit where he had the unhappy duty to travel to the Jones farm, nine miles from Detroit, and to inform Mrs. Jones that she was a widow. Captain Jones was buried in Detroit's Elmwood Cemetery.

Tyler surrendered himself to Marshal Bagg and was taken to jail, first in Port Huron and then in Detroit. On December 13, following a preliminary examination before a commissioner in Young Men's Hall, he was bound over for trial at the next term of the circuit court and returned to jail.[34] Public reaction in Cleveland (the *Concord's* home port), and in Canada was predictably hostile, describing Tyler as a cowardly brute.[35] Queen

Victoria's representatives in Upper Canada remembered all too well that not quite 20 years had passed since the Patriot raids.[36] The governor general directed Lord Napier, the British "Envoy Extraordinaire and Minister Plenipotentiary" to the United States, to begin proceedings to extradite Tyler to Canada for trial under the Webster-Ashburton Treaty of 1842.[37] Napier did make a formal extradition request in January 1859,[38] but he and U.S. secretary of state Lewis Cass temporized, hoping that the extradition question, a tricky issue of sovereignty on both sides, could be avoided if Tyler were convicted in a U.S. court.

Meanwhile, the District of Michigan's district attorney, Joseph Miller, Jr., presented the case to a grand jury of the circuit court, using the testimony of three of the *Concord's* crew. On Thursday, March 24, 1859, the grand jury came before Judge Wilkins, sitting as the circuit court in Young Men's Hall, and "exhibited" an indictment for manslaughter based on a federal statute dealing with homicides committed "within the admiralty and maritime jurisdiction of the United States, and out of the jurisdiction of any particular state."[39] Minutes later, Tyler was brought into court from the Wayne County jail and was arraigned.[40] He was represented by three of Detroit's leading attorneys: George Van Ness Lothrop, Henry N. Walker, and Alfred Russell.[41] Tyler could not possibly have afforded such a powerful defense, and it is likely not a coincidence that the firm of Walker and Russell represented McKnight in the admiralty case.

Immediately after Tyler was arraigned and pleaded not guilty, trial began with the selection of a jury, opening statements, and the testimony of Quinton Morgan, David Brown, and George B. Wilson. The next morning, Miller presented three more witnesses (William A. Moore, Thomas Pennington, and Peter Maley), the defense called Clerk William D. Wilkins, John Dale, and Amos Farmer, and both sides gave their summations. On Saturday, March 26, Wilkins instructed the jury which retired and "after being some time absent return into court and say they find the defendant guilty" of involuntary manslaughter in the commission of an illegal act, but "the jury recommend[ed] the prisoner to the mercy of the court and say that they believe the killing was involuntary and unintentional on the part of the respondent."[42] The maximum penalty for involuntary manslaughter was three years in prison and a fine of $1,000, but on April 4, Judge Wilkins sentenced Tyler to a fine of one dollar and imprisonment for thirty days in addition to the four months he had already spent in the Wayne County jail.[43]

Even before the trial, the case aroused the interest of Michigan's new attorney general, Jacob Howard (the attorney for the defendants in the Timberlake case), whose upstart Republican Party had recently swept control of the state government. Judge Wilkins and all other federal officers in Michigan, including Tyler, were Democrats; indeed in those days of the open spoils system being a Democrat had been a condition of appointment to any federal office for most of the previous thirty years.[44] Observing the progress of Tyler's case, Howard smelled a fix as well as a chance to score political points. Even before Tyler was tried in Detroit, Howard declared the federal court proceeding invalid because, in his opinion, the federal homicide statute did not apply to homicides in Canadian waters,[45] and on February 4, 1859, Howard had Tyler indicted for murder under state law in St. Clair County Circuit Court. The sentence meted out by Wilkins confirmed Howard's suspicions, and when Tyler left jail at the end of his federal sentence on May 4, Howard had him arrested and taken to Port Huron for arraignment and trial. Tyler's attorneys raised as a defense his federal conviction, and Tyler was jailed until the Michigan Supreme Court could resolve this issue at its next session.

The trial and minimal sentence raised suspicions of a fix in the Canadian Parliament as well and did little to improve Canadian-American relations.[46] The governor general insisted on continuing to reserve Britain's treaty right to extradite Tyler,[47] and after Tyler was jailed in Port Huron, a magistrate from Sarnia crossed the river and asked that Tyler be surrendered to his custody for trial in Canada. Tyler's attorneys and Jacob Howard refused to comply.[48]

The Michigan Supreme Court heard arguments of counsel over four days, from June 1 to 4, 1858, and then considered the questions raised for several months before holding, on October 14, that the federal homicide statutes did not apply to a homicide committed in Canadian waters and that therefore the federal proceeding had been a nullity that did not bar state prosecution.[49] Tyler's state murder trial began in Port Huron a few weeks later, before Michigan Circuit Judge Benjamin Franklin Hawkins Witherell. On November 14, 1859, the jury found Tyler guilty of second degree murder, and Judge Witherell sentence him to six years in prison.[50] This result mollified popular opinion in Canada, much to the relief of the American and Canadian governments. Tyler served his sentence in the state penitentiary and returned to the community, working as a messenger in his later days. An 1893 ruling by the U.S. Supreme Court that the federal homicide statute did indeed apply to acts committed on an American ship located in Canadian waters came far too late to help him.[51]

As for the admiralty case, Marshal Bagg finally managed to seize the Concord in January 1860 at the Sault. When her owners did not defend the case, Judge Wilkins entered a default and the ship was sold at auction. By then, McKnight had died and his estate received a mere $287.97.[52] Like most wooden vessels in those days, both ships involved in the collision met bad ends. In October 1862, the General Taylor ran aground at Sleeping Bear in northern Lake Michigan and was a total loss,[53] while in November 1869, the Concord sank in a storm on Lake Erie; three crew members survived with frostbite by hanging on to the mast, which was above water, but five other people died.[54]

The Custom House

When Judge Wilkins moved his courtroom to Young Men's Hall in 1856, he expected it to be just a temporary refuge while the new federal building was completed, but local politics and contractor problems extended his stay to five years. The new building, which came to be called the Custom House, was not ready for the courts until 1861, six-and-a-half years after it was first authorized. Despite the problems and delays, though, the result was a great success that served the federal government for more than a century.

The timing of the city's petitions for a new building was excellent. Before 1850, Congress had authorized the building or purchase of just 41 federal buildings across the country, but policies changed in the early 1850s, and by 1858 another 88 federal buildings had been or were being constructed. Detroit was to be the home of one of eight buildings "for the accommodation of the custom-house, post-office, United States courts, and steamboat inspectors" authorized by Congress in August 1854.[55] Detroit was eager and ready for a federal building to add dignity to the city, but the devil, as usual, was in the details. The authorizing legislation mandated that "the building at Detroit [is] to be erected upon a water [front] lot, belonging to the United States," was to be "eighty-five feet by sixty feet, sixty feet in height from the foundation," and was "to cost not more than eighty-eight thousand dollars." Leading Detroiters objected loudly that the government's waterfront lot was too far from the center of town and, in any case, too small hold a building worthy of the growing metropolis. Petitions, letters, and delegations to Congress resulted in an amendment passed in March 1855 directing the secretary to sell the water lot as well as the bank building and to "apply so much of the proceeds as may be necessary to the purchase of a suitable site for said building . . . and on which the Secretary of the Treasury is authorized to erect said building."[56] The secretary accordingly found and purchased a lot on the northwest corner of Griswold and Larned Streets, a block west of Woodward and a block north of Jefferson, the city's main commercial streets. Having prevailed on that issue, Detroiters turned to size. The new lot was longer than the water lot, and the city lobbied Congress for a longer, more impressive (and thus more expensive) building. In August 1856, after more discussions and politicking, Congress agreed to increase the length by 25 feet and to increase the authorized cost by $30,000 to $118,000.[57]

Detroit's Custom House was one of the last projects undertaken by Ammi Burnham Young during his ten-year tenure as the Treasury Department's first supervising architect. Born in New Hampshire in 1798, Young followed his father into architecture at a young age and became nationally known for projects such as the Vermont State House and the Boston Custom House. In 1852, when the federal building boom began, the Treasury

Department hired him to standardize the designs of federal custom houses, post offices, courthouses, hospitals, and lighthouses. Many of the 34 federal buildings he designed as supervising architect still stand, and several are on the National Register of Historical Places.

Young's development of standardized designs, which he could scale up or down depending on the size of the space available,[58] allowed him to adjust quickly to the changed size of Detroit's Custom House. He completed the working drawings for the smaller version in March 1856,[59] and when Congress authorized changes five months later, he merely stretched the building and added two windows (for a total of seven) to the east and west sides of the second and third floors. Despite his prompt reaction, though, construction was still delayed because the contract had to be rebid to account for the larger size. Then the winning general contractor decided he could not make a profit and withdrew from the project. Excavation of the foundation finally began in June 1857[60] after a new contractor was found, but the cornerstone was not laid until May 1858.[61] At that point, the project was slowed again when Congress delayed appropriations for most federal building projects in the uncertainty over a possible civil war.[62] Detroiters expressed their aggravation over the delays by objecting loudly to "the unsightly fence" around the project, the blocks of stone obstructing the sidewalks, and "the galling fire produced by chisels of stone cutters."[63] Finally, in late 1860, the building was finished and the post office moved in. Several weeks later, on January 29, 1861, Judge Wilkins and his staff were able to settle into their new digs and prepare for the next term.[64]

Young's design for Detroit's Custom House, like most of his custom and court house projects, was in the style of a three-story Italian Renaissance palazzo, a choice that resulted in buildings that "lent an air of simple dignity to the federal government's presence in the community" while also providing more usable space than the Greek temple style popular earlier in the century.[65] The exterior was composed of monumental blocks of ashlar sandstone, three feet thick at the base of the building and two-and-a-half feet thick at the top.[66] Young was one of the first architects to use cast iron extensively, both for fire protection and for strength, and the floors of the Custom House were composed of rolled iron beams supporting brick arches covered with concrete, while iron columns provided interior support.[67] He also used cast iron for stairways, railings, and window shutters; marble for floor surfaces and stair steps; and corrugated iron for the hip roof. Heat was provided by two coal-burning furnaces in the basement, which sent hot air to fireplaces throughout the building and then out ten chimneys that rose above the building's hip roof.

Surviving architectural drawings of the first, slightly smaller design show how Young intended the court facilities to be laid out. He placed the courtroom, which was 55 by 45 feet with a 21 foot ceiling supported by Corinthian columns, on the third story in order to maximize the light coming

Fig. 10. Detroit's 1861 Custom House. (Burton Historical Collection, Detroit Public Library)

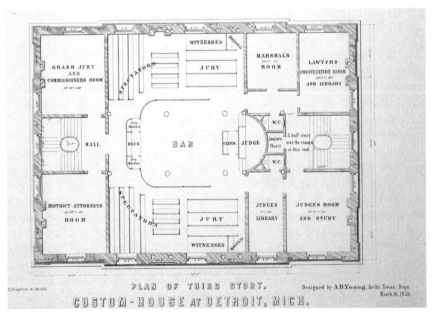

Fig. 11. Preliminary drawing by Ammi Burnham, third story. (Library of Congress)

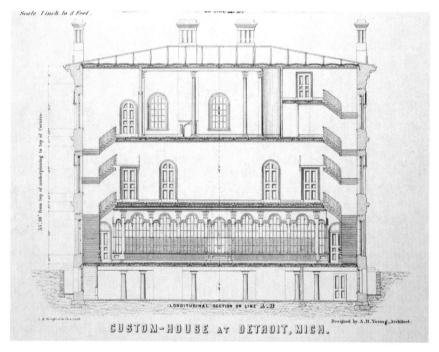

Fig. 12.   Preliminary drawing by Ammi Burnham, longitudinal view. (Library of Congress)

through the courtroom windows (there was, of course, no electricity) and to minimize disruptions by street noise. The third story also contained an office and library for Judge Wilkins, offices for the assistant district attorneys and the marshal, a grand jury room, and a library and consulting room for attorneys. A half-story attic had a room for the petit jury, while the district attorney and the court clerks were housed on the second story. The controller of customs took up the rest of the second story, and the post office was on the first story. Young's design for the courtroom had some unusual features; witnesses waiting to testify sat behind the two jury boxes while anybody testifying from the dock would have his back either to the spectators or to the judge. A reporter also noted that "the Clerk's desk is so high as to preclude all sight of his Honor when seated on the bench. This little defect once remedied, the room will be perfect."[68] The completion and opening of the Custom House to the public does not seem to have been a cause of great public interest or enthusiasm. Less than three months later, though, the Custom House and Judge Wilkins became the symbols of the Union to Detroiters, the place and man they turned to for reassurance as war engulfed the nation.

Notes

1. 10 Stat. 277.

2. James Dale Johnson, *The Detroit City Directory and Advertising Gazetteer of Michigan, for 1855–1856* (Detroit, 1855), 243.

3. There are several biographies of James Jesse Strang, some more sympathetic than others, including: Vickie Cleverley Speek, *"God Has Made Us a Kingdom,": James Strang and the Midwest Mormons* (Salt Lake City, UT: Signature Books, 2006); Roger Van Noord, *Assassination of a Michigan King: The Life of James Jesse Strang* (Ann Arbor, MI: The University of Michigan Press, 2000); and Doyle Fitzpatrick, *The King Strang Story: The Vindication of James J. Strang, the Beaver Island Mormon King* (National Heritage, 1970). I have relied on Van Noord as more even-handed. For more details of the trial see Mary C. Graham and Marian J. Martyn, "Millard Fillmore, George C. Bates, and James Jesse Strang: Why Michigan's Only King Was Tried in Federal Court," *The Court Legacy*, vol. 11, no. 2 (June 2003); David G. Chardavoyne, *The Federal Trial of James Jesse Strang The Court Legacy*, vol. 11, no. 2 (June 2003); David G. Chardavoyne, "The U.S.S. *Michigan:* The U.S. Navy's First Iron Warship" *The Court Legacy*, vol. 11, no. 3 (September 2003), and the court documents, stored in Records Group 21, Records of the U.S. District Court for the District of Michigan, Great Lakes Regional Archives, National Archives and Records Administration, Chicago, IL.

4. Moore's claim was given some credence when word arrived in Detroit, as the trial was about to begin, that a Mormon posse allegedly serving an arrest warrant on Beaver Island had killed Thomas Bennett, a prominent Gentile.

5. Leroy Barnett and Roger Rosentreter, *Michigan's Early Military Forces: A Roster and History of Troops Activated Prior to the American Civil War* (Detroit: Wayne State University Press, 2003), 336, 444–445.

6. A striking legal feature of this trial was the extensive use of deposition testimony in a criminal case. On June 19 and 20, District Court clerk William Wilkins, Judge Wilkins's son, supervised Bates, McReynolds, and Strang on Beaver Island as they took the depositions of fifty witnesses to be used at the trials in Detroit in lieu of their live testimony.

7. *The Steam-boat Thomas Jefferson*, 23 U.S. 428 (1825).

8. Michigan's federal courts were able, though, to hear cases arising on the state's bodies of water if they had some other basis for jurisdiction, such as libels by the United States to enforce federal customs and tax laws or suits between citizens of different states.

9. 5 Stat. 726.

10. *The Propeller Genesee Chief v. Fitzhugh*, 53 U.S. 443 (1852).

11. Admiralty Docket Book B, Records Group 21, Records of the U.S. District Court for the District of Michigan, Great Lakes Regional Archives, National Archives and Records Administration, Chicago, IL.

12. Admiralty Docket Books B and C, Records Group 21, Records of the U.S. District Court for the District of Michigan, Great Lakes Regional Archives, National Archives and Records Administration, Chicago, IL.

13. John Stoughton Newberry, *Reports of Admiralty Cases, argued and adjudged in the District Courts of the United States* (New York: Banks, Gould and Co., 1857) (hereafter cited as "Newb. Adm.").

14. 1 Newb. Adm. 11 (D.C. Mich., 1854).

15. 1 Newb. Adm. 73, 20 F. Cas. 784 (D.C. Mich., 1856).

16. 13 F. Cas. 707 (C.C. Mich., 1856).

17. 1 Newb. Adm. 5, 21 F. Cas. 149 (D.C. Mich., 1852).

18. *Shove's Business Advertiser and Detroit Directory for 1852–53* (Detroit, MI: Free Press Book and Job Office, 1852), 8.

19. James Dale Johnston, *Johnston's Detroit City Directory and Advertising Gazetteer of Michigan for 1855–1856* (Detroit, MI: H. Barns and Co., 1855).

20. See, e.g., James Dale Johnston, *Johnston's Detroit City Directory and Advertising Gazetteer of Michigan, With an Appendix Carefully Revised* (Detroit, 1861), 26.

21. Silas Farmer, *History of Detroit and Wayne County and Early Michigan*, 3rd ed. (Detroit, MI: Silas Farmer and Co., 1890), 710.

22. *Shove's Business Advertiser and Detroit Directory for 1852–53* (Detroit, MI: Free Press Book and Job Office, 1852), 44 ; *The Daily Advertiser Directory for the City of Detroit for the Year 1850* (Detroit, MI: Duncklee, Wales and Co., 1850), 34. There is a single statement, in a gazetteer, that the district court, but not the circuit court, sat in 1859 in the old Odd Fellows Hall, on the west side of Woodward Avenue, between Congress and Larned streets. James Dale Johnston, *Johnston's Detroit City Directory and Advertising Gazetteer of Michigan for 1859* (Detroit, MI: H. Barns and Co., 1859). I have not found any evidence that the district court actually held sessions there, although it is possible because the Odd Fellows Hall did house the U.S. Indian Bureau in the 1850s.

23. *The Daily Advertiser Directory for the City of Detroit for the Year 1850* (Detroit, MI: Duncklee, Wales and Co., 1850), 52.

24. *Detroit Free Press*, June 17, 1856.

25. *Detroit Free Press*, June 18, 1856; Charles R. Morey, "The Fine Arts in Higher Education," *A University Between Two Centuries: Proceedings of the 1937 Celebration of the University of Michigan*, Wilfrid B. Shaw ed. (Ann Arbor, MI: The University of Michigan Press, 1937), 79–89.

26. *Detroit Free Press*, June 19, 1856. The grand jurors were summoned from Eaton, Lenawee, Monroe, Allegan, Kalamazoo, Ingham, Berrien, Calhoun, Jackson, Oakland, Hillsdale, Branch, Genesee, Wayne, and St. Joseph Counties.

27. 179 feet long v. 115; 463 tons displacement v. 234. Descriptions of the ships are based on their U.S. registrations, available online at Maritime History of the Great Lakes, http://www.hhpl.on.ca/GreatLakes/HomePort.asp. (Accessed 9/18/11)

28. *Buffalo Daily Courier*, November 17, 1858.

29. *Detroit Advertiser*, cited in *Buffalo Daily Courier*, November 22, 1858.

30. *Sheldon McKnight, owner of the Propeller General Taylor v. The Brig Concord & her anchors, chains, boats, sails, tackle, apparel, & furniture*, Case No. 641, Admiralty Calendar C, Records Group 21, Records of the U.S. District Court for the District of Michigan, Great Lakes Regional Archives, National Archives and Records Administration, Chicago, IL; *Detroit Free Press*, November 30, 1858.

31. The description of the shooting is based on the trial testimony of Quinton Morgan and David Brown, sailors on the *General Taylor* as reported in the *Detroit Free Press*, March 25, 1859.

32. *Detroit Free Press*, June 26, 1858. Sheldon McKnight (1810–1860) began his career in Michigan as a printer, and went on to be editor of the *Free Press*, Detroit's postmaster, and owner of a fleet of steamships on the upper Great Lakes.

33. Clarence M. Burton, *Detroit Free Press Digest, 1858* (Detroit, MI: Burton Historical Collection, n.d.), 207.

34. *Detroit Daily Advertiser*, December 14, 1858.

35. *Detroit Daily Advertiser*, December 6, 1858.

36. e.g., *Detroit Free Press*, July 30, 1859.

37. 8 Stat. 572, 576.

38. John Bassett Moore, *A Treatise on Extradition and Interstate Rendition*, vol. 1 of 2 (Boston, MA: The Boston Book Company, 1891), 560.

39. 11 Stat. 250. The Wilkins Papers contain two "true bills," one for manslaughter and one for murder under a similar statute, 4 Stat. 115. Indictments, March 24, 1859, March 1859 Folder, Wilkins Papers. It is not known who decided not to arraign Tyler on the murder indictment.

40. Circuit court Journal D, March 24, 1859, circuit court, District of Michigan, Records Group 21, NARA-GL; *Detroit Free Press*, March 25, 1859.

41. *Detroit Free Press*, March 25, 1859. Alfred Russell would himself serve as U.S. district attorney from 1862 to 1869.

42. Circuit court Journal D, March 26, 1859, circuit court, District of Michigan, Records Group 21, NARA-GL.

43. Circuit court Journal D, April 5, 1859, circuit court, District of Michigan, Records Group 21, NARA-GL; *Detroit Free Press*, April 4, 1859.

44. In a letter to President James Buchanan supporting George W. Rice as U.S. marshal, probably written in 1853, Judge Wilkins emphasized that "Col. Rice's sound Democratic principles are well known in this State and he has always been a firm, active and unwavering supporter of the measures and principles of that party." Ross Wilkins to President James Buchanan, undated, *Records Group 60, Unit 350, Records Relating to the Appointment of Federal Judges, Marshals, and Attorneys, 1853–1901; Michigan (East)*, Box 362, Folder 1857–1861, National Archives and Records Administration, College Park, MD. By 1858, the shattering of the Democratic Party over slavery in Kansas had narrowed the required qualification even further to "Lecompton" Democrats who supported President Buchanan against the antislavery faction of Stephen A. Douglas. President Buchanan and southern Democrats supported the Lecompton constitution, adopted in 1857 by pro-slavery forces in Kansas in an election boycotted by anti-slavery residents, who were a majority in the territory. Douglas and many northern Democrats refused to recognize the Lecompton constitution, creating a split among Democrats that opened the door for the new Republican Party and for the election of Abraham Lincoln in 1860. In March 1858, Judge Wilkins assured Buchanan that U.S. marshal Robert W. Davis was not a member of the "Douglas party in this State." Ross Wilkins to James Buchanan, March 30, 1858, *Records Group 60, Unit 350, Records Relating to the Appointment of Federal Judges, Marshals, and Attorneys, 1853–1901; Michigan (East)*, Box 362, Folder 1857–1861, National Archives and Records Administration, College Park, MD. Nevertheless, Davis was replaced by John S. Bagg a few months later.

45. *New York Times*, April 23, 1859.

46. *New York Times*, March 28, 1859.

47. Moore, 560.

48. *New York Times*, May 11, 1859.

49. *People v. Tyler*, 7 Mich. 161 (1859).

50. *Detroit Free Press*, November 15, 1859; *New York Times*, November 16, 1859.

51. *U.S. v. Rodgers*, 150 U.S. 249 (1893).

52. Admiralty docket Book C, Case No. 641, *Sheldon McKnight, owner of the Propeller General Taylor v. The Brig Concord & her anchors, chains, boats, sails, tackle, apparel, & furniture*, Records Group 21, Records of the U.S. District Court for the District of Michigan, Great Lakes Regional Archives, National Archives and Records Administration, Chicago, IL.

53. *Buffalo Daily Courier*, October 10, 1862.

54. *Detroit Free Press*, November 20, 1869.

55. Antoinette J. Lee, *Architects to the Nation: The Rise and Decline of the Supervising Architect's Office* (New York: Oxford University Press, 2000), 48–49.

56. 10 Stat. 643, 674.

57. 11 Stat. 81, 86.

58. Compare, e.g., Young's March 1856 working drawings (Library of Congress, Prints and Photographs Division, Call No. ADE—Unit 2396 [P&P] NA4207, Washington, D.C.) with photographs of the Custom House as built. Also, Young's design for the Wheeling custom house is a smaller scale replication of his design for Detroit. See Lee, 53. In drafting architectural plans, Young would sometimes change only the name of the city.

59. Library of Congress, Prints and Photographs Division, Call No. ADE—Unit 2396 [P&P] NA4207, Washington, D.C.

60. The contractor, Theodore Adams from Harrisburg, PA, was correct. He bid $100,000, and the final construction cost was over $150,000. *Detroit Free Press*, June 24, 1857.

61. *Detroit Daily Advertiser*, May 18, 1858.

62. Lee, 64.

63. *Detroit Daily Advertiser*, November 1, 1858.

64. *Detroit Free Press*, January 30, 1861.

65. Lee, 48–49.

66. W. Hawkins Ferry, *The Buildings of Detroit: A History* (Detroit, MI: Wayne State University Press, 1968), 57–58; *Detroit Free Press*, October 11, 1857.

67. Ferry, 58.

68. Details of the building's interior are derived from Young's March 1856 working drawings and *Detroit Free Press*, January 30, 1861.

CHAPTER 4

The Civil War and the End of the Wilkins Era, 1861–1870

Between 1861 and 1870, the courts of the District of Michigan changed in many ways, not the least of which was the district's division in 1863 into Eastern and Western Districts. The Civil War brought new kinds of cases involving taxes, confiscation of enemy property, conscription, and piracy, as well as old favorites such as counterfeiting, smuggling, and cutting government timber. The number of diversity cases for debt decreased markedly and, for the first time, more cases were filed in the district court than the circuit court. In 1869, Congress made the first substantial structural change in the history of the federal judiciary, creating the position of circuit judge to relieve Supreme Court justices of the duty to ride circuit to attend circuit courts. Finally, in 1870, Judge Ross Wilkins retired after 38 years on the district court, followed by Court Clerks William Wilkins and John Winder.

Into the Fire

For four years, from April 1861 to May 1865, the United States fought a war of unprecedented carnage and brutality. Although in retrospect the Civil War seems to have been inevitable, few people in Michigan felt that way until the federal elections of 1860. The question of slavery had arisen in many shapes during previous decades, and Northern states had always, in the end, acceded to Southern demands or entered into unstable compromises, whether the immediate dispute was over fugitive slaves, the legality of slavery in the District of Columbia, or expansion of slavery into the western territories. Most Americans expected 1860 to be no different, but Southern paranoia and Northern resentment resulted in the shattering of the Democratic Party into Northern and Southern factions, which opened the door for the election by a plurality of the Republican Party's presidential candidate, Abraham Lincoln, and a firm Republican majority in the House of Representatives. Even though Lincoln was careful not to say anything that could be interpreted as a threat to the existence of slavery, and even though he lacked the political means to carry out such a threat when he was inaugurated in March 1861, Southern politicians talked themselves into armed secession. If Lincoln was careful, many other Republicans were not, urging abolition and almost daring the South to secede. Northern Democrats found themselves in between, trying to preserve the Union by avoiding war at any cost.

During the 1850s, Michigan shifted from solidly Democratic to just as solidly Republican. When the 37th Congress convened on March 4, 1861, both of Michigan's senators and all four of its representatives were Republicans Only Wayne County retained a Democratic majority hopeful that secession and war could be avoided by acceding to Southern demands. On January 29, 1861, the same day that they opened the new courtroom, Judge Wilkins and John Winder attended a meeting of Detroit's leading Democratic lawyers, such as George Romeyn, George Van Ness Lothrop, and D. Bethune Duffield, to draft a resolution urging the president to defuse the crisis by affirmatively promising not to interfere with slavery.[1] When news arrived in Detroit on April 13 that South Carolina militia had forced the surrender of Fort Sumter, Judge Wilkins and the other Democrats joined Republican attorneys, such as Halmer Hull Emmons, in organizing mass demonstrations in support of the federal government. The Republican *Detroit Advertiser* did not hesitate to call for armed action, asserting that: "The Stars and Stripes must be sustained at all hazards and at every sacrifice."[2] The Democrat *Detroit Free Press* blamed Republicans' "wretched fanaticism and folly and wickedness" for the crisis, but the newspaper did agree that "it is nevertheless our duty to support the government in a contest for its own preservation."[3] By May, the *Free Press* admitted that it "had become reconciled to the fact that there was no alternative but to fight" and declared that "two confederacies will never live in peace between the Great Lakes and the Mexican Gulf."[4] Nevertheless, throughout the war the *Free Press* was consistent in its fervent opposition to Lincoln's presidency and in its virulent hatred of African Americans.[5]

Faced with the national crisis, the people of Detroit adopted Judge Wilkins and the Custom House as their symbols of the Union. The judge was a featured speaker at most of the public events held to rally the public morale, many held on Griswold Street outside of Custom House. On April 18, for example, a large crowd gathered there, despite heavy rain, to see the Stars and Stripes hoisted to the top of a pole on the building's roof, a highly symbolic event itself in an era when federal buildings did not typically display the national flag. After some preliminary comments by the postmaster, Judge Wilkins addressed the crowd. He warned that: "Providence has added to the number of the original States, but the devil, work-

Fig. 13.   Rally at the Custom House, April 20, 1861. (Burton Historical Collection, Detroit Public Library)

ing through human ambition and passion, is striving to take away from them. In all our wars this flag has floated over our victorious armies."[6] Two days later, Judge Wilkins presided over another ceremony outside the Custom House, in which civilian, military, and naval officers in the city reaffirmed their oath to support the federal government. Thousands of spectators "blockaded the street, crowded the steps, windows and roofs of the buildings in the neighborhood."[7] Judge Wilkins also played a prominent role in rallies held in early May when the First Michigan Infantry Regiment received its colors and left for Washington.

The War Docket

The war changed the relationship between the federal government and ordinary citizens and also the types of cases filed in Michigan's federal courts. Most civil cases before the war, whether filed by the United States or by private parties, were brought to enforce a debt or to prosecute an

Table 4.1   Average Annual Case Filings in the District and Circuit Courts, 1851–1870

Year	Criminal	U.S. Civil	Private Civil	Total
1851–1862	28	12	267	307
1863–1870	281	46	143	470

admiralty libel, while the relatively small number of criminal cases involved, year after year, charges of smuggling, counterfeiting, postal offenses, trespassing, and cutting timber on federal land. During the war, Congress changed this comfortable routine by enacting a myriad of new federal criminal, regulatory, and tax laws designed to help the national government defeat the rebellion. By 1863, the civil and criminal dockets were transformed and remained so into the 1870s, while Judge Wilkins had also to hear 101 petitions for writs of habeas corpus filed in 1863 by men seeking to avoid conscription.

To make matters worse, Judge Wilkins received little help during the war from circuit justices. John McLean, who been a faithful attendee at circuit courts until 1860, died on April 4, 1861, just a few days before the war began. President Lincoln delayed naming a successor until January 1862,[8] when he nominated Noah H. Swayne, a prominent Ohio lawyer who had campaigned heavily for the seat. Swayne attended only one circuit court in Detroit before the District of Michigan was reassigned from the Seventh to the Eighth Circuit on July 15, 1862.[9] Neither of that circuit's justices, John Catron or David Davis, held court in Michigan before January 1863, when Congress returned the district to the Seventh Circuit and Justice Swayne.[10] It appears that Justice Swayne was in Detroit for the June 1863 term of the circuit court, although his name does not appear in any published decision from Michigan until 1866.[11] Because of the press of business, Judge Wilkins seems to have presided alone over both the district and circuit courts throughout the war despite his age (64 years in 1861) and his deteriorating health.

Financing the War

Much of the increase in criminal cases filed from 1863 to 1870 was due to two case types, tax-law violations and smuggling. When it became clear that the war would be neither short nor cheap, the two sides took very different steps to finance their armed forces. The Confederate government, relying on its underlying principle of states' rights, looked to state and local governments to provide the necessary funds. Some Southern states raised taxes, but most borrowed or simply issued more paper money as, eventually, did the Confederate government, resulting in runaway inflation. Before the war, the federal government had always relied on customs duties to finance its modest needs for operations, but those proceeds were negligible, less than $40 million in 1861. Needing huge amounts to win the war (eventually $3 billion), the government paid its suppliers with the first federal paper money, known as greenbacks. Ordinarily such an injection of large amounts of money into the economy would have caused runaway inflation, as it did in the Confederacy, but the federal government soaked up the excess by selling the public war bonds, which promised to pay interest after the war in gold, and by taxing those same citizens on just about everything they owned, bought, did, or sold. From 1863 to 1869, the district court spent an enormous portion of its time enforcing those taxes.

In July 1862, Congress passed a Revenue Act[12] which increased customs duties, created the first federal income and inheritance taxes as well as a Bureau of Internal Revenue, and imposed a raft of new taxes and fees. As amended in 1864, the law imposed monthly taxes on the value of manufacturing businesses, the receipts of transportation companies and public utilities, and surplus funds held by banks and insurance companies; taxes on the gross proceeds of auctions and the sale of slaughtered animals; and stamp taxes on legal and commercial documents, medicines, perfumes and cosmetics, playing cards, matches, photographs, canned goods, gunpowder, feathers, telegrams, leather, pianos, yachts, billiard tables, drugs, patent medicines, and carriages; and annual license fees on bankers, auctioneers, wholesale and retail dealers, pawnbrokers, distillers, brewers, brokers, tobacconists, confectioners, horse dealers, livery stable keepers, cattle brokers, tallow-chandlers and soap makers, coal-oil distillers, peddlers, apothecaries, photographers, lawyers, physicians, and jugglers, defined to include anyone using sleight of hand.[13] Hotels, inns, and taverns paid license fees based on their annual rent. Bowling alleys and billiard parlors paid by the alley or table, while eating establishments, theaters, and circuses paid a flat annual fee. Most of these taxes and fees continued after the war, as the government paid off the bonds and loans, which provided most of its operating funds during the conflict.

The internal revenue system thrust the federal government and the federal courts into unprecedented involvement with the day-to-day lives of ordinary people. In 1863, U.S. district attorney Alfred Russell convinced grand jurors to return 54 indictments alleging violations of the internal revenue laws by retail liquor distributors, hotels, bowling alleys, billiard parlors, theaters, an auctioneer, a manufacturer, nine peddlers, four brokerages, an unstamped check, two unlicensed lawyers, and an unlicensed steamboat engineer. The number of such cases increased in 1864 , but by 1866, there were only 14 tax indictments as the district attorney turned his limited resources to address another consequence of the taxes, rampant smuggling. One of those 14 cases, though, is emblematic of the degree of the federal government's intrusion in day-to-day life: *United States v. Robert Nickel*, in which the defendant was fined for being an unlicensed juggler.

An aspect of these tax prosecutions that troubled contemporaries, but which has become a fact of life in tax matters today, was the use of informers. In the case of the two Michigan attorneys charged in 1863 with practicing law without a federal license, the U.S. paid informers half of the $30 fine paid by each attorney.[14]

A minor source of funds for the war that was used by both sides was the confiscation of property owned by enemies. The Confederate government and its individual states enacted laws in 1861, confiscating the property of citizens of Northern states, including debts owed by Southerners to creditors in the North. Enforcement was active in some jurisdictions, especially in border states, but the laws were a failure overall.[15] The federal government also tried to use enemy property to help finance the war, with similar results. On August 6, 1861, Congress passed a Confiscation Act that authorized federal government to seize any property used in aiding the insurrection and to have it condemned in the district and circuit courts.[16] On July 17, 1862, Congress followed up with a second Confiscation Act[17] which directed the president to seize all the real and personal property, whether or not used in the insurrection, owned by officers of the Confederate forces, any official of the Confederate government or of the government of individual states, and all persons with property located in a loyal state or territory who gave aid or comfort to the Confederacy. In practice, only a small amount of rebel property was ever confiscated, largely because President Lincoln's personal ambivalence about confiscation was communicated to the district attorneys who were assigned the task. Nevertheless, Judge Wilkins did have to rule on a few confiscation cases, including a suit to condemn $4,000 owned by Mrs. Sarah (Sallie) Woodvine Stevenson of Fredericksburg, Virginia, a sister of General Carter Littlepage Stevenson, Jr., "of the Rebel Army, a Public Enemy."[18]

Volunteers and Draftees

For the most part, the people of Michigan supported the Union war effort, although, as in most Northern States, many more did so in order to preserve the Union than to abolish slavery. During the war, 90,048 men from Michigan served in the federal armed forces (all but 598 of them in the army), and 14,855 of them died, including 10,136 who died of disease. Among the Michiganders rallying to the flag in 1861 was William D. Wilkins, clerk of the circuit court and Judge Wilkins's son. Because he had been an officer during the Mexican War, he was offered a commission as captain in the U.S. Army.[19] In August 1861, he took a leave of absence from the court and joined the staff of General Alpheus Williams, a former Wayne County judge and Detroit postmaster who had been assigned the command of a

Fig. 14.   Court Clerk and Major
William D. Wilkins. (Burton
Historical Collection, Detroit
Public Library)

brigade of the Army of the Potomac. During William Wilkins's absence,
J. E. Winder, John Winder's son, acted as deputy clerk of the circuit court.
As adjutant to General Williams, Captain Wilkins was involved in several
battles and was captured twice, at Cedar Mountain, Virginia, in August
1862, and at Chancellorsville, Virginia, in May 1863. On each occasion, he
was incarcerated in the notorious Libby Prison before he was exchanged.
In August 1863, after returning to Union lines for the second time, he
was promoted to Lieutenant Colonel and then resigned due to an injury to
his leg that left him lame.[20] He returned to the circuit court in October of
that year.

The Enrollment Act

Michigan had found it easy to recruit soldiers to fill its quota of the vol-
unteers requested by President Lincoln in 1861, but when the president
called for six more Michigan infantry regiments in July 1862, the response
was less than enthusiastic, and a rumor, planted by Confederate agents
operating out of Canada, that a secret military draft had begun resulted in
a riot in Detroit . Embarrassed by the suggestion that Wayne County was
disloyal, Judge Wilkins led a movement to raise one regiment more than
the president had requested, to be designated the 24th Michigan Volunteer
Infantry and to be recruited solely from Wayne County. A year later, this
regiment played a crucial role in preventing a Union disaster on the first
day of the Battle of Gettysburg.

Although a military draft may have been just a rumor in July 1862, the slow progress toward filling the ranks convinced the federal government to make the rumor a reality. On March 3, 1863, Congress passed the federal government's first military draft act, entitled "an act for enrolling and calling out the National forces, and for other purposes."[21] The first draft selection took place on July 11, 1863, just a week after Union victories at Gettysburg and Vicksburg. Under the act, qualified men could be called up for two years' service in the army or navy to make up any deficiency in their state's response to any presidential call for troops. The Confederacy had been drafting soldiers for more than a year; based on the Southern experience, the federal government anticipated resistance, and it was correct. The draft law was immediately and intensely unpopular. It was viewed as an unwarranted federal intrusion on personal choice and as discriminating against the poor because the law allowed the well-to-do to avoid being drafted by procuring a substitute or by paying a tax of $300. [22]

For several months in 1863, Judge Wilkins spent a large proportion of his time in court dealing with petitions for writs of habeas corpus filed by or on behalf of soldiers. In 1862, he had directed the marshal, Charles Dickey, to serve on the U.S. Army eight writs of habeas corpus on behalf of the parents of boys who had enlisted in the army despite being too young. The judge released all of those overly eager young men back to their parents, whether they wanted to return home or not. The draft, though, greatly increased the judge's habeas corpus business. Between March and September 1863, he issued 101 habeas corpus writs to determine the legality of the army's detention of men selected for the draft and who claimed they were exempt for various reasons—because they were over 45 years old, or were not U.S. citizens, or simply were not the person named in the draft lottery. Judge Wilkins granted most of those petitions, which do not seem to have been hotly contested by the army. The flow of habeas corpus petitions from unhappy draftees stopped abruptly on September 15, 1863, when President Lincoln relieved the federal judges of that burden by the simple, yet constitutionally perilous, step of suspending the right to habeas corpus throughout the United States for different classifications of people, including "officers, soldiers or seamen enrolled or drafted or mustered in."[23]

The Repentigny Seignory

The number of new cases filed in the district court in 1863, including habeas petitions, outnumbered those filed in the circuit court by five to one (309 to 60), but during most of that year Judge Wilkins found himself presiding, alone, over matters in the circuit court, leaving John Winder to note in the district court's journal, day after day: "No business, judge holding Circuit Court." From October through December 1863, though, all of the judge's attention was directed to the docket of the district court and specifically to the trial of Case No. 671, which came to be known as the Repentigny case.[24] The subject of this suit, which one historian has called "one of the most curious that would ever take place in a United States court,"[25] was the validity of a feudal title or "seignory" granted in 1751 by the King of France, over some 214,000 acres (about 18 miles square) along the south bank of the rapids of the St Mary's River. By 1863, this tract was the site of the town of Sault Ste. Marie, Michigan, and of the canal that allowed ships carrying the Upper Peninsula's iron ore and copper to pass from Lake Superior to Lake Huron.

This story begins in 1750, when the governor of New France, the Marquis de la Jonquière, signed an Order of Concession, which granted title to the land on the St. Mary's River to two young officers, the Chevalier Louis le Gardeur de Repentigny and Capitaine Louis de Bonne. This grant, which was ratified by King Louis XV of France in 1751, was the result of a decision by de la Jonquière that the colony needed a new fort on the St. Mary's River to provide a market for furs from Lake Superior and beyond that might otherwise be sold to the British Hudson's Bay Company. As he wrote to the French government in Paris: "[I]n order to thwart the movements that the English do not cease to make in order to seduce the Indian nations of the North, I had sent the Sieur Chevalier de Repentigny to the Saut St. Marie, in order to make there an establishment at his own expense; to build there a palisade fort to stop the Indians of the northern posts who go to and from the English; to interrupt the commerce they carry on; stop and prevent the continuation of the 'talks,' and of the presents which the English send to those nations to corrupt them, to put them entirely in their interests, and inspire them with feelings of hate and aversion for the French." Thus, rather than have the government build and man the fort, de la Jonquiere expected de Repentigny and de Bonne to build the fort and trading post at their own expense, to colonize the area with feudal tenants, and to govern them. De Bonne was a nephew of the governor and captain of his guard, but he had no experience on the frontier and apparently never visited the site. De Repentigny, on the other hand, a veteran of frontier combat who had served at Michilimackinac and other western outposts of New France, made the 800 mile canoe trip from Montreal to his seigniory in 1750 where he built a stockade, and hired a habitant couple as tenants.

Between 1750 and 1754, de Repentigny spent autumns and winters at the Sault, returning east with his load of furs in the spring, but this routine was ended by the resumption of war with Great Britain in 1755 in which de Bonne died. In 1760, France admitted defeat and ceded its claims in North America to Great Britain. The peace treaty offered the French residents a choice: they could remain and have their property interests preserved if they swore allegiance to the British crown. Otherwise, they had 18 months to sell their property to British citizens or lose it. De Repentigny chose to leave and sold property he owned in the east, but he was not able to find a buyer for his half of the Sault seignory. He left Canada with the last French troops and returned to the French army where he had a long career, including service in the American Revolution in Georgia, before he died in Paris in 1786. The widow de Bonne chose to remain in Canada with her young son, P. A. de Bonne, and become British subjects. Soon after the French army left Canada, the British built a fort on the site of de Repentigny's stockade which had burned down. This became an American fort when Great Britain finally vacated the Northwest Territory. The land included in the concession was occupied by the Ojibway (Chippewa) until 1820, when their title was extinguished by a treaty with the United States, except for "a perpetual right of fishing at the falls of St. Mary's, and also a place of encampment upon the tract hereby ceded."[26] Thereafter the United States surveyed the district and sold about 108,000 of the original 214,400 acres to settlers.[27]

In 1841, several people claiming title to the seignory as successors to de Bonne and de Repentigny petitioned Congress for recognition of their land claim.[28] The de Repentigny claimants were the chevalier's great grandchildren: Louise Pauline de Repentigny, Lizette Antoinette le Gardeur de Repentigny, Josephine Lucrece le Gardeur de Repentigny, and Josephine Clavie,[29] all of them French nationals, while the chain of title of the de Bonne claim was more complex. P. A. de Bonne came of age in 1779, and in 1781, he "rendered faith and homage at the Castle of St. Louis, in Quebec, before the governor," one of the conditions of the concession. In 1796, he sold his interest to an American citizen, James Caldwell, who later quitclaimed the interest to Arthur Noble, a British subject. Eventually, the estate of Noble's nephew sold the interest to the current claimant, John Rotton, also a British subject.

The 1841 petition knocked around the Senate before being rejected in 1848. Undaunted, the claimants tried again in 1858, asking Congress to allow them to establish their claims in federal court.[30] This petition gained the support of an influential U.S. senator, Judah P. Benjamin of Louisiana,[31] and, on April 19, 1860, Congress passed a Private Act.[32] The act authorized "the legal representatives of the Sieur de Bonne and of the Chevalier de Repentigny . . . to present their petition to the United States district court for the district of Michigan" and authorized the court "to examine the same." However, the act also provided that, if successful, the petitioners would receive not the land described in the Order of Concession but, instead, warrants for 214,000 acres from the public lands elsewhere. Even so, the potential profit to the petitioners and loss to the United States were enormous.

In January 1861, U.S. Senator Jacob M. Howard, as attorney for the claimants, filed their petition in Detroit.[33] The parties spent the next two and a half years gathering evidence, including taking the depositions of witnesses at Sault Sainte Marie, Montreal, Quebec, Washington, D.C., Paris, and the Island of Guadalupe. Finally, trial began in the Custom House on October 28, 1863, and continued for another 29 days of testimony and argument. District Attorney Alfred Russell tried the case for the United States along with two other Detroit attorneys, Hovey K. Clarke and T. W. Lockwood, while Senator Howard continued to represent the petitioners;[34] nobody seems to have questioned the propriety of a sitting U.S. senator trying a private case against his own government.

During the trial, Howard argued the validity of the grant of the concession under French law applicable in 1750 and pointed to treaties between the United States and France upholding French titles in the former New France. Russell, on the other hand, argued that petitioners' claims had been extinguished in 1760 because de Repentigny and de Bonne's son did not satisfy British laws dealing with the preservation of French titles. However, both Russell and Howard focused the main parts of their evidence and arguments on whether de Repentigny and de Bonne had satisfied the conditions of the concession under the coutume de Paris, as required by the Order of Concession. In particular, did they "improve the said concession and use and occupy the same by their tenants"—i.e., was the stockade erected by de Repentigny a satisfactory improvement, did de Bonne and de Repentigny have to live there continuously, were the habitant couple living on the concession tenants with feudal duties or just employees?

The parties submitted the case to Judge Wilkins on December 9, 1863. He took his time to review the evidence and law, and, on April 5, 1864, ruled in favor of the petitioners. He ruled that (1) the concession was valid under French law because it had been properly granted by de la Jonquière, ratified by Louis XV, and acknowledged by the grantees; and (2) the title was valid as against the United States when granted and so still valid under treaty law. After unsuccessful post-trial maneuvering by Russell (among other things, he wanted the claimants to pay feudal dues to the United States), in 1866 the government appealed the decision to the United States Supreme Court.

Oral arguments were held in the old Senate Chamber in the basement of the Capitol on January 29 and February 1, 1867, with Senator Howard again representing the claimants while District Attorney Russell was joined by U.S. attorney general Henry Stanbery for the United States. On May 6, Justice Samuel Nelson announced that the Supreme Court had reversed Judge Wilkins.[35] The Supreme Court dealt separately with the de Repentigny and de Bonne claims. As to the former, the Court noted that the Chevalier had not fulfilled the requirements of the 1760 treaty regarding preservation of property rights in Canada—he had neither pledged allegiance to the British crown and remained in Canada nor sold the Sault seigniory to a British subject within 18 months. Furthermore, after leaving Canada he had many times complained that he had lost his rights in the

Sault lands in order to remain loyal to France. The Court concluded that de Repentigny had deliberately abandoned his claims to the seigniory and that, consequently, his heirs had no remaining interest.

Although the result was the same, the Court's analysis as to de Bonne was more complex, beginning with the tenancy requirements of the concession. The Court noted that a seignory was a conditional grant, which carried feudal duties to the King. The royal confirmation of the Sault seigniory specifically required the grantees to "improve the said concession and use and occupy the same by their tenants; in default thereof the same shall be united to his majesty's domain"—i.e., rendered void. The evidence proved to the Court that "neither De Bonne nor those claiming under him had taken any steps in fulfillment of the conditions" and that even the efforts of de Repentigny fell far short of what the concession required. However, the Court stated, "we do not intend to put this branch of the case on this ground." Instead, the Court held that the United States had acquired all of the rights of the King of France in the seignory, including the right to reunite it with the King's domain, and that the actions taken by Congress in surveying, selling, and confirming the purchasers' titles to the land constituted just such a reunion, effectively abolishing the seignory.

Confederate Plots and Pirates

Michigan was hundreds of miles from the theaters of war, but it was not immune from the activities of Confederate agents operating with impunity in Canada. Some agents spread Southern propaganda, others acted as agents provocateurs, and one of them devised a plan by which a small band of raiders would attempt one of the most daring operations of the war.[36] In April 1862, the United States opened a camp for prisoners of war on Johnson's Island in Lake Erie's Sandusky Bay. More than 15,000 captured Confederate officers were held in the camp at one time or another, although the highest number at any one time was 3,200. Because the camp was just 15 miles from the Canadian side of the lake, the iron warship U.S.S. *Michigan*, which had been involved in the Strang case, stood guard nearby.

Jacob Thompson, who had been a 12-year U.S. congressman from North Carolina and U.S. secretary of the interior under President James Buchanan, joined the Confederacy in 1861, first as inspector general of the Confederate Army and then, from 1864 as a "confidential agent" stationed in Canada. Thompson developed a plan to disrupt the Democratic national convention in Chicago, but, when that fizzled out, he decided to try to wreak havoc at Sandusky instead. During the summer of 1864, Thompson ordered several conspirators to infiltrate the civilian community at Sandusky while another man, Charles Cole, ingratiated himself with the *Michigan*'s officers. The plan was for a band of armed Confederates gathered in Canada to steal a steamship and sail it to Sandusky Bay. Cole was to drug the officers during a dinner and then signal the raiders who would storm the *Michigan*, use the threat of her 15 cannons to free hundreds of prisoners, and then raid up and down the lakes before seeking asylum in Canada. Thompson, however, was surprisingly indiscreet for a secret agent. He operated openly out of the largest hotel in Windsor, across the river from Detroit, where he was kept under surveillance by American and British agents. One of them, Godfrey Hyams, reported the plot on detail to federal officials in Michigan, who in turn warned Sandusky.

On September 18, 1864, at Detroit, a man giving the name Bennett Burley went on board the small passenger steamship *Philo Parsons*, which operated between Detroit and Sandusky, and asked the captain if he would stop the next day at Amherstburg, Canada, to pick up several passengers. The captain agreed and, on September 19, the *Parsons* welcomed on board 26 men who were, in fact, raiders led by John Beall, an officer in the Confederate Navy. Once the *Parsons* was in Lake Erie, the conspirators took control of her and later seized another small steamer, the *Island Queen*, which they sank. The *Parsons* approached Sandusky in the dead of night, but when Cole did not flash the proper signal from the *Michigan* (because he and several other conspirators had already been arrested), Beall broke off the attack, returned to Amherstburg, and scuttled the *Parsons*. Cole remained in prison until 1866, apparently without ever being tried. Thompson and Beall fled to the Niagara area and kept trying to sabotage the Union war effort until Beall was captured at Niagara Falls, New York, after failing to derail a freight train. He was hanged for espionage just two weeks before the end of the war.

News of the aborted raid spurred Judge Wilkins and District Attorney Alfred Russell into action. Russell focused on Burley, who had incautiously given his real name to the captain of the *Parsons*. The circuit court's grand jury quickly returned an indictment in which Burley was "charged with the crimes of piracy, robbery, and assault with intent to commit murder."[37] Burley, it soon came out, was a young man enjoying somebody else's war. Born in Scotland around 1840, he left home to find adventure and arrived in Richmond early in the war. He joined the Confederate forces, but simple soldiering was too boring, so he turned instead to spying and sabotage, captured a Union steamer in Chesapeake Bay, and raided behind Union lines. Eventually, he was captured, convicted of spying, and sentenced to be shot at Fort Delaware, near Philadelphia. He escaped through the sewer running beneath his cell and made his way to Canada, where he volunteered to assist his Beall with the Johnson's Island plot.

In November 1864, U.S. secretary of state William Henry Seward demanded Burley's extradition from Canada. Russell was concerned that Britain would not recognize the piracy charge, especially against a British subject, so it was arranged that the sheriff of Ottawa County, Ohio, would issue an arrest warrant charging Burley with armed robbery. It seems that, for the sheer fun of it, he had relieved the clerk of the *Parsons* of his wallet at gunpoint before putting him ashore. Canadian authorities arrested Burley in Guelph, Upper Canada, and took him in front of a judge in Toronto for an extradition hearing. Russell sent his assistant district attorney, Henry Billings Brown (a future U.S. district judge and Supreme Court justice) to Toronto with orders to return with Burley. As Brown later remarked, "I had a very lively time with him in Toronto, which was filled with rebels, and for a time it looked as though I should fail to get my man." Burley argued first that as a British subject he was immune from extradition, an argument the court rejected.[38] Burley's other point, that he was an "acting master" in the Confederate Navy and so had committed an act of war, not a crime, also proved fruitless, principally because accepting the "act of war" defense would be tantamount to recognizing the Confederate states as a nation, a step that Great Britain had rejected. On January 20, 1865, the judge ordered Burley extradited on the Ohio warrant, much to the anger of the Confederates who filled the courtroom.[39]

Brown brought Burley back to Detroit where he was arraigned on the federal charges in the Custom House and assigned to a cell in Detroit's House of Correction, where he lived for five months. The warden, Zebulon Brockway, was well aware of Burley's tendency to escape, and he made sure this prisoner was under close guard. He remembered that: "I wakened in the small hours of every night to inspect personally the corridor where he was confined and to note the vigilance of the patrolling guard."[40] Even after the war ended, Burley remained in jail because the federal government was still determined that he should be punished, although, to satisfy Canadian authorities, only for robbery. In July, he was taken (ironically, by the *Parsons*) to Port Clinton, Ohio, to stand trial. The jury deadlocked, likely because the war was over, and Burley was returned to jail to await the Ohio court's October term. He used his charm to be given the run of the jail, and, one day, he just went out a window and escaped back to Canada and then home to Scotland. Upon his return to Great Britain, Burley changed the spelling of his name to Bennet Burleigh and became a famous war correspondent for London's *Daily Telegraph*, reporting on combat in Egypt, the Sudan, West Africa, South Africa, Madagascar, Morocco, Greece, Somalia, Korea, and the Balkans. While Burleigh was covering the Russo-Japanese War, Henry Billings Brown, by then a Supreme Court justice, told reporters that he always watched the news closely to see what reckless adventure Burleigh would indulge in next. Burleigh authored several books on his travels before his death in London in 1914.[41]

The Eastern and Western Districts of Michigan

The most enduring change experienced by Michigan's federal courts during the war was the decision to split the District of Michigan into two judicial districts, denominated the Eastern and Western Districts of Michigan. Since the state's birth, its population had more than tripled, from fewer than 200,000 residents in 1837 to 749,113 in 1860. Moreover, much of that growth was spread across the southern portions of the Lower Peninsula. Although Wayne County, with its growing large manufacturing base, remained the most populous county in Michigan, increasing from 42,756 residents in 1840 to 75,547 in 1860, the U.S. Census of 1860 recorded a significant population in Michigan's western agricultural counties such as Kent (30,716), Kalamazoo (24,646), St. Joseph (21,262), and Van Buren (15,224). At the same time, Chicago and Milwaukee became industrial centers, so that shipping on Lake Michigan soared, as did the number of collisions, mariners' wage disputes, and contract claims which ended up in Detroit's district court, far from the parties and the evidence. Those factors led to a movement for a second district judge or, better yet, a separate district, to hold court in Grand Rapids for the convenience of western Michigan, an idea that had surprising support in Michigan's eastern counties as well as its western.

In February 1862, Michigan's entire delegation to the 37th Congress supported HR 267, introduced in the U.S. House of Representatives by Representative Francis William Kellogg of Grand Rapids, to split the District of Michigan. The bill passed in the House easily in July, but ran into resistance in the Senate, despite being sponsored by Michigan's formidable senator Jacob Howard, a close friend and confidant of President Lincoln. The Senate Committee on the Judiciary opposed the division of Michigan's judicial district on principle. For over a decade, the Senate had been bombarded with bills from practically every state seeking to divide federal judicial districts, but the committee had rejected them all. The senators expressed concerns over the cost of funding another judge, set of court officers, and courthouse, but they also feared that an indirect result of adding districts would be to further burden an over-worked U.S. Supreme Court which was already two years behind in deciding appeals.

The Senate reasoned that adding a district would increase the number of private civil cases filed in the district and circuit courts as attorneys in the new district, now closer to the federal courthouse, would find that it was just as convenient to file cases in the federal courts as in a state court. Because the parties in every civil case filed in a federal were entitled to appeal an adverse decision to the Supreme Court, an increase in cases also meant an increase in appeals. When Howard brought a new bill to the floor for a vote on February 17, 1863, Senator Lyman Trumbull of Illinois, chair of the judiciary committee, remarked dismissively that: "I suppose it will be very convenient to have a court at Grand Rapids, which is a very flourishing town or city, on the western side of the State of Michigan. There is a railroad running right through there to Detroit. You may pass at any time from Grand Rapids to Detroit in ten hours. But still they urge that there is a great deal of maritime business and a great necessity for a court there. They always urge these considerations in every State."[42] Although Howard and Judge Wilkins had locked horns over the case of deputy marshal Tyler, the senator urged passage of the bill for the judge's sake: "I know quite well . . . that the excellent and learned district judge of that district is literally occupied the whole year, early and late, in hearing and determining cases, and in other matters concerned with the discharge of his duties, in which he is as faithful a man as ever I have met with in my life. He spends his whole time in the discharge of his duties; and the business is perpetually accumulating on his hands; and he does all this service learnedly, faithfully, and well, for the small pittance of $2,500 a year. I ought not to say that he does all the business of both of the courts, for the circuit judge comes and assists in holding a circuit court there ordinarily twice a year, but frequently only once a year, and remains there not to exceed a week or ten to twelve days. The great mass of business is thrown on the district judge. He ought to be relieved in some degree from the multitude of cases he is called upon to decide, admiralty cases as well as civil cases."[43] Senator Morton S. Wilkinson of Minnesota voiced his support, but at the end of the day the Senate delayed consideration of the bill.

When Howard brought the bill forward again a week later, other Senators joined the debate. Lafayette S. Foster, of Connecticut, declared that although the people of Michigan were the "bone of [New England's] bone and flesh of our flesh," he had to oppose the bill.[44] William Pitt Fessenden, of Maine, offered his opinion that dividing districts was "rather a matter to make offices than to subserve any other purpose."[45] Senator Fessenden also doubted the need for a second court: "I cannot conceive how it is possible that the maritime business and the business peculiar to the United States courts in the State of Michigan should require anything like another court in that State."[46] New York City, he pointed out, had four times the business of all of Michigan, yet it got by with one court. Iowa Senator James Wilson Grimes joked that if the new court was meant to serve citizens unable to get to Detroit easily, then it ought to be located at Copper Harbor on Lake Superior.

Other senators, such as Lazarus Whitehead Powell of Kentucky, who might have been anticipating their own states' needs for multiple federal courts, supported the bill, and, after the speeches, the bill passed 25 to 11 and became law on February 24, 1863. Congress divided the District of Michigan into the Eastern and Western Districts of Michigan, and assigned Judge Wilkins and his court officers to the Eastern District.[47] The act bisected the Lower Peninsula by a line running roughly north and south from Mackinac. Although Congress included the state capital, Lansing, in the Eastern District, the legislators once more selected Detroit as the only location where the district's courts could hold sessions. The Upper Peninsula was allocated to the Eastern District except for Delta County on the

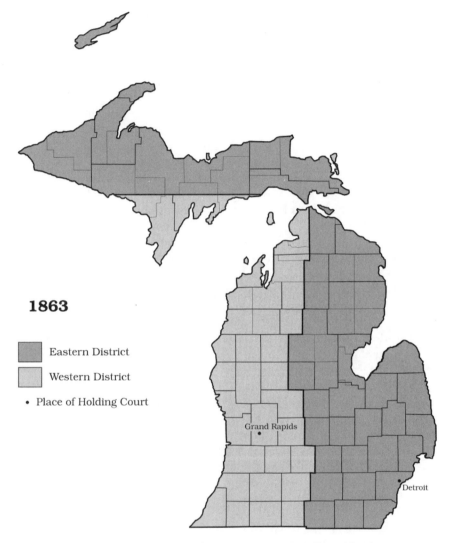

Fig. 15.   The Eastern District of Michigan, 1863. (Ellen White)

north shore of Lake Michigan. The logic of this division was to assign Lake
Michigan and its Michigan coastline on both peninsulas to the Western
District so that its large number of admiralty cases could be heard in Grand
Rapids instead of Detroit. Lake Superior and its Michigan coastline stayed
with the Eastern District because Lake Superior was closer by ship to De-
troit than to Grand Rapids. The original division allocated Calhoun and
Branch Counties to the Western District, but, after complaints from those
counties, Congress returned them to the Eastern District in June 1864.[48]

The War Ends but the Taxes Do Not

The Army of Northern Virginia surrendered at Appomattox Court house, Virginia, on April 9, 1865, and the last ragged Confederate units followed suit in May. Jubilation in the North turned to anguish when news arrived of the assassination of President Lincoln on April 14. By chance, the 24th Michigan Volunteer Infantry of Gettysburg fame was in Springfield, Illinois, when the president's body arrived, and the regiment served as guard of honor during the public viewing and at the funeral. The 24th then headed north, was mustered out of federal service in Detroit, and, like other veterans, found their way home to towns and farms throughout the state.

The war may have been over, but it still had to be paid for; in particular, the holders of war bonds had to be paid back. Consequently, the federal taxes and license fees lingered until 1872, when Congress, at the urging of President Grant, repealed most of them except for the tax on whiskey, which remained in force and became a steady source of income for the federal government. The continuation of war taxes also meant the continuation of a greatly swollen criminal docket. From 1851 to 1862, the district court averaged just 28 new criminal cases per year, but from 1863 to 1869, there were ten times as many criminal cases, an average of 291 per year.[49] Most of the added caseload was due to two categories, tax enforcement and smuggling prevention. In the immediate post-war years, the focus of federal prosecutions was a boom in smuggling, a predictable consequence of the wartime taxes and customs duties. In 1866, for example, 171 of the 296 criminal cases filed involved violations of the customs laws. Later, the focus returned to tax evasion, and in 1870 and 1871, tax cases outnumbered customs cases by 291 to 138. Later in the 1870s, the number of criminal cases returned to lower levels, although liquor-tax enforcement guaranteed they never returned to pre-war levels.

Murder and Adultery at Fort Gratiot

Despite the expanded involvement of the federal government, and the federal judiciary, into areas of law previously reserved to the states, the enforcement of most common-law crimes, such as burglary, robbery, murder, or adultery, remained the responsibility of state and local laws. The major exception to this rule was for criminal acts committed on federal land, including federal military reservations. For example, on July 17, 1866, Judge Wilkins, presiding over the circuit court in Detroit, sentenced Private George Bishop of the 17th U.S. Infantry to be hanged for the murder of a fellow soldier at Fort Gratiot, a military post adjacent to Port Huron. The evidence established that, on May 12, 1866, Bishop and Corporal Frederick Frederickson went fishing in a rowboat on the St. Clair River just offshore from the base. For reasons unknown, Bishop threw Frederickson out of the boat, and the corporal drowned.[50] At first, Bishop claimed that Frederickson had fallen into the river by accident, but after the body was discovered several miles downstream a month later, a coroner's jury found that the death was the result of homicide, and the Eastern District's grand jury indicted Bishop for murder.[51] At the end of the trial, the petit jury returned a guilty verdict, and Judge Wilkins imposed the death sentence, to be carried out on October 7. District attorney Alfred Russell, several of the jurors, and "many other respectable citizens" petitioned President Andrew Johnson to commute Bishop's sentence, which he did by an order dated September 20, 1866, reducing Bishop's sentence to life imprisonment in the state prison at Jackson, Michigan.[52]

The summer of 1866 was an exciting time for gossips at Fort Gratiot, as another federal prosecution for a common-law crime took place at about the same time as the Bishop murder case. On June 13, 1866, George Wilmot and Mary Ann Comby were charged in the district court with committing adultery on a U.S. military reservation.[53] After a short trial, Judge Wilkins sentenced both defendants to six months in the St. Clair County jail.

The Judiciary Act of 1869

On April 4, 1869, Congress made the first major change in the federal judiciary since 1802. The justices of the U.S. Supreme Court had complained since the Judiciary Act of 1789 about the burden placed on them to "ride circuit" over terrible roads and through miserable weather in order to attend circuit courts in each district in their assigned circuits. Congress' reduction of their attendance obligation to one term per district per year in 1844[54] did little to reduce the Justices' complaints, particularly when an increased appellate caseload during the Civil War caused the Supreme Court's docket to fall behind by two to three years. The Judiciary Act of 1869,[55] provided a new type of Article III federal judge, a Circuit Judge, to take over circuit riding from the justices. The act allocated one circuit judge to each of the nine judicial circuits and provided that henceforth circuit courts could be held by the circuit justice, the circuit judge, or the district judge, or by any two of them. Although section 4 of the act also stated that each justice was to "attend at least one term of the circuit court in each district of his circuit during every period of two years," in practice they rarely did. In fact, even the circuit judges found they could not cover all of the circuit courts, and the district judges ended up doing most of the work in both courts.[56]

Changing the Judicial Guard

Although the creation of circuit judges did not always improve the lot of district judges, the Judiciary Act of 1869 also contained a measure much

Fig. 16. Judge Wilkins at retirement, age 71. (Burton Historical Collection, Detroit Public Library)

anticipated by Judge Wilkins, the first retirement plan for federal judges. Section 5 of the act provided that any U.S. judge aged 70 or older who had ten years' or more service on the federal bench could retire and continue, "during the residue of his natural life, [to] receive the same salary which was by law payable to him at the time of his resignation."[57] This was a relief for Wilkins, who had just reached the retirement age on February 19, 1869. He was very tired and unwell, but he could not have supported his large household without his salary, which had been increased in 1867 to $3,500 per year.[58] Shortly before the act became effective on December 6, 1869, Judge Wilkins announced that he would retire on Friday, February 18, 1870, after 38 years as a judge in Michigan and 33 years on the bench of the U.S. District Court. Judge Wilkins's circuit and district clerks, his son William D. Wilkins and John Winder, also resigned effective April 1, 1870.

Unfortunately, Judge Wilkins was able to collect his pension and enjoy his leisure for only two years. On May 11, 1872, he suffered a massive stroke, and died at his home on Jefferson Avenue in Detroit at 1:30 a.m. on May 17.[59] William Wilkins, who became heavily involved with the Detroit School Board after he retired, died in Detroit on March 31, 1882, at the age of 55, having never completely recovered from his Civil War experience.[60] John Winder, known to his friends as "Colonel" Winder and wealthy from his real estate holdings, remained active as a Circuit Court commissioner until he died aged 93 on September 26, 1897, at his home on Woodward Avenue in Detroit.[61]

Notes

1. *Detroit Free Press*, January 30, 1861.

2. *Detroit Daily Advertiser*, April 15, 1861.

3. *Detroit Free Press*, April 14, 1861.

4. Frank B. Woodford, *Father Abraham's Children: Michigan Episodes in the Civil War*, 2nd ed. (Detroit, MI: Wayne State University Press, 1999), 256, quoting the *Detroit Free Press*, May 11, 1861.

5. For examples of the newspaper's acid tongue, see Michael O. Smith, "The First Michigan Colored Infantry: A Black Regiment in the Civil War," (master's thesis, Wayne State University, 1987).

6. *Detroit Free Press*, April 19, 1861.

7. *Detroit Free Press*, April 20, 1861.

8. Lincoln found himself with three Supreme Court vacancies at the outset of the war. In addition to McLean, Justice Peter Vivian Daniel of Virginia had also recently died while Justice Archibald Campbell resigned and returned to his home in Alabama. Lincoln hoped that the war would be short and that by delaying he could name Southerners to replace Daniel and Campbell. Surrency, 37.

9. 12 Stat. 576.

10. 12 Stat. 637.

11. The circuit court journal book for the Civil War period, which would be the best evidence of who presided, is missing. There are no reported cases from Michigan involving Justices Catron or Davis. On June 3, 1863, the *Detroit Free Press* announced that Justice Swayne would attend the June term, but the earliest reported Swayne decision is *The John Fretter*, 13 F.Cas. 672 (C.C. Mich. 1866), allegedly issued on May 12, 1866. That date may be a clerical error, however, as the opinion states it is issued from the District of Michigan rather than from the Eastern District.

12. 12 Stat. 432.

13. Cynthia G. Fox, "Income Tax Records of the Civil War Years," *Prologue Magazine* (National Archives and Records Administration, Winter 1986), http://www.archives.gov/publications/prologue/1986/winter/civil-war-tax-records.html. (Accessed 9/21/11)

14. District of Michigan, District Court Criminal Docket A; Eastern District of Michigan, District Court Criminal Docket B.

15. John Christopher Schwab, *The Confederate States of America, 1861–1865: A Financial and Industrial History of the South During the Civil War* (Chicago, IL: University of Chicago Press, 1901).

16. 12 Stat. 319.

17. 12 Stat. 589.

18. *U.S. v. $4,000, Property of Mrs. Sallie Stevenson, a Public Enemy*. General Stevenson, an 1838 graduate of West Point and a veteran of the Seminole and Mexican Wars, was stationed in Detroit for several years as a young officer. Alpheus S. Williams, *The Civil War Letters of General Alpheus S. Williams: From the Cannon's Mouth*, Milo Quaife, ed. (Detroit, MI: Wayne University Press and Detroit Historical Society, 1959), 333. Stevenson resigned his commission in 1861 to join the Confederate army, in which he rose to the rank of major general.

19. Another Wilkins family member who went off to war was the husband of his grandchild Eleanor, Orlando Poe, a professional soldier who commanded the Second Michigan Volunteer Infantry and then served as chief engineering officer for General William T. Sherman during the Atlanta campaign and the march to the sea. After the war, as the federal government's chief engineer in Michigan, Poe designed and built several lighthouses on the Great Lakes and a new lock at Sault Ste. Marie. Paul Taylor, *Orlando M. Poe: Civil War General and Great Lakes Engineer* (Kent, OH: Kent State University Press, 2009), 27, 38.

20. Alpheus S. Williams, *The Civil War Letters of General Alpheus S. Williams: From the Cannon's Mouth*, Milo Quaife, ed. (Detroit, MI: Wayne University Press and Detroit Historical Society, 1959), 19, 102, 193, 254.

21. 12 Stat. 731.

22. On July 13, a bloody week of rioting broke out in New York City, which was quelled only when several infantry regiments, including one from Michigan, were rushed from the battlefield to Manhattan. There was a race riot in Detroit in 1863 as well, although its relation to the draft is disputed because it occurred before the draft became law.

23. Presidential Proclamation, September 15, 1863. The value of the federal draft was, and is, a subject of considerable debate. Of 195,000 men drafted, only 36,000 men (25,000 of them substitutes) joined the federal armed forces. Alan Nevins, *The War for the Union: The Organized War* (New York: Scribner's, 1971), 8.

24. *In the matter of the Petition of Louise Pauline de Repentigny, Lizette Antoinette le Gardeur de Repentigny, Josephine Lucrece le Gardeur de Repentigny, Agnes Slacke, and the children of Josephine Clavie, deceased: Therese Emilie Clavie, Antoine Clavie, Marie Clorinde Clavie & Marie Octavie Clavie, petitioners v. United States, respondent.* For the facts of this case, I relied on several sources including the opinions and briefs filed in the case as well as Marjorie Cahn Brazer's excellent article, "Feudalism on the Frontier," *Michigan History*, vol. 69 (no. 3, May/June 1985), 32–39.

25. Brazer, 32.

26. Treaty of the United States with the Chippewa, June 16, 1820, 7 Stat. 206.

27. 12 Stat. 838.

28. U.S. Senate Journal, January 14, 1841.

29. After the case was filed, Josephine Clavie died and was replaced by her daughters, de Repentigny's great, great grandchildren: Therese Emilie Clavie, Antoine Clavie, Marie Clorinde Clavie, and Marie Octavie Clavie.

30. S. Bill 259, 35th Congress, 1st Session.

31. Ironically, by the time the case came to trial Judah Benjamin was secretary of state of the Confederacy.

32. 12 Stat. 838.

33. District of Michigan, District Court Admiralty Docket C, Case # 671.

34. *Detroit Free Press*, October 29, 1863.

35. *U.S. v. Repentigny*, 72 U.S. 211 (1866).

36. For more on the Johnson's Island affair, see Woodford, *Father Abraham's Children*, 137–147. Regarding the scope of Confederate plots hatched in Canada, see Hector Willoughby Charlesworth, "Civil War Operation in Canada," *The Canadian Scene. Sketches: Political and Historical* (Toronto: Macmillan, 1927).

37. Shepherd, 45–52.

38. *Re Burley*, 1 Upper Canada Law Journal 34 (Court of Common Pleas of Upper Canada, 1865).

39. *New York Times*, January 21, 1865.

40. Paul W. Keve, "The House of Correction That Detroit Built," *The Court Legacy*, vol. VII, no. 1, April 1999.

41. *New York Times*, June 18, 1914.

42. *Congressional Globe*, 37th Congress, 3rd session, 1018 (February 17, 1863).

43. Id., 1019.

44. *Congressional Globe*, 37th Congress, 3rd session, 1155 (February 21, 1863).

45. Id., 1156.

46. Id.

47. 12 Stat. 660.

48. 13 Stat. 143.

49. Criminal Docket Book A, District Court, District of Michigan; Criminal Docket Books B–E, District Court, Eastern District of Michigan, Record Group 21, NARA-GL.

50. *U.S. v. Bishop*, Eastern District of Michigan, Circuit Court Criminal File No. 188.

51. Western Historical Company, *History of St. Clair County, Michigan* (1883), 614.

52. *U.S. v. Bishop*, Eastern District of Michigan Circuit Court Criminal File No. 188., Presidential Commutation, September 20, 1866.

53. *U.S. v. George Wilmot & Mary Ann Comby*, Eastern District of Michigan District Court Criminal File No. 443.

54. 5 Stat. 676.

55. 16 Stat 44.

56. Surrency, 47.

57. 16 Stat. 45, Sec. 5.

58. 14 Stat. 471. Congress provided that this salary included any expenses or travel costs incurred by the judge.

59. *Detroit Free Press*, May 17, 1872.

60. *Michigan Historical and Pioneer Collection*, vol. 4, 438–439.

61. *Detroit Journal*, September 27, 1897; Robert Budd Ross, *Early Bench and Bar of Detroit: From 1805 to the End of 1850* (Detroit, 1907), 7–14.

PART II

The Industrial Revolution and the Gilded Age, 1870–1900

Between 1860 and 1900, the percentage of the U.S. population character-ized by the Census Bureau as urban[1] doubled from 20 percent to 40 per-cent. Because the overall population more than doubled during that inter-val, the number of urban residents in 1900 (30,214,832) was almost five times what it had been in 1860 (6,216,518). This urban population boom was largely a result of a transformation in the national economy from prin-cipally agricultural to industrial manufacturing, which raised the United States to first place in world manufacturing output in 1890 and drew both rural populations and immigrants (12,000,000 from Europe between 1870 and 1900) to America's urban centers of manufacturing. The nature of industry changed as well—manufacturing by small, owner-operated busi-nesses employing skilled craftsmen gave way to giant corporations using mass production by largely unskilled workers who were supervised by a new managerial class of employees. From 1870 to 1893, the period Mark Twain derisively labeled the Gilded Age in the belief that its prosperity and glitter were superficial,[2] the economy of the United States grew at a rate not equaled before or since. Although the Panic of 1893, a major depression, derailed the Gilded Age and led to calls for reform, by 1900, the economy seemed to have recovered its strength and optimism was high among the rich and the new middle class.

From 1870 to 1900, the Eastern District participated in the population growth and prosperity associated with the Gilded Age, as well as in the economic pain caused by the Panic of 1893, but most of the district's eco-nomic growth came not from large-scale manufacturing, but from the ex-ploitation of Michigan's natural resources by logging and agriculture, and from industries supporting those activities. The most important industry in the Eastern District during this period was logging of the white pine, which grew in vast forests north of the 43rd parallel. Beginning about 1860, Saginaw County became the center of this industry. Immigrants from New England, Canada, and Europe arrived there to fell trees, saw them into boards, and work in other businesses that supported logging. The district's population more than doubled between 1860 and 1900 (466,992 to 1,376,584), and although Wayne County remained the district's most populous county, Saginaw County was second-largest from 1880 to 1910. Other counties associated with the timber industry also grew exponentially, such as Bay and Midland. Even Gladwin, which had only fourteen residents in 1860, increased to 6,664 in 1900.

Following the Civil War, Michigan's second-most important industry was mining, particularly extracting iron and copper ore from huge deposits in the Upper Peninsula. After June 1878, when Congress reallocated all of the Upper Peninsula to the Western District,[3] there was little or no mining for metals in the Eastern District, but mining, like logging, became the basis for transforming Detroit, Pontiac, Lansing, and Flint into manufacturing centers by the beginning of the 20th century. The timber industry attracted wagon and carriage makers who transitioned to railroad cars in the 1890s and eventually to automobiles using iron and copper shipped through the Soo Canal.

CHAPTER 5

The Eastern District in the Post War Era, 1870–1885

The Eastern District, 1870–1885

From 1870 to 1880 the population of the new Eastern District increased by 36 percent to 986,687 and this growth continued to and beyond 1885. This population bump did not seem to result in an increase in the number of cases filed. Although the number of civil cases filed in the circuit court did increase significantly between 1874 and 1885, most cases involved attempts to collect on debts and thus were more likely the result of the Coinage Act of 1873[4] under which the U.S. government no longer issued silver coins, resulting in a reduction in the money supply that forced many debtors to default. Although there were some cases of historical interest during the 1870s, the most important events involved purely judicial matters: changes in the judges, in the courts' jurisdiction, and the question of whether the courts should be held outside Detroit.

Judicial Succession

After 33 years of one district judge, Ross Wilkins, the next 15 years witnessed the appointment of two successive district judges as well as the first U.S. circuit judge for the Sixth Circuit and his successor. In January 1870, President Ulysses S. Grant nominated Detroit attorney Halmer Hull Emmons to be circuit judge for the Sixth Circuit, one of the judgeships created by the Judiciary Act of 1869. Emmons was not the president's first choice, nor was he the first circuit judge for the Sixth Circuit. That honor went to District Judge Solomon L. Withey of the Western District of Michigan. Grant nominated Withey for circuit judge with the apparent plan to open up a vacancy for a deserving Republican in the Western District and to replace Judge Wilkins in the Eastern District with one of two Detroit attorneys, Hovey K. Clark or John S. Newberry, both loyal Republicans. However, after the Senate confirmed Withey and he received his commission, he suddenly decided that he did not want to be away from his family for months at a time holding circuit courts in Ohio, Kentucky, and Tennessee, so he resigned and was allowed to resume his seat as district judge.[5]

For a few days after Withey resigned, there was a fear among Michigan Republicans that the circuit judgeship would go to an attorney from one of the circuit's other states, but they were relieved when President Grant offered the job to Emmons and he accepted. Even so, his appointment was met with mixed feelings in Detroit. Nobody suggested that he was not eminently qualified to be a federal judge; to the contrary he was one of the leaders of the Michigan bar, and had served the Union in Canada during the war, spying on Confederate agents. But he was already 55 years old and not in the best of health, and Detroit Republicans knew that if the circuit judgeship went to a Detroiter, the district judgeship would have to go to a deserving Republican from one of the Eastern District's western or northern counties, and not to Clark or Newberry.[6]

And so it came to pass that, a month after nominating Emmons, President Grant nominated John Wesley Longyear of Lansing to replace Judge Wilkins.[7] Longyear's nomination was very popular out-state, where Longyear was well known as a prominent attorney and former Republican congressman and abolitionist who had provided unwavering support to President Lincoln.[8] Detroit attorneys were more skeptical because they did not know much about him except that, like Emmons, Longyear suffered from "rather feeble health," which frequently kept him from his practice,[9] and that he lacked experience in the admiralty and bankruptcy cases that made up a major portion of the district court's docket. In a short time, Longyear won the doubters over with his quick legal mind, so that he soon was recognized nationally as an expert in those areas of the law.[10] His health, though, did curtail his ability to make a dent on the backlog of matters inherited from Judge Wilkins.

Circuit Judge Halmer Hull Emmons

Born: November 22, 1814, Village of Sandy Hill (now Hudson Falls), New York, to Adonijah and Harriet S. Emmons
Education: Read law
Nominated/Confirmed as Circuit Judge for the Sixth Circuit: January 10/17, 1870 (Ulysses S. Grant)
Vacancy: New Seat
Left Court: May 14, 1877 (Death, Detroit, Michigan)

Halmer H. Emmons stood a spare five feet eight inches tall, energetic and impulsive with straight black hair, "keen black eyes overhung by beetling

Fig. 17.   Judge Halmer Emmons.
(Historical Society for the United
States District Court for the
Eastern District of Michigan)

brows," and a gift for "vituperative profanity." He joined his father and brother in a law practice in Detroit in 1840 and soon became known as one of the leading railroad attorneys in the Midwest.[11] He married Sarah Williams in 1845; they had four children. The stress of work, however, affected his health, and in 1853 he reduced his caseload and sought the peace of rural Wyandotte, Michigan, which remained his home for the rest of his life.

U.S. Supreme Court justice Henry Billings Brown remembered Emmons as "one of the greatest minds I ever came into contact with," but also noted that "he was considered too erratic to be popular as a politician." Attorneys trying cases before Emmons found that he was knowledgeable in the law and patient with long arguments, but that he would not allow wasted time. According to Brown, "Counsel who had been accustomed to trying cases their own way, and consuming all the time they desired, were greatly surprised and shocked when confronted by a judge who insisted upon their trying them in *his* way, and consuming no more time than was necessary for the proper disposition of the case."[12] Emmons's frustration was apparent in an 1875 case involving the bankruptcy of a canal company, in which he castigated creditors for filing suits "which, so far as the court can see, can have no possible purpose other than that of entanglement and delay, the making of unnecessary expense, the creation of cruel obstacles in the way of those financial negotiations which distressed and embarrassed corporations are so frequently compelled to make [and are] so unnecessary, so boldly at war with the opinions and advice of the court."[13]

Fig. 18. Judge John Wesley Longyear. (Historical Society for the United States District Court for the Eastern District of Michigan)

District Judge John Wesley Longyear

Born: October 22, 1820, Shandaken, Ulster County, New York, to Petrus and Jerusha Longyear
Education: Read law
Nominated/Confirmed to District Court: February 7/18, 1870 (Ulysses S. Grant)
Vacancy: Ross Wilkins (Retired)
Left Court: March 10, 1875 (Death, Detroit, Michigan)

After pursuing classical studies at the Lima Academy in Lima, New York, and teaching school for several years, Longyear joined his parents in Mason, Michigan, in April 1844, where he continued teaching school while studying law in the Mason office of Daniel L. Case. He was admitted to the Michigan bar in 1846, and, when Lansing became the new state capital in 1847, he opened a law practice with his brother. In 1849, he married Harriet M. Munro of Eagle, Clinton County, Michigan; they were the parents of three children. In 1862, Longyear was elected as a Republican to the U.S. House of Representatives and was re-elected in 1864. He decided not to seek re-election in 1866 and returned to his practice in Lansing. In 1867, he served as a member of the Michigan Constitutional Convention. After his appointment to the district court, Judge Longyear moved his home to Detroit.

Court Clerks Darius J. Davison, Addison Mandell, and Walter S. Harsha

To replace John Winder and William Wilkins, Judge Longyear selected Darius James Davison as clerk of the district court, and Judge Emmons hired Addison Mandell as clerk of the circuit court; both clerks began work on April 15, 1870. Davison was born in Dundee, New York, in 1828, and his parents moved the family to Union City, Michigan, in 1835. After high school, he attended Albion Seminary (now Albion College) and the University of Michigan, from which he graduated in 1854. He then read law and was admitted to the Detroit bar. A Republican Party stalwart who had been appointed master in chancery by Justice McLean in 1860, he continued as district court clerk for 34 years, until his death in December 1904.[14]

Mandell, also a Detroit attorney, was born in Esperance, New York, in 1816, and arrived in Detroit in August 1836 to study law with Theodore Romeyn. Of medium height and complexion, he was notable for a completely hairless head resulting from a boyhood disease. After joining the bar in 1841, he practiced with Romeyn and then with Jacob Howard, the future U.S. senator. He was a loyal Democrat until the Civil War, when he became a Republican. He was appointed circuit court commissioner and master in chancery in 1843 by Justice John McLean, and was register of the U.S. Land Office in Detroit from 1869 to 1871. After 12 years as circuit court clerk, he resigned on June 5, 1882, due to ill health, although he lived until June 3, 1899, when he died at his summer home near Sandwich, Ontario.[15]

Walter S. Harsha succeeded Addison Mandell as circuit court clerk, and quickly became one of the most distinguished and respected clerks in the federal system. Harsha was born in Detroit in 1849 and educated at the University of Michigan, where he earned two degrees (B.A. in 1871 and M.A. in 1873). He next read law and was admitted to the bar in 1878. Rather than practice law, he became clerk for various state courts and was deputy clerk for Wayne County until his appointment as circuit court clerk. A contemporary described him as "a man of broad mentality, strong initiative and distinct individuality."[16] He was renowned as a sound administrator and as the author and editor of several books on federal court rules and procedure, and he was a successful businessman, but, as we shall see, also something of a crook.

Michigan's Federal Judges v. The Big Four

An eternal theme of U.S. history has been the struggle between the federal government and the states over who decides what the law is. This usually manifests itself in a wrestling match between Congress and state legislatures, but it can also result in a bout between federal and state judiciaries, particularly in the context of the federal courts' diversity jurisdiction. This judicial struggle was on display on January 16, 1872, when Circuit Judge Emmons, District Judge Longyear, and District Judge Solomon Withey of the Western District held a joint session of the circuit courts for the Eastern and Western Districts in the courtroom of Detroit's Custom House.

Their task that day was to hear arguments and decide two cases, one filed in each district, in which the common issue was the meaning of provisions in Michigan's 1850 Constitution. All three federal judges were well aware that a majority of the Michigan Supreme Court, consisting of the nationally respected Big Four (Chief Justice Thomas M. Cooley and Justices James V. Campbell, Isaac Christiancy, and Benjamin F. Graves) had already interpreted those provisions in not one but two recent decisions, just as they knew that Congress and decisions of the U.S. Supreme Court seemed to require them to adopt a state supreme court's decision regarding the meaning of state statutes and constitutions. Yet, they nevertheless ruled that the Michigan Supreme Court's decision was so bizarre, so out of step with reality, and so unfair that it had to be wrong.

The sections of Michigan's 1850 Constitution at issue barred "the state" from helping a private railroad finance its construction. These provisions were a response to the state's painful experience with public finance of railroads and other internal improvements. Michigan's first state Constitution required the state government to build roads, canals, and three railroad lines in order to encourage settlement.[17] That construction plan proved easier to order than to execute. Although two of the railroads were built, the state lost millions in the project through bad luck, bad judgment, corruption, waste, and poor maintenance, and it lost more when it tried to end its misery by selling the railroads to private interests.[18] It was not surprising, then, that when Michigan adopted a new constitution in 1850, it contained three separate sections barring the state from becoming involved financially in any private business or internal improvements.[19]

During the Civil War, even as logging and mining were emerging as the engines driving the state's economy, a majority of families made their living, as they had for decades, by exporting agricultural products, and those farm families came to realize that the most efficient way to move those products was by rail and that the prosperity of their communities depended on access to a railroad line connecting their town or township to the national markets. Beginning in 1863, state legislators began to ignore the constitutional prohibitions and to pass laws authorizing specific local governments to issue bonds to assist railroad construction. Those bills proved so popular that, by 1867, "the Legislature may fairly be said to be afloat on a sea of railroad bills,"[20] amounting to almost four thousand miles of proposed new track financed through the sale of millions of dollars' worth of local bonds.[21] Although Governor Henry H. Crapo warned that the laws were unconstitutional, they kept being passed until the legislature simply passed an omnibus law allowing any local government to get in on the fun.

Inevitably, though, some localities had second thoughts about their undertakings and refused to follow through, citing constitutional prohibitions. Bondholders and their representatives sued in various state courts, and the issue eventually came before the Michigan Supreme Court. In both

People ex rel. Detroit and Howell Railroad Co. v. Township Board of Salem
(1870) and *People ex rel. Bay City v. State Treasurer* (1871),[22] a majority
consisting of Chief Justice Cooley and Justices Campbell and Christiancy
held that railroad-aid acts not only violated the state's constitution, they
were beyond the power of any democratic government to enact because
they authorized the taxing of individual citizens to support a private business. Only Justice Graves voted to uphold the laws.

Press reactions to those decisions were predictably partisan, either intensely hostile or fulsomely adulatory depending on each newspaper's political orientation, but reaction in the bond market and the railroad board-
rooms was uniformly cold terror. Hoping for a better result, holders of the
bonds of defaulting localities sued in the state's two U.S. circuit courts. The
only possible basis for federal court jurisdiction over those cases was diversity of citizenship, so the bondholders, backed by the railroads, arranged
for a bondholder who was a citizen of another state to act as plaintiff. If
there were none, they found a willing candidate and sold him a bond. Thus,
when the township of Pine Grove, in the northeast corner of Van Buren
County, refused to pay principal and interest on its railroad-aid bonds, the
Kalamazoo and South Haven Railroad Company, a Michigan corporation,
transferred Pine Grove bonds to Edward B. Talcott, a citizen of Ohio, who
sued the township in the circuit court for the Western District.[23] When
similar diversity suits were filed in the circuit court for the Eastern District
against Port Huron and Battle Creek, the judges agreed to conduct a consolidated hearing in Detroit.

Today, it would be clear that federal judges sitting in diversity would be
bound by the decisions of the Michigan Supreme Court, unless there were
a contrary federal constitutional provision or statute, thanks to the 1938
decision of the U.S. Supreme Court in *Erie Railroad Co. v. Tompkins*.[24]
Before 1938, though, the choice of which law to apply was somewhat confused. The Judiciary Act of 1789, which first granted the circuit courts
diversity jurisdiction, also specified that "the laws of the several states,
except where the constitution, treaties or statutes of the United States
shall otherwise require or provide, shall be regarded as rules of decision in
trials at common law in the courts of the United States in cases where they
apply."[25] The purpose of this section, which has come to be called the Rules
of Decision Act, was to mollify anti-federalists who feared that federal
judges would usurp local laws, particularly in commercial cases. Within a
few decades, though, the U.S. Supreme Court took a long stride toward
doing just that. In cases such as *Swift v. Tyson* (1842),[26] the Court held
that state law, as used in the Rules of Decision Act, meant state statutes
and constitutions, not common law, that body of judge-made laws that
controlled most legal issues in the tort, commercial, and property cases
that were the bulk of any circuit courts's diversity docket. On the other
hand, as Chief Justice Roger Taney noted, "it is the established doctrine of

this court, that it will adopt and follow the decisions of the State courts in the construction of their own constitution and statutes, when that construction has been settled by the decision of its highest judicial tribunal."[27]

Oral argument took place in the courtroom of the Custom House. The several attorneys representing the bond holders and the local governments were among the cream of Michigan's bar. Appearing for the bond holders were David Darwin Hughes of Marshall, a former Calhoun County prosecutor, prominent Detroit attorneys Theodore Romeyn and Ashley Pond, and University of Michigan professor of law Charles Irish Walker, while the governments were represented by former Judge Samuel T. Douglass, Battle Creek city Attorney Philip H. Emerson, and former Michigan governor and U.S. senator Alpheus Felch. Despite this collection of stars, though, Judge Emmons complained that the arguments were less than stellar, partly because each side started with the assumption that its position was irrefutable. Whatever its quality, the argument seems to have been superfluous because that same day each judge read from the bench a lengthy opinion which he must have prepared beforehand.[28]

As the bondholders had hoped, the federal judges disregarded the decisions of the Michigan Supreme Court and held instead that the bonds in the consolidated cases were valid obligations. Judge Emmons explained at great length (approximately 18,000 words) why, in his mind, the decisions in *Salem Township* and *Bay City*, "[w]ith all respect for the eminent tribunal by which the judgments were pronounced," were not only wrong in every aspect but also so unprecedented that "we believe that since the organization of the state no single judgment has taken the legal mind with such unrelieved surprise as that from which we are now compelled to dissent." In particular, Emmons had no doubt about the state constitutional issue: "That the law is constitutional, and the contracts valid and obligatory upon the municipalities making them, and that it is our duty to enforce them, has been affirmed in nearly every judgment thus far cited." In their shorter opinions, Judges Longyear and Withey preferred to dodge the constitutional issue and agree with Emmons on what seemed to be the fundamental unfairness inflicted by the Michigan Supreme Court's decisions on railroads and on bondholders who had, in good faith, invested their money and assets, only to be hung out to dry by local governments suffering from buyer's remorse. That fairness was their main concern can be inferred from Judge Emmons's concession that the federal courts would tell the holder of a bond created after the state decisions "would be told that those judgments were not subject to criticism here; that this court would administer their doctrines, in all their results, wholly irrespective of our own opinions."

As with *Salem*, press reaction to *Pine Grove* was partisan. The *Detroit Free Press* derided the logic of the federal judges as "an ingenious but not plausible attempt to evade" the duty of federal courts to follow the decision of a state supreme court, while the *Detroit Tribune* predicted that Judge Emmons's opinion "will deepen the regret, already somewhat general, that the State court should have ever taken a contrary view."[29]

The *Tribune* was also confident that holders of bonds issued before the decision in *Salem* could rest easy, but Justice Cooley and his brethren ignored the opinions of the federal judges when the Michigan Supreme Court decided its last railroad-aid case. In *Thomas v. City of Port Huron*,[30] the court held railroad-aid bonds invalid and the authorizing legislation unconstitutional issued even though the bonds had been sold well before *Salem* and regardless of any good faith of, or consideration given by, the bondholders.[31] The state and federal courts never reached an agreement on the validity of railroad-aid bonds, and the issue died a natural death. The Panic of 1873 stalled further railroad construction, and, when the economy improved, railroads turned to other sources of financing such as federal land grants and stock issues. *Talcott* remained important, though, as a forerunner of an era in which federal courts used their diversity jurisdiction and new laws expanding their power to take over cases filed in state courts to create a conservative, business-oriented law of commerce insulated from populist and progressive trends in the laws of the states.

More Judicial Changes

When they took the bench, both Judge Emmons (55) and Judge Longyear (49) were older than the average life expectancy of their era and both had serious medical problems that were aggravated by the strain of their new positions. On March 10, 1875, Judge Longyear died at the age of 54 of stomach cancer (described at the time as "indigestion . . . affecting the heart"),[32] after just three years as district judge. Despite a life-long abstention from alcohol, Judge Emmons suffered from a "feeble constitution," and died May 14, 1877, also of stomach cancer, after a long illness.[33] As Longyear's successor, President Grant nominated Henry Billings Brown, a 39-year-old Detroit attorney who would later become the first of only two Michigan attorneys ever appointed to the U.S. Supreme Court.[34] Two years later, President Rutherford B. Hayes nominated John Baxter of Tennessee to replace Judge Emmons as circuit judge for the Sixth Circuit.

District Judge Henry Billings Brown

Born: March 2, 1836, in South Lee, Massachusetts, to Billings and Mary Amy Tyler Brown

Education: Yale University (B.A.); Yale and Harvard Law Schools (no degree); read law

Nominated/Confirmed to District Court: March 17/19, 1875 (Ulysses S. Grant)

Fig. 19. Justice Henry Billings
Brown. (Historical Society for the
United States District Court for
the Eastern District of Michigan)

Vacancy: John W. Longyear (Died)
Left Court: December 29, 1890 (Confirmed as Associate Justice, U.S.
    Supreme Court)
Death: September 4, 1913, Bronxville, New York

Henry B. Brown arrived in Detroit in 1859 and was admitted to the bar in
1860. A Republican, he thrived after the election of President Lincoln,
winning appointments to part-time work as a circuit court commissioner,
deputy U.S. marshal, and deputy district attorney.[35] Brown came "into
connection with vessel men of all classes, who naturally gravitate toward
the Marshal's office whenever any question arises as to 'tying up' a vessel
to secure a claim,"[36] and when he returned full-time to his private practice
in 1868, he focused his practice on admiralty law, developing a national
reputation.[37] Despite his success, Henry Brown hated the strains of a private law practice, "the uncongenial strifes of the Bar, and the constant fear
lest by some mistake of my own the interests of my clients might be sacrificed."[38] He had weak eyes, hated arguing, and was a bad loser. He found
his escape from many concerns in his marriage to Caroline Pitts, whose
inherited wealth left him financially independent and willing to accept an
appointment to the Wayne County Circuit Court in 1868, despite the low
salary.[39] In 1870, after he lost the next judicial election, he tried to find
another refuge from the practice of law as one of several Republicans who
sought to replace Judge Wilkins, whom he despised, moaning "God, what
a tyrant we have to rule over us!"[40] When that failed, he sought the Republican nomination for Congress in 1872, also without success. Judge Longyear's unexpected death gave Brown another shot at the federal bench,

and his admiralty expertise and his ability to accept the low annual income of a federal judge helped him to win the appointment.

Judge Brown thoroughly enjoyed the change from advocate to judge. Years later, he recalled that: "I was glad to take refuge in the comparative repose of the bench, although it involved the loss of two-thirds of my professional income. . . . The difference in the nervous strain involved gave me an incalculable relief. For the first two years it was a struggle between life and death, but thanks to a good constitution, prudent living and plenty of horseback exercise, my natural vitality triumphed and for twenty-five years thereafter my health continued to improve. . . . The fifteen and a half years I spent as a district judge, though characterized by no act of special importance, were full of pleasurable satisfaction and were not overburdened by work. Indeed I found that I could easily dispose of the business in nine months of the year, and that there was always an opportunity for a summer outing. There are doubtless higher offices, but I know of none in the gift of the government which contributes so much to making life worth the living as a district judgeship of the United States."[41] Although he was "a kind, gentle, and sociable man who enjoyed life to the fullest . . . he was not an intellectual, nor was he prone to deep thought. Pragmatic in nature, Brown relied heavily on personal experience, common sense, and a strong work ethic to guide him through life."[42]

When U.S. Supreme Court justice Samuel F. Miller died in 1890, Judge Brown used his social and political connections to defeat his old boss, Alfred Russell and win the appointment largely because the Court needed a justice who understood admiralty law. Ideologically, Justice Brown was a prototypical, middle-of-the road, post-war Republican. He was assigned most of the opinions in the fields of admiralty and patent law, but he is best remembered for his "separate but equal" opinion for the majority in *Plessy v. Ferguson*. Long notorious for legitimizing segregation, the opinion has in recent years been reappraised because of a recognition that its holding that all races are entitled to equal facilities was, in fact, revolutionary at the time.[43] Justice Brown retired from the Supreme Court on May 28, 1906, because his eyes did not allow him to continue.

Circuit Judge John Baxter

Born: March 5, 1819, in Rutherford County, North Carolina
Education: Read law
Nominated/Confirmed as Circuit Judge for the Sixth Circuit: December 6/13, 1877 (Rutherford B. Hayes)
Vacancy: Halmer H. Emmons (Died)
Death: April 2, 1886, Hot Springs, Arkansas

Judge Baxter spent most of his career before joining the federal bench in private practice in Tennessee. Justice Henry Brown described Baxter as honest and brave, but totally lacking in judicial temperament because "[h]is will was absolutely inflexible . . . a judge who cared even less for authorities than Judge Emmons . . . . He formed offhand impressions and frequently decided upon the strength of them without even listening to an argument. He differed from Judge Emmons in sometimes deciding cases without hearing the party against whom he was about to decide."[44] There are only three published opinions by Baxter as circuit judge in the Eastern District, all dated 1880 or 1881.[45]

The Judiciary Act of 1875:
Federal Question Jurisdiction and Removal

Six years after providing for circuit judges in 1869, Congress passed the Judiciary Act of 1875[46] which significantly expanded the jurisdiction of the circuit courts in two ways intended to allow parties seeking to enforce the growing body of federal law, particularly claims arising under the civil rights acts, access to federal courts and to provide a haven from hostile and obstructive state courts. First, Congress finally granted the circuit courts the power to hear all cases "arising under the Constitution or laws of the United States, or treaties," even if there was no diversity of citizenship or the United States was not party.[47] The act left untouched the power of state courts to hear such cases as well and limited the circuit court to "civil suits in which matter in dispute exceeds $500, exclusive of costs." The second important provision in the 1875 act extended the right to remove cases from state courts to the local circuit court to plaintiffs and to federal-question cases valued at more than $500.

The combination of the two provisions assured that no party could be forced to litigate a case based on a federal law, such as the post-war civil rights acts, in a state court. At first, with few federal statutes on the books, federal-question jurisdiction had little effect on the circuit court's docket. However, by 1910, the exponential growth of federal legislation resulting from the Progressive Movement began to propel the lower federal courts into their present role as the principal enforcers and interpreters of the body of rules and laws that arguably have the greatest impact on the lives of Americans. During the remainder of the 19th century, though, the practical effect of the act seems to have been to alert corporate lawyers to the benefits of using the removal statute to avoid hostile state judges and unfavorable state laws in tort or breach of contract cases filed in state courts. In the calendars of the district and eastern district of Michigan, there is no record of a case being removed until 1868, whereas 220 cases were removed to the circuit court for the Eastern District between 1871 and 1880, including 45 in 1875 and 39 in 1876. However, very few of those cases involved federal questions or were removed by plaintiffs. Instead, they were contract and tort cases in which an individual in the forum state sued a corporation from another state. By removing, the corporation gained the benefit of federal common law and federal judges, both of which tended to be more favorable to business than state laws and judges.[48] Nationwide, filings increased markedly and the judges were hard pressed to keep up. Between 1873 and 1890, the number of cases pending in the district and circuit courts grew from 29,000 to 54,000, while Congress authorized only seven additional judges. The circuit judges were spread so thin that by the 1880s, the district judges were forced to decide 90 percent of the circuit court cases alone, including appeals from their own rulings in the district court.[49] The Eastern District was an exception to the national caseload increase, however. Although the number of private civil cases filed did increase during the early 1870s, they then returned to the level of pre-war filings, and most of the increase was due to an increase in debt-collection cases resulting from the Panic of 1873 and a sudden boom in patent litigation rather than removal or federal question cases.

Intellectual Property Litigation in the 19th Century

Article I, section 8, of the U.S. Constitution empowered Congress "to promote the progress of science and useful arts by securing for limited times to authors and inventors the exclusive right to their respective writings and discoveries." In 1790, Congress began to exercise that power by enacting laws regulating copyrights[50] and patents.[51] Enforcement of both types was allocated to the circuit courts by 1819,[52] but our circuit courts saw very few such cases until after the Civil War. The district's first two patent cases were filed in 1842, and in 1845, Justice McLean and Judge Wilkins issued the District of Michigan's first published patent opinion, *Bryce v. Dorr*,[53] upholding a patent for a process for casting water wheels but limiting the patent holder to nominal damages. Another early case, *Roberts v. Ward*,[54] decided in 1849, although filed in equity, was submitted to a jury, which found that the patent was invalid "because of a want of novelty." In all only thirteen patent cases were ever filed, and only five opinions published, during the life of the District of Michigan.

After the Civil War, the number of intellectual property cases filed increased sharply, and 226 of the 790 civil cases filed in the circuit court between 1870 and 1873 claimed patent infringement, although that number is somewhat deceptive. It was the custom at that time for patent owners to sue dozens of alleged infringers in each federal district, and 185 of those 226 cases involved just two patents. The Goodyear Dental Vulcanite Company sued 98 local dentists claiming infringement of its patent for a dental plate using vulcanized rubber, and Charles L. Hawes sued 87 hotels, which he asserted were using check-in registers that infringed his patent for a register with paid advertisements in the margins.

In 1851, Nelson Goodyear patented a manufacturing process for making a hard rubber which he called Vulcanite. A year later, a Boston dentist, Dr. John Cummings, invented a dental plate made by imbedding false teeth in soft rubber which was then hardened in the Vulcanite process, securing the teeth. He applied for a patent, was turned down, tried again and was rejected. In 1859, Vulcanite dentures from other sources went on sale and gained instant popularity worldwide because it was much cheaper than existing dentures made with ivory or gold and because dentists could easily make the dentures themselves. For the first time, good dentures were available to people who were not wealthy. In 1864, Dr. Cummings finally received a patent for the dental plate and assigned the rights to Josiah Bacon who founded the Goodyear Dental Vulcanite Company, the sole activity of which was to enforce the patent. The company charged dentists a license fee to use the process and a royalty for each denture they made. Many dentists doubted the validity of the patent and found this double-dipping oppressive, so they simply ignored the patents, forcing Cummings to fight a national campaign of suing infringing dentists.

Circuit Judge Emmons upheld the Cummings patent in 1874,[55] and the U.S. Supreme Court affirmed the patent's validity in 1876,[56] but dentists continued to resist the company's demands for payment, and Bacon had to file another 60 cases in the Eastern District alone. The animosity between the Goodyear Dental Vulcanite Company and the dental profession reached a tragic climax in San Francisco on Easter Sunday, April 13, 1879. A dentist named Samuel Chalfant, who had lost his patent infringement case the day before, went to Josiah Bacon's hotel room and shot him dead.[57] Bacon's death and an 1880 decision by the Supreme Court that a dental plate made of celluloid, a plastic, did not infringe the Cummings patent,[58] took the fight out of the company which did not renew the patent before it expired in 1881.

The Charles Hawes patent, which resulted in 118 cases being commenced in the Eastern District between 1872 and 1875, was much simpler in concept but just as time-consuming for the circuit court. In April 1867, Mr. Hawes was granted a patent for "the Advertising Hotel Register," consisting of a book "being constructed so as to have inserted advertisements at the top and bottom, and on the margin of each page, with a blank space for the registering of names of guests, or on each alternate page, leaving the opposite page blank for registering of such names, or on both pages of each alternate leaf, such leaf being sometimes made of bibulous or blotting paper."[59] Just as dentists fought the Goodyear patent, the hotel industry resisted paying royalties, in this instance on the ground the idea was not novel because a register with advertisements had been in use in hotels across Michigan before 1867. In February 1875, less than a month before he died, Judge Longyear ruled in favor of the Hawes patent, holding that the evidence of prior use was not enough to overcome the presumption of a patent's validity.[60]

Copyright cases were even rarer in the Eastern District than patent cases in the 19th century, only two being reported before 1900. Both were filed by the same plaintiff, Detroit's renowned historian, surveyor, and mapmaker Silas Farmer. In 1872, Farmer received a judgment against a map publisher, the Calvert Lithographing, Engraving and Map Publishing Company, of Detroit, which had published copies of 12 of Farmer's maps of certain townships in Wisconsin, Illinois, and Michigan.[61] After reviewing the maps, Judge Longyear determined that the defendant had committed "naked piracy" to the extent they copied Farmer's lines for the township boundaries. He also rejected the argument that, because those boundaries were set by statute, their representation on a map was not subject to copyright: "The defendant, no doubt, had the right to go to the common source of information, and having ascertained those boundaries, to have drawn them upon its map, notwithstanding that in this respect it would have been precisely like complainant's map, (which of course it would have been if they were both correct). But he had no right to avail himself of this very labor on the part of complainant in order to avoid it himself." In the other case, decided in January 1888, Farmer was not quite as successful. He sued over a "pamphlet" consisting of 70 pages of extracts from his 1,024-page history of Detroit, followed by 200 pages of advertising. Judge Henry Billings Brown upheld Farmer's claim, but he enjoined publication of only eleven pages of the pamphlet containing information and facts that were not known before being published in Farmer's book.[62]

Changing the District's Boundaries

On July 19, 1878, Congress approved a law which redrew the boundaries of the Eastern and Western Districts by assigning all of the Upper Peninsula to the Western District.[63] The genesis of this change was a determination by a House committee that the Western District had not lived up to the caseload projections made by its proponents in 1863. Although the caseloads reported in the U.S. attorney general's annual reports for this period are suspect,[64] the Western District consistently reported about half the caseload of the Eastern District. Congressman Jay Abel Hubbell of Houghton, Michigan, campaigned for a third U.S. judicial district encompassing all of the Upper Peninsula, arguing that because most of the filings in the Upper Peninsula were from counties along Lake Superior assigned to the Eastern District, a third district would balance the workload while also relieving his constituents of the need to travel hundreds of miles to Grand Rapids or Detroit to attend a federal court. On the other hand, some members of Congress suggested, as an economy measure, simply

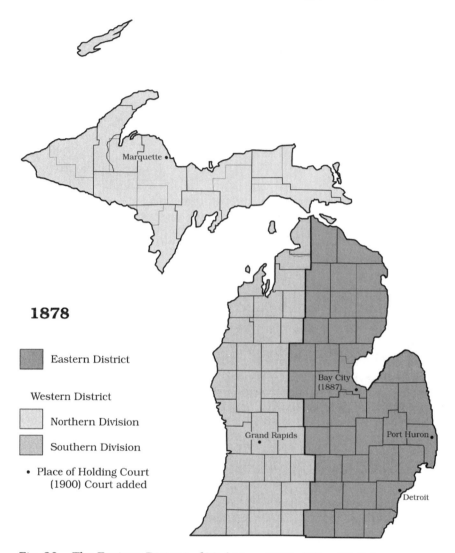

Fig. 20.   The Eastern District of Michigan, 1878. (Ellen White)

consolidating the Eastern and Western Districts into a two-judge district (a suggestion that has been repeated many times).[65] The final result was a compromise that met some of Hubbell's concerns, without satisfying him, and did not increase the budget much. In addition to assigning the entire Upper Peninsula to the Western District, Congress split that district into two divisions and required the district and circuit courts to hold two terms each year in the Northern Division at Marquette.

The Port Huron Federal Building and U.S. Courthouse

The same law that assigned the entire Upper Peninsula to the Western District also contained a piece of political pork relating to the Eastern District, although not one Judge Brown welcomed: a provision that "there shall be" one or more terms of the district court each year "at the United States court room in the city of Port Huron," although Congress fatefully added "in the discretion of the judge of said district court, and at such times as he shall appoint therefor."[66] District court terms in Port Huron were intended to brighten the election prospects of Congressman Omar Dwight Conger, an engineer, lawyer, and judge, who from 1869 to 1881 represented the congressional districts that included Port Huron. As the *Detroit Free Press* wryly noted: "It is insinuated that the provision is not entirely disconnected from Conger's effort to secure a renomination."[67]

In fact, increasing the federal presence in Port Huron had long been a goal for Conger and his constituents. The split of the District of Michigan in 1863 reduced the distance that residents of western Michigan had to travel to find a federal court, but it did nothing for those Michiganders living in the northern counties of the new Eastern District. This was particularly galling to plaintiffs who filed cases in their local state court against a corporation from another state only to have that defendant remove the case to federal court in Detroit. As a first step in their campaign, local boosters petitioned Congress to create a Customs Collection District of Port Huron with its own collector and staff independent of the collector in Detroit. They noted that the population of St. Clair County had practically doubled since 1850 to 26,604 and was still growing, while Port Huron's strategic location at the junction of Lake Huron with the Black and St. Clair Rivers, accessible by water from both north and south, meant that a large portion of the goods imported into Michigan ports were landed there.

In April 1866, Congress did create a new customs district headquartered at Port Huron with its own collector of customs and jurisdiction over Michigan's east coast from the southern end of the St. Clair River to the Straits of Mackinac.[68] When Conger took office in Washington in 1870, he took the next step by sponsoring a bill to appropriate funds to build a federal building in Port Huron. That bill failed, but Conger persisted and on June 10, 1872, Congress finally did authorize the secretary of the treasury "to purchase . . . a suitable lot of ground in the City of Port Huron . . . and to cause to be erected thereon a building suitable for the accommodation of the custom-house, bonded warehouse, and other government offices in that city," at a cost not to exceed $200,000.[69] In March 1873, Congress appropriated a first draw of $100,000 "for purchase of the site and commencing construction."[70] After much argument among residents regarding whether to place the building on a site north or south of the Black River, the southsiders won when the secretary bought a lot at the

Fig. 21.   The Port Huron Federal Building and U.S. Courthouse.
(National Archives and Records Administration)

southeast corner of Sixth and Water Streets for $10,000, of which $5,000 was raised through a subscription by the citizens of Port Huron. Construction, which was supervised by Henry N. Wright of Port Huron and George H. Sease, began in August 1873 and was completed in 1875 at a total cost to the United States of $246,000, appropriated between 1873 and 1877.[71]

The design of Port Huron's federal building was overseen by Alfred Bult Mullett, supervising architect for the Treasury Department from 1866 to 1874. Mullett joined the office of the supervising architect in 1863, during the tenure of his former partner, Isaiah Rogers, whom he worked to undermine until Rogers quit in 1865. Mullett quickly earned a reputation as an interfering, micro-managing authoritarian with an explosive temper. To the *New York Sun*, he was "the most arrogant, pretentious, and preposterous little humbug in the United States. " Nevertheless, Mullett is remembered today for the design of the State, War, and Navy Building (now the Eisenhower Executive Office Building) in Washington, D.C., and other massive "piles" in the French Second Empire style as well as dozens of smaller federal buildings in a variety of styles.[72]

For Port Huron, Mullett and his staff mixed a late Classical Revival design with a French-style dome. The building consists of a ground floor built of limestone from Sandusky, Ohio, and two upper stories built using limestone from Amherst, Ohio, topped by a rotunda with a dome roofed with copper. The building was lighted by gas chandeliers and heated by 17 fireplaces. Since 1875, the Port Huron Federal Building has been renovated and changed many times. The most important exterior change occurred in 1932, when a single-story addition was built at the rear of the building, similar in style to the original structure. During World War II, in a gesture to the war effort, the copper dome was replaced by galvanized copper.

Although Congress had not yet authorized federal court sessions in Port Huron, Mullett's design included a space on the upper floors for a courtroom that was 32 feet high and illuminated by two rows of windows. When Congressman Conger presided over the laying of the cornerstone in October 1874, he promised the people of Port Huron that the courtroom would soon house an annual term of the U.S. District Court to deal with the "very large share of the admiralty business" of the court which originated in the Port Huron customs district. The problem was that Congress decided where federal courts were held and the only venue authorized until then for the District and Eastern District was Detroit.[73] Moreover, like the territorial judges before them, the federal judges resisted holding court anywhere but Detroit[74] not least because Congress, when it set their compensation in 1867, specified that "no other allowance or payment shall be made to them for travel, expenses or otherwise."[75] Besides, Detroit was also the logical location of a federal court. It was the state's largest city, it was the center of banking and other business activity, and was a hub of transportation by water and later by rail.

Conger decided to force the issue by having Congress order the district court to hold terms in Port Huron. He parlayed his support for the June 1878 law to induce the sponsors to add language mandating at least one court term at Port Huron each year and authorized more terms at the discretion of the district judge. By the time the bill passed into law, however, the wording had changed, modifying the mandate to allow the district judge to decide whether to hold court in Port Huron at all. Unfortunately for Conger and Port Huron, Judge Brown and his successors exercised their discretion by staying in Detroit and leaving the building to fill the needs of other federal agencies. Very few court sessions, if any, would be held in Port Huron's lovely federal court room until a century had passed.

Notes

1. The Census defined urban as people living in a town or city with a population of 2,500 or more; the rest of the population was defined as rural.

2. This name comes from a satirical novel written by Mark Twain and Charles Dudley Warner, *The Gilded Age: A Tale of Today* (New York: American Publishing Company, 1873).

3. Section 1, 20 Stat. 175.

4. 17 Stat. 424.

5. *Detroit Advertiser and Tribune*, January 10, 1870.

6. *Detroit Advertiser and Tribune*, January 11, 1870; *New York Times*, February 13, 1870.

7. From 1863 to 1954, Ingham County was assigned to the Eastern District.

8. In 1864, when there was talk of offering to allow the Confederate states to return to the Union but keep their slaves, Longyear declared on the House floor: "Yes, sir, slavery has hung upon the nation like an incubus ever since it has had an existence. It is no part of the body-politic of the nation. It is an excrescence upon it, a horrible disease that has been festering upon its surface, enfevering the entire system, until at last it has struck at the very vitals of the nation; and unless destroyed and entirely removed, the body must die." Speech of Hon. J. W. Longyear of Michigan on the Reconstruction of the Union, in Congress, April 30, 1864 (Washington, D.C.: Lemuel Powers, 1864).

9. *Detroit Advertiser and Tribune*, February 8, 1870.

10. George I. Reed, *Bench and Bar of Michigan: A Volume of History and Biography* (Chicago, IL: Century Publishing and Engraving Company, 1897), 81.

11. *New York Times*, May 15, 1877.

12. Charles A. Kent, *Memoir of Henry Billings Brown: Late Justice of the Supreme Court of the United States* (New York: Duffield and Company, 1915), 25–26.

13. *New York Times*, July 22, 1875.

14. *Detroit Free Press*, December 10, 1904.

15. *Detroit Free Press*, June 4, 1899; Robert Ross, 130.

16. Leake, 799–800.

17. Michigan Constitution (1835), art. 12, § 3.

18. This is a drastically simplified description of a very complex process. For those interested in the gory details, I recommend Robert J. Parks, *Democracy's Railroads: Public Enterprise in Jacksonian Michigan* (Port Washington, NY: Kennicat Press, 1972); and Martin J. Hershock, *The Paradox of Progress: Economic Change, Individual Enterprise, and Political Culture in Michigan, 1837–1878* (Athens, OH: Ohio University Press, 2003).

19. Michigan Constitution (1850), art. 14, § 6 (barring state guarantees of private debt); § 8 (the state "shall not subscribe to, or be interested in, the stock of any company, association, or corporation"); and § 9 (the state barred from being "a party to, or interested in, any work of internal improvement, nor engaged in carrying on any such work, except in expenditure of grants to the State of land or other property").

20. *Detroit Post*, February 16, 1867.

21. *Detroit Free Press*, March 1, 1867.

22. *People ex rel. Detroit and Howell Railroad Co. v. Township Board of Salem*, 20 Mich. 452 (1870); *People ex rel. Bay City v. State Treasurer*, 22 Mich. 499 (1871).

23. It is likely that the energizing figure behind these cases was James F. Joy. As president of the Michigan Central Railroad and front man for a cadre of Boston investors, Joy arranged financing for many smaller roads whose track the Michigan Central then leased in perpetuity. Among those roads were the Jackson, Lansing and Saginaw, and the Kalamazoo and South Haven. Graydon M. Meints, *Michigan Railroads and Railroad Companies* (Lansing, MI: Michigan State University Press, 1992), 8–12.

24. *Erie Railroad Co. v. Tompkins*, 304 U.S. 64 (1938).

25. 1 Stat. 73, sec. 34.

26. *Swift v. Tyson*, 41 U.S.1 (1842).

27. *Nesmith v. Sheldon*, 48 U.S. 812 (1849).

28. The opinions were later published under the name *Talcott v. Township of Pine Grove*, 23 F. Cas. 652 (C.C. D. Mich. 1872).

29. *Detroit Tribune*, January 17, 1872.

30. *Thomas v. City of Port Huron*, 27 Mich. 320 (1873).

31. The U.S. Supreme Court affirmed the decision in *Talcott* in October 1873 in an opinion by Justice Swayne. He noted that: "The question before us belongs to the domain of general jurisprudence. In this class of cases this court is not bound by the judgment of the courts of the States where the cases arise. It must hear and determine for itself." His main point of emphasis, though, was the unfairness of invalidating contracts that everybody had assumed were valid.

32. *New York Times*, March 15, 1875.

33. *New York Times*, May 15, 1877.

34. The other was Frank Murphy, appointed by President Franklin D. Roosevelt.

35. He was a patriotic Republican, but when he was selected for the 1863 military draft he purchased a substitute.

36. Kent, 19–20.

37. Kent, 74. In 1876, a year after his appointment to the district court, Brown published a collection of important admiralty decisions arising in Michigan and northern Ohio. Henry Billings Brown, *Reports of admiralty and revenue cases argued and determined in the circuit and district courts of the United States for the western lake and river districts [1856–1875]* (New York: Baker, Voorhis and Company, 1876). In 1896, while on the Supreme Court, he published a casebook on admiralty law. Idem., *Cases on the Law of Admiralty* (St. Paul, MN: West Publishing Company, 1896).

38. Kent, 23.

39. Kent, 53.

40. Kent, 59.

41. Kent, 23–24.

42. Trevor Broad, "Forgotten Man in a Tumultuous Time: The Gilded Age as Seen by United States Supreme Court Associate Justice Henry Billings Brown," *Michigan Journal of History* (Winter 2005).

43. Justice Brown expressed his own view on the racial divide in 1903: "I know of nothing more ineradicable than racial antipathy, except, perhaps, national antipathy." Kent, 92.

44. Kent, 26–27.

45. *The Mamie*, 8 F. 367 (C.C. E.D. Mich. 1881); *Tarsney v. Turner*, 48 F. 818 (C.C. E.D. Mich. 1880); *The General Burnside*, 3 F. 228 (C.C. E.D. Mich. 1880).

46. 18 Stat., Part 3, 470.

47. The short-lived Judiciary Act of 1801 did grant the lower courts federal question jurisdiction, but it was withdrawn by the Judiciary Act of 1802.

48. Because Republican presidents occupied the White House for 46 of the 54 years between 1861 and 1933, a great majority of the federal judges nominated during that period were also Republicans. In fact, the Eastern District had no district judges appointed by a Democratic president for 66 years, between February 1870

when Judge Wilkins retired and March 1936 when the Senate confirmed Franklin Roosevelt's nomination of Arthur F. Lederle. As a result, federal courts developed a reputation as cold, stodgy, and slanted towards corporations and the rich. See Edward A. Purcell, Jr., *Litigation and Inequality: Federal Diversity Jurisdiction in Industrial America, 1870–1958* (New York: Oxford University Press, 1992).

49. Russell R. Wheeler and Cynthia Harrison, *Creating the Federal Judicial System*, 2nd ed. (Washington, D.C.: Federal Judicial Center, 1994), 16.

50. 1 Stat. 124.

51. 1 Stat. 109.

52. 3 Stat. 481.

53. *Bryce v. Dorr*, 4 F. Cas. 521 (C.C. D. Mich. 1845).

54. *Roberts v. Ward*, 20 F. Cas. 936 (C.C. D. Mich. 1849).

55. *Goodyear Dental Vulcanite Co. v. Willis*, 10 F. Cas. 754 (C.C. E.D. Mich. 1874).

56. *Smith v. Goodyear Dental Vulcanite Company*, 93 U.S. 486 (1876).

57. James Wynbrandt, *The Excruciating History of Dentistry: Toothsome Tales & Oral Oddities from Babylon to Braces* (New York: St. Martin's Press, 1998), 167–169. See the company's press release, *New York Times*, May 4, 1879.

58. *Goodyear Dental Vulcanite Company v. Davis*, 102 US 222 (1880).

59. *Hawes v. Antisdel*, 11 F. Cas. 856 (C.C. E.D. Mich. 1875).

60. Other companies with multiple patent infringement filings included the Birdsell Manufacturing Company (34, farm equipment) and the Hektograph Company (16, writing duplication process).

61. *Silas Farmer v. Calvert Lithographing, Engraving & Map Publishing Co.*, 8 F. Cas. 1022 (C.C. E.D. Mich. 1872).

62. *Farmer v. Elstner*, 33 F. 494 (C.C. E.D. Mich. 1888)(C.C. E.D. Mich. 1888).

63. 20 Stat. 175.

64. See the bibliographical notes.

65. *Detroit Free Press*, June 2, 1878.

66. Section 9, 20 Stat. 177.

67. *Detroit Free Press*, June 2, 1878.

68. 14 Stat. 32.

69. 17 Stat. 387.

70. 17 Stat. 523

71. 17 Stat. 523 ($100,000), 18 Stat. Part 3, 228 ($75,000), 18 Stat. Part 3, 395 ($25,000), 19 Stat. 111 ($36,000), and 19 Stat. 351 ($10,000).

72. Lee, 89–90.

73. The 1836 act of Congress creating the District of Michigan directed that the courts be held at the "seat of government of said State," which was then Detroit. 5 Stat. 61. After the state capital was moved to Lansing in 1847, Congress amended the act to continue Detroit as the court's sole authorized seat. 5 Stat. 176.

74. Before he took the federal bench, Judge Wilkins did ask Senator John Norvell to introduce a bill allowing him to hold court sessions at Mackinac during the summer while his family was vacationing there, but nothing came of it. Letter, John Norvell to Ross Wilkins, January 30, 1837, Box 1(1830–37), Ross Wilkins Papers.

75. 14 Stat. 471.

CHAPTER 6

The Eastern District and the End of the Gilded Age, 1885–1900

The Eastern District, 1885–1900

The post-war boom and the optimism of the Gilded Age continued until they were brought to an abrupt halt by the Panic of 1893, the worst economic crisis that the nation had suffered to that time. Widespread overbuilding of railroads, financed by high-interest bonds that could not be repaid from revenues, resulted in the failure of more than 15,000 companies and 500 banks, a collapse of prices for agricultural products that ruined thousands of farm families, and wide-spread strikes and double-digit unemployment that hit industrial employers and employees alike.[1] Michigan suffered with the rest of the nation, but its recession was deepened by the disappearance of the logging industry and supporting businesses, as the state's last pine forests were cut and lumber companies moved west to Wisconsin and Minnesota. Although the economy began to improve by 1897, it did not fully recover until 1900. The economic distress felt in the Eastern District was reflected in its census figures. Although the district's population reached one million residents in 1890, it grew at a much slower rate during the next ten years than it had during previous decades, and fell to only 57 percent of the state's population, the lowest percentage ever. Most of the district's population growth during the 1890s occurred in Wayne County, while agricultural and timber counties such as Clinton, Lapeer, Livingston, Saginaw, Roscommon, Iosco, and Oscoda lost population.

Judicial activity also decreased somewhat between 1890 and 1900, with filings of private civil cases decreasing by a quarter from the previous decade with the cost of litigation acting as a deterrent. Relatively unaffected by considerations of expense, filings by the U.S. varied greatly in both civil cases (none in 1898, two in 1891, 34 in 1896, and 53 in 1897) and criminal cases (166 in 1895, 30 in 1898, and 1899). For the courts and judges, though, the most important events during this period were the replacement of Judges Brown and Baxter, the decline in the business of the circuit courts, the creation of a new appellate court, and new courthouses in Bay City and Detroit.

Circuit Judge Howell Edmunds Jackson

Born: April 8, 1832, in Paris, Tennessee
Education: University of Virginia, West Tennessee College (A.B. 1849),
    Cumberland University (LL.B. 1856)
Nominated/Confirmed as Circuit Judge for the Sixth Circuit: April 12/12,
    1886 (Grover Cleveland)
Vacancy: John Baxter (Died)
Left Court: March 4, 1893 (Reassigned to U.S. Circuit Court of Appeals for
    the Sixth Circuit)
Death: August 8, 1895, in West Meade, Tennessee

By 1885, the stability in the district and circuit courts under Judge Wilkins and Justice McLean were merely memories, and replacement of the judges every decade or two had become the norm. When Circuit Judge Baxter died while on vacation in Hot Springs, Arkansas, in 1886, at the age of 67, President Grover Cleveland had the first chance, as a Democratic president, to name a judge who would sit on one of the Eastern District's courts since the appointment of Judge Wilkins in 1837 and, as it turned out, the last such chance until 1933. In April 1886, President Cleveland chose another Tennessean, U.S. Senator Howell Edmunds Jackson, to replace Baxter as circuit judge for the Sixth Circuit. Jackson had become a close friend of the president during his Senate term. In 1891, he was automatically transferred to one of the two seats on the new U.S. Circuit Court of Appeals for the Sixth Circuit. In 1893, President Harrison appointed him associate justice of the U.S. Supreme Court. Henry Billings Brown had nothing but praise for Jackson, whom he called an "ideal" judge. There are a dozen published opinions by Jackson sitting in the circuit court for the Eastern District between November 1886 and June of 1892. None of them are of great interest except to the parties, but they show that Jackson, unlike many other circuit judges of that era, was dutiful in his attendance and did not leave the burden of the circuit courts on the district judges.

Another Military Homicide

Twenty years after the Bishop murder case, Judge Brown, presiding alone in the circuit court, was presented with another case of military homicide.

On the evening of July 11, 1887, six prisoners in the stockade at Fort Wayne, downriver from Detroit, were escorted from their cells for their regular inspection. One of them was Arthur Stone, a private in the 23rd U.S. Infantry, who was under sentence of a dishonorable discharge and two years at hard labor for "conduct prejudicial to good order and military discipline." In Stone's case, this military catch-all meant that he had committed the heinous act of wrongfully accusing an officer of stealing a cane.[2] Stone, whose real family name was Saunders, was a very unlikely soldier at a time when many enlisted men were uneducated immigrants and farmers who joined the army because they were hungry or lazy. He, by contrast, grew up in Joliet, Illinois, a member of a wealthy family, had studied Latin, and was fluent in French and German as well as English. He joined the army because of woman troubles back home, and discovered that this romantic impulse was a mistake.

As the prisoners lined up for roll-call, Stone broke from formation and ran toward a six-foot fence that separated the fort from the public road. Hearing a shout, Sergeant of the Guard James Clark loaded his musket and ran around the guard house where he saw that the fugitive was about eighty yards away, out-running his pursuers and likely to make his way over the fence. Clark raised his rifle, fired, and struck Stone "in the back just above the hips, inflicting a wound from which he died in the course of the evening." It seems that Clark and Stone were good friends and that Clark may not have known the identity of his target.

A military court of inquiry absolved Sergeant Clark because he had a duty to fire to stop Stone's escape, although, as one private whispered to a *Free Press* reporter, Clark did not have a duty to hit anything.[3] The reaction of Detroit's civilian population to the incident was outrage that "a man could be shot down like a dog for trying to escape the penalty of an offense not greater than slander." Federal civilian authorities, in the person of District Attorney Cyrenius C. Black and Assistant District Attorney Charles T. Wilkins, the grandson of Judge Wilkins, decided to charge Clark with murder in the circuit court for the Eastern District. Rather than the usual procedure of having a commissioner handle the arraignment, Judge Brown presided as the "committing magistrate." Sergeant Clark, a quiet soldier with a slim face and blond mustache who appeared in full uniform, was represented by three attorneys from Detroit: Sylvester Larned, Allen Fraser, and James C. Smith, while Major Asa Bird Gardiner, a judge advocate of the U.S. Army, appeared to protect the army's interests.[4] After testimony by various soldier witnesses and argument by counsel, Judge Brown announced that he was ready to rule. He confessed to initial doubts that a civil court had jurisdiction over a crime committed by one soldier against another (although he was certainly aware of the precedent of the Bishop case), but opined that the legal authorities he had examined convinced him that he did. He also remarked on the disproportionate punishment imposed on Stone, by "a military code of Draconic severity," but his central concern was whether Stone was justified in firing at a man convicted of what to civilians seemed to be a minor offense, "a crime wholly unknown to the common law." In common law, deadly force was justifiable only to stop a person accused of committing a felony, not a misdemeanor, but the judge reasoned that the distinction between felony and misdemeanor had no place in military law. After a lengthy but inconclusive discussion of the legal authorities, Judge Brown concluded that, even though justification was ordinarily an issue for a jury, he would have set aside a jury's guilty verdict, and so he discharged Clark and returned him to his company.

District Judge Henry Harrison Swan

Born: October 2, 1840 (Detroit, Michigan), to Joseph G. and Mary Catherine Ling Swan
Education: Read law; University of Michigan (no undergraduate degree, M.A. (hon.) 1893, LL.D. (hon.) 1902)
Nominated/Confirmed to District Court: January 13/19, 1891 (Benjamin Harrison)
Vacancy: Henry Billings Brown (Appointed to U.S. Supreme Court)
Left Court: July 1, 1911 (Retired)
Death: June 12, 1916 (Grosse Pointe, Michigan)

When President Harrison appointed Henry Billings Brown to the Supreme Court, he consulted about his successor with Brown as well as with the U.S. senators from Michigan, Francis B. Stockbridge and James McMillan. All of them recommended Henry Harrison Swan, one of Detroit's leading admiralty specialists. However, former Senator Thomas W. Palmer, one of Har-

Fig. 22. Judge Henry Harrison Swan. (Historical Society for the United States District Court for the Eastern District of Michigan)

rison's closest friends, favored Joseph B. Moore, a former state senator and sitting state circuit judge from Lapeer. As late as January 13, 1891, the *Detroit Free Press* reported that the choice was "still to some extent an open one," but later that day the president nominated Swan.[5]

Henry H. Swan , the son of Joseph Grover Swan, a machinist, and Mary Catherine Ling Swan, an immigrant from Germany,[6] was the first district judge born in Michigan. He received his early education in public and private schools in Detroit and then, after three years at the University of Michigan, joined his uncles in running a steamboat business on the San Joaquin and Sacramento Rivers of northern California. He also studied law and was admitted to the California bar in 1867. That same year he returned to Michigan and became partners with one of Michigan's ablest attorneys, the elegant and poetic D. Bethune Duffield, and in 1870 was appointed a part-time assistant to U.S. district attorney Aaron B. Maynard. On April 30, 1873, Judge Swan married Jennie Elizabeth Clark, daughter of a Presbyterian minister; they were the parents of two children. At the time of his appointment, the *Free Press* described Judge Swan as "one of the rare men whose personal characteristics win him the friendship of all who come in contact with him. He never has won or lost a case, no matter how intense the interest was, at the expense of wounding the friendship of those interested on either side."[7]

The U.S. Circuit Courts of Appeals

On March 3, 1891, Congress passed the Evarts Act, which established the United States Circuit Courts of Appeals, nine intermediate appellate courts, one in each circuit, to hear all appeals from decisions of the district courts.[8] In each circuit, the sitting circuit judge, such as Judge Jackson, was reassigned to the circuit court of appeals and was joined by a second circuit judge. Each session of a circuit court of appeals was to be heard by a three-judge panel consisting of the circuit justice and the two circuit judges. Congress did recognize that circuit justices would rarely attend, so the law allowed one of the panelists to be replaced by a district judge, which turned out to be what usually happened.[9] Henry Billings Brown was the first circuit justice of the Circuit Court of Appeals for the Sixth Circuit, and the other circuit judge seat was filled (very snugly) by U.S. solicitor general William Howard Taft, the future president and Supreme Court chief justice.

Even though the Evarts Act ended their appellate function, the old circuit courts remained in existence, causing confusion with the new circuit courts of appeals and preserving the awkward system of dual federal trial courts. The House of Representatives had voted to abolish the circuit courts, but the Senate, in a nod to "extremists who still thought of the pioneer days when the Justices were active on circuit and thus, supposedly, kept the common touch," to circuit court clerks who lobbied feverishly to save their jobs, and to district court clerks who feared that they would be replaced by their circuit court colleagues, convinced the House to retain the circuit courts.[10]

The United States v. Walter Harsha, Round 1

On June 16, 1891, Judges Jackson and Taft appointed Walter Harsha, clerk of the circuit court for the Eastern District, to the position of clerk of the Circuit Court of Appeals for the Sixth Circuit. Harsha held both positions for three years before he returned to Detroit to run the circuit court only. An attorney, Harsha wrote the first set of court rules for a circuit court of appeals, and the Supreme Court was sufficiently impressed that the justices imposed Harsha's rules on the other circuit courts of appeals. Harsha also authored and published an annotated compilation of the rules of the district and circuit courts of the Eastern and Western Districts of Michigan, the Circuit Court of Appeals for the Sixth Circuit, and the Supreme Court.[11]

During his three years as clerk of the Circuit Court of Appeals, Harsha received a salary from that court as well as fees from the operations of the circuit court. He tendered his resignation from the court of appeals in February 1894, but the circuit judges did not accept the resignation until October 1894. After Harsha returned to Detroit, the United States refused to pay him the fees he claimed as circuit court clerk for August and September 1894. The government argued that a federal statute, effective July 31, 1894, barred any federal employee who earned a salary of more than $2,500 from also holding a position paid by fees.[12] Harsha sued for those fees, and Judge Swan awarded him $482.90. The government appealed directly to the Supreme Court, which in 1899 affirmed Harsha's victory on the ground that the statute in question allowed the office-holder to choose which position to retain, and that Harsha's "resignation, coupled with his unequivocal intention to retain the other office, prevented the act of Congress from creating, of its own force, and independently of any action of his, a vacancy in that office."[13] The Supreme Court emphasized that fact that the Circuit Court of Appeals did not accept Harsha's resignation until after the law came into effect was outside of his control and thus irrelevant.

Bay City's 1893 Federal Building and the Northern Division

A decade after Port Huron's ambition to host the district court was thwarted by the passive resistance of District Judge Brown (and then by his successors), the political leaders of Bay City made sure not to leave such a decision to the judges' discretion as they schemed to bring the federal courts even further north and to defeat the similar ambitions of neighboring East

Saginaw. Both cities could point to a booming economy and rapid population growth, as well as the argument that, because they were twice as far from Detroit as Port Huron, effective justice required a local federal court. In 1880, Michigan was the nation's leading lumber state, producing as much as the three next states combined in the vast pine forests extending north and west from Saginaw Bay. For the first time, the state's northern counties were booming both economically and in population growth, although the number of residents remained well below those of the southern counties. Between 1860 and 1880, Bay City grew from 3,164 residents to 38,081, and, Saginaw County increased from 12,693 to 59,095. Lumber drew immigrants, particularly from Poland and Germany, and attracted related industries such as lumber mills, furniture factories, and ship yards, to supplement the traditional fishing and farming. Along with this economic and population growth came political power and local pride.

Both cities decided to conduct a scheme in the opposite order from that used by Port Huron—they worked first to secure a court term and only then to get a federal courthouse. It was obvious that Congress would not authorize the federal courts to sit in both cities, and a bruising battle erupted between Congressmen Spencer O. Fisher of Bay City and Timothy E. Tarsney of Saginaw, conducted on the floor of the House as well as in the cloakrooms. Bay City prevailed in a law passed on February 28, 1887, officially because it was more centrally located than East Saginaw, although the cities are only a dozen miles apart.[14] Bay City's supporters had learned a lesson from Port Huron's disappointment, and Fisher made sure that the act not only *authorized* the courts of the Eastern District to sit at Bay City, it *mandated* that both the district and circuit courts hold two terms in Bay City each year and that the district's U.S. marshal, under the direction of the judges, "rent and suitably furnish rooms at Bay City for the holding of said courts and for the use of the jurors and officers."

Accordingly, Judge Brown ordered that the circuit court hold its first term in Bay City beginning on Tuesday, October 18, 1887. U.S. marshal Galusha Pennell arranged to borrow Bay County's courthouse located on Center Avenue, between Madison and Depot streets. There, on the morning of October 18, Judge Brown ordered the crier to call the circuit court to order. He announced the appointments of William M. Kelly as Bay City's resident deputy clerk for both federal courts and F. A. Myers as crier, and he ordered that J. P. LeRoux, already serving as resident deputy U.S. marshal in Bay City, attend court as well. Judge Brown admitted five local attorneys to the court's bar, and he called the roll of fourteen jurors who had answered summonses to appear for service, although it turned out that two of the fourteen were dead. Because there was not a separate jury pool for Bay City, although two of the summoned jurors were from Saginaw County and two from Bay County, the others had to travel a considerable distance, four of them from Wayne County and one each from St. Clair,

Washtenaw, Hillsdale, Lenawee, Branch, Genesee, and Ingham Counties. Judge Brown called the first two cases, set them for trial on Wednesday, and adjourned. Then the judge, court officers, jurors, attorneys, and spectators accepted the invitation of a local judge to spend the afternoon on his farm on the Kawkawlin River, with the promise that they would be able to return to Bay City in plenty of time to attend the gala reception and banquet organized by the local bar association at the Fraser House, the city's premier hotel.[15]

The all-male banquet was, as the local newspaper declared, "a conspicuous and gratifying success." The guests, in addition to Judge Brown and U.S. marshal Pennell, included Court Clerks Darius Davison and Walter Harsha, U.S. district attorney Cyrenius P. Black, the battling Congressmen Tarsney and Fisher, former Michigan governor David Jerome, state judges from Saginaw, Detroit, and Iosco County, and politicians and attorneys from towns and cities throughout the district. At 9:00 p.m., all attending sat down to "a superb spread," the likes of which is rarely, if ever, seen today. Oysters in the shell and other assorted appetizers were followed by a first course of boiled chicken in oyster sauce, roast beef, Southdown mutton in caper sauce, boiled beef tongue, spring lamb, young turkey in cranberry sauce, escalloped oysters, oyster patties, Spanish puff fritters, and jelly meringue, all washed down with wine. After a restorative glass or two of champagne, the diners soldiered on to the second course of roast wild duck, broiled partridge, chicken salad, lobster salad, baked sweet potatoes, mashed potatoes, sweet peas, mashed turnips, and string beans, all accompanied by Roman punch. Dessert followed for those still a bit peckish: pumpkin pie, cranberry pie, English plum pudding in brandy sauce, Charlotte russe, vanilla ice cream, chocolate cake, coconut cake, sponge cresses, jelly roll, macaroons, fruit cake, angel food cake, grapes, pears, apples, assorted nuts, cheese, coffee, tea, and hot chocolate. Then followed a series of toasts and speeches, jokes and witty repartee (some of which showed that the tension between Saginaw and Bay City had not relaxed), until the celebration wound down at 1:30 a.m.[16] Judge Brown was back on the bench the next morning, and he remained in Bay City for two weeks, tried a half-dozen cases, and adjourned court on November 3, 1887.

Bay City's leaders next turned to the task of convincing Congress to authorize and pay for a federal building to house the courts and other federal agencies. During the banquet, Judge Brown had promised "that he would do all what he could to induce the erection of a government building . . . that would last a hundred years to come." A few days later, he was quoted as remarking that a lot across the street from Bay City's courthouse "would be just the proper spot for the new United States court building."[17] On June 19, 1888, after further lobbying by Congressman Fisher and Bay City postmaster Henry H. Aplin, Congress directed the sec-

retary of the treasury to acquire a site in Bay City and to construct a "substantial and commodious building, with fire-proof vaults, for the use and
accommodation of the United States courts, post-office, customs-office,
internal revenue office, and for other government uses," the total cost not
to exceed $200,000.[18]

Congress did appropriate the full $200,000, the first half in October
1888[19] and the second half in March 1889,[20] but political infighting reminiscent of the comedy which had surrounded Detroit's Custom House
thirty years earlier delayed completion of the building for four years. As
had been the case in Detroit, the first dispute was over the building's location. The Treasury Department preferred to build on the site of the existing
post office, near the southwest corner of Center and Washington Avenues,
to avoid the cost of purchasing a new lot. Local officials, including Congressman Fisher and Bay City Mayor Hamilton M. Wright, held out for a
larger lot further north on Washington Avenue, between Third and Fourth
Streets. The locals prevailed, and, in January 1889, the Treasury Department agreed to pay $40,000 for the northern lot, although a title issue
delayed the transaction for a few months.[21] Next, the federal and local
authorities fought over the choice of building materials. The federal government wanted to use brick in order to keep costs down, but local authorities wanted stone to enhance the building's appearance. Once more,
local opinion prevailed, but with the result that the building was not completed and the post office opened to the public until December 20, 1893,
more than five years after the initial authorization. Even then, the courtroom and offices were still under construction[22] and were not occupied
until the district court began its term on May 15, 1894.[23]

Bay City's federal building was designed by well-known Philadelphia
architect James Hamilton Windrim during his two years (1889–1891) as
the Treasury Department's supervising architect. As with most of the hundred buildings that Windrim designed during his tenure,[24] including Detroit's new federal building completed in 1897, he used his trademark
Romanesque Revival style for the Bay City federal building. Also known as
Richardson Romanesque, it was a broad, romanticized interpretation of a
style of architecture common in the 11th and 12th centuries. From about
1870 to 1900, Romanesque Revival was a common choice in the United
States for public buildings such as churches, courthouses, and university
campuses. The style employed squat pillars, asymmetrical massing, semi-
circular arches over doors and windows, horizontal belts of weathered
stone or brick, often of contrasting color or texture, and high-peaked ga-
bles with irregular outlines. Windrim adopted all of these features to Bay
City's three-story federal building. The design's most striking feature was
a five-story square tower (another Romanesque feature) and rooms richly
appointed with oak paneling and marble fireplaces. The first floor was
given over to the post office and to a small office for the deputy collector of

Fig. 23.   Bay City's 1893 Federal Building and U.S. Courthouse.
(Historical Society for the United States District Court for the Eastern
District of Michigan)

customs, while the courtroom and the offices of the judge, clerk, and marshal occupied the second floor. Other federal agencies and the grand jury
room were on the third floor, under the eaves. The *Bay City Daily Tribune*,
in an article reporting the opening of the building, described the courtroom as "large and well lighted," and assured its readers that it "will be
handsomely fitted." The article also remarked that the building's steam-
heat and ventilation system were "all that could be desired."[25]

The final step in Bay City's plan to ensure a permanent federal court
presence was the work of Congressman Thomas Addis Emmet Weadock,
who replaced Spencer Fisher in 1901 and who, as soon as he was sworn in,
began a campaign to gather support for a law to divide the Eastern District
into two divisions. Initially his fellow legislators and Presidents Benjamin
Harrison and Grover Cleveland were not interested, but he pestered and
maneuvered until he wore them down. The result was a statute enacted on
April 30, 1894 (just two weeks before Judge Swan held the district court's

Fig. 24.   The entrance to Bay City's 1893 Federal Building and U.S. Courthouse. (Historical Society for the United States District Court for the Eastern District of Michigan)

first session in the new federal building's courtroom) in which Congress created the Northern and Southern Divisions of the Eastern District of Michigan.[26] The statute allocated to the Northern Division twenty-three of the district's thirty-nine counties (Cheboygan, Presqne Isle, Otsego, Montmorency, Alpena, Crawford, Oscoda, Alcona, Roscommon, Ogemaw, Iosco, Clare, Gladwin, Arenac, Isabella, Midland, Bay, Tuscola, Huron, Gratiot, Saginaw, Shiawassee, and Genesee), a resident deputy clerk and a resident deputy U.S. marshal. The key provisions for Weadock and the people living

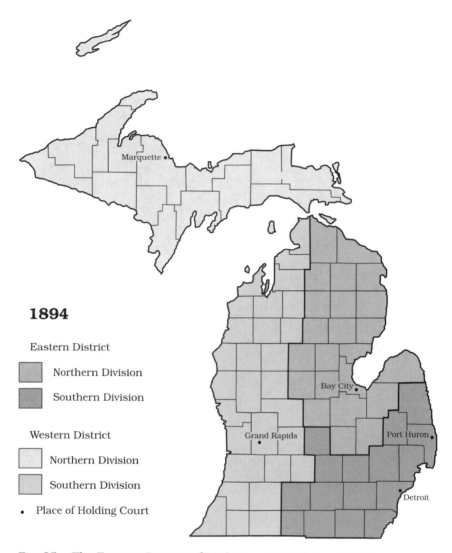

1894

Eastern District

Northern Division

Southern Division

Western District

Northern Division

Southern Division

•   Place of Holding Court

Marquette

Bay City

Grand Rapids

Port Huron

Detroit

Fig. 25.   The Eastern District of Michigan, 1894. (Ellen White)

in the Northern Division were the requirements that all cases arising in the Northern Division must be tried in Bay City using jurors residing in the Northern Division and that the circuit and district courts hold a total of three terms of court in Bay City each year, beginning on the first Tuesdays of May and October plus a special admiralty term beginning in February.

The drive for federal court terms in Bay City began in bright optimism and faith in the growing economy and population of the district's northern counties. Unfortunately, by the time the federal building was completed and the Northern Division created, that optimism had been dashed. The national depression following the Panic of 1893 and the local effects of the end of Michigan's timber boom, as logging companies moved to uncut forests elsewhere, were devastating. The decline of the Northern Division's economy is mirrored by the decline of its percentage of the district's total population. That number peaked at 34.3 percent in 1890, before the split, and thereafter declined to 23.7 percent in 1920 and 17.7 percent in 1950. Since Genesee and Shiawassee counties were reassigned to the Southern Division in 1964,[27] the Northern Division's population has hovered around 13% of the district's total. This loss of population share is also reflective in a decrease in the share of the district's caseload filed in the Northern Division such that early in the 21st century only one of the district's 23 active district and senior district judges is assigned to the Northern Division and there are efforts afoot to consolidate the divisions.

Henry Harrison Swan v. William Howard Taft

The most prominent Eastern District case over which William Howard Taft presided as circuit judge was *City of Detroit v. Detroit City Railway Company*,[28] in which the administration of Mayor Hazen Pingree tried to rid the city of a troublesome company running what Detroiters called a street railway, but what others might call a trolley or tram line. The earliest forms of urban mass transit in Michigan were horse-drawn cars that ran on rails set down in the streets and owned by private corporations that had entered into a long-term contract with the local government. Thus, in 1862 Detroit granted certain individuals about to form a corporation the right to construct and run a street railroad line for 30 years. In 1863, those individuals formed the Detroit City Railway, a new corporation, which under Michigan's general corporation law had a 30-year life span, to build and run the line. In 1879, the city council negotiated with the three street railroad companies running on different city streets for an increase in taxes in return for extending the licenses grants to 1909. In 1882, the Detroit City Railway bought out the other trolley companies and then used a corporate juggling act to transfer all of its assets to a new corporation, the Detroit Street-Railway Company, which nine months later transferred the same assets again to yet another new corporation, the Detroit Citizens' Railway Company, which had a charter that did not expire until 1921. The ownership of the different iterations changed little.

In 1889, the people of Detroit elected the Republican candidate for mayor, Hazen Pingree, a distinguished veteran of the Civil War and owner of a prosperous shoe manufacturing company, principally on his promise to clean up what was known nationally as the most corrupt city government in the country. In 1891, Pingree and the city's working people turned their attention to the street railroad and determined to eject the company, whatever its name, and start again. The company's low wages and long hours had resulted in a violent five-day strike which paralyzed the city, the service was bad, the company paid very little in taxes, and it refused to change from horse power to electricity. Moreover, Pingree was convinced that fares were too high and that the contract extension in 1879 was the result of bribes paid to city councilmen. At Pingree's request, the common council passed an ordinance repealing the 1879 contract extension as illegal under state law because it extended the contract beyond the original corporation's life and that also decreeing that the right to run a trolley system would end on May 9, 1893, the day the original corporation would cease to exist. In March 1892, the city also filed suit in Wayne County Circuit Court for an injunction to force the company to stop running its trolleys and to remove its rails from the streets.

One of the defendants, a New York trust company, removed the case to the U.S. Circuit Court for the Eastern District under an 1887 addition to the removal laws that allowed any defendant in a state court living outside the forum state to remove a case "into the circuit court of the United States [if] it shall be made to appear to such circuit court that from prejudice or local influence he will not be able to obtain justice in such state court."[29] Taft and Swan upheld the removal because of the bitter feelings against the company in Detroit,[30] and then on May 31, 1893, after an initial hearing on the injunction, Judge Taft ruled in favor of the company regarding two of the company's lines but indicated that he would rule for the city on the rest of the company's operations. Judge Swan was appalled and objected vigorously to granting the city any equitable relief that would destroy the company's business without compensation: "The opinion of the circuit judge, in my judgment, in its reasoning and conclusions, is so utterly subversive of the principles of equity that I am unwilling, by my silence, to sanction an apparent assent to what seems to me to be a most inequitable result."[31] Taft replied, in his opinion: "The fact that my Brother Swan, with his legal acumen, long training, and intimate knowledge of the Michigan law, differs with me, gives me much concern, lest I have reached a wrong result. Nevertheless I cannot reconcile any other result to the rules of construction which it seems to me must govern in the case; and it is my duty, therefore, to adhere to the position as stated."

On January 31, 1894, Taft entered the injunction over Swan's dissent,[32] and the defendants appealed to the Circuit Court of Appeals. The Evarts Act barred from the appeals panel any judge "before whom a cause or question may have been tried or heard" below, so Circuit Justice Howell Jackson joined Circuit Judge Horace Lurton, and District Judge George Read Sage of the Southern District of Ohio on this appeal. Attorneys Ashley Pond and Otto Kirchner represented the company, while Charles A. Kent of Ann Arbor (Henry B. Brown's biographer and former Dean of the University of

Michigan Law School) and Saginaw's Benton Hanchett represented the City of Detroit. The Circuit Court of Appeals reversed Taft's decision and upheld Swan's analysis, holding the city had indeed had the power in 1879 to extend the company's franchise beyond the company's lifespan.[33] Although that ended the litigation in federal court, the dispute between the city and the trolley company festered for another twenty-eight years until the city bought the company for $20 million in 1922.[34]

The Chinese Exclusion Acts

On July 15, 1892, John Graves, a circuit court commissioner for the Eastern District, sentenced Wong Wing, Lee Poy, Lee You Tong, and Chan Wah Dong to 60 days of hard labor in the Detroit House of Correction followed by deportation.[35] Their crime: illegal entry into the United States in violation of the Chinese Exclusion Act. At the request of the defendants' attorneys, Judge Swan, sitting alone as the circuit court, issued a writ of habeas corpus which, after a hearing, he dismissed. On appeal, the Supreme Court, in an opinion by Justice George Shiras with a strong concurring opinion by Justice Stephen J. Field, held the Chinese Exclusion Act, and thus the deportation orders, was constitutional except the provision authorizing a commissioner to sentence a defendant to imprisonment at hard labor pending deportation. Hard labor, Shiras and Field agreed, was an "infamous punishment" which, unless imposed following an indictment and trial by jury, violated the Constitution's Fourteenth Amendment.[36] Thus, after a wait of four years, defendants avoided hard labor but not deportation.

From 1882 to 1902, Congress passed several Chinese Exclusion Acts[37] which first limited and then barred the immigration and naturalization of Chinese nationals. To enforce that ban, the acts required all Chinese to prove they were legally in the country by obtaining a certificate and displaying it when challenged by a federal officer. These laws, which were the first significant restriction on free immigration in U.S. history, resulted from an alliance of racial prejudice and a fear that the availability of Chinese laborers drove down wage levels for all workers. The laws proved to be a burden on the federal officers tasked with enforcement, especially on customs officers who were assigned to discover and arrest illegal Chinese and on the circuit court commissioners who held hearings and issued deportation orders.[38]

Between 1882 and 1905, an estimated 10,000 Chinese appealed to federal judges against negative immigration decisions.[39] As with cases under the Fugitive Slave Acts, it is difficult or impossible to tell how many Chinese were deported from the Eastern District because most deportations were not appealed and most of the records kept by commissioners have been lost. However, three calendars kept by commissioners presiding in

Detroit during the relevant period that do survive in the National Archives[40] suggest the scope of enforcement between 1892 and 1903, although the absence of an entry in Graves's journal for the defendants in *Wong Wing*, and the absence of a record for Chong Sam, also the subject of a reported case,[41] underline how incomplete the records are. The earlier calendar (December 21, 1888 to December 19, 1894) records no Chinese cases until June 1891. From then until December 1894, the commissioner reported 100 individual Chinese arrested, of whom 75 were deported, and 25 were released. The later calendar (June 29, 1899 to November 28, 1903), marked "Docket B, Jonathan Graves, U.S. Commissioner, 373 Federal Building, Detroit, Mich.," describes 186 matters in all, none of which are Chinese Exclusion cases until September 23, 1901.[42] Then there are 13 Chinese deportation cases involving 19 defendants, of whom seven were deported and the other 12 released. There are also entries recording a dozen criminal cases, most of them against men with European names, for smuggling Chinese from Canada.

The only positive aspect that might be gleaned from these cases is that the commissioners and Judge Swan seem to have tried to enforce the laws impartially. Of 119 defendants, 37 were released because they proved they were in the U.S. legally. Entries in several of the cases indicate the defendants were represented by an attorney and that an interpreter was present.

Detroit's 1897 Postoffice Building

Despite the Custom House's rugged strength, by 1880 Detroit's federal courts and other federal agencies had outgrown it, particularly the post office. Since the building's opening in 1861, the city's population had more than doubled (and would double again by 1900) and the number of letters and newspapers to be processed had increased even more. Additionally, there was the problem of the Savoyard Creek. This ancient stream had been filled in early in the 19th century, but its bed ran beneath the Custom House and still carried water down to the Detroit River, so that the basement was always damp and unhealthy as well as flooded after heavy rains.[43] Finally, the simple lines of the Custom House were not consistent with the exuberance and optimism of the Gilded Age.

In December 1881, Congressman Henry W. Lord of Detroit introduced a bill to authorize the construction of a new federal building,[44] and in March 1882 the House Committee on Public Grounds and Buildings recommended passage of the bill, noting that "the present building is wholly inadequate" because of Detroit's increased population and business.[45] Two months later, on May 1, 1882 (i.e., six years before approving the Bay City federal building), Congress authorized the secretary of the treasury to erect in Detroit "a building suitable for the accommodation of the courts of the

United States, of the custom house, post office, pension office, and other Government offices in that City." The secretary was given the option of purchasing either a new site or land adjoining the Custom House. If he chose the former the cost was not to exceed $600,000, if the latter the maximum cost was to be $500,000, and in either case the site was to be big enough to allow 40 feet of open space on each side.[46]

In August 1882, Congress appropriated an initial sum of $250,000 to begin the project,[47] but the commencement of construction was delayed for eight years because of disputes over the site and the design. James G. Hill, supervising architect for the Treasury Department from 1877 to 1883, initially decided to save money by building on the site of the Custom House despite "considerable dissatisfaction" in Detroit over that choice because of the flooding problem and because any new building on that site would likely house no more federal employees than the Custom House already did.[48] In 1884, after Hill has been replaced by Mifflin E. Bell, who preferred designs that considered the future needs of the community,[49] Congress decided to allow a local committee to select a new site even though over $100,000 had already been spent acquiring and excavating additional land adjacent to the Custom House. In April 1885, the committee chose an available site northwest of the Custom House bordered by Shelby Street, Lafayette Boulevard, Fort Street, and Washington Boulevard (at that time Wayne Street). In May, Congress raised the maximum cost available for the land and building to $900,000, and, in March 1887 raised it again to $1,100,000.[50]

Even after the site was acquired, though, excavation on the new site did not begin until June 1890, three years after acquisition and eight years after Congress authorized the project. This delay was caused by the difficulty of designing a building acceptable to all parties.[51] James G. Hill's first attempt, unveiled in 1882, was essentially an expanded version of the Custom House with a pitched and gabled roof, but it was withdrawn when Congress authorized the site change. In the spring of 1887, John Moser, working for Hill's successor, Mifflin E. Bell, presented a design that was overwhelmed by a wave of ridicule from both the public and the architectural profession. A Detroit architect called it "an incongruous conglomeration of rubbish," while the *American Architect and Building News* railed against its "preposterous design . . . , an abomination . . . of incongruous parts, no scale and less style." Moser defended his design as "one organic whole, practical and convenient for its work, and probably the best-lighted large Government building in this country,"[52] but the outcry caused Bell to disown it, and when William Freret became supervising architect in July 1887, he assigned C.W. Sommerville to try again. Sommerville came up with a design for a huge building resembling a Gothic cathedral, "but it was found that it was going to cost altogether too much, and it had to be cut down very extensively."[53]

Fig. 26. Moser's preliminary design for Detroit's new Post Office Building. (Historical Society for the United States District Court for the Eastern District of Michigan)

That was the state of affairs when James Windrim became supervising architect in 1889. Taking advantage of the larger site and richer budget than he was working with in Bay City, Windrim designed for Detroit a Romanesque palace. Although the result was visually striking, the complexity of the design details and the use of a great number of imported materials, especially in the interior finishings, contributed to further delays and to the final cost which, rumor had it, exceeded $1.5 million. Windrim's design, 200 feet long by 152 feet wide, called for a basement, four stories for the post office, court and other agencies, an attic under the hipped roof, and a square tower soaring 243 feet, the highest point in the city at that time.[54] The building was roofed with Spanish tile, and stone double eagles, weighing a ton and a half apiece, were perched at the top of each corner, while the dome of the vestibule featured a mosaic of four more eagles with wings outspread.

Fig. 27.   The 1897 Detroit Post Office Building. (Historical Society for the United States District Court for the Eastern District of Michigan)

Construction of the interior was supervised by Peter Dederichs, a Michigan architect who specialized in Catholic churches. The interior was paneled in 20 kinds and colors of marble from the United States, Italy, and France, had tessellated floors and walls, and was highlighted with polished wood and vaulted, painted ceilings. Rooms, corridors and promenades were built around an internal atrium that extended from a skylight separating

Fig. 28.   Detail at the entrance to Detroit's 1897 Post Office Building. (Historical Society for the United States District Court for the Eastern District of Michigan)

the first and second floors to the roof where a stained-glass skylight spread sunshine throughout the atrium and surrounding corridors. The granite-faced basement housed a power plant, which generated steam heat and, another Windrim innovation, electricity for the lights and elevators.[55] The main floor was an immense, pillared, open space given over to the post office while the second floor was assigned to the customs department. Two court rooms and offices for the judges, the clerk, the district attorney, and the U.S. marshal occupied the third floor, and the fourth floor was home to other federal agencies, the marine hospital service, and a dormitory. A large space in the attic intended for the grand jury was reached by a secret winding stairway inside the walls of the circuit judge's courtroom so that witnesses could give evidence to the grand jury in secret. After a few years, the grand jurors' complaints about meeting in the attic (which had no elevator and inadequate ventilation) resulted in their being moved to another room and the attic being relegated to storage space.

As remarkable as the building's exterior and the marble hallways were, the two courtrooms, both on the third floor were each beautiful in its own way. The walls, bench, jury box, and other appointments of the everyday Byzantine-style courtroom for the district judge were paneled in solid Indian mahogany "fancifully and artistically carved by masters."[56] The courtroom intended for the occasional sessions of the circuit court, what came to be known as the "million dollar courtroom," was one of the most exuberant and luxurious court facilities ever built in the United States. The wide arched marble door frames, with their delicate and intricate designs and hand-carved massive mahogany doors, led into a large room with walls clad in thirty kinds of marble and replete with symbolic ornamentation.

Fig. 29.   The "million dollar" circuit courtroom. (Walter P. Reuther Library, Wayne State University)

Fig. 30.   Rear of the "million dollar" circuit courtroom. (Historical Society for the United States District Court for the Eastern District of Michigan)

Fourteen-foot ivory marble columns flanked either side of the judge's mahogany bench, each "surmounted by lions, four in number, bearing on their backs the globe, or world, emblematic of the strength of justice."[57] Because the columns were so delicate, it took three shipments from Italy to get an intact pair.[58] In the wall behind the bench were three marble arches surmounted by a frieze of female heads symbolizing the purity of justice, while another marble frieze wrapped around the room with lion heads at intervals, 35 to a side, no two of which were identical. Like the doors, the woodwork in the courtroom was all polished mahogany. The wainscoting of the courtroom was of massive slabs of marble, and there were marble slabs set in the tiled floors. The ceiling was a barrel vault, and tiers of windows, the upper tier in stained glass, lighted the room.[59]

Even after the design was approved, construction was so painfully slow that the building was not completed and ready for occupancy until more than 15 years after it was first authorized. The post office opened for business on November 27, 1897, and the court facilities were ready for the next regular terms of the district and circuit courts. Because of the long delays in construction, though, the building was already too crowded to hold all

Fig. 31.   Bench in the "million dollar" circuit courtroom. (Historical Society for the United States District Court for the Eastern District of Michigan)

of Detroit's federal employees. In July 1898, not even a year after the new building opened, Congress rescinded a directive to sell the Custom House,[60] and, in June 1906, authorized an addition to the post office building, covering up the park space, which was not completed until 1913 at a cost of $395,000.[61] However even with the addition, the building was bursting at its seams within a decade.

Notes

1. For a detailed analysis of the Panic of 1893, see Charles Hoffmann, *The Depression of the Nineties: An Economic History* (Santa Barbara, CA: Greenwood Press, 1970).

2. See Peggy Miller, "Truth, Justice, and the Military Way," *The Court Legacy*, no. 2 (October 1993), and from Judge Brown's opinion, *U.S. v. Clark*, 31 F. 710 (C.C. E.D. Mich. 1887).

3. *Detroit Free Press*, July 12, 1887.

4. *Detroit Free Press*, August 2, 1887.

5. *Detroit Free Press* January 13 and 14, 1891. As a consolation, President Harrison appointed Moore to a commission to establish a reservation for the Mission

Indians in California. In 1895, Moore was elected to the Michigan Supreme Court where he served for 30 years.

6. George I. Reed, *Bench and Bar of Michigan: A Volume of History and Biography* (Chicago: Century Publishing and Engraving Co., 1897), 403.

7. *Detroit Free Press*, January 14, 1891.

8. 26 Stat. 826. The Evarts Act also established a uniform annual salary of $5,000 for all U.S. district judges. Previously, Congress set the salary for each district court separately.

9. The main purpose of the Evarts Act was to relieve the Supreme Court of its historic duty of hearing every appeal of a civil case decision from every district, a burden which, in 1890 alone, added 623 new appeals to the Court's docket. The act did this by providing that decisions of the Circuit Courts of Appeals were to be final for diversity, patent, and admiralty cases unless that court or the Supreme Court certified the case for further appeal. This change reduced the appeals filed in the Supreme Court to 275 in 1892.

10. I. Scott Messinger, *Order in the Courts: A History of the Federal Clerk's Office* (Federal Judicial Center, 2002), pp. 36–37, quoting Felix Frankfurter and James M. Landis, *The Business of the Supreme Court: A Study in the Federal Judicial System* (New York: MacMillan 1928), 100.

11. Walter S. Harsha, *Rules of the United States Courts for the Districts of Michigan; Rules of the United States Supreme Court and of the United States Circuit Court of Appeals for the Sixth Circuit* (Detroit: n.p., 1891).

12. 28 Stat. 162, 205.

13. *U.S. v. Harsha*, 172 U.S. 567 (1899).

14. 24 Stat. 423.

15. *(Bay City) Evening Press*, October 18, 1887.

16. *(Bay City) Evening Press*, October 19, 1887.

17. *(Bay City) Evening Press*, October 24, 1887.

18. 25 Stat. 194.

19. 25 Stat. 505.

20. 25 Stat. 939.

21. *Bay City Times*, January 22, 1889; idem., March 22, 1989.

22. *Bay City Daily Tribune*, December 19, 1893.

23. *Bay City Times Press*, May 15, 1894.

24. Lee, 149.

25. *Bay City Daily Tribune*, December 19, 1893.

26. 28 Stat. 67.

27. 78 Stat. 1003.

28. *City of Detroit v. Detroit City Railway Company*, 60 F. 161 (C.C. E.D. Mich. 1894).

29. 25 Stat. 433.

30. *City of Detroit v. Detroit City Ry. Co.*, 54 F. 1 (C.C. E.D. Mich. 1893).

31. *City of Detroit v. Detroit City Ry. Co.*, 56 F. 867 (C.C. E.D. Mich. 1893).

32. *City of Detroit v. Detroit City R. Co.*, 60 F. 161 (C.C. E.D. Mich. 1894).

33. *Detroit Citizens' St. Ry. Co. v. City of Detroit*, 64 F. 628 (6th Cir. 1894).

34. See George B. Catlin, *The Story of Detroit*, rev. ed. (Detroit, MI: The Detroit News, 1926), 615–634.

35. These are the names and spellings in the record. The courts were not very good at transcribing Chinese names into English sounds, and Chinese defendants often gave false names to the authorities, so the identity of these and other defendants in Exclusion Act cases likely will remain unknown. The court may also have made up names: two defendants deported in 1892 are recorded as "Jon Do & Dik Ro." Calendar for December 21, 2888–January 22, 1894, 26, U.S. Commissioner Calendars 1879–1905, Eastern District of Michigan, Records Group 21, NARA Chicago.

36. *Wong Wing v. U.S.*, 163 U.S. 228 (1896).

37. As commonly used, the term Chinese Exclusion Acts included the Chinese Exclusion Acts of 1882, 22 Stat. 58, and 1884, 23 Stat. 115; the Scott Act of 1888, 25 Stat. 476; the Geary Act of 1892, 27 Stat. 25; the McCreary Act of 1893, 28 Stat. 7; the Chinese Exclusion Act of 1902, 32 Stat. 176; and the Chinese Exclusion Extension Act of 1904, 33 Stat. 428.

38. Section 13 of the Scott Act authorized "any justice, judge, or commissioner of any United States court" to issue arrest warrants, hold hearings, and order deportations. 25 Stat. 476, 479.

39. Roger Daniels, *Coming to America: A History of Immigration and Ethnicity in American Life*, 2d ed. (New York: Harper Perennial, 2002), 271.

40. The calendars are preserved at the National Archives and Records Administration, Great Lakes Division, in Chicago. Record Group 21, Eastern District of Michigan, U.S. Commissioner Calendars, 1879–1905, 3 vols.

41. *U.S. v. Chong Sam*, 47 F. 878 (E.D. Mich. 1891).

42. Assuming the early handwriting is by Graves, a clear change in handwriting indicates that another commissioner took over the calendar in January 1902.

43. U.S. House Report 320, 46th Cong., 3rd Sess., February 19, 1881.

44. *Detroit Free Press*, December 17, 1881.

45. *Detroit Free Press*, March 2, 1882.

46. 22 Stat. 96.

47. 22 Stat. 304.

48. Robert Budd Ross & George Catlin, *Landmarks of Wayne County and Detroit* (Detroit: Evening News Association, 1898), 569–571.

49. Antoinette J. Lee, *Architects to the Nation: The Rise and Decline of the Supervising Architect's Office* (New York: Oxford University Press, 2000), 136.

50. 23 Stat. 338; 24 Stat. 468.

51. Underlying the criticism of the designs was a struggle over just who should design federal buildings, the office of the supervising architect or private firms. After years of bitter dispute, in 1893 Congress passed the Tarsney Act, 27 Stat. 468, which allowed the supervising architect to open the design of federal buildings to private architects, but this rarely happened before the Tarsney Act was repealed in 1912. See Lee, 163–187.

52. *The American Architect and Building News*, XXI: 595 (May 21, 1887), 595.

53. Testimony of E.T. Avery before the U.S. Senate Committee on Public Buildings and Grounds, January 5, 1889.

54. The tower top was designed to serve as a weather station, although it was never used for that purpose.

55. *Detroit Free Press*, November 8, 1897; Lee, 148.

56. *Detroit Free Press*, November 8, 1897; *Detroit News*, January 4, 1931.

57. See Alison M. Dawe, "The Eastern District Courthouse, Circa 1897, and the 'Million Dollar Courtroom,'" *The Court Legacy*, vol. IX, no. 1 (September 2001), 6–10.

58. Arthur J. Tuttle to Fred Woodworth, September 22, 1925, Custodian file, Box 23, Tuttle Papers.

59. *Detroit Free Press*, November 8, 1897.

60. 30 Stat. 598.

61. The initial appropriation in June 1906 was $325,000, 34 Stat. 774, followed by another $70,000 in 1913.

PART III
Decades of Tumult, 1900–1945

The first five decades of the 20th century witnessed events in the world at large, in the United States, in Michigan, and in the Eastern District, that changed practically everything. Little of that change was predictable in 1900, although life for most people was not as rosy as nostalgia tends to portray it. Poverty and disease were endemic in both the industrial and rural regions. Medicine was primitive, infant-mortality rates high, there were no antibiotics, and the average life expectancy of an American was less than 50 years. The average industrial employee worked 59 hours each week and in some industries capital and labor were in a shooting war. On the other hand, a majority of the 76 million Americans (including ten million immigrants) were confident in the future. The depression triggered by the Panic of 1903 was over and the United States led the world in industrial production. Republican Senator Mark Hanna announced: "Furnaces are glowing, spindles are singing their song. Happiness comes to us all with prosperity."[1] The short war with Spain was over and the nation found itself the owner of a small overseas empire. Nobody imagined that the next five decades would find the United States sending millions of troops overseas to fight two world wars and worrying about the possibility of a third (indeed, the very concept of a world war would have stunned most Americans in 1900), facing an unprecedented wave of criminality and corruption born of a well-meant prohibition law, and enduring a Great Depression that dug much deeper and lasted far longer than any economic bust to that time. Nor would they have guessed that the United States would emerge from all of those events as one of the world's two great powers facing each other with the power to destroy the world.

The forces that molded the nation during those decades also changed the federal courts forever. Congress abolished the old circuit courts, but the march of time abolished the Eastern District's old district court just as completely. The district court of the 19th century, in which a single district judge and a few staff disposed of a few hundred admiralty and criminal cases in a few months each year, was on the way out, to be replaced by a multi-judge court working all year to try to make a dent in the grossly swollen dockets produced by an aggressively reformist Congress, new bodies of law passed to help win two wars, the dislocations of the Great Depression, and above all Prohibition, which strained the court to its limits.

CHAPTER 7

Progressive Legislation and the First World War, 1900–1920

The Eastern District, 1900–1920

From 1900 to 1920, the population of the Eastern District soared by more than a million to 2,456,159, fueled by the birth and rapid growth of the motor vehicle industry in Detroit and, to a lesser extent, in Pontiac, Flint, and Lansing. Although Oakland, Genesee, and Ingham counties all doubled in population, 80 percent of the overall increase occurred in Wayne County (+828,852), most of them living in Detroit whose population, 994,000, made it the fourth-largest city in the nation, soon to pass Philadelphia into third place. Population totals were not the only measure of changes in the Eastern District. The number of registered motor vehicles in the United States grew from 8,000 in 1900 to 9.2 million in 1920 (and would exceed 23 million by 1930); most of them were manufactured in Michigan. The auto plants' insatiable need for unskilled labor drew a new tide of immigration to Michigan from Europe, particularly from Germany, Poland, and Russia. By 1915, three-fourths of Detroit's residents were immigrants or the children of immigrants, and half of the city's population could not speak English.[2] The city's African American population increased from 4,000 in 1900 to 40,000 in 1920. "Native" Michiganders, who were the descendants of earlier waves of immigration, were profoundly uneasy about the habits and loyalty of the newcomers.

There were two obvious changes in the courts' dockets between 1891 and 1920. The number of private civil filings halved due to a sudden dearth of new admiralty cases beginning in 1898, while the number of criminal cases tripled due to wartime criminal laws introduced in 1917 and at the beginning of Prohibition.[3] The number of U.S. civil cases changed slightly, but the types expanded to include cases based on new federal statutes

Table 7.1   Average Annual Case Filings in the District and Circuit Courts, 1891–1920

Fiscal Years	Criminal	U.S. Civil	Private Civil	Total
1891–1900	64	18	311	393
1901–1910	71	21	147	239
1911–1920	207	29	121	357

passed in the spirit of the Progressive Era to reform businesses, governments, and morals.

Progressive Era Legislation

During the Progressive Era, a period extending roughly from 1885 to 1920, newly-emergent middle and professional classes sought social and legal reform in all aspects of life, local and national, private and public, using modern scientific methods. A major tenet of the Progressives was greater regulation of business by the federal government on the grounds that state and local governments had proved powerless to affect large corporations operating across state lines. Presidents and Congress responded with a long list of statutes, beginning with the Interstate Commerce Act and the Sherman Antitrust Act in the 1880s and the Railroad Safety Appliance Act in the 1990s, then accelerating in the early 1900s with laws regulating public and private activities previously unregulated or left to state and local enforcement, such as the Pure Food and Drug Act and the Meat Inspection Act (both passed in 1906), the Railroad Hours of Service Act (1907), the Federal Employers Liability Act (1908), the Opium Exclusion Act (1909), the White Slavery (Mann) Act (1910), the Harrison Narcotics Tax Act and the Clayton Antitrust Act (both 1914), and the National Motor Vehicle Theft (Dyer) Act (1919). The effect of these laws on federal court dockets was palpable but absorbable before World War I, but war legislation and then the National Prohibition (Volstead) Act, which capped the Progressive Era, finally inundated the court's docket.

Carrie Davison, Clerk of the District Court

One of the most notable court events of the first decade of the century involved neither cases nor judges but, instead, the clerks of the district and circuit courts. In 1904, Judge Swan appointed Carrie Davison to succeed her father as clerk of the district court, likely the first appointment of a woman as clerk of any federal court. Darius ("Davy") Davison was clerk of the district court for more than 34 years, from 1870 when he succeeded John Winder until his death on December 9, 1904, just weeks before his

Fig. 32.   District Court Clerk
Darius Davison. (Burton Histori-
cal Collection, Detroit Public
Library)

77th birthday. Judge Swan immediately announced that the new clerk of
the district court would be the chief deputy clerk, Darius Davison's daughter Carrie Davison.[4] Born in Detroit in 1863, she joined the clerk's office
as a deputy clerk in 1890, and in 1901, she was appointed to be her father's chief deputy clerk. Although it is likely she was the first woman to

Fig. 33.   District Court Clerk
Carrie Davison. (Historical
Society for the United States
District Court for the Eastern
District of Michigan)

be appointed the clerk of a federal court, it appears her appointment was popular. Contemporary reports described Ms. Davison as "well known, very capable, and well liked by all attorneys who have had business dealings in the United States district court,"[5] and "a favorite of the attorneys, district court officials, and men of large business affairs."[6] She was also "the only woman in the United States honored with such an office.". She held the position until December 31, 1911, the day the circuit court was abolished. Judge Alexis C. Angell, who succeeded Judge Swan, gave the job of clerk of the consolidated district court to Elmer Voorheis, a deputy circuit court clerk. Ms. Davison then returned to her position as chief deputy clerk, which she held for the next 20 years.[7]

The United States v. Walter Harsha, Round 2

Another event during the 1900s brought the court shame rather than pride. Walter Harsha won his first encounter in court with the Justice Department, but in the second he lost the case as well as his reputation. In 1906, when Harsha had been clerk of the circuit court for 24 years, the U.S. Department of Justice began what at first appeared to be a routine audit of the circuit court's finances. Since 1789, the income of federal clerks had come solely from the fees paid into the courts for various services (and a per diem if they traveled). Eventually Congress decided that some clerks were earning too much and in 1841 and 1842 passed laws that required clerks to remit to the Treasury any fees received, net of expenses including the pay of a deputy clerk, in excess of $3,500 for the clerk of a district court and $2,500 for the clerk of a circuit court. For most clerks this limit was irrelevant because they earned far less, but for clerks of busy courts this was a problem that some solved by charging higher fees and reporting only a portion to Washington. In response, Congress enacted a fixed fee schedule in 1853, but some clerks were able to charge for services separate from their court duties and keep the full amount, particularly fees relating to naturalization. In a court in a large city full of immigrants, such fees were a gold mine, but in 1898, Congress shuttered the mine by requiring clerks to turn over to the Treasury all fees charged for naturalization. Again, some clerks looked for other schemes to supplement their income.[8]

As part of the cat and mouse game between the clerks and Congress, the Justice Department began auditing and investigating the operations and financial accounting of individual clerks. Justice Department special investigator Charles De Woody was assigned to review the clerks of the Eastern District. After an intensive review of 1,000 cases filed over Harsha's entire tenure, De Woody reported that over several years, Harsha had embezzled up to $30,000 by routinely inflating his estimated fees for certain services, such as preparing records for appeal, having the parties pay in advance, and keeping the excess.[9] When the Justice Department made the report public in March 1909, Judge Swan suspended Harsha and ordered him to turn over his personal files, and when Harsha refused, Swan threatened to hold him in contempt.[10] Harsha's niece, Jennie Wright Jones, deputy clerk in Bay City, also came under suspicion and resigned.[11] On April 18, 1909, the *Detroit Free Press*, which had treated the investigation and court proceedings as headline material, reported that Harsha would be allowed to resign to avoid further publicity, although he was not given any promise of immunity and the resignation did not end his troubles.[12] Deputy Clerk Elmer W. Voorheis became temporary custodian of the circuit court clerk's office pending appointment of a new clerk.

The government claimed that Harsha had promised to repay any deficiencies in his accounts, but after resigning, he refused to do so.[13] The United States sued Harsha and the surety on his fidelity bond in the circuit court seeking an accounting and enforcement of the bond. The government's bill of particulars covered 27 years and 2,181 cases in which it was alleged that Harsha had overcharged litigants. Judge Swan recused himself and the Circuit Court of Appeals designated District Judge Arthur C. Denison of the Western District to preside instead. The proceedings dragged on while Judge Denison was appointed to the Sixth Circuit,[14] and it was not until January 1913 that District Judge Clarence W. Sessions, who had replaced Judge Denison in the Western District, ruled in favor of the government and entered a judgment against Harsha. In the end, Harsha paid the government $11,862.87,[15] a substantial amount at a time when a U.S. district judge's annual salary was $6,000.

Although compensation by fees net of expenses had once been the standard for all non-judicial employees of the courts, by this time the district court clerks were alone in that regard. Harsha's case and others like it convinced Congress that it was time to put court clerks on a salary and for the government to assume the costs of the clerk's office. On February 17, 1919, Congress passed the Salary Act[16] which provided that clerks of the district court would receive an annual salary of between $2,500 and $5,000, that all fees earned were to be paid to the Treasury, and that the Treasury would reimburse the clerk for all of expenses including deputy clerks and clerical personnel. Most district court clerks supported the change to salaries because it increased and stabilized their income; the others went along with it, although the loss of fees was substantial for clerks of the busier districts.[17]

Circuit Court Clerk Martin J. Cavanaugh

The circuit court clerk's position remained vacant for a month after Harsha's resignation while the judges of the Circuit Court of Appeals decided what to do about a replacement. They ultimately left the decision to their colleague Judge Henry Franklin Severens. He considered many candidates who had indicated their interest, but in May 1909, he appointed a man who had not asked for the job, Ann Arbor attorney Martin J. Cavanaugh.[18] A native of Manchester, Michigan, and an 1887 graduate of the University of Michigan, the new clerk was one of the best known Democrats in a thoroughly Republican Michigan because of his unsuccessful campaigns for election to Washtenaw County Circuit Court and the Michigan Supreme Court.

Martin Cavanaugh's tenure as clerk of the circuit court lasted less than four years. On March 3, 1911, Congress passed the Judicial Code of 1911 that abolished the circuit courts as of January 1, 1912, and transferred their pending cases and remaining jurisdiction to the district courts.[19] The traditionalists, clerks, and other champions of the circuit courts who had preserved them in 1891 had finally lost their battle. Judge Angell decided to demote Carrie Davison to deputy clerk and to appoint his personal secretary, Deputy Clerk Elmer W. Voorheis, as the new clerk of the district court. Voorheis, whose own career would also end in public disgrace, was born in 1869 near Ypsilanti, Michigan. He graduated from Adrian College and the Detroit College of Law and, after a very short time in private practice, joined the clerk's office.

Judge Swan Retires

As he approached the age of 70, Judge Swan appeared to be overwhelmed by his caseload. Although the circuit and district courts were technically held in a few terms each year, the courts' journals show that for most of his tenure, Swan worked year-round holding both courts, usually without the circuit judge.[20] Nevertheless, he kept his head above water only because of the decrease in admiralty cases. In February 1910, a litigant complained to President William Howard Taft that Swan refused to schedule a hearing on his six-year-old patent case. According to the litigant, Swan explained "that he has worked beyond his ability, and that he could not hear all the cases which came before him, he heard some and put others off, and in response to the question by counsel if he heard cases in rotation, he said 'not always.'"[21] Although the president understood that Judge Swan intended to remain on the bench until he qualified for a pension in January 1911,[22] he began the search for Swan's successor immediately. Several candidates applied for the job, but they were considered political hacks, and qualified attorneys seemed to be put off by the low annual salary. This was the case for the preferred choice of Detroit's legal community, Alexis C. Angell, who declined to apply because he had a young family and could earn much more in his corporate practice.[23] When no other suitable candidate emerged after Swan retired, Taft decided to nominate Angell whether he wanted the job or not. Angell tried to refuse, but Taft leaked news of the nomination to the Detroit newspapers, guessing that Angell did not want to be seen to contradict the President of the United States. After Angell accepted the inevitable and wired his acceptance, Taft wrote back congratulating Angell and noting that he had already sent the nomination to the Senate, "in order to bring a leverage on you."

District Judge Alexis Caswell Angell

Born: April 26, 1857 (Providence, Rhode Island) to James B. and Sarah
    Swope Angell
Education: University of Michigan (A.B. 1878, LL. B. 1880, LL.M. (hon.) 1930)
Nominated/Confirmed: February 25/March 2, 1911 (William H. Taft)
Vacancy: Henry Harrison Swan (Retired)
Left Court: June 1, 1912 (Resigned)
Death: December 24, 1932

Alexis Caswell Angell had an immaculate background for a scholar. His father was a renowned professor of languages at Brown University, and then president of the University of Michigan from 1871 to 1916. Judge Angell's wife, Fanny C. Cooley, was the daughter of Michigan Supreme Court justice Thomas C. Cooley[24] who was also, at that time, Jay Professor of Law at the University of Michigan's Law Department. In 1890 and 1891, Alexis Angell edited new editions of his father-in-law's great works, *A Treatise on the Constitutional Limitations* and *The General Principles of Constitutional Law in The United States of America*, and taught courses in constitutional and domestic relations law at the University of Michigan's Law

Fig. 34.   Judge Alexis Caswell Angell. (Historical Society for the United States District Court for the Eastern District of Michigan)

Department. His practice, though, was long on corporate law and short on criminal law and litigation.

Judge Swan did all he could to make things easier for Judge Angell. For a month before Angell took over, Swan worked until after midnight, with the help of Judge Denison of the Western District, to reduce the number of pending cases. Once on the bench, Judge Angell also worked hard and managed to close 33 U.S. civil cases, 59 criminal cases, and 113 private civil cases. District Attorney Arthur J. Tuttle managed to get 45 of the criminal defendants to plead guilty, and only six criminal cases required jury trials. These results were very similar to what the septuagenarian Judge Swan had accomplished over the previous few years, but Angell nevertheless complained to President Taft that: "The pressure of work is heavy beyond all expectation & business is increasing beyond all hope of keeping up with it." He also told Taft that: "I have found much of the work of the office utterly distasteful," which may be a reference to the 14 Mann Act prostitution cases filed during his tenure.

The last straw seems to have been the criminal trial of the Bathtub Trust, a cabal of manufacturers of bathtubs and "sanitary porcelain" who were alleged to have conspired to violate the Sherman Antitrust Act. The trial by jury of 13 companies and 24 individuals began, in the splendor of the million-dollar courtroom, on February 6, 1912. Not only was the trial complex and exhausting for Judge Angell, an assistant district attorney imported from Washington to try the case publicly excoriated the judge's evidentiary rulings as well as his jury instructions. Overwhelmed, Judge Angell submitted his resignation to President Taft on March 12, 1912.[25] The next day, after the jurors reported that they could not reach a verdict, Angell declared a mistrial and discharged the jury.[26] The short, unhappy reign of Judge Angell ended on July 1, 1912, when he formally resigned to return to private practice in Detroit. In 1917, admirers put his name on the ballot for the Detroit Board of Education. He won easily without campaigning and served for several years, although he disliked the politics and compromises of public office.

District Judge Arthur J. Tuttle

Born: November 8, 1868 (Leslie, Ingham County, Michigan), to Ogden
    Valorous and Julia Elizabeth McArthur Tuttle
Education: University of Michigan (Ph.B. 1892, LL.B. 1895)
Nominated/Confirmed: August 2/6, 1912 (William H. Taft)
Vacancy: Alexis Carswell Angell (Resigned)
Left Court: December 2, 1944 (Died)

Within a month after Judge Angell's abrupt resignation, 22 men applied to be his successor, including two sitting justices of the Michigan Supreme Court, Charles A. Blair and Flavius L. Brooke, and the district attorney for the Eastern District, Arthur J. Tuttle. Brooke drew by far the most endorsements and recommendations, including more than 100 letters and tele-

Fig. 35.   Judge Arthur J. Tuttle.
(Bentley Library, University of
Michigan)

grams now in the files of the Justice Department's appointment clerk, and also had the support of Michigan's Senior Senator, William Alden Smith. Tuttle had fewer supporters, but one of the strongest was Michigan's other senator, Charles E. Townsend, whose campaign Tuttle had managed.[27] On the other hand, the Detroit Bar Association refused to endorse either man, writing to the president that Brooke and Tuttle "have pleasing personalities but it is questionable whether anyone of them has the training necessary for satisfactory discharge of the duties of a Federal Judge in this part of the world."[28] Although Townsend was slightly less senior than Smith, he lived in the Eastern District while Smith lived in the Western District, and Smith eventually conceded control of the nomination to Townsend, who advised the president to nominate Tuttle.

Judge Angell's precipitate departure from the bench was fortunate for the court and the district. Angell was ill-equipped to deal with the pressures that the next decades would impose, whereas Judge Tuttle seemed to be born to deal with the crises to come. He proved to be one of the most energetic, forceful, and hard-working judges ever to grace the court; indeed, for the first ten years of his 32-year career as a federal judge, he was the district court, its only judge, its undisputed administrative voice, and its public face. Even when the court grew from one judge to five, it was his leadership and his intense interest in every aspect of the court and its administration that steered the court safely through conditions sometimes approaching chaos.

Tuttle grew up on the family farm in Leslie, Michigan, south of Lansing. He earned his undergraduate and law degrees from the University of Michigan, and then returned to Leslie where he opened a private practice and also served as president of the Bank of Leslie and director of the local telephone company. In 1898, he was elected prosecuting attorney of Ingham County (a part-time office) and opened a law office in Lansing. During his two terms as a prosecutor, he distinguished himself by convicting the state's quartermaster general and the assistant quartermaster of embezzling military property. In conducting those prosecutions, he was fearless, even subpoenaing Michigan governor Hazen Pingree as he ran for a train. In 1907, Tuttle joined a Lansing law firm, and he served in the Michigan Senate from 1908 to 1910, where he drafted legislation providing free education to children living outside of incorporated cities and villages. He then focused on his private practice until 1911, when President William Howard Taft appointed him the district attorney for the Eastern District of Michigan. In March 1903, Judge Tuttle married Jessie Beatrice Stewart, daughter of William K. Stewart, of Grande Pointe, Michigan, and the Tuttles soon had two daughters. Their family life was idyllic until Mrs. Tuttle died suddenly of a pulmonary hemorrhage on August 24, 1912, just 12 days after the Senate confirmed Tuttle's appointment as district judge; he never remarried.

Judge Tuttle was a complex man. He was conservative even for a Republican of that era and solemn, sometimes harsh, on the bench, yet he was also extremely social and much admired by those who knew him personally. He was a "joiner" who belonged to "44 fraternal, civic, benevolent, patriotic, law, and scholastic societies,"[29] including his college fraternity for which he served a term as national president.

He had a conservative's strict view of his role in relation to the law and believed in the deterrent effect of imposing maximum sentences. A friend remembered him as having "what I call a mental integrity, a conscience of the mind. The rule that governed him was his respect for the law as supreme arbiter. He had intense political and social convictions, but when the law and the statute did not square with them, he sternly repressed those convictions. He never let his judgments be swayed by them or his prejudice."[30] Yet he often worked behind the scenes to temper the effect of his rulings, and he kept track of the defendants he sentenced, corresponding with prison wardens about their activities in prison and offering to find a job for every one of them who asked for his help, even during the Depression when jobs were scarce.[31] He encouraged his daughters to become lawyers, and after graduation from the University of Michigan Law School in 1930, they established the state's first all-woman law firm.

Although a man of ordinary size for his time (five foot eight inches and 175 pounds in 1922[32]), Judge Tuttle seemed to have an unlimited store of energy and curiosity. He was interested in a wide variety of subjects, and, if he was interested, he formed strong opinions which he could not keep to himself. Instead, he dictated long letters (often eight or ten typed, single-spaced pages) setting out his views. As he admitted in one of them, "I am just so constituted that when I see something that looks as if it were not right, if it has to do with my own country, I have to visit with someone about it."[33] His ability to administer a court, dictate long diatribes, spend day after day in court trying cases, be an attentive father, and still enjoy his social life was aided immeasurably by the two women who served as his secretaries during his 32 years on the bench. Tuttle brought Julia M. Baldwin with him when he came to the court from the district attorney's office. In 1925, as Prohibition rendered life in the court ever more hectic, he added Josephine M. Bowman. Ms. Baldwin died in about 1930, but Ms. Bowman was still running his life when Judge Tuttle died in 1944.[34]

Cleaning Up the Docket

A few months after they settled into their work, Judge Tuttle and Clerk Elmer Voorheis addressed an administrative problem that had dogged the court for decades. Forty years earlier, in March 1873, Congress directed the attorney general to report annually regarding certain matters, including "the number of causes, civil and criminal, pending during the preceding year in each of the several courts of the United States."[35] The attorney general then passed the buck to the district attorneys to collect and forward the pertinent statistics. According to the attorney general's report for the year ending on June 30, 1912, the Eastern District had pending 39 U.S. civil cases, 39 criminal cases, and 4,764 private civil cases. Although it was true that the number of private civil cases filed between 1900 and 1912 had exceeded the number closed in those years by some 350 cases, Tuttle and Voorheis were convinced that they did not have 4,764 cases of any kind waiting to be tried. Their investigation of the court's records confirmed their belief and discovered the cause of the discrepancy. From the first, the reports to the attorney general were inaccurate, for two main reasons. First, beginning before the Civil War, district and circuit clerks had failed to formally close hundreds of cases in which there had been no activity for years, usually because the defendants could not be served or the case was settled privately. As a result, those cases were still reported as open and pending in 1912. Second, beginning in 1876, somebody, either Clerk Darius Davison or District Attorney Sullivan McCutcheon or both, routinely overstated the number of the admiralty cases filed each year by up to several times the actual number recorded in the district court's official admiralty calendars. In 1876, for example, the offical court calendar recorded the filing of 134 new admiralty cases, but the annual report claimed there were 690. The next year, 161 admiralty cases were filed according to the calendar records but 836 were reported. In just ten years, from 1876 to 1885, the number of admiralty cases reported exceeded the number in the calendars by 3,143 cases. In April and July 1913, and again in 1916, Judge Tuttle issued general orders dismissing thousands of abandoned cases and reduced the number of admiralty cases to those actually in the calendars, so that the report for 1916 honestly stated that the district court had pending only 240 private civil cases of all kinds, including admiralty cases.

United States v. Kellogg Toasted Corn Flake Co.

Not all of the fruits of Michigan's industrial development were made of steel and rubber. In 1906, Will K. Kellogg formed a company in Battle Creek, Michigan, to adapt mass production and national marketing to the manufacture of a breakfast cereal made of toasted corn. The Kellogg Toasted Corn Flake Company prospered and soon left its competitors behind.[36] Part of the company's marketing strategy was to sell only to jobbers (distributors) who promised to resell to retailers at a price fixed by the Kellogg Company and unilaterally to stop dealing with any jobber who sold at a different price. In 1911, in *Dr. Miles Medical Co. v. John D. Park and Sons*,[37] the U.S. Supreme Court held that such a pricing scheme, today called resale price maintenance, in which retailers promised in writing to sell only at the prices set by the manufacturer, was an agreement in restraint in trade that violated the Sherman Antitrust Act. In December 1912, on the authority of that decision, the U.S. attorney general sued the Kellogg Company and its top officers (Will Kellogg, his brother Wilfred, and Andrew Rose) in the district court in Detroit seeking an injunction barring Kellogg's resale price maintenance scheme. The attorney general also certified the case to be "of general public importance" and invoked the Expediting Act,[38] which assigned the case to a three-judge panel for decision as soon as possible, with an appeal directly to the Supreme Court. For some reason, after 16 months this "expedited" case was still at the stage of motions to strike or dismiss the complaint. On April 14, 1915, a panel consisting of Judge Tuttle and Circuit Judges John W. Warrington and Loyal E. Knappen denied the defendants' motions and held that neither the company's patents nor the lack of a written contract with the jobbers distinguished this case from *Dr. Miles*.[39] Rather than fight on in the Supreme Court, the Kellogg Company conceded and agreed to the injunction, entered on September 20, 1915. Perhaps Kellogg should have persevered. Just four years later, in *United States v. Colgate*,[40] the Supreme Court held that a resale price maintenance scheme identical to Kellogg's did not violate the Sherman Act because the seller did not make the purchasers "agree" to resell at the mandated price, but only terminated jobbers if they sold at a different price. Generations of antitrust attorneys had to explain this subtle distinction to confused clients until the Supreme Court overruled *Dr. Miles* in 2007.[41]

The Eastern District in the Great War

In August 1914, the British, German, Russian, and Austro-Hungarian Empires, the Republic of France, and the Kingdom of Italy, along with a bevy of smaller nations, muddled into a war like none ever experienced before. In the first month, the belligerents suffered almost a million casualties, and by the end, four years later, the total killed, wounded, and missing exceeded 38 million combatants and civilians. The United States entered the war on April 16, 1917, and suffered 322,000 dead and wounded servicemen before the war ended on November 11, 1918; of 175,000 Michiganders in the armed forces, 5,000 died and 15,000 were wounded. As it would during World War II, the Eastern District increased its industrial output tremendously. In addition to providing trucks, guns, equipment, and supplies for the American forces, businesses found themselves, soon after the war began, supplying arms and equipment to the belligerents. Because of the Royal Navy's blockade of German ports, most of those goods were sold to the Allies (Britain, France, Russia, and Italy).

For the district court, the years during which the United States was at war (fiscal 1917 through fiscal 1919) involved new laws, ramped up emotions, and a doubling of the criminal and U.S. civil dockets. As soon as it declared war, Congress passed several new laws intended to prepare the nation for the struggle against the Central Powers, including the Selective Service Act,[42] the Espionage Act,[43] the Sedition Act,[44] and the Food and Fuel Control Act.[45] Each of these laws raised new legal and constitutional issues, and each of them also raised the hackles of one group of the district's residents or another. The Selective Service Act, which provided most of the increase in criminal cases, was particularly controversial as was the Sedition Act which criminalized a wide range of expression critical of the war and the federal government.

United States v. Albert Kaltschmidt

Even before April 1917, though, the war came to the district court. Hundreds of thousands of the Eastern District's people were immigrants or children of immigrants, most from a country now at war. Some of those residents returned to Europe to fight, but most chose to stay in this country. Many of those who stayed provided moral or physical support to their homeland's war effort. Most of those residents limited their protests to holding rallies, raising money, and trying to convince the U.S. government and other Michiganders, themselves deeply split between pacifism and preparedness, that the best path to peace was complete neutrality (if German or Austrian) or joining the Allies (if British). A few others decided to do more.

On June 20, 1915, a bomb destroyed the Peabody Company's war plant in Windsor, Ontario, and police found another bomb at the Windsor Armory set to explode at the same time. Within days, Canadian authorities arrested two German immigrants, Charles Respa and William Leffler, who confessed to setting the bombs and implicated, as their leader, a German national and businessman residing in Detroit, Albert Kaltschmidt.[46] Investigators from the U.S. Department of Justice had been watching Kaltschmidt since the war began a year earlier and had even questioned him, but they had found no evidence that he had done anything illegal.[47] Even after Respa and Leffler confessed, the U.S. was stymied both because Canada refused to bring them to Detroit to testify and because it was doubtful that any U.S. law expressly prohibited anybody from spying against another country, or even blowing up one of its buildings.

The federal investigators' scrutiny of Kaltschmidt became even more intense in December 1915 when the U.S. deported the German military attaché in Washington, Count Franz Joseph Hermann Michael Maria von Papen zu Köningen and confiscated his luggage which contained 126 check stubs showing payments to agents, including several to Kaltschmidt.[48] When the United States entered the war, federal agents immediately arrested Kaltschmidt at his salt plant in Marine City, Michigan.[49] A month later, in May, the Eastern District's grand jury indicted Kaltschmidt and 12 others under the Neutrality Act, essentially the same law used against the Patriots 80 years earlier, alleging that conspiring to blow up buildings in Canada constituted a "military expedition or enterprise."[50] Later, the indictments were amended when evidence surfaced that the group had also planned to dynamite targets in the United States, including the Detroit Screw Works and the railroad tunnel under the St. Clair River.

The trial of Kaltschmidt and five other defendants began on December 6, 1917, before Judge Tuttle in the million dollar courtroom of the 1897 Post Office. Security was extraordinary, with armed soldiers on guard inside the building and even inside the courtroom when the prisoners were being moved. District Attorney John Kinnane prosecuted and the defendants were represented by many of the best criminal defense attorneys in the city, including former U.S. Senator James Murtha, Lazarus Davidow, H.W. Bailey, and S. Pointer Bradley. After Charles Respa, William Leffler, and two other confessed members of the conspiracy, Richard Hermann and William Jarosch, fingered Kaltschmidt, Pointer Bradley was left with only a jurisdictional argument—that the civil courts had no power to try spies: "The testimony all has tended that they were spies, not military invaders, and this civil court is not the place in which spies should be tried." Kaltscmidt's enjoyment of this technical distinction must have been blunted by Bradley's next words: "Since the beginning of the war, spies have been tried in military courts *and shot down like dogs.*"[51]

At 2:00 a.m. on Saturday, December 22, 1917, after deliberating for 14 hours, the jury convicted Kaltschmidt on all three counts of the indictment, acquitted Franz Respa, Charles's father, and found the other defendants guilty on at least one count.[52] As soon as the verdicts were read, Judge Tuttle sentenced each defendant to the maximum allowed, which he complained was "utterly inadequate." For Kaltschmidt, that meant a sentence of four years in Leavenworth and a fine of $20,000; the others received lesser sentences. To Judge Tuttle's great disgust, Kaltschmidt served only three years of his sentence because the Justice Department released and deported him in February 1921, reasoning that the U.S. was not at war when he committed his sabotage and that he was a German citizen acting for his government.[53]

The Selective Service Act

When the U.S. entered the war, the Regular Army consisted of about 100,000 men and the National Guard about 120,000, but the army planned to build an expeditionary force of five to eight million soldiers. President Wilson preferred an all-volunteer force, and former president Teddy Roosevelt, the old Rough Rider, offered to raise and lead a volunteer army to Europe. However, volunteer enlistments were initially slow, and neither Wilson nor Roosevelt had a real understanding of complexity of the task ahead. Instead, the government decided that a draft would be fairer and more effective. On May 18, 1917, Congress, passed the Selective Service Act, also known as the Conscription Act,[54] which required all men between the ages of 21 and 30 (expanded in August 1917 to between 18 and 45) to register for the draft. On the day of the first draft registration, June 5, 1917, 380,000 men registered in Michigan, and eventually, this "most important of the war laws"[55] contributed more than half of the 4.8 million men who served in the U.S. armed forces during the war. During the first months, though, the local draft boards struggled to process draftees amidst confusion and controversy. About half of the men called up in the first draft asked for exemption, thousands simply did not show up to be inducted, and a large portion of those who did appear were rejected as physically unfit. More than 300,000 men across the nation tried to avoid or resist the draft, and this single statute added more than 160 criminal prosecutions to Judge Tuttle's docket between July 1917 and June 1919 as well as more than seventy habeas corpus petitions from draftees seeking release from the army.[56]

Hoping to discourage resistance to registration, Judge Tuttle and District Attorney John Kinnane began trying the first cases brought for failing to register in July 1917 and quickly disposed of 20 of them. In each of those cases, the jury found the defendant guilty and in each case but one Judge Tuttle imposed the maximum sentence, a year in the Detroit House of Correction and an order directing the defendant to register for the draft.[57] Having made his point with the first 20 cases, Judge Tuttle had to try only seven more draft cases during and after the war. Instead, he accepted 105 guilty pleas and gave lighter sentences to defendants who appeared before him later. In 1919, the war over, two of the last draft defendants received only 30 and 60 days in jail.

Most of the draft cases filed in the district court involved men who did not want to be drafted for personal reasons or who believed they qualified for one of the act's exemptions. Some defendants though opposed the draft and American participation in the war on political and moral grounds. Although the act allowed conscientious objectors to serve in non-combat military positions, about 2,000 men nationally refused to cooperate in any way. One such was Detroit attorney Maurice Sugar, a leader of Michigan's militant branch of the Socialist Party of America, which characterized the war as a dispute among capitalists fought by working men. He and ten other Socialists were indicted for refusing to register and for conspiring to counsel others not to register. The basis for the conspiracy charge was a resolution published on May 27, 1917, in *The Michigan Socialist* magazine which declared: "In the name of the workers, who will bleed but not benefit, we pledge ourselves to oppose registration for conscription by refusing to enroll upon registration day, and we call upon all workers to refrain from signifying their willingness to kill the workers of any other nation. Better the freedom of a prison cell than slavery in the interest of commercialism. . . . WILL YOU CRINGE LIKE A COWARD OR STAND UP LIKE A MAN? . . . Better a prison cell than the blood of innocent workers on your hands. BE A MAN."[58]

The defendants, represented by Detroit attorney Joseph B. Beckenstein, moved to quash the indictment on several constitutional grounds including that the act resulted in slavery or involuntary servitude contrary to the Thirteenth Amendment to the Constitution, constituted class legislation, "deprive[d] the courts of the United States of the power to pass upon the exemptions provided for in said act, was "not an exercise of any power conferred upon Congress by the Constitution," and "calls out the militia for a purpose not authorized by the Constitution." On July 8, 1917, Judge Tuttle predictably rejected all of the defendants' arguments, whereupon Sugar adopted the unusual tactic of pleading guilty, and, after receiving the maximum sentence of a year in prison, filing a motion in arrest of judgment. Judge Tuttle rejected that motion as well, the Sixth Circuit affirmed his conviction, and, on November 4, 1918, exactly one week before the Armistice which ended the war, the Supreme Court rejected his petition for review.[59] Sugar spent ten months of his one-year sentence in the Detroit House of Correction and was also disbarred, although he emerged from jail as a Socialist hero and later regained his law license.[60]

The trial of five of the defendants on the conspiracy charge began on August 10, 1917. The jury began deliberating at 6:00 p.m. on August 16, continued all night and the next morning, and just after noon on August 17 returned a verdict acquitting all five defendants.[61] The government then settled with the other defendants, including Sugar, who was allowed to serve his one-year sentence for conspiracy concurrently with his sentence for failing to register.[62]

Another type of challenge to the draft came from resident aliens. The Selective Service Act applied only to U.S. citizens and to aliens who had applied for citizenship, but many local draft boards tried to conscript all aliens in order to fill their quotas. During the war, the district court received at least 76 petitions for writs of habeas corpus from aliens seeking to be released from the army. Judge Tuttle routinely denied those petitions but was troubled by those draft boards which seemed intent upon forcing aliens, particularly enemy aliens, into the armed services. After he had upheld governmental authority in public, he often approached the Army discreetly to obtain the petitioner's discharge. As he put it: "If the purpose [of the draft boards] be to force an alien into the army, in order that an American citizen may be kept at home, it is unpatriotic. It would deprive the country of the services of an American soldier and give in lieu thereof an unwilling alien. If the motive be patriotism, it is of the misguided and short-sighted brand. Assuming that to thus take advantage of the opportunity, afforded by a technical form of law, to trap an unwilling alien into the military service of this country can be justified on moral or equitable grounds, what is thereby gained? The result of each such case is to inject into our brave American army one unfriendly alien, and, in the present case, an alien enemy. Men of the type and spirit of this petitioner would make a poor army to champion the cause of liberty for the nation whose representatives had accorded them such treatment in bringing them to the colors."[63]

The Espionage and Sedition Acts

Freedom of speech in wartime is always a difficult subject. Maurice Sugar and his co-defendants were charged under the Selective Service Act, but until 1918 there was no federal law against speech critical of the war effort unrelated to the draft. Then on May 16, 1918, Congress passed the Sedition Act[64] which amended the Espionage Act of 1917[65] to criminalize a wide range of speech, including speech opposing or criticizing the war, the draft, the military, the government, or the Constitution. On orders from Washington, District Attorney John Kinnane indicted 22 persons who spoke out against the war. These indictments presented Judge Tuttle with a dilemma. He supported the war effort and sincerely believed that the amount of "disloyal," defeatist, and anti-war speech in the Eastern District was dangerous, and his interpretation of the scope of constitutional protection of free speech was far narrower than ours ninety years later. He did disagree, however, with the Justice Department's use of the Sedition Act to stifle all anti-war dissent. His solution was to instruct juries trying Sedition Act cases that defendants were guilty only if they acted with the intent to injure the United States and did, in fact, cause "palpable" injury. The Justice Department cried foul, but Tuttle persevered.

In the few Sedition Act cases in which the jury did convict, Tuttle gave stiff sentences but, as with the alien draft cases, worked behind the scenes to mitigate the punishment somewhat. William Powell, for example, was an American citizen with German parents who complained loudly and often about the war, the government, and war bonds, to the great annoyance of his neighbors, most of whom were German immigrants. They turned him in and, on July 24, 1918, Powell became the first defendant in the Eastern District to be convicted under the Espionage Act. Tuttle imposed the maximum sentence, 20 years in prison and a $10,000 fine, and excoriated Powell in an emotional tirade that was apparently influenced by the death in aerial combat just ten days earlier of Quentin Roosevelt, youngest son of Theodore Roosevelt. Judge Tuttle described Powell as "more dangerous than a German fighting in the ranks," and he thundered: "The life of one man in this war is of no more importance than a fly-speck. Why should mercy be shown to you when the sons of our presidents are dying for our country? Even you, disloyal as you are, can be of service to this country, if by making an example of you we teach others of your stamp that their actions will not be tolerated."[66] That same morning, though, Tuttle met privately with Powell's attorney and explained that although imposing the maximum sentence was his duty because of "too many of our citizens and residents making disloyal utterances," he would quietly reduce the fine to (a still daunting) $5,000, if paid at once.[67] Eventually, Powell's sentence was commuted to two years and he was released from Leavenworth in April 1919, after serving less than a year. In August 1918, Tuttle gave the same sentence to two more defendants, Anthony J. Stopa and Mojick Fieron, for statements opposing participation in the war ("Young men are fools if they join the Army to be shot down like dogs"), although both asserted their loyalty to the United States. Both sentences were commuted to five years by President Wilson and then to time served by President Harding in December 1921.[68] After the war, Tuttle admitted that to a friend in his war cases he "made all the sentences about four times what I would have made" in order to send a message to the public.[69] To another correspondent the judge explained that: "We were in the midst of a great war; it was necessary for the courts and for everyone to stand by our country and to crush everybody and everything which stood in the way of the laws of our land."[70]

Bribery and Theft

Judge Tuttle first made an impression on the people of Michigan when as Ingham County prosecutor he pursued and convicted well-placed officials and state militia officers who profited illegally from the purchase of military supplies and materials during the Spanish-American War.[71] During and after World War I he revisited the subjects of theft and bribery involving war materiel. On March 19, 1918, army Captain Ralph A. Pillinger and a civilian, Ralph S. Windhorst, were arraigned on the charge of seeking bribes in negotiating contracts for the construction of buildings at Camp Custer. A jury convicted Windhorst of the charges after a brief deliberation. Judge Tuttle expressed his regret that he could not impose the death penalty on Mr. Windhorst and then pronounced a sentence of two years in Leavenworth and a $10,000 fine.[72] Captain Pillinger was not so lucky. He was tried by court martial, convicted, and sentenced to 21 years in prison. The prosecutor in Pillinger's court-martial was Lieutenant Frank Murphy, who would soon join John Kinnane's staff and would go on to a brilliant career as Wayne County circuit judge, Detroit mayor, Michigan governor, U.S. attorney general, and U.S. Supreme Court justice.[73]

After his discharge from the army, Murphy became an assistant district attorney and was assigned to the prosecution of several individuals charged with bribery and defrauding the United States.[74] This case, described by Judge Tuttle as "the most remarkable ever tried in the Eastern District of the Federal Court,"[75] has a very modern ring, with public corruption, a bugged hotel room, the defense of entrapment, and challenges to evidence under the Fourth Amendment. The chief defendant was Grant Hugh Browne, a New York businessman who, with the connivance of Major Lester Waterbury, offered bribes to Captain Soterious Nicholson and Lieutenant Bolivar Reamy, the officers in charge of sales of surplus military goods in Detroit, in order to buy the goods for about half their true value. Unfortunately for the others, Reamy was honest and immediately reported the bribe offer to the Justice Department. Agents began a sting operation and, in an investigative first, placed a dictograph in Browne's room at Detroit's Statler Hotel to record him discussing his scheme with Reamy and Nicholson. After the agents followed Browne to rural Rochester, Michigan, and observed him delivering $5,000 in $100 bills to Nicholson, they swooped in and arrested Browne, Nicholson (who immediately confessed), and other alleged conspirators.

When trial began on December 2, 1919, Kinnane and Murphy faced a defense team which Kinnane called "the greatest array of counsel . . . ever assembled in a court," although the best known of the defense attorneys, Thomas B. Felder, would be convicted of conspiracy to obstruct justice in another case.[76] Judge Tuttle kept the attorneys in court without a dinner break until 8:30 p.m. to finish jury selection.[77] The trial that followed was extraordinarily long and complex for that era—more than six weeks of testimony, 60 witnesses, and 400 exhibits. Browne's main defense was that he was the innocent victim of government entrapment and had never intended to commit a crime. The dictograph transcript and the papers he was carrying when arrested discredited that defense, so his counsel objected to their admission because they had been obtained without a warrant. Judge Tuttle rejected all of the defense objections to this evidence, and the jury, after nine hours' deliberation, found Browne, Waterbury, and

Nicholson guilty, although other defendants were acquitted. Tuttle sentenced Browne to two years in prison and Waterbury to 18 months; and the Sixth Circuit affirmed both convictions.[78] Nicholson received a fine of $1,000 but no prison time.

The Food and Fuel Control Act

Even more controversial than the Selective Service Act or the Sedition Act was the Food and Fuel Control Act, also known as the Lever Act.[79] From its passage in August 1917 until its repeal in December 1920, the Lever Act gave two administrators selected by the president (Herbert Hoover and Harry Garfield) almost absolute power over the nation's food and energy supplies, including the power to set prices, license distributors, limit civilian sales, and punish hoarders and profiteers, all with the goal of conserving resources and maximizing the supplies available for the armed forces and the European allies. During the war, the controls essentially worked, and consumer prices remained low even though supplies were limited.

In 1919, after the war, prices for food and other commodities began to increase sharply. In August, President Wilson asked Congress to extend the Lever Act and to increase penalties on hoarders and profiteers. At the same time, U.S. attorney general A. Mitchell Palmer announced that he intended to use the Lever Act "to hunt down the hoarders of and the profiteers in food."[80] Always a team player, John Kinnane reported to Palmer, the very next day, that his office was "devoting practically its entire energies to this work." The results of Kinnane's raids were impressive, including the seizure of millions of eggs, 300,000 pounds of butter, and 30,000 pounds of poultry. In April 1920, however, Judge Tuttle stopped Kinnane in his tracks by joining other district judges in holding that the maximum price provisions of the Lever Act were "too vague, indefinite, and uncertain to satisfy constitutional requirements or to constitute due process of law."[81] The Supreme Court affirmed Tuttle's decision in February 1921.[82]

Notes

1. *The Nation*, August 30, 1900.
2. Lawrence I. Kiern, "War and the law in Detroit, 1917–1919" (Ph.D. diss., University of Connecticut, 1996), ix, http://digitalcommons.uconn.edu/dissertations/AAI9717516. (Accessed 10/7/11)
3. Although the Volstead Act did not come into effect until January 1, 1920, half way through fiscal year 1920, the federal courts, as we shall see, were enforcing state prohibition much earlier.
4. *Detroit Times*, December 10, 1904. Her official date of appointment was December 14, 1904.
5. *Detroit Free Press*, December 15, 1904.

6. *Detroit Times*, December 15, 1904.

7. *Detroit Free Press*, June 25, 1928.

8. I. Scott Messinger, *Order in the Courts: A History of the Federal Clerk's Office* (Federal Judicial Center, 2002), 20–45.

9. *Detroit Free Press*, April 18, 1909.

10. *Detroit Free Press*, March 30, 1909, April 6, 1909.

11. *Detroit Free Press*, April 16, 1909.

12. Harsha was far from the only clerk under scrutiny at that time, as the fee system had allowed petty theft to creep into many offices of the clerk. In 1912, Attorney General George Wickersham reported that "'serious irregularities' had been found in the operations of 28 clerks in the previous year, almost all of which involved the improper collection of fees. Ten clerks had resigned after such irregularities had come to light; six had been indicted; and three were convicted and removed from office." Messinger, 41.

13. *Ogden (Utah) Standard*, June 16, 1909.

14. The delay was also due to Denison's concerns about the case's complexity. On April 27, 1911, Denison refused to even attempt to try the case before a jury because it was so complex that a jury trial would be a farce that might take four months to complete. Instead, he stayed all proceedings and urged the parties to refile the case in equity so it could be referred to a master in chancery. *U.S. v. Harsha*, 188 F. 759 (C.C. E.D. Mich. 1911).

15. *Annual Report of the Attorney General of the United States* (1913), 48. *Detroit Journal*, January 4, 1913.

16. 40 Stat. 1182.

17. Messinger, 41-45.

18. *Detroit Free Press*, May 19, 1909.

19. Judicial Code of 1911, ch. 13, sec. 289; 36 Stat. 1087, 1167.

20. See Law and Equity Journals, Circuit Court, Eastern District of Michigan, 1890–1911, NARA-Great Lakes.

21. Edward C. Marshon to President William H. Taft, February 15, 1910, Michigan Eastern, Judge, General 1911 folder, *NARA RG 60, Unit 357, Appointment Clerk, Applications & Endorsements, 1901–1933, Michigan Eastern*, Box 452.

22. Judge Swan's 70th birthday was October 2, 1910, but he did not satisfy the other requirement for a pension, 20 years' service on the bench, until January 18, 1911.

23. Levi Barbour to President William H. Taft, December 29, 1910, Michigan Eastern, Judge, General 1911 Folder, *NARA RG 60, Unit 357, Appointment Clerk, Applications & Endorsements, 1901–1933, Michigan Eastern*, Box 452.

24. Judge and Mrs. Angell were the parents of three sons and three daughters.

25. *New York Times*, March 13, 1912.

26. The first trial of the Bathtub Trust defendants ended with a hung jury. A second trial resumed on February 3, 1913, before District Judge Clarence Sessions of the Western District, and ended with the conviction of all of the defendants. Judge Tuttle was disqualified from presiding over the retrial because he had assisted in prosecuting the first trial. Defendants were convicted and fined a total of $51,000. *Annual Report of the United States Attorney General (1913)*, 11; *New York Times*, February 15, 1913.

27. List of Applicants, June 24, 1912, *Records Group 60, Unit 357, Appointment Clerk, Applications & Endorsements, 1901–1933, Michigan Eastern*, Box 452, Michigan Eastern List of Applicants Judge 1912, NARA College Park, Maryland; Aaron J. Veselenak, "Arthur J. Tuttle: 'Dean of the Federal Bench,'" *The Court Legacy*, 7, no. 2 (September 1999), 6-11.

28. Sidney T. Miller, president, Detroit Bar Association, to President Taft, June 19, 1912, *Records Group 60, Unit 357, Appointment Clerk, Applications & Endorsements, 1901–1933, Michigan Eastern*, Box 452, Michigan Eastern List of Applicants Judge 1912, NARA College Park, Maryland.

29. *Detroit Free Press*, December 4, 1944.

30. Veselenak, 8.

31. Letter, Tuttle to attorney general, May 27, 1919, Judge Additional 1 file, Box 20, Tuttle Papers. Judge Tuttle also provided elderly Baseball Hall of Fame member Samuel Luther Thompson with a source of income during the last years of his life by employing Thompson as his court crier.

32. Order Form, Judicial Robes File, Box 23, Tuttle Papers.

33. Letter, Tuttle to warden of Leavenworth, December 29, 1939, Lockhart criminal file, Box 48, Tuttle Papers.

34. Both women used only their initials (JMB) on most of their communications with the judge and other staff, leading researchers to no end of confusion.

35. 17 Stat. 578.

36. Willis F. Dunbar and George S. May, *Michigan: A History of the Wolverine State*, rev. ed. (Grand Rapids, MI: Eerdmans Publishing Company, 1980), 464–465.

37. *Dr. Miles Medical Co. v. John D. Park and Sons*, 220 U.S. 373 (1911).

38. 32 Stat. 823.

39. *U.S. v. Kellogg Toasted Corn Flake Co*, 222 F. 725 (E.D. Mich. 1915).

40. *United States v. Colgate*, 250 U.S. 300 (1919).

41. *Leegin Creative Leather Products, Inc. v. PSKS, Inc.*, 551 U.S. 877 (2007).

42. 40 Stat. 76.

43. 40 Stat. 219.

44. 40 Stat. 553–554.

45. 40 Stat. 276.

46. *New York Times*, July 29, 1915.

47. Kiern, 140.

48. Von Papen's memoirs describe Kaltschmidt as "a person who could be trusted, and I instructed him to make plans for attacks on the [Canadian Pacific] railway. He had, however, much bigger ideas and wanted to blow up munitions factories." Grant W. Grams, "Karl Respa and German Espionage in Canada During World War One," *Journal of Military and Strategic Studies*, vol. 8, issue 1 (Fall 2005), 4.

49. *New York Times*, April 7, 1917.

50. *New York Times*, May 23, 1917.

51. *Detroit News*, December 20, 1917.

52. *New York Times*, December 22, 1917.

53. *New York Times*, February 19, 1921.

54. 40 Stat. 76.

55. *Annual Report of the U.S. Attorney General (1918)*, 24.

56. Kiern, 231, 239.

57. In the 20th case, the defendant, a Navy veteran, had re-enlisted after his arrest. Kiern, 243.

58. *The Michigan Socialist*, 1:46 (May 27, 1917) (Capital letters in the original).

59. *U.S. v. Sugar*, 243 F. 423 (E.D. Mich. 1917), *aff'd*, 252 F. 79 (6th Cir.), *cert. den'd*, 248 U.S. 578 (1918).

60. Christopher H. Johnson, *Maurice Sugar: law, labor, and the left in Detroit, 1912-1950* (Detroit: Wayne State University Press, 1988), 71–72.

61. *Detroit News*, August 17, 1917. The acquitted defendants were Saul M. Parker, Max A. Yagman, Herman Aberly, Philip Travis, and Arnold Fuhrer.

62. Kiern, 264-271.

63. *Ex parte Blazekovic*, 248 F. 327 (E.D. Mich. 1918).

64. 40 Stat. 553–554.

65. 40 Stat. 219.

66. *Detroit Free Press*, July 24, 1918.

67. Tuttle to Richard Raudabaugh, August 6, 1918, Box 73, Tuttle Papers.

68. *New York Times*, December 24, 1921.

69. Arthur J. Tuttle to Richard Raudabaugh, April 19, 1919, Box 73, Tuttle Papers.

70. Arthur J. Tuttle to O. L. Smith, April 24, 1931, quoted at Kiern, 244

71. Catlin, 643-645.

72. *Manchester (Michigan) Enterprise*, May 16, 1918.

73. Sidney Fine, *Frank Murphy: The Detroit Years* (Ann Arbor, MI: The University of Michigan Press, 1975), 43.

74. *U.S. v. Browne & Waterbury*, E.D. Mich. Case #6569 and #6599.

75. *Detroit News*, March 5, 1920.

76. *Time Magazine*, February 9, 1925. Besides Felder, the defense counsel included Alfred J. Murphy, William C. Manchester, Levi Cooke, William L. Wemple, James McNamara, and Harry Helfman. *Detroit Free Press*, December 3, 1919.

77. *Detroit Free Press*, December 3, 1919.

78. *Browne v. U.S.*, 290 F. 870 (6th Cir. 1923).

79. 40 Stat. 276.

80. Fine, *Detroit*, 60.

81. *Detroit Creamery Co. v. Kinnane*, 264 F. 845 (E.D. Mich. 1920), *aff'd*, 255 U.S. 102 (1921).

82. *Kinnane v. Detroit Creamery Co.* 255 U.S. 102 (1921).

CHAPTER 8

The Red Scare and Prohibition, 1920–1934

Anarchists in the Attic

As the world returned to peace, Americans had every reason to be optimistic about the future, but that optimism was tested by a series of events that raised the specter of a violent revolution akin to that in Russia. First was a series of bombings the press blamed on "bolsheviks," a catch-all for left-wing foreigners, whether violent or not.[1] On December 30, 1918, bombs exploded at the homes of three prominent citizens of Philadelphia; nobody was injured. Then, in late April 1919, 30 mail bombs were sent to federal judges, members of Congress, businessmen, and officials, including Supreme Court Justice Oliver Wendell Holmes, Jr., U.S. Attorney General A. Mitchell Palmer, J. P. Morgan, Jr., and John D. Rockefeller. Only one bomb exploded, raising the alarm. The others were intercepted by alert postal officers. A few weeks later, on June 2, 1919, bombs exploded in eight cities. One bomb in Washington, D.C., destroyed the home of Attorney General Palmer and almost killed Assistant Secretary of the Navy Franklin D. Roosevelt, who was walking by Palmer's home. Another source of public anxiety about "bolsheviks" was a series of bitter strikes in key industries, which broke the relative peace that labor and capital had observed during the war. A general strike by 65,000 workers in Seattle in February 1919 led to warnings, by labor and by business, of a national shutdown on July 4, but they proved to be just talk. Racial violence erupted in the District of Columbia and in Chicago, the Boston police went on strike, and the U.S. House of Representatives refused to seat Victor L. Berger, elected from Wisconsin, because of his socialism, German ancestry, and anti-war viewpoints.

By the autumn of 1919, the Red Scare was in full flower, and Palmer, who aspired to the presidency, decided to take advantage of it. During the night of November 7 and throughout November 8, federal agents across the country arrested 450 members of the Union of Russian Workers (U.R.W.), a social club for Russians who professed anarchism. In Detroit, agents seized 75 U.R.W. members on immigration charges and sent 55 of them to Ellis Island. Although most of the men from Detroit were released, some were among the 249 U.S. citizens and immigrants of Russian origin placed on board the S.S. *Buford* (called by the press the Soviet Ark) and shipped to Russia. Encouraged by the favorable publicity he received over the November raids, Palmer struck again, on January 2 and 4, 1920, arresting 4,500 men and women across the country. In Detroit, 550 "radicals" were arrested in raids organized by the Justice Department's chief agent in the city, Arthur L. Barkey, assisted by the Detroit police and the Michigan state constabulary. A prime target of the raids was a meeting hall for anarchists known as the House of the Masses, located above a saloon. In their enthusiasm, the agents arrested the men and women drinking in the saloon as well as the occupants of the House of the Masses. On January 4, federal officials in Detroit raided again and arrested 280 more men and women.

There was then no federal prison or jail in the Eastern District, and Detroit's jail and police precinct houses took only 200 of the prisoners, including all of the women. The rest of the men were taken to the 1897 Post Office Building, herded up to the attic on the fifth floor, and deposited in the corridors on three sides of the atrium. Fifteen immigration agents began interrogating the prisoners, looking for alien terrorists but often finding citizens (including 12 veterans) and aliens with no sinister connections. The grilling was slow, and the prisoners waiting their turn were stuck in the attic with little food, water, space, or toilet facilities. On Tuesday, January 6, when the men had been in the attic for up to four days, the *Detroit News*, which demonstrated a good deal more sympathy for the prisoners than did the *Free Press*, published an eye-witness account of "[a] spectacle never before recorded in Detroit's history."[2] The reporter described "a condition on Monday close to the chaotic," 600 men milling about in the attic corridors, squeezed in between the walls and railings overlooking the atrium. There were no windows and the only light came from the atrium's opaque skylight "and a few dim globes." Those men on the railing side could look down at the glass ceiling over the post office on the first floor, but most of them could see nothing except walls and their fellow prisoners. "Scores were lying on the floor, others paced about in the restricted space, stepping over the bodies of their companions. . . . Most sleep on the bare floor without washing or shaving, stand in long lines waiting for access to the one drinking fountain, and line up in a similar manner to reach the solitary toilet. . . . For food they have had the lunches brought in by hundreds of their relatives and friends—supplemented when necessary by certain supplies furnished by the Government." The prisoners were separated from the stairs by guarded steel doors, and officers kept their visitors away from the railings on the lower floors so they could not communicate with them, although their shouts and songs disturbed Judge Tuttle in his courtroom on the third floor. The interrogators worked around the clock and were themselves disheveled and exhausted. The *News* concluded: "And so the inquisition went on far into the night. Soon another Soviet Ark will sail, and thus its human freight is being garnered."

The attic lacked central heating, but that was the least of the prisoners' problems, living among 600 sources of body heat, sweat, and urine, the last sprayed on the walls by men who could no longer wait. After keeping them in squalor for six days, the Justice Department released about 400 men as totally innocent, sent 50 more to Detroit Police precincts and then marched 140 bedraggled, unwashed, unshaved men through the wintery streets to the basement of Detroit's Municipal Building, where they were kept for another week in a "bull pen" with a stone floor, one window, and wooden benches.[3]

Almost all of the men were eventually released, and by the middle of 1920 the Red Scare was over. Public revulsion against Palmer's methods ended his chances of a run at the presidency, although many people, including Frank Murphy, still supported his candidacy. Even when a bomb hidden in a horse-drawn cart exploded on Wall Street at 12:01 p.m. on September 16, 1920, killing 38 people and wounding hundreds more, the public outside New York kept surprisingly calm. Their full attention had been drawn to a new phenomenon: the constitutional ban on the manufacture, sale, or transportation of alcoholic beverages known as a Prohibition.

The Eastern District, 1920-1934

Without question, nothing had as great an impact on the operations of the District Court for the Eastern District of Michigan as the Eighteenth Amendment to the U.S. Constitution and the National Prohibition (Volstead) Act,[4] which went into effect on January 17, 1920.[5] Over the next dozen years enforcement of Prohibition would swell the court's docket by a factor of ten or more, with one result being that after 80 years of operating with one district judge, by the time the Eighteenth Amendment was repealed in 1933, the court had three district judges and a new courthouse.

Fiscal year 1917 (July 1, 1916 to June 30, 1917) was the last year that the number of cases filed was relatable to the previous 70 years. Even in 1917, a good many of the new criminal and U.S. civil cases were based on Progressive Era statutes rather than the traditional sources of cases, but the total was only 10 percent more than the average for the previous 20 years. Then, from 1917 to 1919, civil and criminal filings increased by about 50 percent, principally because of criminal cases enforcing the war acts. Although this increase was a strain on Judge Tuttle, it was nothing compared to what was on the horizon. During the Prohibition Era (1918–1933),

Table 8.1   The Effect of Prohibition on Annual Average Criminal and Civil
Filings, 1910–1933

Fiscal Year	Criminal	U.S. Civil	Private Civil	Total
1910–1917	107	29	125	261
1918–1933	1,200	623	245	2,068

criminal filings increased 11 fold compared to 1910–1917, while over those same periods U.S. civil cases increased by 21 times. The number of U.S. civil and criminal cases filed in 1930 alone (3,735) was more than in Judge Tuttle's first ten years in office (3,690). The judge's sole consolation was that the number of private civil cases remained fairly stable until 1928, although even those numbers grew substantially after the Great Crash of 1929 and especially after the banking crisis of 1932.

Results from 1931 give a good idea of the Northern Division's docket during Prohibition.[6] Of the 355 criminal defendants indicted (a small decrease from 1930), 337 were charged with liquor-law violations, while no other type of crime accounted for more than 3 indictments. Most of the defendants (57 percent) resided in Saginaw or Genesee County, while Bay County accounted for only 6 percent. During 1931, 330 defendants pleaded guilty and 18 were tried, all of whom were convicted. The longest criminal trial, on a charge of bank embezzlement, lasted seven weeks. Judge Tuttle sentenced 262 defendants to county jails for an average of 344 days (maximum sentence five years; minimum 21 days), fined 66 defendants an average of $464 (maximum $2,300; minimum 1 cent), placed nine defendants on probation, and dismissed two cases at the request of the U.S. district attorney. In addition to the criminal docket, civil plaintiffs filed 105 cases in the Northern Division in 1931, an increase over prior years, and there were also 312 new bankruptcies, an increase of 66.7 percent over 1930, a consequence of the deepening Depression.

Judge Tuttle v. the 1897 Post Office Building

When Detroit's 1897 Post Office Building opened, it was too small to fulfill its purpose of bringing all of Detroit's federal agencies under one roof, forcing Congress to scrap plans to sell Custom House.[7] Even after an addition was completed in 1913, the growing number of federal employees enforcing the growing number of federal laws, culminating with the the advent of Prohibition, kept office space at a premium in Detroit as well as in Bay City and Port Huron. Because Judge Tuttle spent only a few weeks each year in Bay City and no time at all in Port Huron, though, Detroit's federal building became the natural object of his ire. By 1922, he found the competition among federal agencies over every square foot of that building intolerable

Fig. 36.　Judge Tuttle in the 1897 district courtroom. (Bentley Library, University of Michigan)

as even the airy, four-story atrium, which brought light and beauty into the building's interior, became an inter-agency battlefield. First agencies lined employee desks along the corridors facing the atrium well, but the maneuvering soon escalated when at least two agencies began to place planking over the skylight between the first and second floors with the idea of adding desks, chairs, typewriters, adding machines, and telephones. These activities drove Elmer Voorheis and Judge Tuttle to distraction because of the "appalling" noise and increased traffic in the corridors. Because the building's heating system worked far too well, the building was too hot, even in winter, and the judge had to prop open the courtroom doors. Doing this made court sessions bearable, but only made the noise problem worse.[8]

Eventually, the judge entered an injunction barring all use of the corridors for business.

A more difficult problem arose when Charles Simons joined the court as a second district judge in 1923. The supervising architect had provided two courtrooms, but as Tuttle explained to the building's custodian in 1925, there was not enough office space for Judge Simons, much less their frequent visiting judges, and his own chambers were overflowing. The master in chancery and the master's secretary occupied the reception room in Tuttle's chambers, Tuttle used the middle room, and his secretary, Ms. Baldwin, was in a third room. When there was a visiting judge, Tuttle would hold non-jury trials in his office so the visitor could use the "million dollar courtroom," but because they shared Tuttle's office, interruptions during non-jury trials were common.[9] Tuttle also complained that he had no robing or breakroom adjoining the million dollar courtroom and no separate judge's door. Before and after sessions, and every time he adjourned court in between, he had to walk about 120 feet through the corridors on the third floor, accosted every step of the way by attorneys and other people wanting something from him. But complain as he might, Tuttle's dream of a new federal building was stymied by a Congressional moratorium until 1933.

Enforcing State Prohibition

Judge Tuttle was presented with the district court's first prohibition cases even before the effective date of the Volstead Act, cases based, in a circular way, on Michigan criminal law. The people of Michigan had long had a love-hate relationship with alcohol. During most of the 19th century, Michigan was one of the heaviest drinking places in the country, yet it was also the home of some of the earliest temperance societies and other organizations opposed to drinking. State and local governments were a battlefield between prohibitionists on one side and thirsty consumers and the liquor lobby on the other, but even when temperance forces were able to pass legislation barring or limiting the sale of alcohol, breweries, distilleries, and saloons in many parts of the state stayed open and the public kept drinking.[10] On November 6, 1916, after an energetic campaign led by business and religious leaders, including the evangelist Billy Sunday, a small majority of the electorate voted to prohibit the manufacture and sale of alcohol in the state effective May 1, 1918.[11]

This "dry" victory was widely credited to the fact that the law did not prohibit or criminalize alcohol consumption, but instead allowed individuals to import and consume "vinous, malt, brewed, fermented, spirituous, or intoxicating liquors."[12] However, before Michigan's ban went into effect, Congress enacted the "Reed Amendment,"[13] which provided for criminal penalties (a fine of $1,000 or six months in prison and, for a subsequent offense, up to a year in prison) for violations of the Webb-Kenyon Act,[14] prohibiting the import of alcoholic beverages into a dry state, including Michigan.[15] So, on May 1, 1918, the importation of alcohol into Michigan became a federal crime to be enforced in the district court.

May 1, 1918, also saw the birth of the "Avenue de Booze," as hundreds of Detroiters, most of whom probably thought they were acting within the law, traveled south on the Dixie Highway to Toledo, in "wet" Ohio, to buy beer and liquor. The roadways and inter-urban railways were filled with amateur smugglers returning home with shopping bags and suitcases full of gin and beer. As is usually the case with illegal activity, the amateurs were soon replaced by professionals such as the Billingsley brothers, Logan, Sherman, and Ora, who had records for liquor smuggling in three states before they came to Michigan. The brothers developed and supplied a customer base of 35 restaurants and bars in Detroit for the beer and whiskey they transported by truck. Although experienced, the boys were not very smart; Sherman and Ora were arrested by undercover federal agents in September 1918 as they transported 1,500 quarts of whiskey into Michigan from Ohio. They were charged under the Reed Amendment and went to trial in January 1919 before Judge Tuttle. The jury did not buy their defense that they were simple grocers who had been entrapped by unscrupulous police officers. The brothers were convicted on all 23 counts of the indictment, and Judge Tuttle sentenced each of them to two and a half years in Leavenworth. The Circuit Court of Appeals did not believe their story either and affirmed the convictions.[16]

When Judge Tuttle sentenced the Billingsley brothers, he expressed his disgust at their disregard for the law: "You fellows have got it into your heads . . . that it was smart to defy the laws and you thought you could get away with it here."[17] Tuttle could hardly have anticipated that a substantial number of otherwise law-abiding residents of the Eastern District (such as Henry and Georgia Gardner, my otherwise staid and respectable grandparents) would develop the same attitude towards Prohibition or that most of them (like my grandparents) would get away with it easily. He was also unlikely to anticipate the dark side of the Roaring Twenties. State prohibition introduced the Eastern District to gangland turf battles, as the Giannola and Vitale gangs left bodies strewn throughout Detroit's east side from 1918 to 1920.[18] Although those killings were not within the district court's jurisdiction, they were a warning to all law enforcers of the violence to come as hundreds of people in the Eastern District, including dozens of law officers, would die before Prohibition ended.

Fighting a Losing Battle with John Barleycorn

One of the reasons for the flood of cases that swept through the district court beginning in January 1920 was simple geography. Throughout the

Prohibition years, the sale of alcoholic beverages for export was legal in the Province of Ontario, and the Eastern District shared a waterway with the province that stretched some 400 miles from the southern outlet of the Detroit River to the northern shores of Lake Huron. Along the Detroit and St. Clair Rivers the waterway was less than a mile wide, and both shores were dotted with small harbors, inlets, and streams where smugglers could operate with impunity. Moreover, thousands of railcars passed from Ontario to Michigan daily by ferry or in two underwater tunnels. Soon after Prohibition came into effect, booze was pouring over the international border on its way to the cities of the Eastern District as well as places like Chicago, Cleveland, and Milwaukee. Smuggling was not the only source of illegal alcohol. Thousands of illegal breweries and stills operated in the Eastern District as well as tens of thousands of drinking establishments, known locally (then and now) as blind pigs. Despite almost daily raids by state and federal officers, new blind pigs opened faster than they could be closed down. Legal breweries, licensed to brew low-alcohol "near" beer were easy fronts for the manufacture and sale of real beer. Detroit journalist Malcolm Bingay famously remarked that: "It was absolutely impossible to get a drink in Detroit unless you walked at least ten feet and told the busy bartender what you wanted in a voice loud enough for him to hear you above the uproar."[19] At the same time, the resources available to enforce Prohibition were not adequate for the job.

While federal law enforcement agencies attacked the illegal importation and manufacture of alcoholic beverages, closing down blind pigs was usually the responsibility of local governments. These governments found themselves overwhelmed. Officials trying to do their jobs found that they could not close down even half of the blind pigs; they had to decide where to focus. Each of Detroit's mayors during Prohibition, no matter his political affiliation or attitude toward Prohibition, eventually conceded that there was only one workable strategy, a form of extra-legal regulation. Blind pigs that operated with regard for the community—those that set up far from schools and churches, kept out gambling and prostitution, and refused to serve teenagers—were tolerated. Those that were not community-minded were busted up in police raids conducted without warrants, in which nobody was arrested but every barrel, bottle, piano, table, chair, and other item on the premises was smashed.[20]

A Multi-Judge District Court

Characteristically, Judge Tuttle shouldered the burden of his swollen caseload with both energy and loud complaints. In the spring of 1919, even before Prohibition bloated his docket, he began a campaign to embarrass Congress and the Circuit Court of Appeals for the Sixth Circuit into approving a second district judge position. Congress had always been reluctant to increase the number of district judges and had not authorized a second judge for any district court until 1903.[21] Tuttle dictated long letters that were alternately whiny and argumentative, prompting the senior judge of the Sixth Circuit, Arthur Denison, to write him on March 29, 1919, expressing his court's concern that Tuttle was exhausted and needed a rest.[22] The suggestion that he lacked the strength of body and will to perform his job outraged Tuttle who, on March 31, wrote to Sixth Circuit Judge John Wesley Warrington to deny that he needed a rest ("I'm able to do four men's work every day") even though, as he explained, he had been holding jury trials non-stop for two-and-a-half years and worked all day and late every night, including Sundays.[23] On the other hand, in April, he complained to District Judge John Milton Killits, of the Northern District of Ohio, that: "I am very tired and have been for a long time," because he held jury trials four days per week, heard chancery cases on Saturdays and motions on Mondays, and wrote his opinions and correspondence at night and on Sundays.[24]

Several weeks later, on May 27, 1919, Tuttle wrote Attorney General Palmer, who had not yet turned his attention to red-baiting, a letter remarkable both for its length and for its vehemence.[25] His stated purpose in this 3,000-word letter, which was accompanied by a nine-page "brief" and three additional tables of statistics, was to obtain a raise in salary from $110 to $150 per month for his secretary, Ms. Baldwin, who had given her notice. Much of the material, though, dealt with the immense amount of work *he* performed even with her help and how, "[d]uring the past seven years I have sacrificed all recreation. I have sacrificed social matters and home life in order to meet these pressing duties." He explained that he held five terms of court each year and "had a jury in practically continuous session for years." In the brief, he reminded Palmer that "the predecessor of the present resident judge" (Judge Angell) resigned after 11 months "because the burden was too heavy to carry. . . . The resident Judge [himself] has had no real vacation since he was appointed, August 6, 1912. He holds court with a jury on Tuesday, Wednesday, Thursday, and Friday each week, including the summer seasons, hears patent and general chancery cases and admiralty cases on Saturday, and on Monday takes care of motions, receiverships, bankruptcy cases, arraignments, sentences, and miscellaneous matters. He often sits for jury cases and hearings evenings. By using a Dictaphone he writes all his opinions and answers all his correspondence at nights and on Sundays. During the one year here in question, 2,240 letters were dictated by him," among them lengthy letters on each prisoner up for parole or pardon, including attempts to find them a job after release. He also noted that he spent one day each month, until late at night, just on naturalization petitions. Palmer must have wondered how such a busy man could find the time to dictate such a long letter. It is telling that Judge Tuttle and his devoted secretaries kept all of his letters complaining about the amount of work in a file titled "Additional Judge, 1," demonstrating that his goal was not just sounding off or obtaining more visiting judges. He wanted one or more additional judges permanently assigned to the district.

Judge Tuttle's campaign first bore fruit on September 14, 1922, when Congress included the Eastern District among 24 districts given a second judgeship.[26] Judge Tuttle welcomed the help even though these positions were not permanent: the authorizing law provided that "[a] vacancy occurring more than two years after the passage of this Act . . . shall not be filled unless Congress shall so provide." In January 1923, President Harding nominated Detroit attorney Charles Casper Simons to the new position, although, like many other great federal judges, Simons was not the first choice of politicians responsible for recommending a nominee. In a December 6, 1922, *Detroit Free Press* article, Simons was not among the several names suggested as likely nominees, such as Michigan's attorney general Merlin Wiley, Michigan Circuit Judge Henry Mandell, and U.S. District Attorney Earl J. Davis.[27] Just three days later, though, the *Free Press* announced that U.S. senators Charles Townsend and James Couzens, "in what comes as a surprise to Michigan circles," had urged President Harding to nominate Simons.[28] The *Detroit News* seemed to have a better handle on the politics of the story, explaining that Simons "long has been one of the principal supporters of Mr. Townsend in Detroit and he is a son of David W. Simons who, as a member of [Detroit's Common] Council was a close political friend of Mr. Couzens."[29]

District Judge Charles Casper Simons

Born: May 21, 1876 (Detroit, Michigan), to Mr. and Mrs. David Simons
Education: University of Michigan (L.B. 1898, LL.B. 1900)
Nominated/Confirmed: January 31/February 6, 1923 (Warren G. Harding)
Vacancy: New Seat
Left Court: February 2, 1932 (Appointed to the Sixth Circuit)
Died: February 2, 1964, at Detroit, Michigan

Judge Simons, Michigan's first Jewish federal judge, was the son of immigrant parents who fled Russia to escape anti-Semitic persecution. His father began a scrap metal business with one horse and a wagon, and rose to prominence in Detroit's business, banking, and political circles. Charles Simons followed his father's footsteps into public service as Michigan's youngest state senator, Wayne County circuit court commissioner, and delegate to the Constitutional Convention that wrote Michigan's 1908 Constitution. He was also a member of countless charitable and civic organizations. His law practice emphasized service to the public, representing indigents and recent immigrants. In 1906, Judge Simons married Lillian Bernstein, a schoolteacher and social worker. They had no children, and both left most of their estates to charities. In February 1932, President

Fig. 37.   Judge Charles Casper
Simons. (Historical Society for the
United States District Court for
the Eastern District of Michigan)

Hoover appointed Judge Simons to the U.S. Court of Appeals for the Sixth
Circuit, where he remained until his death at the age of 88. His 41 years of
service remain one of the longest careers in the history of the federal
courts.

As the court's caseload continued to grow in the mid-1920s, Judge Tuttle renewed his pleas for help, and this time the attorney general agreed,
noting in his annual report for 1926, "We add to our recommendations
previously made by one in favor of a new district judge to be created for the
Eastern District of Michigan, where the present judicial force of two judges
is wholly inadequate."[30] On March 3, 1927, Congress responded by authorizing a third judgeship (second permanent) for the Eastern District,[31] and
three months later President Calvin Coolidge filled the position with a recess appointment of Michigan Circuit Judge Edward Julien Moinet of St.
John's, Michigan.

District Judge Edward Julien Moinet

Born: July 14, 1873 (Louisville, Ohio), to Julien J. and Adeline Savageot
    Moinet
Education: University of Michigan (LL.B. 1895)

Fig. 38.　Judge Edward Julien Moinet. (Walter P. Reuther Library, Wayne State University)

Recess Appointment/Confirmed: June 13/December 6, 1927 (Calvin Coolidge)
Vacancy: New Seat
Left Court: February 28, 1946 (Retired)
Died: December 23, 1952, at St. John's, Michigan

Judge Moinet was the Eastern District's first judge since Ross Wilkins to come to the district court with judicial experience; in fact, that experience was crucial to his appointment. Like Judge Simons, Judge Moinet's name was not among those supposed to be under consideration. Senator James Couzens's first choice was U.S. representative Earl Michener of Adrian, Michigan, but President Coolidge would not nominate a sitting congressman. Couzens next suggested Wayne County Circuit Judge Thomas M. Cotter, but U.S. attorney general John G. Sargent objected. Detroit's bar recommended their colleague James V. Oxtoby, but he declined. Finally, knowing that Sargent preferred to recommend rural state judges for district judgeships, Couzens suggested Moinet, and Sargent agreed.[32]

After graduation from law school, Judge Moinet engaged in a small-town private practice in Ithaca and then in St. Johns. On October 30, 1897, he married Eda M. Steel, with whom he had two children. From 1909 to 1913 he was also Clinton County prosecutor, and from 1913 until his appointment to the federal bench he was a judge of Michigan's 29th Judicial Circuit Court (Clinton and Gratiot counties).[33] Mrs. Eda Moinet died in 1942, and two years later Judge Moinet married Virginia Lee Monteith.

Still Judge Tuttle was not finished. In May 1930, at the end of a fiscal year in which the number of new civil and criminal cases exceeded 3,000, ten times the pre-war rate, he sent a telegram to Congressman Earl Michener of Michigan explaining that the district court's criminal calendar was behind one year, its civil calendar behind two years, he was holding court more than six hours per day, and the court had enough work to keep five judges busy.[34] Once again Congress gave in and on February 20, 1931, authorized a fourth judgeship (third permanent) for the Eastern District.[35] A week later, President Herbert Hoover nominated former Wayne County Circuit Judge Ernest Aloysius O'Brien to fill that position.

District Judge Ernest Aloysius O'Brien

Born: July 1, 1879 (Detroit, Michigan), to James and Mary Ann Brennan O'Brien
Education: Detroit College (B.A., 1898); Detroit College of Law (LL.B., 1905)
Nominated/Confirmed: February 26/March 2, 1931 (Herbert Hoover)
Vacancy: New Seat
Left Court: October 9, 1948 (Died)

The first Roman Catholic on the bench of the Eastern District, Judge O'Brien was a descendant of early Detroit settlers. After graduating from Detroit College (now the University of Detroit-Mercy) O'Brien became a reporter for the *Detroit Tribune* and later worked as a draftsman for De-

Fig. 39. Judge Ernest Aloysius O'Brien. (Historical Society for the United States District Court for the Eastern District of Michigan)

troit's water department while saving money for law school. He married Elizabeth Dee on September 16, 1909. They were the parents of two sons. In addition to his law practice, Judge O'Brien was very active in Catholic and other civic organizations. In 1921, he led the fight to quash a proposed Michigan law that would have closed all Catholic schools in the state. For his public service, he was knighted as a member of the Order of St. Gregory by Pope Pius XI.[36] In January 1928, Michigan governor Fred W. Green appointed him to a seat on Wayne County Circuit Court, but he was defeated in the election the following November. He returned to private practice until called to the federal bench at the recommendation of his former law partner, Congressman Clarence J. McLeod, and Senator James Couzens. According to the *Detroit Free Press*, "Jews and Protestants . . . acknowledge his vigilant militancy in helping to stamp out religious intolerance and his championing of freedom of worship and free speech."

Whatever relief Congress gave the district by adding a third permanent judgeship was lost in February 1932, when President Hoover elevated Judge Simons to the U.S. Circuit Court of Appeals for the Sixth Circuit. Because his district judgeship had been temporary, it expired when he left the district court,[37] and Judges Tuttle, Moinet, and O'Brien had to carry on without him until Congress awarded the district new judgeships in 1935 and 1938.

The Corruption of Public Officials

One of the worst results of Prohibition was the widespread corruption among city, state, and federal officials. This further diminished whatever confidence the public had in government after the scandals of the turn of the century that fueled the Progressives and helped newspapers thrive with reports of theft, bribery, and collusion in local governments. The amount of money involved in illegal liquor pushed the scale of temptation and corruption to new heights that did not exempt federal agents fighting the booze trade. Customs agents were bribed to look the other way, and not just in isolated instances.[38] In 1931, gangster Peter Licavoli was convicted of conducting massive and systematic bribery of customs agents; Judge Moinet sentenced him to two years in Leavenworth.[39] The separate Prohibition Service had its own problems, including its public image. In November 1929, Judge Tuttle wrote to the district's prohibition administrator suggesting some aggressive steps the agency should take in general and in a particular case, and admonished the administrator that: "If the agents would do that, they would elevate their own station as public officers from that of individuals who merely buy and guzzle liquor, to that higher plane of one who thinks, analyzes and investigates in a logical manner."[40]

The district court itself was not immune from rumors of corruption. Soon after the court moved into the Recreation Building in 1931, while the new courthouse was being built, an embarrassing string of acquittals in important cases raised an alarm among judges and prosecutors about jury integrity in the court's temporary home. In January 1932, the *Detroit News* reported that federal officials were concerned that they could not control "hangers-on" in the building who might try to communicate with jurors in order to try to fix cases.[41] The *News* reported that prosecutors were "incensed at several acquittals by juries recently in cases where the federal authorities were sure the evidence for conviction was conclusive," particularly the case of one Alois Albers, who had been arrested in a house where agents found ten barrels of beer. The jury deliberated only 40 minutes before returning a verdict of not guilty of possession of alcohol and keeping a public nuisance. Enraged by the verdict, Judge Simons dismissed the 12 Albers jurors from the court's standing jury venire, telling them: "I am amazed that you should have reached this verdict. The evidence against the defendant was undisputed and I don't see how you could have found him not guilty." The *News* claimed that U.S. district attorney Gregory Frederick was investigating another possible reason for some of the acquittals: rumors that two deputy U.S. marshals and three other federal court "attachés" shepherded jurors across the river to be "entertained on liquor parties in Canada by professional bondsmen." Frederick and F.B.I. special agent O.G. Hall questioned the officers and the Albers jurors, but with no success.[42] The jurors scoffed at the idea of parties in Canada, telling the *News* that their acquittal was due to the government's failure to prove that Albers had any control over the premises where the beer was discovered.

Corruption reached high up into the ranks of local government in the district as mayors and other city officials were caught in the prohibition net. One of the most notorious was the city of Hamtramck's first mayor, pharmacist Peter Jezewski. In 1900, Hamtramck was a farming village a few miles north of Detroit with a population of about 3,000. By 1922, it was an dynamic industrial city with a population of 49,000 and was home to 150 brothels, 400 saloons, and open gambling. It was also the headquarters of the treacherous Chester "Big Chet" Le Mare (sometimes recorded as La Mare), known as the Vice King of Hamtramck, who ran all of the city's illegal activities from his Venice Café.[43]

By 1923, Le Mare's operations and the corruption in Hamtramck's government had become so notorious that Michigan governor Alex Groesbeck ordered the state police to take over the city government. Federal agents joined in the clean-up and 45 men, including several saloon owners; Mayor Jezewski; Max Wosinski, the city's director of public safety; and police lieutenant John Ferguson were indicted in the district court for violating the Volstead Act. According to the indictment, three of the defendants obtained a license to make legal, low-alcohol beer at the West Side Brewery, but instead made real beer and sold it to the saloonkeepers. Jezewski, Wosinski, and Ferguson were accused of providing protection to the scheme, promising that "they would have nothing to fear from the Hamtramck police."[44] The evidence also showed that Jezewski shook down the saloon keepers to pay his campaign expenses.

Six of the 45 defendants pleaded guilty, but the others chose to go to trial before Judge Tuttle. District Attorney Delos G. Smith and a special assistant from the Justice Department, John B. Marshall, prosecuted. At the end of the trial, Judge Tuttle directed a verdict of not guilty for five defendants, and the jury found three defendants not guilty and the other 31 guilty. In July 1924, Judge Tuttle sentenced Jezewski, Wosinski, John Ferguson, and three managers at the West Side Brewery to two years' imprisonment. Bertha Johnson, owner of the Hamtramck Inn and the only woman among the defendants, was sentenced to serve four months in the Detroit House of Correction. Other defendants received sentences of between three months and 13 months in prison.[45] Nineteen of the defendants, including Jezewski and Wosinski, appealed, and the Sixth Circuit reversed the convictions of five saloon keepers, but affirmed the convictions of the other appellants.

In 1926, Le Mare found himself in district court, where he was convicted of violating the Volstead Act.[46] Judge Simons initially sentenced him to a fine and a year in federal prison, but when Big Chet turned on his considerable charm and promised to go straight, the judge reduced the custodial sentence to probation. Le Mare did keep his promise for a while, but returned to crime in 1930, when he took over the west side mob and began a war with the east side mob. During this war, Le Mare's men blundered by killing two neutral mobsters by mistake, with the result that 15 of Le Mare's men were gunned down and he fled to New York. He incautiously returned to Detroit in February 1931, only to be killed, in the best mob tradition, by a shot in the back fired by his own bodyguard.[47]

Flint, the home of Buick, was also a center of bootlegging and corruption. Years later, the resident deputy clerk of the Northern Division, Clarence S. Pettit, remembered that, during Prohibition, the federal court in Bay City received 130 prohibition cases from Flint every month.[48] The citizens of Flint had a well-founded belief that the city's government, like that of Hamtramck, was thoroughly corrupt. The district attorney and his deputy in the Northern Division tried to clean up the mess by going after the head of the organization, but in the end they failed.

On a cold afternoon in February 1932, Flint mayor William H. McKeighan, police chief and city manager Caesar Scavarda, and five Flint police officers drove north along Dixie Highway to the Ridotto Building, the temporary U.S. courthouse in Bay City, to be arraigned in the third-floor ballroom by Pettit in his position as U.S. commissioner. This was a high-profile case that had the potential to disrupt more than just the Flint government. Besides being mayor, McKeighan was also the leader of the Republican Party in Genesee County, a power in party circles across Michigan, and a likely candidate for governor in 1932. This was also a matter of some delicacy for Judge Tuttle, a prominent Republican who had run in the party primary for U.S. Senate in 1924. Newspapers reported, accurately or not, that Tuttle ordered Pettit to keep the court open until 5:30 p.m. so that McKeighan could finish his day's work in Flint, drive to Bay City, and then drive to Lansing for a Republican political dinner.[49]

The defendants were charged with conspiring to violate the Volstead Act by accepting large bribes to provide protection to bootleggers and saloons in Genesee County. Judge Tuttle denied a defense motion to quash the indictment,[50] but the trial went poorly for the prosecutors, and on April 12, 1932, the jury acquitted all of the defendants.[51] McKeighan did run in the 1932 primary election for governor, but lost. He seemed to have more luck in courts than in the polls; during the 1940s he was indicted in a state court for violations of Michigan's liquor laws, but the judge in that case directed an acquittal.

Judicial Robes

Although we tend to picture all judges as wearing flowing black robes, in fact judicial robes were not common in American trial courts during the 18th and 19th centuries except along the eastern seaboard. Although the justices of the U.S. Supreme Court adopted robes early on, many Americans objected to judicial robes as they were considered symbols of British oppression, and most state and federal judges west of the Appalachians did not begin to wear robes until well into the 20th century.[52] The Eastern District of Michigan was no exception: its judges presided in court without robes until 1925.

Although a traditionalist and a westerner in many ways, Judge Tuttle also believed that judicial robes would contribute to the dignity of the court and justice system. Soon after he came on the bench in 1912, he began lobbying his fellow district judges in the Sixth Circuit to agree to wear judicial robes. Although he was the Eastern District's only judge and could have decided on his own to wear a robe in court, he feared that doing so alone would be seen as a sign of judicial arrogance or as a mere fashion statement.[53] In 1917, a slim majority of the district judges in the Sixth Circuit did vote to wear robes, but some judges, such as Andrew McConnell January Cochran, of the Eastern District of Kentucky, were so opposed that the majority decided to wait.[54]

In 1924, after Judge Simons ascended to the bench, Detroit and Wayne County bar organizations urged both judges to pass a court rule requiring robes for judges while in court. Ever frugal, Judge Tuttle first checked with the Department of Justice to determine if the government would pay for robes. The department noted that this was the first time they had been asked the question and that no money had ever been appropriated for that purpose. "Sorry, no funds appropriated" was the department's standard initial objection to practically every requisition Tuttle submitted, but, upon reflection, bureaucrats agreed that the department would pay for robes if not too many judges asked for them.[55] On February 10, 1925, Judges Tuttle and Simons held a joint session in which, after speeches by representatives of the bar, they signed the new court rule mandating robes for district judges in court beginning on March 3, 1925.[56]

Sapiro v. Ford, the Trial of the Century?

On March 15, 1927, in the district courtroom of Detroit's 1897 Post Office Building, trial began in the libel case brought by lawyer and financier Aaron Sapiro against Henry Ford.[57] Presiding over the trial was District Judge Fred M. Raymond of the Western District of Michigan, who had been appointed to the bench by President Calvin Coolidge just two years before. When the suit was filed, Judge Tuttle, who oversaw the allocation of cases between himself and Judge Simons, assigned the case to himself. After a year of pretrial jockeying by attorneys, in August 1926, Tuttle informed all concerned that he would start the trial in September. Attorneys for Ford then asked Tuttle to recuse himself because Tuttle was biased against Ford. Juggling an overflowing docket, Tuttle was only too happy to agree. The Sixth Circuit assigned district judges from Ohio to handle pretrial matters and then Judge Raymond for the trial.

Fig. 40.   Aaron Sapiro. (Walter P. Reuther Library, Wayne State University)

Fig. 41.   Henry Ford. (Historical
Society for the United States
District Court for the Eastern
District of Michigan)

Henry Ford is still a well-known name around the world, but Aaron Leland Sapiro is not. In 1920s, though, Sapiro was famous both as a lawyer
and as the primary proponent of farmers forming cooperatives to market
their crops in order to eliminate middlemen and increase farmers' profits.
By 1925, 825,000 farmers, ranchers, and dairies were members of cooperatives, and Sapiro made a very nice living representing them. In essence,
both Ford and Sapiro understood how to profit from marketing to the
masses, but Ford believed that Sapiro and cooperatives were a threat to
the ruggedly independent, yeoman farmer of myth dear to Ford's heart.
Also, Ford was willing to share his anti-Semitism with the world through
his newspaper, the *Dearborn Independent*. In 1924 and 1925, the *Independent* ran a series of articles that accused Sapiro and other Jewish businessmen of conspiring to monopolize American agriculture, defraud farmers and consumers, and deliver stolen profits to "international speculators"
and "communists," terms used by anti-Semitic publications interchange-
ably with "Jews." Ford was not nearly alone in his beliefs: "Ford's campaign
against the Jews, as historians have recognized, reflected the renewed
racial tribalism that characterized post–World War I American society. A
rising tide of private social discrimination spilled into the public realm
after the armistice, affecting the racial, religious, and ethnic dimensions of
Jewish identity."[58] By 1925, Sapiro had endured silently long enough and
sued Ford for libel in the district court.[59]

On March 15, Ford's attorney, U.S. senator James A. Reed of Missouri,
the father of the Reed Prohibition Amendment, and Sapiro's successful
Detroit trial attorney, William Henry Gallagher, selected a jury of six men

and six women and testimony began. Although newspapers billed it as the trial of the century, the proceedings disappointed both as drama and as effective trial presentation. Judge Raymond blocked Gallagher from presenting evidence of Ford's anti-Semitic views, Ford himself did not testify, and Reed presented no evidence to support Ford's claims of an international conspiracy to destroy American farming. Instead, the defense tried to show that Sapiro was dishonest and a money-grubber. None of it was very compelling, and the jury struggled to stay awake. By April 14, Senator Reed was exhausted and took to his bed.

During the ensuing recess, one of the jurors gave an interview to the local Hearst paper, the *Detroit Times*, and the judge declared a mistrial even though Sapiro was ready to continue with 11 jurors. Before a new trial could begin, Ford let it be known through back channels that he was ready to settle. His wife, Clara, and son, Edsel, had long been embarrassed by the articles and urged him to end the suit. Ford apparently caved in to all of Sapiro's settlement demands, including a published apology to all Jews, retraction of all charges in the articles, and payment of Gallagher's fee, said to be $50,000. Ford quietly hired Jewish lawyer and scholar Louis Marshall, a founder of the American Jewish Committee, to draft his apology, published in the *Detroit News* in July 1927.[60] Although Detroit's trial of the century turned out to be mundane theater, its importance lies in the publication of Henry Ford's apology, an act of repentance which many consider a pivotal event in Jewish history in the United States.

A Courthouse Building Boom, 1930-1934

The addition to Detroit's 1897 Post Office Building was completed in 1913, just as Congress began what turned out to be a 13-year moratorium on new federal buildings. Then, in 1926, in the midst of a post-war economic boom, Congress passed a Public Buildings Act,[61] which appropriated $50 million for new buildings in Washington, D.C. (including the present Supreme Court and Federal Triangle complex) and $15 million for projects approved before 1913, but not fully funded. The act also authorized the secretary of the treasury to spend up to $100 million for new federal office and post office buildings at his discretion. Although the secretary did not exercise his discretion in favor of the Eastern District until 1930, by 1934 the district had a major addition to the Port Huron Federal Building and new federal buildings in Bay City and Detroit.

1932 Extension of the Port Huron Federal Building

In March 1931, Congress authorized the secretary of the treasury to enter into contracts for hundreds of public buildings, including the extension and remodeling of the Port Huron Federal Building at an estimated cost of

Fig. 42.   The Port Huron Federal Building showing the addition at the
rear. (Library of Congress)

$115,000.[62] The result, completed in 1932, was a one-story addition at the
rear of the building designed to match the style of the original building's
ground floor.[63]

1933 Bay City Post Office and Federal Building

On July 3, 1930, Congress appropriated $475,000 to demolish Bay City's
old federal office building and to begin erecting a new one on the same site,
although the secretary of the treasury was given the discretion to buy a
new site instead.[64] The demolition began more than a year later, on August
14, 1931, with the dynamiting of the building's tower.[65] The new building
was dedicated on June 6, 1933. In the interim, the post office and the district court were housed, to the satisfaction of Judge Tuttle,[66] in Bay City's
Ridotto Building, a three-story brick structure built in 1890 on the southwest corner of Center and Madison avenues. The district court was held
on the building's third floor, which was "devoted to an immense public
assembly hall, . . . fitted with a stage, . . . and [could] comfortably seat
nearly 500 people. Adjacent to this are reception and toilet rooms, dining
rooms and every convenience necessary."[67]

Bay City's new building was one of the last overseen by James Alphonso Wetmore, acting supervising architect of the Treasury Department from 1915 to 1934. Wetmore was not an architect, but a skilled administrator who supervised the design and construction of more than 2,000 federal projects, leaving the actual designs to his staff.[68] For the new Bay City building, Wetmore's architects chose a neo-classical exterior, dignified but simpler and less cluttered than Romanesque, reflecting both hard economic times and changed aesthetic tastes. As in most Wetmore buildings shared by a post office and a court, the post office occupied the first floor while the district court's facilities, including the courtroom, the judge's chambers, offices for the resident assistant district attorney and deputy U.S. marshal, and the clerk's office were on the second floor and could be reached by elevators and stairways at both ends of the post office. A secondary courtroom and office suite were provided on the third floor for the bankruptcy referees.[69] The district court's courtroom was 43 feet wide, 62feet long, and two stories (20 feet) high. In addition to electric lights and chandeliers, natural lighting was provided by five long windows on its east wall. The windows were covered over at one time in the building's history, but have recently been restored. The district judge entered the courtroom from chambers by a door behind the raised bench.

The new building, formally known as the Bay City Post Office and Federal Building,[70] was dedicated at the beginning of the district court's May

Fig. 43.   The 1933 Bay City Post Office and U.S. Courthouse. (Library of Congress)

term, which had to be delayed a month to Tuesday, June 6, 1933, in order to get everything finished. After the usual routine of opening the Bay City term (swearing in the grand and traverse juries, calling the calendar, and docketing the cases for trial),[71] the court adjourned for the dedication ceremony attended by "more than six hundred persons," including Sixth Circuit Court of Appeals Judge Charles Simons, the three district judges (Tuttle, Moinet, and O'Brien), state judges, and attorneys from throughout the Eastern District.[72] The dedicatory address was given by Thomas A. E. Weadock, former mayor of Bay City and U.S. congressman who had been instrumental in the creation of the Northern Division in 1894. Another speaker was State Circuit Judge Paul V. Gadola, Sr., whose son, Paul Jr. would become a U.S. district judge in 1988.

That evening, most of the crowd from the dedication joined the judges at the Hotel Wenonah, on the southeast corner of Center Avenue and Water Street. The banquet, a simple meal of fruit cocktail, cream of tomato soup, steak with potatoes and green beans, ice cream, and cake, contrasted strikingly to that celebrating the first court session in 1887, further proof of how times and tastes had changed since the Gilded Age.[73] The theme of the 1933 banquet was a tribute to Judge Tuttle and his 25 years on the federal bench. The Michigan Bar presented to the court a life-size portrait of the judge Tuttle, painted by Roy C. Gamble, a well-known Detroit artist,[74] which now hangs in the Bay City courtroom, along with those of three other district judges who are closely associated with that courtroom and the Northern Division: Frank Picard, James Harvey, and James Churchill.

1934 Detroit Post Office and Federal Building

As in the 1890s, Detroit's federal building project began before Bay City's but ended later. The project began in March 1929, when Congress authorized the expenditure of $1,715,000 to build a 15-story federal office building on the site of the Custom House, at Larned and Griswold streets,[75] but the building would not have included space for the court or other major agencies. Local business and civic leaders objected on the grounds that "a city its size deserves and needs [a] first class federal building" that could accommodate the needs of all federal agencies for years to come, preferably on the site of the 1897 Post Office Building. They went so far as to hire Robert O. Derrick, a 40-year-old Detroit architect responsible for the design of the Henry Ford Museum in Dearborn and notable buildings in Grosse Pointe, to draw up plans for "a suitable building of monumental size" at an estimated cost of $4.9 million. This proposal had the support of both of Michigan's U.S. senators, James Couzens and Arthur Vandenberg.[76] In December 1929, Representatives Robert Clancy and Clarence McLeod accompanied a delegation of Detroit boosters to the Treasury De-

Fig. 44.   The Recreation Building. (Historical Society for the United
States District Court for the Eastern District of Michigan)

partment to present Derrick's plans, which were approved by Supervising
Architect James A. Wetmore and his staff. In July 1930, Congress appropriated $5,650,000 to demolish the 1897 Post Office Building and erect
Derrick's building in its place.[77] Once again, Congress decided to spare
the Custom House rather than to sell it to help pay the bill for the new
building.

The next problem was to find a suitable location for the district court to use during the expected two to three years of demolition and construction. The courtroom in the Custom House had been chopped up into smaller spaces, so the Treasury Department solicited bids, resulting in a free-for-all among the owners of downtown office buildings who were hurting during the Depression. Already, though, Judge Tuttle had his eye on the Recreation Building, located directly across Lafayette Boulevard from the 1897 Post Office Building. Located on the northwest corner of Lafayette and Shelby, the Recreation Building was a seven-story brick edifice designed by famed Detroit architects Smith, Hinchman and Grylls. When it opened for business on October 1, 1917, its six upper floors held 103 billiard tables and 88 bowling alleys. Advertised as "the largest building in the world devoted exclusively to billiard rooms and bowling alleys," it also housed "a liberal scattering of refreshment fountains and cigar stands" as well as various retail stores on the ground floor including a drug store and lunch counter, a barber, a laundry, and a "public shine and hat works."[78] In 1919, Detroit's Chamber of Commerce hailed the Recreation Building as "the greatest recreational temple in the world," "a great civic asset" and "the recreational center of Detroit."[79] There were lower bids, and the Recreation Building could not accommodate the district attorney or other agencies, but Judge Tuttle believed that the shortest move would be the best and that the open architecture of the billiard halls could easily be converted into courtrooms and offices. The three other district judges disagreed strongly and complained that because the court would occupy only two of the building's seven stories, the building's usual activities would continue on the other floors including "large gambling games."[80] As usual, Tuttle prevailed,[81] and the Recreation Building's fourth floor was transformed into chambers and courtrooms for the four judges as well as a separate office for the master in chancery, a jury room, and two rooms for prosecutors when court was in session.[82] Clerk Elmer Voorheis occupied two rooms on the third floor, while District Attorney Gregory H. Frederick and his staff, as well as the court's stenographers, were housed in the Lafayette Building across from the Recreation Building on Shelby Street.

Demolition of the 1897 Post Office Building began in late 1931, the cornerstone of the new building was laid in October 1932, construction was complete in March 1934, and the tenants moved in between May 15 and 27. On June 27, the building was dedicated at a gala outdoor ceremony which included a speech by Postmaster General James A. Farley.[83] The Detroit Post Office and Federal Building, now the Theodore Levin United States Courthouse, is ten stories high (184 feet from the street to the roof) and covered the entire block excepting sidewalks. Its monolithic appearance from the street is belied by an open center court above the second floor. The exterior is faced with polished black granite at its base and smooth-cut limestone above, in art deco/art moderne style that emphasizes the

Fig. 45.   The 1934 Detroit Post Office and Federal Building, now the
Theodore Levin U.S. Courthouse. (Library of Congress)

clean and stripped-down cubic forms with restrained, geometric ornamentation.[84] The building features relief figures of eagles above the entrances and several ornamental bas-relief sculptural panels and medallions, by Detroit architectural modeler Corrado Joseph Parducci, which depict various agencies and activities of the federal government."[85]

In 1934, the raised first story accommodated the post office with public counters along a central marble walkway below a domed, hand-painted ceiling. The district court was located on the seventh and eighth stories, which contain six judicial suites and double-height courtrooms, four on the seventh story and two on the eighth story.[86] The seventh story also housed a library described by Judge Tuttle as "the finest room in this entire building. It is finished in the best manner. The furnishings in it are of high grade. The tables, the chairs and the entire outfit are of high type and of the kind needed for a very high-grade library."[87] Its only deficiency was that it had no books.

As the most senior judge, Tuttle was assigned to the suite on the northeast corner of the seventh story where, at his insistence, the million dollar courtroom from the 1897 Post Office had been reassembled in all of its

Fig. 46. Wall panel by Parducci. (Historical Society for the United States District Court for the Eastern District of Michigan)

glory. Judge Moinet joined him on the seventh story, which also accommodated the clerk of the court, while the eighth story housed Judge O'Brien, in one of the two court suites, and the offices of the district attorney, the marshal, the probation officer, and the court reporters as well as the grand-jury room.[88]

Judge Tuttle was very happy about the trouble-free reconstitution of his courtroom, but just about everything else about the new building displeased him. The building's custodian, Wilbert Garred of the Treasury Department, was the unfortunate recipient of a storm of memos and letters detailing Tuttle's unhappiness, particularly over the deletion of two stories from Derrick's design, probably for budget reasons. Because that meant the building had less office space, judges had to cede some on their precious seventh and eighth floors to other federal agencies such as the Automobile Labor Board, which took over one of the four judicial suites on the 8th floor, including the courtroom (there were then only three district judges). Judge Tuttle reminded Garred that: "I urged the Treasury Department to build some rooms in this building for uses of that kind. I urged them to build additional stories so that we would not be bothered every time some official from Washington rolled into Detroit and wanted to have a place of business. . . . I wrote them that the Government had made that kind of a mistake for a hundred and fifty years . . . [instead] we have the usual poor Federal Building which is too small, the Referees in Bankruptcy are without a toilet, the Clerk has a row of offices which look more like a bowling alley than they do like the offices for a clerk of the United States District Court in a busy district."[89] A few months later, the judges reluctantly agreed to allow the Federal Home Owners Loan Corporation to use 8,720 square feet on the 7th and 8th floors, including two court-rooms on the 8th floor, although they refused to give up their library. They complained that: "It is really an imposition on us that this building was built so small that this situation is forced upon us. We protested against it, we urged that the building be made larger, our requests were ignored, and we find ourselves in the situation described."[90] Judge Tuttle also be-moaned the decision to delete plans for the "well-equipped lunch room on the top floor of the new federal building." He explained that such a cafe-teria would "take care of a class of people who are at heart good people, but at the same time they are poor, they have little money to spend for food and they do not have much time to eat their food."[91]

Space was not his only complaint. The Treasury Department had speci-fied the judge's carpets, furniture, and other furnishings, including 34 cus-pidors for the seventh and eighth stories,[92] but the quality left Tuttle un-satisfied. He rejected the "Kleerflax" carpeting installed in his chambers as "totally unsuitable,"[93] and he chided Garred for the lack of custodial care for the bankruptcy referees and their staff housed on the 10th floor. He demanded to know whether the Treasury Department was willing to keep the building clean or would Tuttle have hire his own janitors to clean up after Garred's janitors.[94] Tuttle also demonstrated his characteristic impa-tience with bureaucrats in his response to a form request for information on how much electricity his chambers used and where it was generated: "I know nothing more about the quantity or origin of the electricity used in my office for light than I do about the oxygen used for breathing."

Notes

1. For detailed accounts of the Palmer Raids and the events surrounding them, see Anthony Read, *The World on Fire: 1919 and the Battle with Bolshevism* (New York: W. W. Norton and Co., 2008), and Beverly Gage, *The Day Wall Street Exploded: A Story of America in Its First Age of Terror* (New York: Oxford University Press, 2009).

2. *Detroit News*, January 6, 1920.

3. Sidney Fine, *Frank Murphy: The Detroit Years* (Ann Arbor, MI: University of Michigan Press, 1975), 68-69; Read, 315.

4. 41 Stat. 305.

5. In April 1919, the Michigan legislature added possession and importation to the state prohibition law, essentially making Michigan "bone dry" in advance of the effective date of the Volstead Act. Michigan Public Laws No. 53 (1919).

6. Details are from the *Bay City Daily Times*, January 1, 1932.

7. H.R. Rep. 2811, 54th Cong., 2d Sess. (February 5, 1897), recommending re-tention of the Custom House because "the new building is inadequate for the accom-modation of the offices of the appraiser, pension agent, engineer department, marine and steamboat inspectors, Life-Saving Service, and other Government offices . . . ."

8. Arthur J. Tuttle to Charles E. Townsend, April 1, 1922, Federal Building Changes file, Box 23, Tuttle Papers.

9. Arthur J. Tuttle to Fred L. Woodworth, September 22, 1925, Custodian file, Box 23, Tuttle Papers.

10. See David G. Chardavoyne, "Intemperate Habits and Appetites: Temperance Laws in Early Michigan," *The Court Legacy*, vol. XIII, no. 2 (September 2005), 8.

11. Philip P. Mason, *Rum Running and the Roaring Twenties: Prohibition on the Michigan-Ontario Waterway* (Detroit, MI: Wayne State University Press, 1995), 14–15.

12. Michigan Public Law No. 338 (1917).

13. The Reed Amendment is part of the Postal Appropriations Act of 1917, 39 Stat. 1058, 1069.

14. 37 Stat. 699.

15. For a detailed explanation of the political maneuvers that took the United States into and out of Prohibition, see Daniel Okrent, *Last Call: The Rise and Fall of Prohibition* (New York: Scribner, 2010).

16. *Billingsley v. U.S.*, 274 F. 86 (6th Cir. 1921).

17. *Detroit News*, January 24, 1919.

18. Paul R. Kavieff, *The Violent Years: Prohibition and the Detroit Mobs* (Fort Lee, NJ: Barricade Books, 2001), 5-21.

19. Malcolm Bingay, *Detroit is my Home Town* (Indianapolis, IN: Bobbs-Merrill, 1946), 323.

20. Larry D. Engelmann, "A Separate Peace: The Politics of Prohibition Enforcement in Detroit, 1920–1930," *Detroit in Perspective: A Journal of Regional History*, vol 1, no. 1 (Autumn 1972), 51, 54.

21. Erwin C. Surrency, *History of the Federal Courts* (New York: Oceana Publications, Inc., 1987), 290.

22. Arthur Denison to Arthur J. Tuttle, March 29, 1919, "Judge, Additional 1" file, Box 20, Tuttle Papers.

23. Arthur J. Tuttle to John Wesley Warrington, March 31, 1919, "Judge, Additional 1" file, Box 20, Tuttle Papers.

24. Arthur J. Tuttle to John Milton Killits, April 5, 1919, "Judge, Additional 1" file, Box 20, Tuttle Papers.

25. Arthur J. Tuttle to U.S. Attorney General Alexander Mitchell Palmer, May 27, 1919, "Judge, Additional 1" file, Box 20, Tuttle Papers.

26. 42 Stat. 837.

27. *Detroit Free Press*, December 6, 1922.

28. *Detroit Free Press*, December 9, 1922.

29. *Detroit News*, December 9, 1922. Judge Simons was not formally nominated until January 31, 1923, because the president waited until he had recommendations for all of the new judgeships added in 1922. *Detroit Free Press*, February 1, 1923.

30. 1926 Annual Report of the Attorney General of the United States, 9.

31. 44 Stat. 1380.

32. *Detroit News*, June 14, 1927.

33. At that time, Clinton and Gratiot Counties were assigned to the Eastern District of Michigan. In 1954, Congress reassigned those counties to the Western District.

34. Arthur J. Tuttle to Representative Earl Michener, May 27, 1930, Additional Judge file, Box 28, Tuttle Papers.

35. 46 Stat. 1197.

36. *Detroit Free Press*, October 10, 1948.

37. 42 Stat. 837.

38. *Scriber v. U.S.*, 4 F.2d 97 (6th Cir. 1925).

39. Kavieff, 42-45. Moinet also sentenced Joseph Moceri, Roy Pascuzzi, Joe Pascuzzi, and Sam Goldberg for conspiracy to violate prohibition laws, May 21, 1930. *Id.* 46.

40. Arthur J. Tuttle to Prohibition Administrator, November 27, 1929, Prohibition Dept. file, Box 31, Tuttle Papers.

41. *Detroit News*, January 7, 1932.

42. *Id.*, January 8, 1932.

43. Kavieff, 55.

44. *Jezewski v. U.S.*, 13 F.2d 599 (6th Cir.), certiorari denied as *Ross v. U.S.*, 273 U.S. 735 (1926).

45. *Bay City Times and Tribune*, July 18, 1924.

46. *Le Mare v. U.S.*, 19 F.2d 1019 (6th Cir. 1927).

47. Despite all of this crime and violence, in 1930, Detroit was judged to have the lowest death rate of any large city in the world. *Detroit News*, February 26, 1931.

48. *Bay City Times*, May 18, 1952, 10.

49. *New York Times*, February 18, 1932.

50. *U.S. v. McKeighan*, 58 F.2d 298 (E.D. Mich. 1932).

51. Detroit's city government was no better and was pursued by state and local law enforcement. Beginning in 1940, Wayne County Circuit Judge Homer Ferguson conducted a one-man grand jury investigating bribery of city officials. The result was more than 150 defendants receiving jail sentences, including Detroit mayor Richard Reading, his son Richard, Jr., Wayne County sheriff Thomas Wilcox, and Wayne County prosecutor Duncan McCrea. Kavieff, 200.

52. Stephen C. O'Neill, "Why Are Judges' Robes Black?" *The Court Legacy*, vol. XI, no. 1 (February 2003), 5.

53. Transcript, February 10, 1925, Judicial Robes file, Box 23, Tuttle Papers.

54. Edward Sanford to Arthur J. Tuttle, February 21, 1917, Judicial Robes file, Box 23, Tuttle Papers.

55. U.S. Department of Justice to Arthur J. Tuttle, January 12, 1925, Judicial Robes file, Box 23, Tuttle Papers.

56. Transcript, February 10, 1925, Judicial Robes file, Box 23, Tuttle Papers.

57. For a detailed account of the case, see Victoria Saker Woeste, "Detroit's Trial of the Century: *Sapiro v. Ford*, 1927," *The Court Legacy*, vol. VIII, no. 2 (September 1999).

58. Victoria Saker Woeste, "Insecure Equality: Louis Marshall, Henry Ford, and the Problem of Defamatory Antisemitism, 1920–1929," *The Journal of American History*, vol. 91, no. 3 (2004), 877.

59. Sapiro claimed that he chose the Eastern District in order to force Ford to testify.

60. *Detroit News*, July 8, 1927.

61. Also known as the Elliot-Fernald Act, 44 Stat. 630.

62. 46 Stat. 1552, 1600.

63. Matthew Heron and Matthew Dawson, "Port Huron Federal Building," part 2, *The Court Legacy*, vol. XIII, no. 1 (February 2005), 10.

64. 46 Stat. 893.

65. *Bay City Daily Times*, August 15, 1931.

66. Arthur J. Tuttle to acting chief clerk, U.S. Supreme Court, October 1, 1931, Additional Judge file, Box 28, Tuttle Papers.

67. Bay City Board of Trade, *Bay City Illustrated* (Gregory Printing Company, 1898). The Ridotto was built by Frank and Fremont Chesbrough to provide a more refined venue for ballroom dancing than the town's rough saloons frequented by lumberjacks on a spree. When ballroom dancing lost popularity, the hall was converted to a vaudeville house. After the new federal building opened, the Northeastern School of Commerce took over the third floor. Although it was described in 1898 as "practically fire proof [sic]," the Ridotto Building was destroyed by fire on April 1, 1940. Dale Patrick Wolicki, *The Historic Architecture of Bay City, Michigan* (Bay City, MI: Bay County Historical Society, 1998), 154.

68. "Art: Cornerstone Man," *Time Magazine*, December 10, 1934.

69. Some of the accommodations in the building's upper stories have changed over time. In 2011, only the elevator and stairway on the north end are open to the public, the deputy clerk's office and counter are on the third floor, and the former bankruptcy courtroom is used by the U.S. Magistrate Judge. Facilities for the Bankruptcy Court and the U.S. Attorney have moved to rented space in buildings in Bay City.

70. Unlike the district's other courthouses, which are owned and operated by the General Services Administration, the Bay City Post Office and U.S. Courthouse is owned and operated by the U.S. Postal Service.

71. *Bay City Sunday Times*, June 4, 1933; Judy Christie, "Bay City and Its Courthouses," *The Court Legacy*, vol. XIII, no. 1 (February 2005).

72. *Bay City Times*, June 7, 1933.

73. Program from Bay City testimonial dinner, June 6, 1933, Obituary and Tributes File, Box 106, Tuttle Papers.

74. *Bay City Times*, June 7, 1933.

75. 45 Stat. 1657.

76. *Detroit Times*, December 2, 1929.

77. 46 Stat. 896.

78. *Detroit Evening Journal*, September 21, 1917.

79. *The Detroiter*, January 13, 1919, 33.

80. Robert West to Arthur J. Tuttle, September 3, 1931, Federal Building file, Box 33, Tuttle Papers.

81. Letter, October 1, 1931, Arthur J. Tuttle to acting chief clerk, U.S. Supreme Court, Federal Building file, Box 33, Tuttle Papers.

82. *Polk's Detroit City Directory, 1931–1932* (Detroit, MI: Polk and Co., 1931), 36, 1673.

83. Wilbert Garred to tenants, May 5, 1934, Federal Building file, Box 33, Tuttle Papers.

84. http://www.gsa.gov. (Accessed 9/5/11).

85. Id.

86. As the number of judges has grown, so has the number of courtrooms. In 2011, there are 24 courtrooms on floors 1, 2, 6, 7, and 8.

87. Judges to Wilbert C. Garred, September 26, 1934, Federal Building file, Box 33, Tuttle Papers.

88. Memorandum, Wilbert C. Garred to tenants, April 26, 1934, Federal Building file, Box 33, Tuttle Papers.

89. Arthur J. Tuttle to Wilbert C. Garred, June 15, 1934, Federal Building file, Box 33, Tuttle Papers.

90. Arthur J. Tuttle to Wilbert C. Garred, September 26, 1934, Federal Building file, Box 33, Tuttle Papers.

91. Arthur J. Tuttle to Charles R. Dickerson, April 4, 1934, Federal Building file, Box 33, Tuttle Papers.

92. Memo, January 23, 1934, Furniture and Carpets file, Box 33, Tuttle Papers.

93. Arthur J. Tuttle to Wilbert C. Garred, August 8, 1934, Custodian file, Box 33, Tuttle Papers.

94. Arthur J. Tuttle to Wilbert C. Garred, June 15, 1934, Custodian file, Box 33, Tuttle Papers.

CHAPTER 9

The Great Depression and the New Deal, 1932–1940

The Eastern District, 1934–1940

The Eastern District's rapid increase in population during the 1920s did not continue during the following decade. The 1930 U.S. census found 3.53 million residents in the district, an increase of just under 1.1 million since 1920. By 1940, though, the total had increased by only 340,000 as the worldwide depression slowed job creation and immigration. Most of the district's population increase from 1920 to 1940 occurred in southeastern Michigan, which increased to 63 percent of the total, while other counties were stagnant during both decades. The Great Depression, which began with the Crash of 1929, hit Detroit and other industrial cities of the district particularly hard. For example, between 1929 and 1932, production of motor vehicles in the United States and Canada plummeted from 5.6 million to 1.4 million, employment levels in Detroit-area auto plants dropped from 90 percent to 20 percent, and the value of a share of the common stock of General Motors Corporation collapsed from $72 to $8.[1]

Prohibition cases decreased after 1932, but were still a substantial factor in the court's load of new cases until 1934. In 1933, the number of new U.S. civil cases filed was down about 20 percent from its peak, but was still, at 1,092, more than a thousand more than the number filed in 1916. The same applied to criminal filings (1,415), down 40 percent from their zenith, but still 1,300 more than in 1916. The number of new private civil cases was still relatively small, 465, but its filings were increasing as the others decreased. By 1937, the mix of cases had changed greatly, with only 188 new U.S. civil cases, 591 new criminal cases, and 890 private civil cases. More than half of the 6,248 "private" civil cases filed from 1934 to 1940 were not so private, nor did they represent an enduring trend. Instead, they were collection suits by court-appointed receivers of failed Michigan banks against defaulting borrowers, and by 1942 they were gone.

Failed Banks and the Court under Scrutiny

In 1934 and 1935, the bench of the Eastern District saw itself under attack as too sympathetic to local bankers and as hostile to the federal government. Judge O'Brien, in particular, was accused publicly of being unable to give the United States a fair trial, and the Justice Department paraded his wife's finances before the press. In the end, the judges of the Sixth Circuit, in an order similar to that directed to another Eastern District judge 40 years later, removed Judge O'Brien from the cases in question, even as it reassured him that he had done absolutely nothing meriting removal.

When the stock market bubble burst in November 1929, the economy reacted much as it had in 1837, 1873, and 1893, and would again in 2008: credit dried up, property values crashed, depositors withdrew funds, and banks closed. There were 1,350 bank failures nationwide in 1930, 2,293 in 1931, 1,453 in 1932, and 273 in January 1933.[2] Nearly 200 banks closed in Michigan. Detroit was reduced to six banks, none of them stable because their assets consisted largely of loans made on the inflated value of real property and corporate securities, which were now worth only a small fraction of the balances owed to the banks. In addition, worried depositors had lost faith in banks and were withdrawing their savings, leaving money that could have been used to restart the economy stuffed under mattresses. Initially, President Hoover refused to use the power and assets of the federal government to alleviate the depression in general and the bank failures in particular, but he finally did agree to the creation by Congress, in January 1932, of the Reconstruction Finance Corporation (RFC) which was to make loans to struggling banks, railroads, farm mortgage associations, and other businesses. The RFC was slow to act, though, and, in order to stop runs on state banks, Michigan governor William Comstock closed all state-chartered banks temporarily. Other states followed Michigan and declared bank holidays for their own state banks. On March 6, 1933, two days after his inauguration, President Roosevelt closed all banks across the country. Three days later, Congress passed the Emergency Banking Relief Act,[3] which affirmed the bank closure order and ordered the comptroller of the currency to examine all national banks, reopening only those which were sound. The act also promised, in effect, to guarantee deposits at all reopened banks. With this start, a combination of government and private efforts eventually restored the public's confidence in the banks.[4]

Both of Detroit's two large bank holding companies, the Detroit Bankers Company and the Guardian Detroit Union Group, had applied for and received loans from the RFC, but neither reopened after the national bank holiday; instead they were placed in federal receivership. Examiners for the receivers discovered evidence that some of the bank groups' officers and directors had misrepresented to the RFC the balance sheets of their banks, in order, the government charged, to delude both the public and the RFC into believing that the banks were sound. In June 1934, the Eastern District's grand jury indicted 13 executives of the two banking groups for conspiracy to defraud, and in August the grand jury brought additional indictments against 28 executives of the bank groups. For some reason, though, the top executives and directors of the banking groups, which included prominent auto industry figures such as Edsel Ford, Fred Fisher, and Roy D. Chapin, were not charged.[5]

While this was going on, the banks' receivers were filing hundreds of suits in the district court to recover on defaulted loans made by the closed banks in happier days. At first, the receivers, who were federal appointees, seemed content to let the judges of the Eastern District try their cases. Then the judges began to hear that the receivers were complaining to the comptroller of the currency and the attorney general that federal judges sitting in Michigan should not hear the cases because they all had business dealings of one kind or another with the banks. Judge Tuttle asked the receivers to draw up a list of cases they did not want the resident judges to hear, and he then directed the clerk to assign those cases to visiting judges whenever the court could obtain one, which was not often. This procedure smelled, to the defendants' attorneys, like judge shopping by the government. When the criminal indictments came down, there were rumors among members of the local bar that the government was going to seek to disqualify all three (Republican) resident district judges from hearing the criminal bank cases and bring in a recent Roosevelt (and thus Democratic) appointee from another court instead.[6]

It was the custom of Judge Tuttle at that time, as senior judge, to direct Clerk Elmer Voorheis to allocate all cases on a particular subject to a single judge. As president of a bank with deposits in the failed banks, he disqualified himself from the criminal bank cases and instead assigned them to Judge O'Brien. The special prosecutor, Guy K. Bard, brought in from California, asked Tuttle to disqualify O'Brien as well, asserting that Mrs. O'Brien was in default on loans made by the defendants' bank and that Judge O'Brien knew two of the defendants socially. Bard also alleged that somebody had heard Judge O'Brien make disparaging remarks about the investigation that resulted in the indictments and that O'Brien was "undoubtedly personally biased and prejudiced against the government and biased and prejudiced in favor of the defendants."[7] O'Brien admitted the first two claims and denied the third. He also advised Bard that he had "looked into his heart," and decided he held no prejudice either way in the case. When Judge O'Brien refused to step down, Bard filed a written recusal request that contained all of the allegations. On January 8, 1935, O'Brien refused once more to recuse himself, and then the behavior of the Justice Department became odd.

Three weeks after O'Brien's refusal, on January 27, 1935, Bard told the press that "the necessary preliminaries bearing upon the assignment of a judge not disqualified to hear the issues involved have now been disposed of," and expressed himself ready to begin the first trial,[8] which seemed to indicate that he had put the recusal issue behind him and would accept O'Brien as trial judge. Just another week later, though, U.S. attorney general Homer Stile Cummings called a news conference in Washington, in which copies of the affidavits containing the claims against Judge O'Brien were distributed, suggesting that the department was not finished with recusal after all. Then, instead of seeking appellate review of O'Brien's recusal decision, the prosecution went forward with the first trial.

Trial of the first three defendants, prominent bankers John Ballantyne, Herbert Chittenden, and John Hart, supposed to be the prosecution's strongest cases, began on March 26, 1935. On April 6, after nine days of testimony and argument, the jury, after deliberating for less than two hours, acquitted the defendants on all counts.[9] The prosecutors complained to the press that Judge O'Brien's instructions to the jury were so erroneous that they had made conviction impossible, and they questioned whether the judge was capable of giving the government a fair trial. Specifically, they complained that the judge had instructed the jury that the defendants were not charged with criminality in its ordinary and accepted meaning, but that to convict the jurors had to find that the defendants acted with criminal intent.[10] This was not a fair summary of the judge's charge, at least as published in the *Detroit Free Press*: Judge O'Brien merely noted that the defendants were not charged "with misappropriation of funds, of misapplication of funds, or of embezzlement." Thus, he continued: "There is no charge in this case of any criminality in its ordinary and accepted meaning, but there is a charge of a violation of a criminal phase of the Federal banking laws as they apply to a federal bank."[11] He did comment on the evidence and on what facts were disputed, as was then common in most American courts, but he certainly did not direct a verdict. Nevertheless, on May 10, the Justice Department petitioned the Sixth Circuit to disqualify Judge O'Brien. A month later, a panel of Sixth Circuit judges issued a "memorandum" in which they explained that, based on the facts before them, there seemed to be no grounds to disqualify Judge O'Brien. They also noted, however, that: "the fact remains that an embarrassing situation has arisen . . . which may afford a pretext for uncalled for criticism of the respondent [Judge O'Brien] and the District Court, but which could be relieved if the respondent should voluntarily withdraw from further participation in the hearing of the cases."[12] Judge O'Brien declined to take the circuit judge's suggestion,[13] and, on June 29, 1935, the Sixth Circuit ordered him to recuse himself from all bank cases,[14] an order which the U.S. Supreme Court declined to review.[15]

A few months later, Attorney General Cummings asked that Judges Tuttle and Moinet recuse themselves from all bank cases as well as accept temporary transfers to another district so that a visiting judge could try the remaining criminal bank cases. Republican voices, such as *Time* magazine, chose to interpret this request as tantamount to a vote by President Roosevelt of no confidence in all Republican federal judges. The furore was such that, when President Roosevelt nominated Arthur F. Lederle in February 1936 to the Eastern District's new fourth judgeship, the Senate confirmed Lederle subject to his pledge not to accept the criminal bank cases that were still awaiting trial. In the end, Judges Tuttle and Moinet were not sent into exile, and District Judge Patrick T. Stone of the Western District of Wisconsin, a Roosevelt nominee, was assigned as visiting judge to try the cases.[16] Some defendants were convicted, one of them, Herbert Wilkin, was fined, and Judge Stone dismissed charges against 22 others.[17] The district court, its honor unsullied, but a bit tarnished, returned to its business.

This ordeal did not shake Judge O'Brien's gentle sense of humor that he demonstrated in a 1938 opinion disposing of an otherwise obscure tax case involving Detroit's very exclusive Yondotega Club. The issue before him was whether the Yondotega was a social club, whose dues were taxable as income, or merely a luncheon club, whose dues were not taxable. Judge O'Brien ruled that it was a social club, despite its sumptuous menu, including, as he described it, the club's "succulent steaks and the pluperfect pickled pig knuckles." He noted that: "We don't eat or drink only for the purpose of living. Of course, we've got to do both to live, but when men congregate together, they do that incidentally. . . . I think the heart and the soul of the organization is that congenial people, people of like interests, meet for the purpose and benefit and the pleasure of solace of companionship, rather than the more or less animal function of eating food. . . . It is the companionship that sometimes makes the function of eating endurable. One would rather have—and I am speaking for myself—a crust with Shakespeare than a Lucullan banquet with Al Capone."[18]

Congress Adds Two Judgeships

When Franklin D. Roosevelt became president in March 1933, a great majority of federal judges had been appointed by Republican presidents. In the District and Eastern District of Michigan, for example, eight district judges had been appointed by Republicans and only one, Judge Wilkins, by a Democrat. During his 12 years in office, FDR restored a balance by appointing a record 193 federal judges, including 134 district judges. Only two of those appointments were to the Eastern District, however. In August 1935, Congress authorized filling "any existing vacancy and any vacancy which may occur any time hereafter" in the 14 temporary judgeships created in 1922, including the seat vacated by Judge Simons when he went to the Sixth Circuit.[19] Then, in May 1938, Congress authorized 12 more district judge positions including one for the Eastern District.[20] Thus, in just 16 years, the district court expanded from one judge to five.

District Judge Arthur Frederick Lederle

Born: November 25, 1887 (Leland, Michigan), to John Edward and Christina Marie Dunkelow Lederle
Education: Michigan State Normal School (now Eastern Michigan University) (B.A. 1909); Detroit College of Law (LL. B. 1915); University of Detroit (now Detroit-Mercy) School of Law (LL. M. 1923)
Nominated/Confirmed: February 20/March 3, 1936 (Franklin D. Roosevelt)
Vacancy: New Seat[21]
Senior Status: July 1, 1960
Died: April 29, 1972

The selection of Arthur F. Lederle as the Democratic Party's first nomination to the Eastern District's district court in a century was seen as a victory for the "younger branch" of the state party (George Schroeder, George Sadowski, John Dingell Sr., John Lesinski, Louis Rabaut), "clipping the wings" of national committeeman Horatio Abbott, who wanted the nomination to go to Frank A. Picard of Saginaw[22] who had to wait three more years to join the federal bench.

Fig. 47.   Judge Arthur Frederick Lederle. (Historical Society for the United States District Court for the Eastern District of Michigan)

Judge Lederle was one of 12 children of a farming family. After receiving his B.A., he became a teacher in River Rouge and Detroit. In 1911, he married a fellow teacher, Margaret Bailie Matthews of Ludington. After receiving his law degrees, he was appointed assistant corporation counsel (i.e., assistant city attorney) for the city of Detroit where, except for a year (1933–1934) spent as a special assistant Michigan attorney general, he remained until his appointment to the district court. He was very active in Democratic politics in Michigan until his appointment. Judge and Mrs. Lederle had no children, but they shared a strong commitment to education. From 1927 to 1946, Judge Lederle taught at what is now Wayne State University Law School, which honored him in 1952 with the degree of LL.D. The couple established scholarship funds at Eastern Michigan University and the University of Detroit-Mercy, and Judge Lederle left his entire estate to the Arthur F. Lederle Scholarship Fund at Wayne State University Law School.

District Judge Frank Albert Picard

Born: October 19, 1889 (Saginaw, Michigan), to Alfred de la Chapelle and
    Zepherine Lagault Picard
Education: University of Michigan (L.L.B. 1912)
Nominated/Confirmed: February 9/23, 1939 (Franklin D. Roosevelt)
Vacancy: New Seat
Senior Status: March 31, 1961
Left Court: February 28, 1963 (Died at Saginaw, Michigan)

At his death, the *Bay City Times* described Judge Picard as "one of the century's most colorful figures in the federal judiciary."[23] The passage of time has done little to dispute that assessment: in his personal and public lives, Judge Picard was one of a kind. He was born, the seventh of eight natural children (plus two step-sons) of hotelkeeper parents, both of whom had emigrated from Quebec to Saginaw in the 1860s. Known to family and friends as "Zip," Frank tried to join his brothers' aerialist troupe, the Flying Picards, but when his father refused to allow it, Frank turned his energy to school sports and music. In 1907, he captained Saginaw High to the school's first state football championship, and played three seasons at the University of Michigan.[24]

After graduating from Saginaw High in 1907, Judge Picard worked for two years as a reporter before enrolling in the Law Department at the University of Michigan. He graduated with a law degree in 1912, worked for a year as an assistant to the Saginaw County prosecutor, and then began a private practice. During World War I, he served as a captain in the U.S. Army, but did not see combat. He joked that: "I chased the war all over Europe. Never could catch up with it." In June 1921, Judge Picard married Ruth Caroline Doersan, daughter of another French-Canadian family which had settled in Saginaw. They had four children, two boys and two girls.

In 1920, he ran for lieutenant governor on the Democratic slate but lost. He ran for U.S. senator in 1934 against incumbent senator Arthur Vanden-

Fig. 48.   Judge Frank Albert Picard. (Historical Society for the United States District Court for the Eastern District of Michigan)

berg, basing his campaign on his own support for President Roosevelt and Vandenberg's ties to Prohibition and the past. He lost, but the unexpectedly small margin bolstered his reputation as a leading Democrat in largely Republican Michigan.[25] When the fifth judgeship was created for the Eastern District, he sought the nomination from President Roosevelt and Michigan's Democratic U.S. senator Prentiss Marsh Brown, despite the district judge's relatively low annual salary, then $10,000. Because Judge Picard kept his home in Saginaw, Judge Tuttle happily handed off to him the Northern Division's docket as well as a Detroit caseload.

Scandal and Tragedy in the Court

After Elmer W. Voorheis was appointed clerk of the district court, he quickly established a reputation as an excellent administrator, and Judge Tuttle came to rely on him completely for all matters relating to his office. Voorheis hired employees, established procedures, collected fees, and, after Judge Simons joined the bench, assigned cases between the judges with minimal input from them. By the mid-1930s, however, Voorheis and the performance of the clerk's office, flooded with Prohibition cases and having to satisfy four busy judges, had deteriorated. Voorheis himself appeared to be overwhelmed by the pace of the work. Judge Tuttle noted that: "In recent years, he has not been as strong physically as he formerly was and yet his burdens have increased beyond description. During the day he is just pulled and hauled until I don't see how he is able to stand up under the strain."[26] Morale in the clerk's office was low, procedures were ignored, attendance was spotty, and record-keeping was slipshod. Voorheis delegated practically no responsibility to his chief deputy or any other employees, assigned all tasks himself, and refused to let employees help each other. Attendance and punctuality were inconsistent, and employees ignored his orders that they occasionally work overtime. At the same time, Voorheis's health deteriorated, and he spent most of 1936 in Florida recuperating.

During his absence, the Department of Justice began an investigation of his office and accounts, and discovered a series of discrepancies reminiscent of the Harsha era. According to a memo from Judge Tuttle to the other judges, Voorheis admitted to having some personal scandal in his past that increased his need for cash even as his fee compensation was converted to a salary in 1919. For whatever reason, he began to steal. One relatively minor source of graft was charging new citizens for naturalization certificates and other immigration forms that were supposed to be free. His main fraud, though, was the same one practiced by Walter Harsha. Although most fees for filing or other clerk services were fixed, the charge for the preparation of a case's record on appeal varied according to the amount of work and paper involved. Attorneys asking for an appeal record would pay in advance based on an estimate by Voorheis who then insisted on assembling and preparing the appellate records himself. Like Harsha, he simply exaggerated the cost, remitted the proper fee amount to the court, and kept the rest for himself. Over the years, this graft amounted to about $34,000. Voorheis also had all of the printing required for the record done by a single company, which then kicked back 10 percent of the charge.[27] In early December 1936, Justice Department investigators advised the judges of what they had found, and on December 8, the judges officially ordered Voorheis to stop charging for immigration materials, to return the stolen funds, and to "devote your time exclusively to that work until it has been completed."[28]

Two weeks later, while the judges tried to contain the scandal, they and the rest of the city were shocked by an incident the court could not possibly keep quiet. At 2:30 p.m. on December 21, 1936, the district court's 53-year-old master in chancery, William S. Sayres, Jr., jumped to his death from the 28th floor of Detroit's Book Cadillac Hotel, landing in Michigan Avenue in front of hundreds of Christmas shoppers. Described as "a genial, lovable person," Mr. Sayres had accomplished much despite having to spend most of his life in a wheelchair as the result of contracting polio before his first birthday. He graduated from the Detroit College of Law in 1909, and when his condition deterred potential clients, he earned a living writing appellate briefs for other attorneys. He then returned to Detroit College of Law where he served first as secretary and then as dean. During that time, Judge Tuttle often referred difficult matters for him to try as a special master, and in 1917, the judge appointed Sayres as the court's full-time master in chancery, a position in which he took evidence and issued opinions cases involving patent, tax, and corporate issues, supervised corporate receiverships, and did whatever else he was assigned. He was compensated in the old-fashioned manner, by fees approved by the assigning judge from which he paid his expenses, including the salary of his stenographer, Miss Grant.

Sayres had suffered a series of strokes during 1936 and had twice tried to order poison, presumably to end his life, only to be thwarted by his nurse and attendant of 17 years, Oscar Hartung. On the day of his death, Sayres worked in his office in the morning, and at noon told his secretary that he thought he would go to the hotel to have lunch and take a nap. Hartung wheeled Sayres the two blocks to the Book Cadillac where he asked for a room with a river view. Because the hotel was a half mile from the Detroit River with several office buildings in between, that meant a room on an upper floor. Sayres ordered lunch and then asked Hartung to pick up some Christmas packages. A few minutes after Hartung left the room, Sayres apparently managed to open a window, crawl out onto a four-foot ledge, and throw himself down into the street. There is no evidence that his death was related to the clerk's office investigation. According to Hartung, Sayres "had attempted to poison himself some time ago,"[29] and it is more likely that he simply no longer wanted to endure his physical condition.

As the New Year arrived, the judges had to turn their attention back to Elmer Voorheis, and they decided that he had to go. He resigned effective March 31, 1937, giving, as a public reason, "my ill-health, which has been known to you for months."[30] He also promised to return $37,000, representing the $34,000 in overpayments plus interest. In a private conversation with Judge Tuttle, Voorheis said: "I want to tell you of a dreadful thing which happened about ten years ago and which might have placed me in worse disgrace than I now find myself. It will explain to you the reason why I have done some of these things in order to get money." Judge Tuttle replied that he would listen at the appropriate time, but that: "I do, of course, feel greatly disappointed and sorry for what you have done."[31] As had been the case with Harsha, resignation did not end Elmer Voorheis's troubles. Until then, the true reason for his departure had been kept out of the newspapers, but on April 5, 1937, the investigators gave the story to the press which, of course, made the whole affair public.[32] Voorheis retreated to his Detroit home where he died of a series of heart attacks on August 20, 1938, at the age of 69.

Word of the pending vacancy in the clerk's office had leaked out months earlier, and dozens of attorneys applied for the job. In the end, the judges appointed an attorney who did not apply, a former court administrator and state judge, George M. Read. Just three days short of his 53rd birthday when he was sworn in on April 1, 1937, "Judge" Read, as Tuttle always referred to him, was a graduate of the University of Michigan and the Detroit College of Law. From 1909 to 1927, he was registrar of the juvenile division of Wayne County Probate Court, and he served as judge of that court from 1927 until 1932, when he returned to private practice. He would remain as clerk of the district court until 1951, although he took a leave of absence in 1946 to serve a term as secretary general of the Allied military tribunals at Nuremberg.

United States v. Anthony Chebatoris

Like *Sapiro v. Ford*, the 1937 murder trial of Anthony Chebatoris in the Bay City court is more important for the result than for the trial itself. The defendant's guilt was never in doubt, and if *U.S. v. Chebatoris* remains in the public consciousness 70 years later, it is not because of any dramatic twists and turns in the courtroom, but because of the dramatic events that followed: the first execution in Michigan in over a century and the futile efforts of Michigan governor (and future U.S. Supreme Court justice) Frank Murphy to move the hanging out of the state.[33]

Anthony Chebatoris had been a criminal practically since his birth in 1898. He stood less than five feet, six inches tall (the reporters covering the trial described him as "diminutive"),[34] but he was a ruthless thug with a long history of violence who had served 15 of the previous 17 years from 1920 to 1937 in prison for armed robbery and other crimes, was wanted in Pennsylvania for a bank robbery, and was a suspect in another case in Kentucky. While in Michigan's Marquette prison, Chebatoris met Jack Gracy, ten years his junior and another career criminal who had spent most of his life in prison for armed robberies and attempted escape. They became friends and after they were released from prison, they teamed up to do what bank robbers do when they get out—plan another bank robbery.

The Dow Chemical Company deposited its $75,000 payroll twice a month in the Chemical State Savings Bank of Midland, Michigan, 20 miles west of Bay City. Gracy cased the bank and reported back to Chebatoris that it was an easy mark with no security. Early on the morning of September 29, 1937, they left Hamtramck in separate cars and drove north to Corunna, west of Flint, where they left one car and continued north to Midland in the other, a blue Ford sedan. They were armed with a .38 caliber Smith and Wesson revolver, a sawed-off shotgun, and a rifle. After parking the Ford at an angle in front of the bank, they waited for a few minutes, then, at about 11:30 a.m., they entered. Both men wore hats pulled down to hide their faces, Chebatoris with the revolver hidden in his short blue denim jacket while Gracy concealed the shotgun under his long dark coat. Chebatoris left the rifle in the car, probably because it was impossible for him to carry it into the bank without its being seen. Inside the bank, Gracy walked up to Clarence H. Macomber, the bank's 65-year-old president who

Fig. 49.   The Midland Chemical State Savings Bank and Dr. Hardy's office. (*Midland Daily News*)

stood out with his striking white hair and goatee. Macomber was talking with his daughter, Clair, when Gracy jammed the barrel of the shotgun in his ribs. Macomber reacted quickly, grabbed the barrel, and pointed it toward the door. While Gracy wrestled for control of the shotgun, Chebatoris drew his revolver and threatened Macomber as patrons yelled and screamed. When Macomber continued to struggle, Chebatoris shot him once in the left side of his chest. Paul D. Bywater, a young cashier, ran up to help Macomber, and Chebatoris shot him in the stomach. Realizing that their plan was in shreds, the robbers raced back to their car and jumped in. Chebatoris swung the car around and started to drive southwest down Benson Street toward the bridge over the Tittabawassee River.[35]

While casing the bank and Midland, Gracy failed to discover that because there had already been a dozen armed bank robberies in Michigan that year, Midland County sheriff Ira M. Smith had deputized several downtown businessmen, one of whom, Frank L. Hardy, a dentist and war veteran, had an office on the second story above the Levine Mattress Manufacturing Company, next to the bank. As Chebatoris drove the Ford away, Hardy grabbed his .35-caliber deer rifle and fired three shots, the last of which went through the rear window and hit Chebatoris in the arm, causing

Fig. 50.   Interior, the Midland Chemical State Savings Bank. (*Midland Daily News*)

him to lose control and crash into a parked car and then a guardrail. Chebatoris grabbed the rifle as he and Gracy jumped out and ran down the street. Chebatoris looked right and saw a man in the Midford Garage with a visored hat: Henry Porter, a 55-year-old truck driver from Bay City wearing a company uniform. Chebatoris apparently mistook Porter for a policeman because he aimed the rifle at him and fired, sending the lead slug tearing deep into Porter's stomach.

The robbers next tried to steal a car driven by Irene Stolsmark, a local woman who had her baby with her. As she fled on foot with the child, Hardy fired another round, which missed but convinced the robbers to keep running. At the Benson Street bridge, they tried to hijack a Nehil Lumber Company truck, but Hardy's sixth and last shot, from 150 yards, blew off the top of Gracy's head, killing him instantly. Chebatoris ran northwest along the Pere Marquette Railroad's railbed and then, nearing exhaustion, jumped into a car belonging to a member of a street-repair crew. One of the crew, Richard Van Orden, jumped on the car's passenger-side running-board and grabbed the rifle from the front seat, just as Sheriff Smith ran up to the car and pulled Chebatoris out. As the dust settled,

Jack Gracy was dead, Clarence Macomber, and Tony Chebatoris had flesh wounds, and Paul Bywater and Henry Porter were badly wounded. After two anxious weeks, Bywater was able to pull through, but Henry Porter developed an infection from debris in his belly wound, impossible to treat in that time before antibiotics were widely available, and died of peritonitis on October 11 at Bay City's Mercy Hospital.

If the robbery had occurred a few years earlier, Chebatoris would have been arraigned in Midland County Circuit Court and charged with robbery and first-degree murder. Under Michigan law, his maximum sentence would have been life in prison without the possibility of parole. Michigan had never experienced an execution as a state, and the last execution during its territorial period had occurred more than a century earlier. The state legislature had banned capital punishment for murderers since 1847, the first English-speaking jurisdiction to take that step.[36] In 1934, though, Congress reacted to the wave of bank robberies across the country by passing the National Bank Robbery Act,[37] which made the robbery of a federally chartered bank a federal offense and allowed a jury to impose the death penalty on any bank robber who killed a person while robbing a bank or while "avoiding or attempting to avoid apprehension for the commission of such offense."[38] In 1935, Congress increased the scope of the act to include banks with federally-insured deposits,[39] which included the Chemical State Savings Bank. The significance of those federal laws was well known to the Eastern District's 59-year-old district attorney, John Camillus Lehr, who had assisted in drafting the act during his term in Congress from 1933 to 1935. Within days of the botched robbery, Lehr convened a federal grand jury in Bay City, which indicted Chebatoris for attempted bank robbery and assault. A week after Henry Porter died, Lehr had the indictment amended to add the charge of capital murder under the bank act.[40]

Justice could move swiftly in those days in a high-profile criminal case, and Chebatoris's trial on the murder indictment began on Tuesday, October 26, 1937, less than a month after the botched robbery, two weeks after Porter's death, and just one week after the addition of the murder charge. The venue was the four-year-old Bay City courtroom above the post office with Judge Tuttle presiding. John C. Lehr and Assistant District Attorney John W. Babcock prosecuted, while two stars of the Bay City bar, Dell H. Thompson and James K. Brooker, agreed to Judge Tuttle's request that they represent Chebatoris without a fee. It was very unusual for Tuttle to obtain counsel for a criminal defendant. In 1935, in response to an inquiry from the Justice Department regarding his method of appointing attorneys for indigent criminal defendants, he asserted that: "I have not made such an assignment in at least ten years." In minor matters, he explained, he discussed the issue with the defendants in open court, and they always agreed to proceed without counsel. If the possible penalty exceeded five

Fig. 51.   Chebatoris enters the court's basement by the back stairs.
(*Midland Daily News*)

years, he insisted the defendant retain counsel, and they always did so
somehow. He added that, in his experience, 99 percent of defendants are
guilty.[41]

Today, just picking a jury in a murder case can take weeks, but in *U.S.
v. Chebatoris* the entire trial, including jury selection, took only three days.
On October 26, jury selection using a venire of men and women from the

Northern Division resulted in a panel of 12 regular jurors, consisting of seven women (five housewives, a restaurant operator, and a store official) and five men (three farmers, a hotel owner, and a retail grocer), plus another housewife as an alternate. Four of the jurors were from two of the division's metropolises, Bay City and Saginaw, but the rest were from small towns and villages such as Alpena, Alabaster, Freeland, Onaway, and Houghton Lake. On October 27, as Chebatoris sat impassively at the defense table, his arm still in a sling, John Babcock presented the opening statement for the prosecution, took the jury through the facts, and "declared the government will demand the extreme penalty upon conclusion of the trial."[42] After the defense attorneys reserved their opening statement, seven prosecution witnesses, including Clarence Macomber and Frank Hardy, described the events as they remembered them. On the morning of October 28, the government presented another seven witnesses to complete the chain linking Chebatoris to Porter's death, and then rested. Defense counsel called no witnesses and confined themselves, on both days, to a cross-examination highlighting inconsistencies among the stories told by the prosecution witnesses.

The trial proceeded quickly, and Babcock began the closing argument for the government before noon on October 28, summarizing the evidence in a thunderous voice. Then it was the turn of Brooker, for the defense, who spoke calmly yet forcefully for less than ten minutes. He began by telling the jurors: "You're on the spot, you've got to take it." He admitted that Chebatoris was guilty of the robbery attempt, but argued that there was insufficient evidence that his client, rather than Dr. Hardy or some other vigilante, fired the fatal shot. He also reminded the jury of Michigan's traditional distaste for capital punishment, a comment that drew an objection from Babcock, which Judge Tuttle sustained. Lehr then rose and gave the government's rebuttal, shouting at Chebatoris, the jury, and the audience as he denounced the defendant as "a brutal slayer, a sly, sneaking, human beast" and admonished the jurors that they had "the responsibility of protecting innocent American citizens against bandits, gangsters, and ruthless beasts." At 1:05 p.m., the jurors retired to deliberate. After taking breaks for lunch and dinner, they returned to the courtroom with a verdict at 8:25 p.m. As foreman Ira Akins, the hotel owner from Houghton Lake, rose to announce the verdict, Chebatoris remained impassive, as he had for the entire trial, chewing gum incessantly and rarely paying attention to what was being said. In the packed but silent courtroom, Akins read the verdict aloud: "We find the defendant guilty as charged, and direct that he be punished by death." Akins later told the press that the jury was unanimous for guilt on the first ballot but that it took six more ballots before they agreed on the death sentence.

There was little doubt that Judge Tuttle would accept the jury's verdict and sentence Chebatoris to death. He favored giving armed bank robbers

Fig. 52.   Jury foreman Ira Akins. (*Midland Daily News*)

the stiffest sentence allowed by law. As he explained to the father of a convicted bank robber who sought a sentence reduction for his son, there had
been a lot of bank robberies in the Eastern District until he started to give
only the maximum sentence, and afterwards there were few.[43] He had
often bemoaned the absence of a death sentence in the sedition and sabotage cases he tried during World War I, and he had a particular hatred of
armed, daylight bank robberies, which too often ended in gunshots and

death. In 1921, as part of a panel of judges and prosecutors, he recommended that the federal government support the states in passing laws to confiscate all firearms less than three feet long and to make it a felony to manufacture, sell, use or own such a weapon. Although he was a lifelong hunter and gun owner, he urged that: "If we could clear the country of small firearms, we would eliminate 90 percent of premeditated, violent crimes."[44]

Before his guards took Chebatoris back to his cell in the Saginaw County Jail in the early hours of October 29, Judge Tuttle admonished them to keep the defendant safe so that he would not escape legal punishment. Chebatoris was stripped to his underwear before being locked in, and three deputy sheriffs and a state trooper stood guard outside the cell, but Chebatoris somehow found a way to hide a small piece of a razor blade. At about 5:00 a.m., he slashed his right wrist and arm four times and made a three-inch gash that just missed his throat. He was rushed to Saginaw General Hospital in critical condition, but he had botched his suicide as badly as he had botched the robbery, and he was well enough on November 1 to be driven to the United States Detention Farm at Milan, Michigan, to recover further and await his sentence.

While the trial was going on, the press, the public, and Michigan governor Frank Murphy had assumed that, if sentenced to death, Chebatoris would not be executed in Michigan. An amendment to the banking law, enacted by Congress less than five months earlier, in June 1937, provided that: "The manner of inflicting the punishment of death shall be the manner prescribed by the laws of the State within which the sentence is imposed. . . . If the laws of the State within which sentence is imposed make no provision for the infliction of the penalty of death, then the court shall designate some other State in which such sentence shall be executed in the manner prescribed by the laws thereof."[45] This seemed to rule out Michigan and require Judge Tuttle to designate that Chebatoris be executed elsewhere, possibly in Ohio or Indiana. However, while Chebatoris waited in Milan and Judge Tuttle prepared for his annual deer hunt, District Attorney Lehr was trying to find a way to keep the execution in Michigan. On November 9, he announced that he had "discovered" that Michigan had a criminal law first enacted in its earliest days that punished treason with death by hanging.[46] This, he asserted, was enough to justify executing Chebatoris in Michigan by hanging, although he also noted that he had to check with Attorney General Homer Cummings.

Judge Tuttle shot his buck, his 20th annual kill, and arranged for its head to join several others on the walls of in his chambers in Bay City.[47] On November 30, Chebatoris was driven back to Bay City from Milan and brought into court to be sentenced. He stood silent and motionless, shackled to a guard, as Judge Tuttle formally sentenced him to death by hanging inside Milan prison on July 8, 1938. Holding the execution at Milan was a severe disappointment to Governor Murphy and other opponents of the death penalty in Michigan. Murphy did not hide his hatred for capital punishment, no matter how despicable the crime or the criminal: "The act of putting a noose around a man's neck and hanging him until he is dead is uncivilized. That he too is uncivilized does not excuse it."

Judge Tuttle would have none of it, stating that he had "neither the power nor the inclination" to move the execution.[48] It appears, though, that it was his inclination, and not his power, that made up his mind. On June 22, 1938, less than three weeks before the execution date, Murphy wrote to President Franklin D. Roosevelt, a friend and supporter,[49] asking that Chebatoris's sentence be commuted to life in prison or that, at least, the execution be moved to another state.[50] On July 6, 1938, two days before the execution, District Attorney Lehr received an order from Washington to inform Judge Tuttle that the federal government had no objection to moving the execution.[51] Tuttle rejected the offer, stating that "it would not be in good taste to select the territory of a neighbor for the performance of an unpleasant duty."[52]

Meanwhile, at Milan, planning for an execution by hanging continued, under the supervision of the Eastern District's U.S. marshal, John J. Barc. One major decision for Barc was who would be the hangman. The June 1937 law authorized Barc to obtain "the services of an appropriate State or local official or employ some other person for such purpose, and pay the cost [of conducting the execution] in an amount approved by the Attorney General." Because no living Michigan official had ever hanged anybody, Barc hired George Phillip Hanna of Epworth, Illinois, an experienced and dedicated executioner. Hanna, a wealthy farmer then aged 64, was nearing the end of a long career in which he had hanged more than 70 people. He used his own scaffold and trap door, and prided himself on minimizing the prisoner's suffering and on not accepting a fee for his services. Barc asked Midland County sheriff Ira Smith, who had captured Chebatoris, if he would pull the lever to release Hanna's trap door. Smith accepted, he said, as a matter of duty rather than for any personal satisfaction. Judge Tuttle, on the other hand, declined to witness the execution which he had ordered, and, instead, sent Richard F. Doyle, his chief U.S. probation officer, with instructions to report on the events in writing.

Exactly what happened at Milan on that early morning is not clear. Doyle's detailed report to Tuttle corroborates the official story that everything went perfectly and by the book.[53] According to Doyle, the 23 witnesses to the execution (himself; assistant U.S. attorney John Babcock; three U.S. marshals; Sheriff Smith; Warden John J. Ryan; representatives of the Department of Justice and of the FBI; other law officers; four physicians; two chaplains; three reporters; Hanna, his assistant, Sheriff Chester A. Pyle of White County, Illinois; as well as their friend, Ollie R. Weaver, a deputy sheriff from Vanderburg County, Indiana) watched in silence as

Chebatoris went quietly to his death. H. M. Kelly of the Associated Press reported the same story: "The execution party of twenty-three entered the specially built hanging chamber at 5:04 A.M. and Chebatoris, with head erect, walked firmly up the thirteen steps to the platform. He smiled at the chief executioner [Hanna] and appeared entirely calm. The trap was sprung at 5:08. The Rev. Lee Laige [sic], a priest from a near-by parish, walked beside Chebatoris to the gallows and chanted in Latin during the death march, a surprising development, because the prisoner had spurned all religious consolation until yesterday. After the hanging the priest said: 'Now he can have a Christian burial.'"[54] The *Bay City Times* added that Sheriff Smith did pull the lever to trigger the trap door and that Chebatoris's heart continued to beat for five minutes before it began to weaken. When it stopped, the body was taken to the jail's morgue.[55]

That was the story that was communicated to the public, but the man in charge of all federal prisons at that time, James V. Bennett, told quite a different tale. In his autobiography, Bennett recalled receiving a panicked telephone call from Warden Ryan at 2:00 a.m. on July 8. Bennett asked if the hanging was over, and Ryan told him; "I wish to God it was. The hangman arrived about an hour ago. He's gloriously drunk and he's got three friends with him, just as potted. We've given him enough coffee to sober him up a bit, but he says he isn't going to do the job unless we let his friends watch. He wants them to see what a 'pro' he is." Bennett reminded Ryan that according to federal prison rules, if an executioner could not or would not proceed, the warden was to perform the office instead. Ryan refused to be the hangman, but Bennett ordered him to get it done somehow. According to Bennett, Ryan tricked the hangman into believing his friends were watching, and then, after the execution, threw the drunks out of the prison.[56] Bennett says he ordered Ryan to keep the debacle quiet, and if Bennett's account is true, Ryan may have convinced Doyle and the other witnesses to keep the problems secret. Perhaps Doyle, whose job was in Tuttle's hands, wanted to spare Tuttle's feelings, or he may have given the judge an accurate oral report, while his written report was cleaned up for posterity. On the other hand, the behavior attributed to Hanna seems out of character and Bennett, who also hated capital punishment, may have exaggerated.

After the execution, the press reported that Chebatoris's family refused to claim the body and that he would be buried in an unmarked grave. In fact, he was buried in Marble Park Cemetery, just west of Milan, where his headstone, inscribed "In Loving Memory," can still be seen.

The First Law Clerk

The district judges' need to name a replacement for William Sayres as master in chancery gave them an opportunity to cure another personnel situation, this one involving the court's first law clerk. In 1882, when Associate Justice Horace Gray joined the Supreme Court from the Supreme Judicial Court of Massachusetts, he introduced to the federal courts his practice of hiring a recent law-school graduate for a year or two to perform legal research, construct drafts of opinions, and provide other legal and clerical services. Initially, Gray paid for what he called his "secretary" from his own pocket, but when, in 1886, Congress agreed to pay for a stenographer for each justice of the Supreme Court,[57] he used that money instead. In time, the other justices of the Supreme Court adopted this policy, and, in 1919, Congress provided funds specifically to hire each justice a legally-trained "law clerk" in addition to a stenographer.

The Supreme Court's experience was so successful that in 1930, Congress authorized the hiring of one law clerk for each judge of the Circuit Courts of Appeals and in 1936 one for each district judge "when he deems the same to be necessary," at a salary not to exceed $2,750 per annum. Always conscious of cost, though, Congress provided that only 35 clerks could be hired by district judges during the fiscal year ending June 30, 1937 and even then only if the circuit's senior circuit judge issued a certificate of need.[58] The senior judge of the Sixth Circuit promptly authorized one law clerk for the four district judges of the Eastern District, and Judge Tuttle immediately wrote to Henry Moore Bates, dean of the University of Michigan Law School, for a suitable candidate. Bates recommended third-year student Donald L. Quaife, praising his intelligence, his accomplishments in scholarly competitions, and his capacity for hard work. In April 1936, Judge Tuttle informed Dean Bates that the judges had taken his recommendation and hired Quaife as the court's first law clerk beginning on July 1, 1936, the first day of the 1937 fiscal year.[59] Quaife did begin work that day, but two weeks later the Department of Justice informed Tuttle that Congress had appropriated no money to pay the law clerks it had authorized the courts to hire. Judge Tuttle exerted his salesmanship to convince Quaife to stay on, promising that he would find money for him somehow. Early in 1937, Quaife ended his career as a law clerk and took over Sayres's office, staff, and duties, although not his title. Instead, Quaife worked for several years under a "gentlemen's agreement" with Tuttle. From the fees allowed by the court for his work as a master, Quaife was to receive a salary, pay the salary of Sayres's secretary and the other expenses of his office, and then deposit any surplus in a fund to buy books for the court's library.[60] Donald Quaife and Judge Tuttle retained a warm relationship for the rest of the judge's life, so much so that Quaife named his first child Arthur in the judge's honor.[61]

In 1940, Congress decided that some senior circuit judges were too generous to their district courts in approving law clerks and so limited their appointment to only two in any circuit.[62] In a few years, though, law clerks proved their worth, and Congress did not include that limitation in the 1945 appropriations, which the district judges took as authority for each of them to hire a law clerk. The clerks were so useful that after a few years, district judges began to replace their court criers with a second, "crier" law clerk, and today in the computer age some have dispensed with a stenographer and hired a third law clerk instead.

Bankruptcy Business

Analysis of the size of the civil and criminal dockets does not explain the full burden of work imposed on the judges of the Eastern District during the 1930s. The Great Crash of 1929 and the resultant Great Depression also spawned a tremendous increase in the number of commercial and individual bankruptcies, which took up an important amount of judicial time and resources. Article I of the Constitution empowers Congress to establish "uniform laws on the subject of Bankruptcies,"[63] but until the 20th century bankruptcy was only sporadically a part of the courts' work. Acts passed in 1800, 1841, and 1867 were all repealed in a relatively short time, although not before the 1841 and 1867 laws added 685 and 1611 cases, respectively, to the district court's caseload. The fourth bankruptcy law, enacted in 1898,[64] proved to be more durable, surviving until it was replaced in 1978. The 1898 act was also noteworthy in that it allowed businesses as well as individuals to seek protection from creditors, and the addition of section 77[65] in June 1934 introduced reorganization as a possible remedy for insolvent corporations.

During its first decades, the 1898 act did not substantially impact the district judges. Until the 1930s, the number of cases was relatively low, although increasing (from 177 in 1899, to 392 in 1917, and to 863 in 1928), and most debtors were individuals who had no assets. Each district judge was allowed to appoint as many bankruptcy referees "as may be necessary" to two-year terms "to assist in expeditiously transacting the bankruptcy business." Referees were compensated by the fees paid by the parties, performed most of the judicial and administrative tasks necessary to keep the system running, with the district judge getting involved only when a referee's decision was appealed. Then the Crash of 1929 and the Depression resulted in a huge increase in the number of bankruptcy cases filed, from 962 in fiscal 1929 (before the crash) to a peak of 2,649 in 1934. The referees did manage to keep the routine cases moving, most of which were no-asset or low-asset cases requiring little or no judicial attention, and managed to close more cases than were filed each year beginning in 1935.[66]

The corporate reorganizations, the so-called section 77b cases, were a different matter, however, taking up the judges' time, out of proportion to their number in the overall docket, and it seems that the judges rather enjoyed the experience. Although section 77b authorized the district court to keep management in place or to appoint a trustee to run the corporation, with broad powers either way, the judges of the Eastern District took a much more active role, at least during the section's first two years. In January 1936, the Associated Press ran a story which appeared across the country, including in the *New York Times*,[67] describing how, under the auspices of section 77b, the Eastern District's judges were happily engaged in operating "a distillery, a pickle factory, a university, a big manufacturing concern, numerous hotels and apartments and two hot-dog stands." Although each of the 250 companies under reorganization had a trustee in bankruptcy directly in charge of day-to-day operations, the judges, according to this article, were "[a]lmost daily called upon to decide whether new equipment should be purchased for one of the eight breweries under their control, whether the lunch wagon could improve business by putting in a new coffee urn, or if a Federal court notice should be sent John J. Doe ordering him to pay up his rent." The article quoted Judge Tuttle as remarking that: "Having a liking for business as well as law, I have enjoyed handling the cases," and concluded by noting that, as they spoke, the trustees for the distillery were before Judge O'Brien asking "if it would be all right to go into the manufacturing of vodka."

The Administrative Office of the United States Courts

Although each district judge had always jealously controlled the management of his docket independently, since 1789 judicial budgets had been controlled by Congressional appropriations and the oversight of a succession of executive-branch departments: the Treasury Department from 1789 to 1849, the Interior Department from 1849 to 1870, and then the Justice Department until 1939. By the 1930s, one of the major concerns of a majority of federal judges was the involvement in the operation of the courts of the attorney general and the Justice Department even as their representatives appeared before the judges in court as litigants. Judge Tuttle expressed those concerns in 1935: "Now, in my judgment one of the misfortunes that has grown up is not that the judges do not listen enough to the Attorney General of the United States, but that they listen too much. . . . The judges can't receive a sheet of paper or a lead pencil at the expense of the Government without a requisition which passes through the office of the Attorney General. The judges can't have a clerk of the court except one who is approved by the Attorney General. The judges can't raise the salary of their secretary a hundred dollars without getting the approval of the Attorney General. . . . I think that we have got started wrong when we fix the lawyer for the United States as the individual to whom the judges have to go for anything and everything they get. . . . I am pointing out . . . that there is a danger and that we ought to be careful to see that the Attorney

General does not control and dominate the judges. There is danger that
. . . the judges will get to saying their prayers to the Attorney General."[68]

Four years later, Congress responded to such complaints by Tuttle and
other judges by creating the Administrative Office of the United States
Courts.[69] The act appointed the director of the administrative office as "the
administrative officer of the United States courts [to] have charge, under
the supervision and direction of the conference of senior circuit judges,[70]
of . . . [a]dministrative matters relating to the offices of the clerks and other
clerical and administrative personnel of the courts," including taking over
the gathering of data regarding the dockets of the district courts, disburs-
ing funds appropriated by Congress, providing equipment and supplies,
and "[t]he providing of accommodations for the use of the courts and the
various officials and employees covered by this chapter."

Notes

1. Darwyn H. Lumley, *Breaking the Banks in the Motor City: The Auto Industry,
the 1933 Detroit Banking Crisis and the Start of the New Deal* (Jefferson, NC: Mc-
Farland and Co., 2009), 15.

2. Lumley, 13.

3. 48 Stat. 1.

4. Bald, 406–409.

5. Lumley, 32.

6. Arthur J. Tuttle to Earl C. Michener, May 20, 1935, Ernest O'Brien file, Box
34, Tuttle Papers. At this time Judge Simons had been appointed to the Sixth Circuit and had not been replaced on the district court.

7. *New York Times*, February 3, 1935.

8. *New York Times*, January 27, 1935, sec. 2, 15.

9. *Detroit Free Press*, April 7, 1935. The defendants were represented by Detroit
attorneys Clifford Longley, O. L. Smith, David Crowley, and George Burke.

10. *New York Times*, April 7, 1935, sec. 2, 2.

11. *Detroit Free Press*, April 7, 1935.

12. *U.S. v. O'Brien*, 6th Cir. Case No. 7101, Memorandum, June 5, 1935, 11.

13. *U.S. v. O'Brien*, 6th Cir. Case No. 7101, Response by Judge O'Brien, undated.

14. *New York Times*, June 30, 1935; *Detroit Free Press*, June 30, 1935, 1, 5.

15. *O'Brien v. U.S.*, 296 U.S. 637 (1935).

16. *Time*, April 20, 1936.

17. (St. Petersburg Florida) *Evening Independent*, June 10, 1937, 12.

18. *Yondotega Club v. United States*, 384 C.C.H. 1938 Fed. Tax Serv., par. 9134
(E.D. Mich. 1938).

19. 49 Stat. 659.

20. 52 Stat. 584.

21. Whether this is a new seat or a continuation of Judge Simons's seat is pure
semantics.

22. *Detroit Free Press*, February 27, 1936.

23. *Bay City Times*, February 28, 1963.

24. Bentley Historical Library, Online Database, University of Michigan Football Rosters. Picard was on the team for three years (1909–1911), including one with the varsity, as a 140-pound quarterback under coach Fielding Yost. He also exhibited musical talent. As a child, he teamed with his sister as a song-and-dance act at county fairs and he later turned to song writing.

25. In addition to his private practice, he also served as Saginaw's city attorney (1924–1928), as first chairperson of the Michigan Liquor Control Commission (1933–1934), and as first director of the Michigan Unemployment Compensation Commission (1938–1939). As the first chairperson of the Michigan Chapter of the Christian-American Palestine Committee, he worked to promote the establishment of the State of Israel.

26. Arthur J. Tuttle to J. C. Austin, October 28, 1935, Clerk of the Court Detroit file, Box 33, Tuttle Papers.

27. *Detroit News*, April 5, 1937.

28. Judges to Elmer Voorheis, December 8, 1936, Clerk of the Court Detroit file, Box 33, Tuttle Papers.

29. *New York Times*, December 23, 1936, 14.

30. Elmer Voorheis to judges, March 31, 1937, Appointment file, Box 33, Tuttle Papers.

31. Arthur J. Tuttle memo, February 16, 1937, Clerk of the Court Detroit file, Box 33, Tuttle Papers.

32. *Detroit News*, April 5, 1937; *Detroit Free Press*, April 6, 1937.

33. Except as noted, the facts of the Chebatoris case are based on accounts in the *Bay City Times*, photographs in the archives of the *Midland Daily News*, and two articles, Margaret A. Leaming, "An Occurrence at Milan—Michigan's Last Execution," *The Court Legacy*, Issue 3, April 1994,. 1; Aaron J. Veselenak, "Making Legal History—The Execution of Anthony Chebatoris," *The Court Legacy*, vol. VI, no. 2, Fall 1998, 7.

34. E.g., *Bay City Times*, July 8, 1938.

35. Neither the bridge nor that portion of Benson Street exist today.

36. David G. Chardavoyne, *A Hanging in Detroit* (Detroit, MI: Wayne State University Press, 2003).

37. 48 Stat. 783.

38. 48 Stat. 783, sec. 3: "Whoever, in committing any offense defined in this Act, or in avoiding or attempting to avoid apprehension for the commission of such offense, or in freeing himself or attempting to free himself from arrest or confinement for such offense, kills any person, or forces any person to accompany him without the consent of such person, shall be punished by imprisonment for not less than 10 years, or by death if the verdict of the jury shall so direct."

39. 49 Stat. 684, 720.

40. The indictment was amended once more, on October 26, just before the trial began, to cure a technical defect.

41. Arthur J. Tuttle to Department of Justice, July 23, 1935, Department of Justice file, Box 33, Tuttle Papers.

42. *Bay City Times*, October 27, 1937.

43. Arthur J. Tuttle to McComber, February 8, 1943, Lockhart criminal file, Box 48, Tuttle Papers.

44. *New York Times*, October 23, 1921.

45. 50 Stat. 304.

46. Michigan's treason law was not a secret although it had never been enforced.

47. *Bay City Times*, November 23, 1937.

48. See, e.g., *Time*, July 18, 1938.

49. President Roosevelt appointed Murphy to be governor-general of the Philippines (1933), U.S. attorney general (1939), and associate justice of the U.S. Supreme Court (1940).

50. Fine, *New Deal*, 428–429.

51. Fine, *New Deal*, 429.

52. Chebatoris file, Box 48, Tuttle Papers.

53. Report, Richard F. Doyle to Arthur J. Tuttle, July 9, 1938, Chebatoris file, Box 48, Tuttle Papers. The witnesses to Chebatoris's execution were: himself; U.S. marshals John H. Grogan, John D. Page, and John J. Barc; U.S. attorney John W. Babcock; Warden John J. Ryan; T. De Boskey of the Justice Department; John Bugas, F.B.I.; Ira M. Smith, Midland County sheriff; Thomas C. Wilcox, Wayne County sheriff; H. W. Pickert, Detroit commissioner of police; Chaplains W. S. Nelson and Father Lee Paige; reporters Steve Richards (U.P.), Howard Handleman (I.N.S.), and H. M. Kelly (A.P.); physicians Max O. Wolfe (U.S. Veterans Bureau), G. R. Heidenrich, B. H. Shallow, and C.W. Balser; executioner George Phillip Hanna, Epworth Illinois; and his guests Chester A. Pyle, sheriff of White County, Illinois; and Ollie R. Weaver, deputy sheriff of Vanderburg County, Indiana.

54. H. M. Kelly's story for the Associated Press was carried by the *New York Times*, July 9, 1938, and other publications.

55. *Bay City Times*, July 8, 1938.

56. James V. Bennett, *I Chose Prison* (New York: Alfred A. Knopf, 1970), 161.

57. 24 Stat. 254.

58. 49 Stat. 1140.

59. Arthur J. Tuttle to Henry Moore Bates, April 9, 1946, Law Clerk Folder, Box 35, Tuttle Papers.

60. e.g., *Kellogg Switchboard & Supply Co. v. Michigan Bell Telephone Co.*, 71 F. Supp. 365 (E.D. Mich. 1947).

61. It is indicative of the formality of their relationship, though, that Quaife's wife never met Tuttle. Author's interview with Mrs. Eleanor Ropes, December 2009.

62. 54 Stat. 210.

63. U.S. Constitution, art. I, § 8.

64. 30 Stat. 544.

65. 48 Stat. 911.

66. In 1935, of 2,325 liquidation cases closed, 1,775 had no assets to distribute to creditors, and the average gross recovery in the other 650 cases, individual and corporate, was only $1,500.

67. *New York Times*, January 12, 1936, sec. 2, 3.

68. Arthur J. Tuttle to Earl C. Michener, May 20, 1935, Ernest O'Brien file, Box 34, Tuttle Papers.

69. 53 Stat. 1223.

70. The Conference of Senior Circuit Judges, formed by statute in 1922, is now the Judicial Conference of the United States.

CHAPTER 10

The Second World War, 1940–1945

The Eastern District, 1940–1945

In 1940, the Eastern District was slowly emerging from the Great Depression, but the recovery was not obvious to many people who were still unemployed or considered themselves to be underpaid. Nationally, unemployment was close to 20 percent. In the automobile industry, the unemployment rate hovered around 50 percent. Many workers counted among the employed were on a part-time schedule. Although the district's population continued to grow, it did so at the slowest rate since 1890–1900. World War II changed all of that. Between the ramping up of the armed forces and new jobs created by war industries that popped up throughout the district, unemployment became a memory, even as hundreds of thousands of people throughout the eastern United States migrated to the district. Over the entire decade from 1940 to 1950, the district's population grew by nearly a million people to 4,826,865, an increase of 25 percent, as Wayne County alone added 420,612 residents, followed by Oakland (added 141,933), Macomb (added 77,323) and Washtenaw (added 53,796).

World War II did not swell the district court's docket as the Great War had, and the burden on each judge was thankfully less. In fact, each judge's caseload during World War II was substantially smaller than during the previous five years, largely because bank-receiver suits largely disappeared after the United States entered the war. On the other hand, new U.S. civil cases more than tripled during the war years because of claims brought on behalf of the Office of Price Administration (OPA), which was created by an executive order in August 1941 to control prices and ration tires, automobiles, shoes, nylon, sugar, gasoline, fuel oil, coffee, meats, processed foods, and many other raw materials and finished goods critical to the war effort. OPA enforcement suits, which included both civil and crimi-

Fig. 53. Detroit Tigers game, 1940. L–R: Judge O'Brien, Judge Picard, Justice Frank Murphy, Judge Moinet, Judge Simons. (Walter P. Reuther Library, Wayne State University)

nal cases, began with just a trickle but grew to 703 in 1945, fully 45 percent of U.S. civil and criminal cases filed that year. Other "war" crimes such as contractor fraud under the Contract Renegotiation and the Contract Termination Acts, and draft dodging under the Selective Service Act[1] brought the total to more than two-thirds of 1945's criminal and U.S. civil filings.[2]

Hitler's Erstwhile Buddy

Between September 1, 1939 and December 6, 1941 the war in Europe was on the mind of every American, but the fighting was far away. Echoes of

Table 10.1   Civil and Criminal Filings by Fiscal Year (July 1 to June 30), 1940–1945

Fiscal Year	Criminal	U.S. Civil	Private Civil	Total
1940	507	211	290	1,008
1941	362	294	695	1,351
1942	574	139	705	1,418
1943	567	251	253	1,071
1944	664	264	195	1,123
1945	722	743	206	1,671

the military and political events across the Atlantic did mange to occasionally reach Michigan, such as Judge Tuttle's hearings on the naturalization petition of Kurt Georg Wilhelm Ludecke, an early convert to the National Socialist Party who had written a popular book describing his friendship with Adolph Hitler. In *I Knew Hitler*, Ludecke boasted of his close personal friendship with the Fuhrer and with other Nazi officials, writing that Hitler's "appeal to German manhood was like a call to arms, the gospel he preached a sacred truth." However, he claimed that their relationship ended in 1933 when he ran afoul of his leader and spent eight months in prison.

Upon his release, Ludecke emigrated to the United States where, charming and educated, he lived off wealthy Americans who were not bothered by his continued praise for Nazi racial doctrines. He married a woman from Detroit, and in October 1938, filed a petition with immigration authorities there to obtain U.S. citizenship as the spouse of an American citizen with three years residence in the United States.[3] Naturalization commissioner Robert Wilson recommended denying the petition, and Ludecke appealed to Judge Tuttle. After a preliminary hearing on June 16, 1939, Judge Tuttle adjourned the petition so that he could read Ludecke's book.

By the time the hearing resumed on December 5, Britain and France were technically at war with Germany, although little fighting had occurred. In court, Tuttle read aloud from Ludecke's book and then described the author as a "gambler and crook," "anti-everything," and "as dumb as an oyster in the shell." Asked about his current beliefs, Ludecke said he had changed ("Even pagans have become Christians") and commented cryptically: "Americans should realize that they should do something to bring about certain reforms before it is too late." Tuttle adjourned the hearing again for two weeks to allow Ludecke to obtain counsel.[4] When he returned to court on December 18, the petitioner promised Tuttle that he was a "new Ludecke," but Tuttle was skeptical: "I believe I can still see signs of [the old Ludecke] popping up again."[5] The judge indicated that he was going to deny the application with prejudice, declaring that: "You're just a cheap politician and a hanger-on. You would have remained in Germany if you could have obtained a job from the Nazi party."[6] Tuttle entered his official opinion and order denying Ludecke's petition with prejudice on February 26, 1940.[7] After Germany declared war on the United States, Ludecke was interned for the rest of the war.

Judge Tuttle, Henry Ford, and the United Automobile Workers

In 1933 and 1934, the struggle between labor and management over unionization and collective bargaining exploded into general strikes, factory seizures, and violence. Fearing greater unrest, in July 1935 Congress passed the National Labor Relations Act (also known as the Wagner Act) for the purpose of "encouraging the practice and procedure of collective bargaining and by protecting the exercise by workers of full freedom of association, self-organization, and designation of representatives of their own choosing, for the purpose of negotiating the terms and conditions of their employment or other mutual aid or protection."[8] The General Motors Corporation reached an agreement with the United Automobile Workers (UAW) in February 1937, after a series of strikes including the Flint sit-down strike; Chrysler signed a contract a month later. By 1941, only the Ford Motor Company among Detroit's Big 3 remained a hold-out, largely due to the aging Henry Ford's virulent anti-unionism, translated into action by his brutal assistant, Harry Bennett.

Most of Michigan's judicial battles on unionization took place in state courts, and the district court remained on the sidelines, partly because of the Anti-Injunction Act of 1932,[9] which barred federal courts from entering an injunction in a labor dispute. However, the act furnished an exception if the judge found, after hearing witnesses testify in open court, "with opportunity for cross-examination," that "unlawful acts have been threatened and will be committed and will be continued unless restrained," and that the petitioner had no adequate remedy at law. In April 1941, Judge Tuttle invoked that exception to enter an injunction against the UAW.

On April 2, 1941, Bennett fired eight employees at Ford's River Rouge complex in Dearborn, Michigan, because they were UAW members. Word of the firings spread quickly, and a majority of the Rouge's 50,000 employees left work, although some stayed, including many African Americans who felt they owed loyalty to Ford for their jobs. The complex was surrounded by picketers, streets leading to the area were blocked, cars were tipped over, and fights erupted between white and black employees at the gates of the plant. As the strike continued on April 3, I. A. "Cappy" Capizzi, attorney for the Ford Motor Company, came to the district court seeking a restraining order to prevent the UAW from interfering with the company's operations. Judge Tuttle began a hearing without notifying the union and heard testimony from three witnesses. Two Dearborn police officers, Chief Carl Brooks and Inspector Charles Slamer, testified that they were powerless to stop the strike because of the size of the crowds surrounding the facility. Edward Riley, who identified himself as a Ford employee, testified that the strikers barred him from entering the plant's administration building. The union's attorney ran into court in the middle of proceedings and asked for a postponement for a few hours to gather witnesses to contradict the company's testimony. Despite the statutory mandate that each side be able to cross-examine witnesses, Judge Tuttle refused and entered the restraining order, saying that: "I think that this is a great emergency if you or I want to go to the Ford plant and we are stopped and maybe beaten up. When thousands block the street, tip over cars, and so on, I think it's time all of us recognized it is an emergency and that all of us did everything possible to put a stop to it."[10]

On April 8, Judge Tuttle began a hearing on Ford's request to make the restraining order permanent. State and federal officials, who were meeting with representatives of the company and union to settle the dispute,[11] urged Tuttle to delay the hearing, but he refused. Told by union counsel William Henry Gallagher (who had represented Aaron Sapiro against Henry Ford 15 years earlier) that the request came from Michigan's governor Murray Van Wagoner, a Democrat, Tuttle replied: "You can respect his wishes if you want to, but I don't have to. Governors come and go in this State, but I'm on the bench all the time."[12] Turning back to the hearing, Tuttle grilled Laurence A. Lyons, the commander of the Michigan State Police unit on the scene, asking why he had not dispersed the strikers by force. Lyons replied that he could have cleared the streets, but only at the cost of three or four hundred deaths. Asked by the judge if he feared for his life and those of his men, Lyons replied: "We get paid to get killed, but we would consider it a blot on the name of the community if riot and bloodshed occurred."

The union kept up the pressure for ten days. As they had during the Sapiro trial, Henry Ford's wife, Clara, and son, Edsel, convinced Ford to settle, and he agreed to concessions that went beyond union demands. On June 21, the Ford Motor Company became a closed shop, meaning all employees had to be union members, and the company initiated a "dues check-off" provision, which would allow union dues to be deducted from payroll and sent directly to the union. The company thus leaped to the forefront of labor-management relations.

In August 1941, the automobile industry was ordered to begin switching production from civilian vehicles to military vehicles and weapons. The attack on Pearl Harbor in December 1941 finally brought the United States into the war and on February 10, 1942 the manufacture of civilian automobiles ended for the duration. Ironically, Ford found its union contract a great advantage in attracting the additional workers necessary to produce tanks, trucks, and bombers. Although Judge Tuttle ended his hearing, the UAW was not forgiving. At its next national convention, union delegates passed a resolution calling on Congress to impeach Judge Tuttle.[13] The union's stated grounds were that he had slandered the CIO and had denied citizenship to immigrants based solely on their membership in the CIO, but there was little doubt that the Ford restraining order was the impetus. As the UAW certainly anticipated, Congress ignored its resolution.

Treason on Trial

Certainly the court's most noteworthy wartime case was the capital treason trial of Detroit tavern owner Max Stephan.[14] Born in Cologne, Germany, in 1892, Stephan left school at the age of 14 and apprenticed as a grocer. He served in the German army before and during World War I, and after the war spent time as a police officer before turning to his life's work of running a saloon. In 1928, he emigrated to Windsor, Ontario, and a year later his wife, Agnes, followed. They used a mail-drop scheme to convince U.S. authorities that they had lived in the United States for five years, and in 1935 they both became U.S. citizens. Max opened a German restaurant and meeting hall in a ramshackle frame building across East Jefferson Avenue from Detroit's Belle Isle park. The couple lived above the restaurant and their establishment became a favored gathering place for the city's German immigrants, particularly those who still had a sense of allegiance towards Germany.

On the morning of April 18, 1942, four months after the attack on Pearl Harbor, Max Stephan received a telephone call from one of those German loyalists, Margareta Bertelmann. She told him that she had at her home a German pilot who had escaped from a prisoner-of-war camp in Canada and needed help. Mrs. Bertelmann, who had never sought U.S. citizenship, was one of a group of women who provided knitting and food packages to

Fig. 54.   Max Stephan. (Walter P. Reuther Library, Wayne State University)

German prisoners of war in Canada. By law, the packages had to include a return address, and thus her name and address became known to the POWs. At Bertelmann's apartment, which consisted of the upper floor of a duplex house at 259 Philip Street in Detroit, Stephan met 22-year-old *Leutnant* (second lieutenant) Hans Peter Krug whose *Luftwaffe* Dornier-17-Z bomber had been shot down over England during the Battle of Britain. He was captured and shipped to Canada with other captured Germans to what the Canadian authorities in all innocence termed officially a "concentration camp" at Bowmanville, Ontario, east of Toronto. On April 15, 1942, Krug escaped and, posing as a French sailor (though he spoke no French), he managed to reach Windsor two days later. In the early hours of Saturday, April 18, 1842, he paddled a rowboat with one oar across the Detroit River to Belle Isle, then walked across the bridge to the U.S. mainland. After a couple of false starts, he found the Bertlemann residence and rang the bell.

Krug asked Stephan for help in making his way to neutral Mexico where German diplomats could return him to Germany and the war. After Stephan drove Krug to his restaurant, which Krug had walked past unknowingly earlier that morning, he suggested that Krug take a walk around downtown Detroit, which, strangely, the fugitive did. Later, Stephan took Krug to several cafes and bars where he bought the pilot drinks and food, even though Krug's photo was prominently displayed on the front page of Detroit's newspapers and on wanted posters. They made an odd pair, the short, middle-aged, and doughy tavern owner and the young, fit, coldly handsome flier. When asked, Stephan said Krug was a friend from Milwaukee or "one of Meier's boys,"[15] although he did tell the truth to another German immigrant, Theodore Donay. Among their stops was 54 Duffield Street, a frame, two-story house kept as a brothel by Alvina Ludlow, where Stephan paid $3 for Krug to have a brief session with an aging prostitute. As evening fell, Stephan offered to have Krug speak at the next evening's meeting of a German social club at the restaurant. Krug wisely declined, and Stephan arranged for him to spend the night at the Field Hotel near his restaurant. The next morning, Sunday, April 19, Stephan bought Krug a chicken dinner, gave him some money, and put him on a Greyhound bus to Chicago.

At least one person, Dietrich Rintelin, Donay's sales clerk, reported Krug's presence to the Detroit office of the Federal Bureau of Investigation, which apparently did nothing until Sunday night when agents raided Stephan's restaurant and arrested him. Stephan quickly caved in during interrogation and gave a detailed written confession. Agnes Stephan, Margareta Bertelmann, and Theodore Donay were also arrested. The story broke in Detroit's newspapers on April 21, with high praise for the FBI, but the next day's headlines reported that federal officials had lost track of Krug. His meandering escape led him from Chicago to Philadelphia, New

York, Pittsburgh, Dallas, and San Antonio, where a suspicious hotel clerk turned him in on May 1. Under the Geneva Convention, Krug could not be charged with escape, so the FBI returned him to Canada. Agents kept in contact, stroking his considerable ego, and managed to convince him to testify at Stephan's trial, even though, under the Geneva Convention, he could not be forced to reveal the names of people who assisted him or what they did.

Max Stephan was initially charged only with harboring an illegal alien, but on May 23 U.S. attorney general Nicholas Biddle announced that the government would ask the Eastern District's grand jury to indict him for committing treason, defined by the U.S. Constitution as "levying war against [the United States], adhering to their enemies, [or] giving them aid and comfort."[16] The grand jury obliged on June 18,[17] and Judge Tuttle arraigned Stephan the next day. At the same time, Theodore Donay was being arrested, arraigned before Judge Moinet, and charged with misprision of treason, i.e. with failing to report Stephan's treasonous acts. It seems likely that Donay is the only person ever charged by the United States with that crime.

Stephan's trial began on Monday, June 29, 1942, after Judge Tuttle settled behind the bench in a hot and humid million-dollar courtroom. The government was represented by the same men who had prosecuted Tony Chebatoris five years earlier, District Attorney John C. Lehr and his assistant, John Babcock. Max Stephan had a difficult time finding an attorney willing to represent him, but Verne C. Amberson of Detroit, a 1907 graduate of the University of Michigan Law School and a veteran of World War I, volunteered to take the case. After a jury of six men and six women was sworn in and John Lehr gave the government's opening statement, proofs began with preliminary testimony to establish for the record the undisputed facts that Max Stephan was a U.S. citizen and that the United States was at war with Germany.

The prosecution's star witness was Hans Peter Krug, recently promoted to *Oberleutnant* (first lieutenant), who marched into the courtroom resplendent in his dark blue *Luftwaffe* dress uniform trimmed in silver threads, regulation white shirt and black tie, and with the swastika displayed prominently on his pilot's badge and on his hat. He flashed a Nazi salute to Judge Tuttle and then told his story in a cold voice, with frequent displays of arrogance. Why Krug chose to testify is a mystery. As a POW he did not have to, and he insisted on the stand that he was there to testify on behalf of Max Stephan. Perhaps he was just young, self-important, and easily flattered by the FBI, or perhaps he just wanted a few more days away from the boredom, squalor, and bad food of the POW camp. Whatever his reasoning, his performance sank Max Stephan, whose only chance for acquittal, if he ever had any, was to convince the jury that he had just been trying to help a poor lost boy, and not, as he was charged, giving aid

Fig. 55. Lt. Hans Peter Krug. (Walter P. Reuther Library, Wayne State University)

and comfort to the German war machine. Instead of a lost boy, the jury saw a living example of the fanatical Nazi who featured prominently in the popular press. Krug spent four hours on the stand, split between June 29 and 30. Then the government called witnesses to establish that Krug was a POW and had escaped, while others, including Mrs. Ludlow and the prostitute, testified to seeing Stephan and Krug together.

On Wednesday, July 1, the government rested, and Amberson, who had cross-examined most of the prosecution witnesses, surprised spectators who packed the courtroom by declaring that the defense would rest without calling any witnesses of its own. When court resumed on Thursday, July 2, Judge Tuttle began by announcing that, after reflecting overnight, he was striking all testimony and other references to Krug's visit to the brothel. Apparently, he wanted a more family-friendly transcript for posterity. He then directed John Babcock to begin the prosecution's closing argument. Babcock, florid and emotional, contrasted Stephan's oath of citizenship with the signers of the Declaration of Independence, reminded the jurors of Stephan's enduring love for the *Vaterland*, and showed them how the facts brought out at trial led to only one possible verdict, guilty. In his summation for the defense, Amberson tweaked the government for relying on a Nazi officer's testimony, admitted that there were no facts in controversy, and identified the real issue to be whether there was any evidence that Max Stephan had acted with the intent to harm the United States. John Lehr's rebuttal completed the arguments, and Judge Tuttle instructed the jurors and sent them to the jury room to deliberate. The jury's first ballot was 11 to 1 for conviction, but only because the foreman, Jerry Armstrong from Emmett in the Thumb, wanted to make sure they discussed the evidence. The second ballot was unanimous, and, at 5:35 p.m., about 80 minutes after the jury withdrew, they signaled that they had reached a verdict. When the cast of characters reassembled, Armstrong announced that they found Stephan guilty as charged. Judge Tuttle set the sentencing date for a week later, court was adjourned, and Stephan was returned to the federal prison at Milan.

In fact, it took a month before Tuttle was satisfied that he knew enough about Max Stephan to decide on the sentence. Although the U.S. Constitution defined treason, it left the punishment to Congress, and in 1942, that punishment was death or imprisonment for not less than five years and a fine of not less than $10,000. The judge reviewed a report from his probation officer, which listed several liquor-law violations as well as the Stephans' scheme for becoming citizens. He also interviewed Max Stephan twice, with counsel present. It was not until August 6, the 30th anniversary of the judge's elevation to the bench, that Stephan returned to the million-dollar courtroom to be sentenced.

After asking Stephan if he had anything to say, Judge Tuttle read aloud a 45-minute explanation for his decision. He noted that Krug had intended to return to Germany and bear arms against American boys. He praised the loyalty of most German-Americans and declared that the sentence he imposed had to send a message to any other disloyal Americans. Obviously referring to his experience with spies in World War I, he explained that only a death sentence would have the desired effect because it was well-known that spies and subversives convicted during that war were released when it ended. Tuttle concluded by directing that Stephan be returned to Milan where, on November 13, 1942, "the said defendant [shall] be by the United States Marshal hanged by the neck until he, the said Max Stephan, is dead."

Appeals delayed the execution. On December 12, 1942, the Sixth Circuit affirmed the verdict and sentence, so a new attorney for Stephan, Nicholas Salowich, sought review by the Supreme Court, based on an issue that had not been raised at trial. In his written confession, Stephan had claimed that, before he sent Krug on his way, he asked one of his customers, William Nagel, Detroit's retired U.S. postmaster, what to do. According to Stephan, Nagel told him to go ahead because Krug would be caught soon enough anyway. Nagel denied it all. On April 5, 1943, the Supreme Court ruled that there was no basis for reversing the decision, and a new execution date was set, but it too was delayed. Finally, all appeals exhausted, Tuttle set the execution for July 2, 1943, a year after the verdict.

Judge Tuttle received hundreds of letters regarding his sentence, most congratulating him, but a few asking for mercy. There is no indication that Tuttle ever wavered in his belief that he had done the right thing, but other members of the federal government were quietly in favor of a commutation to life in prison. John Lehr's rebuttal argument at trial suggested that the prosecutors were in favor of prison and a fine when he stated that some traitorous acts, although they could not be excused, did not warrant the death penalty. After the trial, Lehr let it be known that he included Stephan's acts in that category. U.S. Supreme Court justice Frank Murphy, who, as governor of Michigan, had asked that Anthony Chebatoris be executed outside Michigan, wrote President Roosevelt asking for clemency for Stephan, as did U.S. Circuit Court of Appeals Judge Learned Hand and Solicitor General Charles H. Fahy. On July 1, just hours before the execution, the president did commute Stephan's sentence to life in prison, much to the disgust of Judge Tuttle, who wrote the president pleading that Stephan's citizenship not be revoked for fear that after the war he would be released and deported like Albert Kaltschmidt. Tuttle need not have worried, as Max Stephan never left the United States or even the federal penal system. He died of cancer on January 13, 1952, aged 59, at the Springfield, Missouri, hospital for federal prisoners.

In May 1943, Hans Krug returned to Detroit and the district court, this time to Judge Picard's courtroom, to testify in Theodore Donay's trial for misprision of treason. Krug was no help to this defendant either as he testified that Stephan had told Donay who Krug was when they met. Krug argued with Judge Picard (who frequently mentioned his two sons in military service), and at one point refused to answer questions, although he changed his mind after a discussion with his FBI handlers. After the trial, Krug returned to the P.O.W. camp in Canada. He tried to escape once more, but was quickly recaptured. In 1946, he returned to Germany and eventually became a successful businessman. After a short trial, Donay was convicted and sentenced to a $1,000 fine and six and a half years in prison, in addition to the year he had spent at the Milan prison awaiting trial. He served his sentence and upon his release was allowed to remain in the United States while he appealed the revocation of his citizenship certificate. In September 1949, Judge Lederle denied his petition to restore his citizenship, and Donay appealed to the Sixth Circuit. In April 1950, as the Court of Appeals was considering the matter, Donay traveled to California, where he rented a small boat from a marina on Catalina Island, 20 miles offshore from Los Angeles. He failed to return on time, and several hours later the boat was found empty and drifting eight miles from the island.[18] His disappearance was ruled a suicide, although there were news reports of a mysterious submarine surfacing in the general area at a time Donay might have been in the boat. A month after Donay's disappearance, the Sixth Circuit affirmed Judge Lederle's ruling revoking Donay's citizenship.[19]

Spy or Pawn?

If there was no real doubt about the facts in Max Stephan's treason case, the same cannot be said for another high-profile espionage case that dragged on for nine years, even after the war ended. The story begins early on the morning of August 24, 1943, when six FBI agents knocked on the door of the Detroit home of Heinrich and Marianna von Moltke, a Wayne (now Wayne State) University professor and his wife.[20] Although Professor von Moltke was a naturalized U.S. citizen and the couple had lived in Detroit for many years, his wife, described as "greying, talkative [and] poesy-minded,"[21] had never sought to become a citizen. Agents ordered Mrs. von Moltke to accompany them to their local office where she was fingerprinted, photographed, and examined by a physician. From there she was placed in solitary confinement and, according to her later statement, questioned "persistently but courteously" by FBI agents for 11 hours daily for four days and told only that she was being held indefinitely "as a dangerous enemy alien" who "was not allowed to see an attorney."

Mrs. von Moltke was one of five persons arrested in Detroit that morning as members of an espionage ring alleged to be led by trained Nazi spy Grace Buchanan-Dineen, a Canadian citizen and graduate of Vassar College who claimed to be a French countess, and by Jugoslavian-born Theresa Behrens. Both were alleged to have used their contacts in Detroit's social circles to collect intelligence for Germany about Detroit's war plants. The arrests caused a sensation in Detroit and across the country. *Time* magazine marveled at the "storybook" plot,[22] and the *New York Times* carried a lengthy report of the charges against the bogus countess and her minions.[23] Meanwhile, Wayne University fired Heinrich von Moltke from his position teaching German, even though he was not charged with anything.

Twenty-five days after her arrest, Mrs. von Moltke, who, ironically, was a real German "Grafin," or countess who never used her title, received a copy of an indictment charging her with conspiracy to violate the Espionage Act of 1917.[24] Although the indictment alleged that other defendants spied on specific targets, as to Mrs. von Moltke it alleged only that she "met and conferred with" one or more of the other defendants and that she "introduced" someone to one of the defendants. Three days later, 28 days after being arrested, Mrs. von Moltke and another defendant were arraigned before Judge Moinet. Because they had no lawyer, Moinet directed an attorney who was sitting in the courtroom to "help these two women out," and, taking the attorney's advice, she stood mute and was ordered detained at the Wayne County jail.

Judge Moinet promised to appoint permanent counsel for her, but never did, and the FBI continued to interrogate her without counsel present. She later claimed that during those interrogations an agent told her that she could be guilty of conspiracy just by being present when the other defendants schemed, even if she did not know what was going on. For that or for some other reason, she was convinced to plead guilty and was taken to court on October 7, 1943. Judge Moinet was busy, so the district attorney took her to Judge Lederle. At first, Lederle refused to accept the plea because she lacked counsel, but after she told him that her plea was voluntary and agreed to sign a form waiving her right to counsel, he did allow her to plead guilty. The proceeding took "five minutes during an interlude in another trial."

Before she could be sentenced, Mrs. von Moltke tried to change her plea back to not guilty. Judge Moinet denied her petition and, on November 14, 1944, sentenced her to four years in prison. In early 1946, with the war over, Mrs. von Moltke petitioned for a writ of habeas corpus against A. Blake Gillies, superintendent of the Detroit House of Correction, on the grounds that she had been deprived of access to counsel when she pleaded guilty. Judge O'Brien denied the petition because he found that her waiver of counsel had been voluntary and that federal officials "were meticulous in safeguarding the rights of the petitioner."[25] O'Brien noted that: "The petitioner is a woman obviously of good education and above the average in intelligence. Her knowledge of English was fluent and ample. She had discussed the case with various people before the plea of guilty was entered."

The Sixth Circuit affirmed Judge O'Brien in March 1947, although Circuit Judge McAllister dissented strongly, pointing out the coercive nature of her detention and interrogation.[26] On June 2, 1947, the U.S. Supreme Court granted *certiorari* just two weeks before Mrs. von Moltke was released from prison and almost four years after she was arrested. Although free, she continued to challenge her conviction in order to avoid deportation. On January 19, 1948, a majority of the Supreme Court agreed with Judge McAllister and remanded the case to the district court to review the validity of her waiver of counsel. Justice Hugo Black warned that courts trying such emotional cases had to be careful: "We were waging total war with Germany. She had a German name. She was a German. She had been a German countess. The war atmosphere was saturated at that time with a suspicion and fear of Germans. . . . If found guilty, she could have been, and many people might think should have been, legally put to death as punishment for violation of the Espionage Act. . . . Anyone charged with espionage in wartime under the statute in question would have sorely needed a lawyer; Mrs. von Moltke in particular, desperately needed the best she could get."[27] Justice Felix Frankfurter was particularly concerned that the FBI agents may have convinced her that she could be guilty of conspiracy without knowing any wrong was occurring.

In March 1949, Mrs. von Moltke got her new hearing on her plea before Judge Picard. After listening to testimony over five days, Judge Picard (the fourth district judge on the case), dismissed the writ. He held that she had been aware of her rights and that the agent's alleged bad legal advice occurred after she had already decided to plead guilty. The Sixth Circuit affirmed, with Judge Mcallister once again dissenting.[28] On April 21, 1952, the Supreme Court affirmed by an equally divided court,[29] ending Mrs. von Moltke's legal fight just short of nine years after her arrest.

As for the other alleged spies, Buchanan-Dineen pleaded guilty and was sentenced to 12 years in federal prison. Behrens also pleaded guilty and received a 20-year sentence. In February 1944, both women testified against Dr. Frederick W. Thomas, a Detroit obstetrician. On the stand, Buchanan-Dineen revealed that she had been arrested in March 1942 by the FBI and worked as a double agent since. Thomas was convicted by a jury on February 24, 1944, after a four-week trial presided over by Judge Moinet, although his conviction was reversed on appeal and he was not retried.[30] Buchanan-Dineen was paroled in 1948 and deported to Canada.

The Boys in the Bund

The German-American Bund was the last incarnation of a Nazi front organization that began in 1924 in Chicago as the Free Union Teutonia. As the organization grew, it included youth, social, and paramilitary groups that mirrored their German counterparts. At its height, in February 1939, the Bund held a rally in Madison Square Garden where 20,000 members in Nazi-style uniforms adorned with swastikas gave the Nazi salute, waved American flags, and listened to their "fuhrer," Fritz Kuhn, rant against Jews. Not long after, though, Kuhn was convicted of embezzling money from Bund contributions, and the organization went into decline and dissolved just before the attack on Pearl Harbor.

Detroit, with its large population of German immigrants, had a very active chapter of the Bund. In 1944, District Attorney John C. Lehr petitioned the district court to revoke the naturalized citizenship of seven men who had been Bund members. Following a hearing, Judge Moinet, in an opinion that provides a detailed history of the Bund, granted the petitions and revoked the respondents' citizenship.[31] He held that "Adherence to the program of the German-American Bund and its predecessor organizations is incompatible with being well disposed toward the good order and happiness of the United States of America." Although the judge conceded that mere membership in the Bund was not enough to set aside a naturalization, "the nature and extent of membership or participation of the defendant in the activities of the German-American Bund and its predecessor organizations and knowledge on the part of the defendant of the real purposes of the Bund may be considered along with other proof by the court in determining whether or not fraud existed at the time of the defendant's naturalization." Judge Moinet found that each of the respondents had lied in taking the oath of citizenship when he swore allegiance to the United States and renounced "absolutely and forever all allegiance and fidelity . . . to the German Reich."

The Death of the Dean of the Federal Bench

On November 8, 1944, Judge Tuttle grudgingly endured his 76th birthday. Although his mind was still sharp and his temperament remained crusty, his vaunted physical condition had deteriorated. He had been a patient for several weeks in Detroit's Henry Ford Hospital for treatment of arthritis. He characteristically tried to keep his docket running via letters and notes to his staff, although he refused all visitors. Judge Tuttle died in the hospital on December 3, 1944, and was buried at Woodlawn Cemetery in his native Leslie, Michigan, next to his parents and his wife. Two days after his death, his long-time secretary Josephine M. Bowman replied to a note of condolence from the director of the Administrative Office of the U.S. Courts: "No one could be associated for so many years with such a kind and considerate employer as Judge Tuttle without becoming deeply attached to him, and I grieve at his passing. But I remind myself of his own philosophy, so often expressed to others, that one should not grieve because of loss at such a time, but rather rejoice in the good fortune of having had the long association. The influence which Judge Tuttle unconsciously exerted upon those of us who worked with him was so good and great that we shall never be able to evaluate it. For that helpful influence, and for many pleasant and happy memories, I am deeply grateful."

District Judge Arthur A. Koscinski

Born: April 1, 1887 (Posen, Poland), to Anthony and Mary Lula Koscinski
Education: St. Mary's College and Seminary, Orchard Lake, MI; University of
    Michigan Law School (LL.B. 1910)
Nominated/Confirmed: June 4/July 17, 1945 (Harry S. Truman)

Fig. 56. Judge Arthur A. Koscin-ski. (Historical Society for the United States District Court for the Eastern District of Michigan)

Vacancy: Arthur J. Tuttle (Died)
Senior Status: April 30, 1957
Left Court: November 21, 1957 (Died)

President Roosevelt selected Detroit attorney Arthur A. Koscinski to suc-ceed Judge Tuttle. Roosevelt died before the approval process was com-plete, and President Truman made the nomination. The second judge of the Eastern District born in Europe, Koscinski and his parents emigrated from Poland to Detroit in 1889. After law school, he went into private prac-tice with his brother Leopold, which he maintained until he became a dis-trict judge. He had a long history of public service, ran unsuccessfully as the Democratic candidate for Michigan secretary of state in 1944, and served on many state, county, and city commissions. In 1913, Judge Kos-cinski married Blanche C. Kruse of Manistee, Michigan; they had three children.

Judge Picard and the Portal-to-Portal Case

Because Judge Picard is so strongly identified with the court's Northern Division, many people assume that he tried that courtroom's most famous case, the capital murder trial of Anthony Chebatoris. In fact, Picard was not yet a district judge in 1937, when Judge Tuttle sentenced Chebatoris to death. Judge Picard's two best-known cases, the Smith Act trial in 1954 and his 1943 decision on the portal-to-portal rule, were part of his De-troit docket and proceedings in those cases took place in the 1934 Detroit

Federal Building. The Smith Act trial, to be discussed later, is better remembered today, but the portal-to-portal case, which had tremendous social and economic implications at the time, was the case that obituary writers recalled at the time of his death in 1963.

Before 1938, it was common for industrial employers to require employees to arrive for work long before their shift began, sometimes just so that they would be poised at their posts and ready to begin production when the whistle blew to start the shift, but in other companies to perform such tasks as unloading supplies needed that day from railroad boxcars or warehouses. It was also customary for employers not to pay employees for this extra time unless there was a local contract or practice to the contrary. In June 1938, Congress passed the Fair Labor Standards Act (FLSA),[32] which established national minimum hourly wage standards and mandatory overtime pay for time worked more than a weekly maximum (initially 44 hours, then reduced, in steps, to 40 hours) for employees involved in producing goods for interstate commerce. Employers resisted the new law as an intrusion in their relationship with their employees; and even some union leaders resented the federal interference in their negotiations with management. In 1941, in *U.S. v. Darby*,[33] the Supreme Court held the FLSA constitutional, but the decision and the language of the FLSA itself left many questions unanswered, including just which activities had to be included in any time subject to the minimum wage and the statutory work week. Did the FLSA mandate a "portal-to-portal" rule, which began counting the minutes when an employee entered the plant, or did it allow an employer to count only the formal shift time, or did it mean something else? For most employers and employees struggling through the Great Depression, this issue was a source of contention, but was not foremost on their minds.

In the spring of 1941, the Mount Clemens Pottery Company, a subsidiary of the S. S. Kresge Company which produced chinaware for sale at Kresge stores, was in the midst of labor turmoil. The Michigan branch of the Congress of Industrial Organizations (CIO), led by August Scholle, was trying to organize the plant's 1,200 employees. In April, Scholle called a strike that lasted for three weeks until management agreed to hold a recognition election. In November 1941, when no election had been scheduled and management fired 12 union leaders, Scholle led the employees out for an extended strike. Ultimately, the strike failed, partly because Michigan governor Murray Van Wagoner, a Democrat, sent in the state police to break up picket lines, and in March 1942, the employees returned to work without a union. While the strike was on, though, Scholle decided to use the FLSA as a bargaining chip by suing the company for a host of violations regarding minimum wages and overtime pay.[34] When he could interest no Michigan attorney in the case, Scholle enlisted veteran labor attorney Edward Lamb from Toledo, Ohio.

Lamb's complaint filed in the district court in Detroit included a claim that the company required its production employees to begin work 14 minutes before the shift officially began, to stay at their work stations 14 minutes after their lunch break began, to return to their work stations 14 minutes before the lunch break ended, and to remain at work for 14 minutes after their shift ended, all without pay. The company conceded that employees clocked in and out before and after their shift, but argued that this was necessary to avoid a crush at the time clocks and that the employees were not required to begin or continue work out of shift time, except for "preliminary work" necessary to prepare for the beginning of the shift.[35] It seems that, at least initially, the positions of the parties were moderate: the employees did not argue to be paid for every second they were at the plant, and the company did not insist on paying them only for the actual shift time. This happy state did not last long.

The case was assigned to Judge Picard who appointed Donald Quaife as special master to take proofs and report to him. Quaife held extensive fact-finding over 23 days of testimony and, in March 1943, prepared a detailed report that recommended dismissing the suit. Quaife found that the employees were not required to work the extra 56 minutes per shift that Lamb had alleged, although they did perform some preliminary work, and he concluded that this time ought not to be not included in an FLSA calculation as a matter of law. He also recommended that the extra time not be a basis for damages in this case because there was no evidence except the employees' timecards as to how much time any individual employee spent on preliminary work, as opposed to standing around. Thus, Quaife concluded that any award of damages would be speculative.[36]

Although he had appointed Donald Quaife to be the master, Judge Picard apparently had his own ideas as to how to analyze the evidence. Instead of accepting or rejecting Quaife's report, Judge Picard reviewed the evidence himself, including a detailed analysis, entry by entry, of hundreds of timecards. In an opinion dated June 30, 1943, Picard held for the employees, but with qualifications: instead of adopting the portal-to-portal rule, he based his ruling on the time, according to his calculations, that production work really started, as opposed to when workers arrived at the plant or when their shift began.[37] Because most of the employees were paid by the piece, Picard assumed that each work group would begin as soon as its members were present, without regard to when the shift officially began: "It is apparent, therefore, that practically every member of the entire shift was ready to work at from 5 to 7 minutes before the hour and it does not seem probable that with compensation set by piece work, and the crew ready, that these employees didn't start to work immediately." On the other hand, he found that, on average, it took the employees seven minutes after clocking in to walk to their stations. He also found that the employees spent a minute or two each shift donning special apparel. From all of his detailed computations of averages, based on Quaife's meticulous fact-finding, Judge Picard held that each employee at the Mount Clemens Pottery Company was entitled to be paid, and to receive credit toward overtime, from clock-in to clock-out (essentially, without using those words, portal-to-portal), less seven minutes travel time per shift. On that basis, he entered judgment against the company in the amount of $2,415.74 plus attorney fees and costs.

Picard's decision did not create any immediate public interest. He, himself, seemed to feel that he had, for the most part, confirmed Quaife's report. The employees did not get rich, and, given the wartime labor shortage, the company might have licked its wounds, paid the judgment, modified its procedures, and gone on with its business. Instead, Mount Clemens Pottery Company appealed. At first it seemed to be a sound move. On May 21, 1945, the week after V. E. Day, the Sixth Circuit reversed Judge Picard's ruling and ordered the case dismissed. The Court of Appeals held that, because there was substantial evidence to support Quaife's report, and because Quaife had not committed clear error, Judge Picard was obligated to accept Quaife's conclusions. The appellate court also rejected Judge Picard's use of an "arbitrary formula" that "produced a judgment based upon surmise and conjecture." Instead, the court explained, "the burden rested on each of the plaintiffs here to prove by a preponderance of the evidence that he did not receive the wages that he was entitled to receive under the Fair Labor Standards Act, and to show by evidence, not resting upon conjecture, the extent of overtime worked. It does not suffice for the employee to base his right to recovery on a mere estimated average of overtime worked. To uphold a judgment based on such uncertain and conjectural evidence would be to rest it upon speculation."[38]

The employees, with little to lose, sought review from the Supreme Court, which granted *certiorari*. On June 10, 1946, the Court reversed the decision of the Sixth Circuit, although it did not entirely uphold Judge Picard's ruling either.[39] During the years since Lamb first filed suit, the Court had considered the portal-to-portal issue twice in mining cases, and had held that walking underground from the pit head to the mine face was dangerous and undeniably work, for which the miners had to be compensated.[40] The Court now had to decide how much further the FLSA was meant to go. In an opinion by Justice Frank Murphy, the Court first rejected Picard's formula for deciding when "productive work" took place and also agreed with the Court of Appeals that he should have accepted Quaife's report on that issue. Murphy also explained, however, that this error was moot because the proper measure under FLSA was not just time when productive work occurred but "all time during which an employee is necessarily required to be on the employer's premises, on duty or at a prescribed workplace." In this case, said Murphy, such compensable time included "the time necessarily spent by the employees in walking to work on the employer's premises, following the punching of the time clocks," as well as "certain preliminary activities after arriving at their places of work, such as putting on aprons and overalls, removing shirts, taping or greasing arms, putting on finger cots, preparing the equipment for productive work, turning on switches for lights and machinery, opening windows and assembling and sharpening tools." In essence, portal-to-portal.

The Supreme Court also dealt with Quaife's concern about the sufficiency of the evidence of individual claims for damages. Murphy agreed that the employees had the burden of proof, but he also held that it was the employer's duty to keep adequate records of each employee's work time, and that if an employer failed to do so, the employee was relieved of the duty to prove damages precisely. Finally, the Court gave the employer a break: finders of fact were to use a *de minimis* standard, "so that insubstantial and insignificant periods of time spent in preliminary activities need not be included in the statutory workweek." The Court then remanded the case back to Judge Picard to scour the record and to make such further findings as to damages as the evidence warranted.

At first, the Supreme Court's decision went almost unnoticed except by the pottery company and its employees. Then Scholle spread the word, and, in a few months, portal-to-portal was front-page news across the nation. Unions began filing suits everywhere seeking back-pay, reaching back as far as the statutes of limitations would allow. The damages alleged in the suits filed by the end of 1946 exceeded $1 billion nationally (and $38 million in Detroit alone), and they increased quickly to $5 billion by February 1947.[41] The *Wage Earner*, a newspaper published in Detroit by the Association of Catholic Trade Unionists, whooped that all industrial employees could expect to recover up to $1,000 each. The newspaper also noted the irony that, had the CIO succeeded in unionizing the company, the suit likely would have been dismissed voluntarily and the pay issue dealt with in collective bargaining.[42] Conservatives blamed Picard for opening up this can of worms, even though it was the Supreme Court's interpretation of the FLSA that precipitated what they saw as a dire crisis. Senator James Eastland of Mississippi went so far as to call for Picard to be impeached because he had, Eastland alleged, stated in open court that he wanted employees to get all that was due them.[43] For his part, Picard, who had resumed hearings on the case in February 1947, was frustrated by the difficulties in complying with the Supreme Court's directive and by the intransigence of the parties.

Although nothing came of Eastland's bluster, Congress did act to vitiate the effect of the Supreme Court's ruling. Representative John W. Gwynne, a Republican from Iowa, introduced a bill with two goals in mind: to invalidate all existing FLSA overtime claims, and to limit portal-to-portal claims in the future. The bill, which became the Portal-to-Portal Act of 1947,[44] barred *all* claims for minimum wages or overtime pay based on work done before the act's passage on May 14, 1947. It also provided that, for work performed after that date, no claims could be made for "walking, riding, or traveling to and from the actual place of performance of the principal activity or activities which such employee is employed to perform" or "activities which are preliminary or postliminary to such principal activity or activities." Besides creating a new word, postliminary, Congress essentially replicated Judge Picard's emphasis on the productive process rather than on time spent on the employer's premises. Future cases would shift the balance that Congress intended to achieve by expanding the interpretation of what kind of work constitutes a principal activity, but Judge Picard's name would remain associated with the portal-to-portal concept.

Notes

1. 54 Stat. 885. Unlike 1917, there was little or no organized opposition to World War II or to the draft except among a few American Nazis. See, e.g., *U.S. v. Baecker*, 55 F. Supp. 403 (E.D. Mich. 1944). The district court had fewer than 300 draft cases during and just after the war, some of which involved the rights of returning veterans under the act rather than draft evasion.

2. Although much of the business of the OPA and other federal agencies was crucial to the war effort, some of their activities involved the federal government in minute details of private lives, and some of the cases seem a poor use of the district judges' time. For example, in *Bowles v. Slater*, 64 F. Supp. 387 (E.D. Mich. 1945), a case brought for the OPA, the question facing Judge Moinet and Donald Quaife, sitting as a special master, was whether landlords in Pontiac violated the Emergency Price Control Act by ending their policy of discounting one dollar from the monthly rent of tenants who paid on the due date or who had rented from the same landlord for two years. After a trial and hearings before both the master and the judge, the court ruled in favor of the OPA and ordered the defendants to refund a couple of dollars in discounts to each eligible tenant.

3. Eastern District of Michigan Naturalization Petition 119289. Except as indicated otherwise, facts are from Judge Tuttle's opinion of February 26, 1940, published in *Petition of Ludecke*, 31 F. Supp. 521 (E.D. Mich. 1940).

4. *New York Times*, December 6, 1939.

5. *Time Magazine*, January 1, 1940.

6. *German Studies Review*, vol. 26, no. 3 (10/2003), 597.

7. *Petition of Ludecke*, 31 F. Supp. 521 (E.D. Mich. 1940). It did not help Ludecke's case that in his book he described Detroit and its suburbs as "the least delightful scene to which my travels ever carried me." Kurt G. W. Ludecke, *I Knew Hitler: The Story of a Nazi Who Escaped the Blood Purge* (New York: Charles Scribner's Sons, 1937), 194.

8. 49 Stat. 449, codified, as amended, at 29 U.S.C. §§ 151–169.

9. 47 Stat. 70.

10. *New York Times*, April 4, 1941.

11. Their effort became more complicated when officials of the American Federation of Labor (A.F.L.) tried to intervene in the negotiations. The U.A.W. had been a member of the AFL but had broken away in 1938 to become part of the more mili-

tant Congress of Industrial Organizations (CIO). The AFL sent a former president of the CIO to Detroit to stake a claim to represent the automobile workers. In the election which followed Ford's agreement to accept a union, the UAW easily defeated the AFL backed option. The AFL and CIO merged in 1955, by which time both organizations were part of mainstream American life.

12. *New York Times*, April 9, 1941.

13. *New York Times*, August 14, 1941.

14. Except where I indicate another source, I have relied on James R. Wilson, *No Ordinary Crime: An Authentic Tale of Justice Influenced by War Hysteria* (Swartz Creek, MI: Broadblade Press, 1989) for a meticulously detailed account of the events of the Max Stephan case.

15. If Stephan had been capable of wit, one might think that "Meier's boys" was a reference to *Luftwaffe* personnel, whose commander, Herman Goering, promised that, if Allied bombers ever appeared over Berlin, Germans could call him Meier.

16. U.S. Constitution, art. III, § 3.

17. *U.S. v. Max Stephan*, District Court Criminal No. 26619 (1942).

18. *Ludington (Michigan) Daily News*, April 3, 1950.

19. *Donay v. U.S.*, 181 F.2d 1010 (6th Cir. 1950).

20. These facts are taken from the opinion of the Supreme Court in *Von Moltke v. Gillies*, 332 U.S. 708 (1948).

21. *Time*, September 6, 1943.

22. *Time*, September 6, 1943.

23. *New York Times*, August 25, 1943.

24. 40 Stat. 217.

25. *Ex parte Von Moltke*, 72 F. Supp. 994 (E.D. Mich. 1946).

26. *Von Moltke v. Gillies*, 161 F.2d 113 (6th Cir. 1947).

27. *Von Moltke v. Gillies*, 332 U.S. 708 (1948).

28. Facts from *U.S. v. von Moltke*, 189 F.2d 56 (6th Cir. 4/6/1951).

29. *Von Moltke v. Gillies*, 343 U.S. 922 (1952).

30. *New York Times*, January 22, 1944; February 25, 1944; *Detroit Free Press*, February 25, 1944. In September 1945, the Sixth Circuit reversed Thomas's conviction for error in the jury instructions and remanded for a new trial. *Thomas v. U.S.*, 151 F.2d 183 (6th Cir. 1945). In June 1949, the government asked that the indictment be dismissed because essential witnesses were no longer in the United States. *1949 Annual Report of the U.S. Attorney General*, 4.

31. *U.S. v. Baecker*, 55 F.Supp. 403 (E.D. Mich. 1944). The defendants were August Baecker, Herman Guenther, Jakob Josef Karr, Paul Gies, John Henry Berthold Schreiber, Fritz Streuer, and Fritz Bruno Ebert.

32. 52 Stat. 1060, codified at 29 U.S.C.A. 201 et seq.

33. 312 U.S. 100 (1941).

34. *The (Detroit) Wage Earner*, December 20, 1946.

35. *Anderson v. Mt. Clemens Pottery Co.*, E.D. Mich. Case No. 2582.

36. The complete text of Quaife's report was published in the *Detroit News*, December 29, 1946. Quaife also rejected other claims by plaintiffs relating to wages paid to women, charity deductions, and deductions for materials and tools. I am indebted to Quaife's widow, Mrs. Eleanor Ropes, who donated Quaife's extensive working files on this case to the court's historical society.

37. *Anderson v. Mt. Clemens Pottery Co.*, 60 F. Supp. 146 (E.D. Mich. 1943).

38. *Mt. Clemens Pottery Co. v. Anderson*, 149 F.2d 461 (6th Cir. 1945).

39. *Anderson v. Mt. Clemens Pottery Co.*, 328 U.S. 680 (1946).

40. *Tennessee Coal, Iron & R. Co. v. Muscoda Local No. 123*, 321 U.S. 590 (1944); *Jewell Ridge Coal Corp. v. Local No. 6167, United Mine Workers of America*, 325 U.S. 161 (1945).

41. *Detroit News*, December 29, 1946; *Time*, January 6, 1947; *Chicago Daily Tribune*, February 8, 1947.

42. *The (Detroit) Wage Earner-*,December 20, 1946 .

43. *New York Times*, January 21, 1947.

44. 61 Stat. 84, codified at 29 U.S.C. 251 et seq.

PART IV

The Era of Grand Expectations, 1946–1976[1]

In 1945, after surviving two world wars, the lawlessness of Prohibition, the Great Crash of 1929, and the deepest, longest depression in American history, many Americans yearned for a peaceful, secure, "normal" life, in which they could live comfortably without cares, raise healthy families, and prosper. A life where all problems were easy to solve. That such normalcy had never really existed outside of *Love Finds Andy Hardy* did not matter to them. Other Americans, particularly returning veterans, wanted to break with the past and make a better, modern world. What both groups received was enormous economic growth that raised their standard of living to new heights, vast scientific and technological advancements, the birth of suburban society, and the development of television, the invention with the greatest impact on society during the years between the automobile and the personal computer.[2] During this period, Americans and the federal courts also had to come to grips with Communism, racial discrimination, alienation of the young, and drugs.

CHAPTER 11

The Pursuit of Happiness and Communists, 1946–1960

The Eastern District, 1946–1960

As the war faded into the rearview mirrors of the first private automobiles manufactured since 1941, the population of the Eastern District continued to grow, from 3.87 million in 1940 to 4.83 million in 1950, and to 5.54 million in 1960. As in the past, Wayne County led the growth from 1945 to 1960, but a new phenomenon, the migration from Detroit to suburban communities rising from the farmlands of Oakland and Macomb counties, was also apparent. After peaking at 1.85 million residents in 1950, Detroit decreased to 1.67 million in 1960, while the suburbs added more than 900,000 residents. The bare numbers do not tell the full implications of this migration. Although the migration was initiated by veterans and their families seeking a solution to the city's severe housing shortage and fueled by generous federal loan guarantees, almost all of the people moving to the suburbs from Detroit were white, while a growing percentage of those remaining in Detroit were black.[3] In the following decades, this dichotomy would be the source of much of the region's problems.

The Eastern District remained the home of an industrial force with few equals, as a 1952 committee of Michigan lawyers bragged: "In the lower half of the eastern district lies what has been described as the greatest concentration of industrial development the world has yet seen, and which is expanding at a phenomenal rate. It includes the industrial areas of the Detroit metropolitan district and those of Flint, Pontiac, Midland, Jackson, Battle Creek, Saginaw, and Bay City, while practically every town and hamlet has its industrial plants." The report also referred with pride to Lansing, "an important industrial city," and to Calhoun County, which "embraces three important industrial cities, namely Battle Creek, Albion, and Marshall."[4]

From 1946 to 1960, the district court averaged 1,832 new civil and criminal cases per year, fairly evenly divided among criminal (685), U.S. civil (591), and private civil (556), of which the Northern Division contributed only 10 percent.[5] For many years after V J Day, war-related cases were a significant part of the district court's civil and criminal dockets. For example, the OPA and the Office of the Housing Expediter (HPE), which took over enforcement of federal rent-control laws from the OPA in May 1947, added 2,408 cases to the court's U.S. civil docket from 1946 to 1953, and the U.S. attorney (as the district attorney was now called) filed 3,014 cases between 1950 and 1960 to collect defaulted loans guaranteed by the federal government, most of which had been made to veterans. Additions to the private civil docket included traditional commercial cases, but for the first time those cases were outnumbered by personal injury cases, principally involving automobile accidents,[6] while during the first years after the war there were also numerous cases filed under wartime laws regulating rents and veterans' rights. For most of the 1950s, cases characterized as "fraud and other theft" were the largest component of the criminal docket followed far behind by violations of the liquor-tax and narcotics laws.

From 1946 to 1954, the court had five district judges, although Judge Koscinski was ill for many years before his death in 1957 and could not manage a full share of the docket. In 1954, Congress added a sixth judgeship. President Truman made his second and third appointments to the district court (Theodore Levin in 1946 and Thomas P. Thornton in 1949), and President Eisenhower made four nominations (Ralph M. Freeman in 1954, Clifford P. O'Sullivan in 1957, Frederick W. Kaess in 1960, and John Feikens in 1960) although only the first three were confirmed. There were also two changes of leadership in the office of the clerk during this period. On March 1, 1951, Frank J. Dingell was sworn in as the new clerk of the district court, replacing George Read.[7] Dingell, the brother of then U.S. representative John D. Dingell, Sr. (and the uncle of U.S. representative John D. Dingell, Jr.), was born in St. Joseph, Missouri, in 1890 and was a career federal employee, having previously worked for the Treasury Department and the Federal Housing Administration. Frank Dingell retired in 1958 and died on November 21, 1959.[8] He was succeeded as clerk by long-time deputy John J. Ginther, who had joined the clerk's office in 1935.

Veterans' Re-employment Rights

Most of the civil cases filed under the Selective Service Act did not involve draft dodgers, but rather the right of veterans to return to the jobs they held before the war "or to a position of like seniority, status, and pay unless the employer's circumstances have so changed as to make it impossible or unreasonable to do so."[9] For example, in *Sullivan v. Milner Hotel*

Co.,[10] plaintiff Dorothea L. Sullivan left her job as a receptionist and switch-board operator with the Milner Hotel chain in January 1944 to enlist in the U.S. Marine Corps. When she was honorably discharged in November 1945, she asked Milner to restore her job. Milner refused, and she sued. Judge Lederle held that the act entitled plaintiff to be restored to her position with back pay. These cases were not always so easy to decide, particularly when seniority was an issue. In *Droste v. Nash-Kelvinator Corp.*,[11] the U.S. attorney sued Nash-Kelvinator on behalf of an honorably discharged veteran who, although re-employed, had not received "super seniority," i.e. seniority above all others in his job who were not also veterans of World War II. The U.A.W., which represented the plant's employees, intervened on the part of the company to protect its contractual seniority system, and the Veterans of Foreign Wars intervened to support the veteran. This case, like *Sullivan*, was assigned to Judge Lederle who held that the act did not raise veterans over all non-veteran employees. Instead, it gave each veteran "the full benefit of whatever added rights he might have acquired if he had remained in his position instead of being inducted into the service." He pointed out that many "essential" employees were not allowed to enlist, and he concluded that "Congress did not intend to penalize these essential employees by reducing their seniority status, for it is well known that without the services of the essential employees in production, it would have been impossible to carry the war through to a successful conclusion."

The Politics of a Judicial Appointment

Many judicial appointments have political overtones, but in most cases political maneuvers are carried out behind a gentlemanly facade. The nomination and appointment of Theodore Levin to the district court turned into a public battle among Democrats that was anything but gentlemanly. Although in 1919 Congress had created the concept of an older judge "retiring" yet remaining active on the bench (what is now known as senior status), no Eastern District judge took advantage of the law until Judge Moinet did so effective February 28, 1946. Under the law, this allowed President Truman to nominate a new district judge to occupy Judge Moinet's former seat. His choice of Detroit attorney, Theodore Levin, who became one of the district's great judges, resulted in the most contentious intra-party judicial selection in the history of the federal courts in Michigan.

By 1946, the selection of a nominee for the federal bench had become the prerogative of those U.S. senators from the forum state who belonged to the president's political party. If no such senator existed, the rules were not clear. In 1946, the president was a Democrat, but both of Michigan's senators were Republicans, while only six of the state's 17 representatives were Democrats. As a result, the multiple factions of Michigan's Democratic Party fought over the nomination to succeed Judge Moinet. Congressional district organizations and unions pushed Frank Fitzgerald, a Detroit attorney and former candidate for U.S. senator; the Democratic County Chairmen's Association favored Detroit attorney Frank Schwartz, a party stalwart, a frequent candidate for office, and a delegate to the party's national convention; while powerful U.S. Representative John Lesinski, Sr. supported Representative Louis C. Rabaut of Grosse Pointe, with whom he had served in Congress since 1935.

On July 3, 1946, the *Detroit Free Press* noted that "some members of the [congressional] delegation have been urging Theodore Levin," although the paper also quoted the chairman of the County Chairmen's Association as saying that: "We are not supporting him."[12] Nevertheless, on the day that article appeared, and to the consternation of all of the state's Democratic factions, President Truman did nominate Theodore Levin. The reaction among Michigan's Democrats was immediate and vehemently negative. They inundated the president with letters and telegrams beseeching him to withdraw Levin's nomination because, they alleged, Levin had never been active in the local Democratic Party organization and was, in fact, a closet Republican. One Fitzgerald supporter, Patrick Nertney, went further and claimed that Levin was "a well-known Detroit Republican" who had campaigned for Republican presidential nominee Alf Landon in 1936.[13] Another Michigan Democrat warned the president that the appointment would "defeat, discourage, and alienate practically all of the groups of administration forces in Michigan," while another called the appointment "a grave error and a disservice to the Federal Court and to the people."[14] The president also received a telegram opposing Levin signed with the names of Walter Reuther and other officers of the United Automobile Workers (later denounced by Reuther as a forgery),[15] which claimed that "Labor is up in arms" over the nomination, that Levin was being "supported by big business interests who are strongly anti-labor," and that "Labor in Michigan is prepared to carry their protest to the polls if this appointment of Levin is carried through."[16]

Levin's lack of involvement in Democratic affairs had come up before. In 1935, Philip Slomovitz, the editor of Detroit's *Jewish News*, recommended Levin to Congressman John Dingell, Sr. for the federal bench when Congress created the Eastern District's fourth judgeship, but Dingell had gently rebuffed him. This was the first opportunity for an appointment to the district court by a Democratic president in a century, and Dingell noted that "there are too many men of good qualifications who have Party service records of from twenty to thirty years," whereas Levin had practically none.[17] In 1946, Slomovitz renewed his campaign to gain Representative Dingell's support, arguing both Levin's qualifications and the dearth of Jews receiving federal appointments in Michigan recently. Dingell was won over, and he quietly gained the support of E. Cyril Bevan and Clara Van Auken, Michigan's members of the Democratic National Committee. Responding to claims that Levin was a Republican, they reassured President Truman that Levin and his family had performed grassroots work on each of President Roosevelt's four campaigns, as well as on Frank Murphy's campaigns for governor, that Levin was a progressive, and that he was better qualified for the position than any other candidate.

Just days after Levin's nomination was announced, 700 delegates met in Lansing for the annual Democratic State Convention. The nominations of Levin and of Raymond W. Starr for the district court bench in the Western District overshadowed all other issues.[18] Bevan reported to President Truman that "a rabble-rousing campaign was organized by Messrs. Hook [U.S. representative Frank Hook of Ironwood], Fitzgerald, et al. in the course of which every stop was pulled on the subject of religious prejudice and race prejudice, and it was the element that could be appealed to on this score that were receptive."[19] Van Auken and Bevan also became targets at the convention as a resolution calling on them to resign from the Democratic National Committee was blocked only by "a hasty adjournment" on a voice vote.[20] When Truman did not withdraw the Michigan appointments, Hook demanded a hearing before the Senate Judiciary Committee to oppose both nominations.[21] As to Levin, Hook and other opponents raised a new claim, alleging that in 1935, Levin had defrauded holders of insurance policies issued by the Detroit Life Insurance Company.[22] Levin, who had been the attorney of a man trying to acquire the company, testified on this issue for four hours in a closed hearing. A majority of the committee approved his appointment, and Levin was confirmed by the full Senate.

President Truman never explained why he stuck with Levin in the face of such broad opposition, but he rarely did change his mind. As David Halberstam explained, "He was not afflicted by inner doubts. He made his decisions quickly and cleanly by listening to the evidence and the best advice of those around him, and he did not look back."[23] It is likely that having received a recommendation from a Congressman he respected and trusted as well as from the state's two national committee members, he made a decision that was much less important to him than many others he faced as president. Once made, he was not willing to be seen to change his mind in the face of complaints from the unruly factions of a splintered state party.

District Judge Theodore Levin

Born: February 18, 1897 (Chicago, Illinois), to Joseph and Ida Rosin Levin
Education: University of Detroit School of Law (LL.B. 1920; LL.M. 1924)
Nominated/Confirmed: July 3, 1946/July 25, 1946 (Harry S. Truman)
Vacancy: Edward J. Moinet (Senior Status)
Left Court: December 31, 1970 (Death)

Fig. 57. Judge Theodore Levin.
(Historical Society for the United
States District Court for the
Eastern District of Michigan)

One of the eight children, Theodore Levin sold newspapers on the streets of Detroit as a young boy and later worked in a machine shop to earn money for college. Following law school, he entered the practice of law with his brother Saul, joined later by Morris Garvett and Louis Dill. Levin married Rhoda Katzin of Chicago on May 21, 1925, and they had four children.[24] Judge Levin felt a strong sense of duty to immigrants who had been displaced to the United States by the upheavals in Europe following World War I. During the 1930s, Levin was part of a group of immigration lawyers who challenged Michigan's Alien Registration and Fingerprinting Act and succeeded in having it declared unconstitutional by a panel of three U.S. judges.[25] Levin also served as a member of the executive board of the National Refugees Service Administration and an officer of the Michigan Commission on Displaced Persons. In 1933, Levin was appointed special assistant attorney general in an investigation into the Michigan Bank Holiday, and, from 1944 to 1946, he served as a member of the Selective Service Appeal Board.

Judge Levin served as chief judge of the court from 1959 to 1967. He achieved national renown for his work on the Judicial Conference of the United States, and he was the creator of the court's sentencing council, which was adopted by other courts to reform standards for criminal sentences imposed in federal courts. He was an able administrator and skillfully resolved conflicts among judges and court staff, which gained him great respect. He had a remarkable talent, too, for resolving difficult legal cases with "practical and often unorthodox solutions." Judge Wade McCree remembered that: "He was very much a gentleman with a courtroom decorum that was the epitome of what a courtroom should be."

The Chief Judge of the District Court

In 1948, Judge Lederle became the chief judge of the district court, a new title created by Congress, although the idea of a *primus inter pares* had been around since 1919 in the title senior district judge.[26] Initially, the chief judge was simply "the district judge senior in commission," but in 1958, Congress directed that the chief judge was to be replaced upon reaching the age of 70, and in 1982, specified that, regardless of age, the chief judge is to be replaced after seven years in the position.[27] In whatever manner a chief judge leaves the position, the successor is the court's district judge with the greatest seniority who has not yet turned 65. The 1958 legislation also gave the title senior judge its current meaning: a judge who has retired from active service but who carries an active caseload, usually between 100 percent and 50 percent of that of an active district judge in that district.

Congress has never made clear the exact duties of a chief judge. The old senior district judge "was generally expected to exercise whatever administrative authority or power was necessary, however vaguely it might be defined,"[28] and the 1948 act was little more specific as to a chief judge's duties other than to "have precedence and preside at any session which he attends." In practice, the administrative duties of the chief judge of a district court have increased steadily so that by the beginning of the 21st century the chief judge was assigned only a partial caseload. To this writing, 15 judges have served as the district court's chief judge.[29]

District Judge Thomas Patrick Thornton

Born: March 8, 1898 (Somerville, Massachusetts), to Patrick Joseph and
    Sarah Ann O'Malley Thornton
Education: Tufts University, Syracuse University, Fordham University,
    University of Detroit School of Law (LL.B. 1926)
Military: U.S. Navy (World War I)
Nominated/Confirmed: January 13/31, 1949 (Harry S. Truman)
Vacancy: Ernest O'Brien (Died)
Senior Status: February 15, 1966
Left Court: July 1, 1985 (Died)

When Judge O'Brien died on October 9, 1948, President Truman nominated as O'Brien's successor the district's U.S. attorney, Thomas Patrick Thornton, known since his college days as Tiger Thornton for his tenacity and aggressive play on the football field. He completed his education in 1926, with a law degree from the University of Detroit, where he was also a swimmer and a diver, and was later inducted into the University of Detroit Hall of Fame and named to their all-time football team. Upon graduation, he began a private practice in Detroit. In 1937, he joined the staff of

Fig. 58.   Judge Thomas Patrick
Thornton. (Historical Society for
the United States District Court
for the Eastern District of
Michigan)

the district attorney for the Eastern District and remained there until he
was appointed to the bench of the district court, serving as chief assistant
from 1944 to 1947 and as U.S. attorney from 1947 to 1949. Judge Thornton
married Margaret Florence Beaudin in 1946. Four years after her death in
1976, he took a second wife, Rose Garland.

The Trial of the Michigan Six

In 1953, Judge Picard presided over a trial in the Detroit courthouse in
which six officials of the Communist Party of the USA (CPUSA) were charged
with violating the Alien Registration Act of 1940, popularly known as the
Smith Act, by conspiring to teach and advocate the overthrow of the government of the United States by force or violence. This trial, known as the
Little Smith Act Trial, or the Trial of the Michigan Six, was one of a series
of prosecutions of leaders of the CPUSA, conducted in federal courts across
the country, which so disrupted the party's leadership and finances that it
never recovered. For the most part, prosecutors in those cases did not try
to prove that the defendants themselves advocated the violent overthrow
of the government. Instead, they tried to connect the defendants with positions taken by the CPUSA decades earlier, using documents from the earlier era and the testimony of former party members who, to the defendants'
consternation, were revealed as informants for the FBI.

The Smith Act was the product of decades of worldwide political turmoil which left many people in the late 1930s believing that democracy

Fig. 59.   The Michigan Six. L–R: Wellman, Winter, Schatz, Allan, Dennis, Kaplan/Ganley. (Walter P. Reuther Library, Wayne State University)

was a spent force and that the future belonged to the winner of the contest between Communism and National Socialism, exemplified by the Spanish Civil War. By the autumn of 1939, that calculus was further complicated by the Nazi-Soviet Non-Aggression Pact, followed two weeks later by Germany's invasion of Poland and the beginning of World War II. In the midst of this chaos, Representative Howard Worth Smith (Democrat, Virgina) introduced a bill (one of a hundred anti-alien/anti-sedition bills on the House docket in the 76th Congress) that made it a felony "to knowingly or willfully advocate, abet, advise, or teach the duty, necessity, desirability, or propriety of overthrowing or destroying any government of the United States by force," or "to organize or help to organize any society, group, or assembly of persons who teach, advocate, or encourage the overthrow or destruction of any government in the United States by force or violence."[30] Congress passed the Smith Act with near unanimity,[31] and President Franklin D. Roosevelt signed it into law on June 28, 1940, a week after France surrendered to Germany and two weeks after the remains of the British army were evacuated from Dunkirk. Democratic governments in Holland, Belgium, Poland, and Czechoslovakia had long since fallen to the Nazi *Blitzkrieg*.

Ironically, although the CPUSA was likely one of the intended targets of the Smith Act, and the Party mounted protests against its passage, the Party enthusiastically supported the first Smith Act prosecutions because they were against the Party's left-wing rival, the Trotskyist Socialist Workers' Party (SWP). The CPUSA also supported the second Smith Act prosecution, begun in 1942, against 31 American Fascists who were vocal critics of the president and who were accused of conspiring with Germany to cause subordination in the American armed forces. After the war, however, the focus of Smith Act prosecutions became the CPUSA.

On January 17, 1949, a Smith Act trial that came to be known as the Battle of Foley Square began in the U.S. district court for the southern district of New York against the CPUSA and 12 of its national leaders. Although there was little or no evidence against the individual defendants, they chose to conduct a so-called "Dimitrov" strategy, focused on offering a defense of their political philosophy instead of trying to prove their innocence, intending to demonstrate they could not get a fair trial in a capitalist court. After a raucous trial, the jury convicted all of the defendants. The U.S. Court of Appeals for the Second Circuit affirmed the verdicts,[32] and the U.S. Supreme Court, on June 4, 1951, also affirmed the convictions and held that the relevant sections of the Smith Act were constitutional.[33]

The success of the Foley Square case led to indictments against officials of the CPUSA across the country. On September 22, 1952, a grand jury in the Eastern District indicted Saul Wellman, Nathan Kaplan (also known as Nat Ganley), Thomas De Witt Dennis Jr., Phillip Schatz, William Allan and Helen M. Winter, all leaders of the Michigan District off the CPUSA and members of the CPUSA National Committee.[34] The case was assigned to Judge Picard who, like his political mentor Franklin Roosevelt, had no sympathy for the defendants' politics. He was, though, determined to conduct a fair trial and, above all, to avoid the circus atmosphere that characterized the Foley Square trial.

When trial began on October 29, 1953, the prosecution was led by the district's recently appointed U.S. attorney, and future U.S. district judge, Frederick W. Kaess, assisted by a young Justice Department attorney, William G. Hundley, who had helped obtain convictions in a Smith Act case in Pittsburgh. Ernest Goodman, a well-respected Detroit labor attorney and civil libertarian, initially agreed to represent all of the defendants.[35] When they advised him, however, that they intended to replicate the New York defendants' disruptive "defense," he refused to continue as counsel. Finally, it was agreed that Goodman would represent three of the defendants, leaving the other three free to represent themselves. George W. Crockett, Jr., one of Detroit's most prominent African American lawyers and himself a future judge and member of Congress, assisted in the defense, but Goodman bore the brunt of the day-to-day grind through the long months of preparation and trial.

Although Judge Picard asserted in opening the trial, and instructed the jurors, that the case was not about the defendants' political beliefs, only Goodman seems to have taken him seriously. As in the Foley Square trial, the prosecution attacked the CPUSA and its politics instead of any violation of the Smith Act by the defendants. Those defendants who represented themselves used the trial, for their part, as a vehicle to defend the Party and Communism. Only Goodman addressed the serious questions of whether the defendants were guilty of advocating violence and whether the Smith Act, as written or as applied, violated the First Amendment and endangered the civil liberties of all Americans. The government's case was much the same as that presented in New York. First the prosecution presented a Communist document from the 1930s or earlier, then an expert witness, usually a former Party member, testified to what the document meant to Communists. Then the prosecution presented former Party members, FBI plants and paid informers, who testified that the present CPUSA advocated the same views set out in the documents. As in New York, the identity of the prosecution witnesses, people whom the defendants knew and trusted, including the Michigan chapter's former membership secretary, Berenice Baldwin, was a demoralizing shock.

Goodman tried to convince the jury of the weakness of the prosecution's case. He pointed out the antiquity of the documents and the fact that none of them implicated any defendant during the period charged in the indictment. He also attacked the government's reliance on informants. In a startling move, Goodman was able to prove that two of those informers, former Party members Milton Santwire and Steve Schemanske, had, in addition to receiving money from the government to spy on the CPUSA, also been paid by the Ford Motor Company to spy on its employees, a violation of the National Labor Relations Act. Goodman established that the United States and Ford had paid the prosecution's witnesses a total of $172,650. Those payments, Goodman argued, showed where the informers' loyalty lay: "They are not in court primarily to give facts but rather to reveal or conceal them as they think will be most helpful to their employer and most harmful to the persons against whom they are paid to inform."

Despite Goodman's heroic efforts, the jury convicted all six defendants. On February 19, 1954, Judge Picard fined each of them $10,000 and sentenced them to prison terms: Nat Ganley, five years (the maximum); Saul Wellman, four years and eight months; William Allen and Thomas De Witt Dennis, Jr., four years and six months; Phillip Schatz, four years and four months; and Helen Mary Winter, four years. In addition to pronouncing sentence, Judge Picard addressed the defendants at length, a speech which received national exposure when it was published in *U.S. News & World*

Report. He told the defendants that he felt pity for them, not anger or hate, and that while he admired their abilities, he could not understand the mental processes that had brought them to Communism. He also compared them favorably to the prosecution's witnesses, noting that the defendants had no divorces among them while the informers had 11. What did clearly arouse Judge Picard's ire was the defendants' complete subjugation to the Soviet Union. He simply could not understand, or forgive, their willingness to do whatever they could to support the Soviet Union and to take whatever twists and turns shifting Soviet policy mandated. His disgust led him to offer to suspend the sentence and provide transportation for any defendant who preferred to live in the Soviet Union rather than serve his or her sentence.[36] None of the defendants took him up on his offer. What was missing from Judge Picard's comments, and indeed from the trial itself, was any reference to even the slightest evidence that these defendants, or even the CPUSA, did indeed advocate the violent overthrow of the government. An uninformed observer present in the judge's courtroom that day might easily have concluded from the judge's comments that the defendants were, as they alleged, being jailed merely for their belief in a "foreign" political philosophy.

Ernest Goodman appealed the verdicts for the defendants, but, in November 1955, the U.S. Court of Appeals for the Sixth Circuit affirmed, holding that the evidence was sufficient to sustain the jury's conclusion that defendants were members of a conspiracy to teach and advocate violent overthrow of government. [37] The appellate court also held that the Smith Act was constitutional and that the three-years statute of limitations did not bar their conviction for having helped organize the CPUSA, which even the government admitted had been created no later than 1945, because, under the Smith Act, every step taken in furtherance of the conspiracy constituted a new act of "organizing." Goodman petitioned the U.S. Supreme Court for a writ of certiorari, and, while he and the defendants waited, things changed.

The Red Scare of the 1950s was waning, at least as it applied to the CPUSA, largely because most Americans no longer saw it a threat to democracy. Being an American Communist was no more acceptable than it had been for the last decade, and external communism was still a serious concern, but the CPUSA had become an impotent joke. The Party, whose candidates drew 103,000 votes in the 1932 presidential election and claimed 100,000 members in 1939 and 60,000 in 1948, was, by the summer of 1958, "a nearly dead party of only 3,000 to 6,000 members."[38] Because of this changed perception of the Party, or for some other reason, the government's unbroken string of Smith Act convictions began to come apart. In October 1956, the U.S. Supreme Court vacated the conviction of several Communists tried in Pittsburgh because of perjured testimony,[39] and then, in June 1957, the Supreme Court dealt further prosecutions a crippling blow by vacating convictions on the constitutional and limitations grounds urged by Goodman in the Detroit trial. A week later, the Supreme Court granted Goodman's petition for certiorari, vacated the judgment, and remanded the case to the Sixth Circuit.[40] In March 1958, the Sixth Circuit dismissed the organizing charge as untimely but found there was enough evidence on the advocating charge to warrant a new trial and remanded the case to the district court.[41] The Justice Department considered proceeding, but prosecutors Kaess and Hundley advised against it, noting that, under the new rules, the evidence available was insufficient to obtain an "advocating" conviction. In September 1958, Judge Picard granted Kaess's motion to dismiss the remaining counts of the indictment. Six years after they were arrested, the defendants were free, but not without irreparable damage to their lives and their finances. Prosecutor Hundley later admitted that he took no pride in his part of the case which, he joked, he never included on his resume.[42]

A Sixth Judgeship and a Smaller District

From 1920 to 1937, the Eastern District averaged 878 new civil and criminal cases filed annually per judge, one of the highest caseloads of all district courts during those halcyon years. However, even as Congress authorized a fifth judge for the district in 1938, its caseload was declining and remained below the per-judge average for all districts until 1950. That did not mean that the Eastern District's judges were not busy, though, because the national average grew from 329 to 413 new cases per judge between 1941 and 1952, causing judges and the AOUSC to urge Congress to authorize a major increase in district judgeships. On February 10, 1954, Congress reacted by authorizing three new circuit judgeships and 27 new district judgeships, including one district judge each for Michigan's two districts (the sixth for the Eastern District and the second for the Western District).[43] At the same time, Congress transferred five counties (Ingham, Branch, Calhoun, Clinton, and Hillsdale) from the Eastern District to the Western, a move deemed necessary to justify the Western District's second judgeship because it added 387,067 residents (8.1 percent of the Eastern District's 1950 total population) to the Western District.[44]

Selecting the nominee for the Eastern District's sixth judgeship became a bone of contention between Michigan's two U.S. senators, both Republicans. Senator Homer Ferguson wanted attorney William B. (Buck) Giles of Detroit, while Senator Charles E. Potter wanted Carl Smith Sr. of Saginaw. According to Senior District Judge John Feikens, who was then chairman of the Republican Party in Michigan, both senators were intractable, leaving an opening for U.S. Postmaster General Arthur Summerfield of Flint, himself former chair of the Michigan Republicans and a close ally of President Eisenhower. Summerfield convinced Ferguson and Potter to agree to

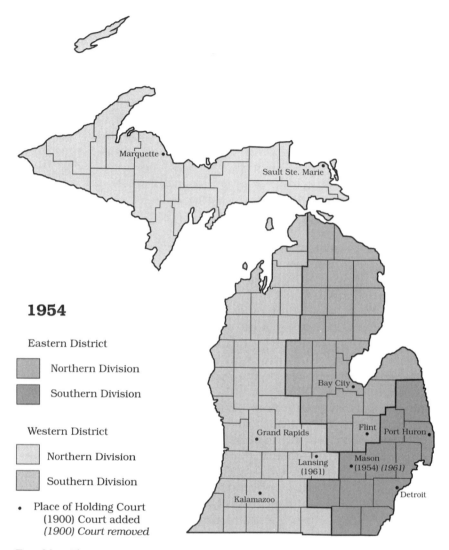

1954

Eastern District

Northern Division

Southern Division

Western District

Northern Division

Southern Division

• Place of Holding Court
(1900) Court added
(1900) Court removed

Marquette •

Sault Ste. Marie

Bay City

Grand Rapids   Flint   Port Huron

Lansing   Mason
(1961)   •(1954) *(1961)*

Kalamazoo   Detroit

Fig. 60.   The Eastern District of Michigan, 1954. (Ellen White)

accept a compromise candidate, Ralph M. Freeman, a Flint attorney who
represented Summerfield's huge Chevrolet dealership.[45]

District Judge Ralph McKenzie Freeman

Born: May 5, 1902 (Flushing, Genesee County, Michigan), to Horace Burton
and Laura Delia McKenzie Freeman

Fig. 61.   Judge Ralph McKenzie
Freeman. (Historical Society for
the United States District Court
for the Eastern District of
Michigan)

Education: University of Michigan Law School (LL.B. 1926)
Nominated/Confirmed: May 10/June 8, 1954 (Dwight D. Eisenhower)
Vacancy: New Seat
Senior Status: July 1, 1973
Left Court: March 29, 1990 (Died)

Ralph Freeman was indelibly connected to the City of Flint and Genesee
County. He graduated from Flint High School and worked at a General
Motors plant in Flint while attending the University of Michigan. After receiving his law degree, he returned to Flint to open a private practice. In
1928, he joined the office of the Genesee County prosecutor and was
elected to one term as county prosecutor (1931–1932). He then returned
to private practice until he was appointed to the district court in 1954. On
August 13, 1938, Freeman married Emmalyn Ellis. Although they had no
children, Judge Freeman became a member of the Flint Board of Education (1935–1949) and served consecutively as secretary, vice president,
and president. To honor his service, the board named a new school the
Ralph M. Freeman Elementary School. Judge and Mrs. Freeman established several scholarship endowments at the University of Michigan's Flint
campus, where Judge Freeman's judicial papers are archived. Judge Freeman became one of the most respected and diligent judges on the district
court, serving as chief judge from 1967 until 1972. He continued hearing
cases until shortly before his death.

Stanley Wloch Shoots at Judge Picard

Two years after he sentenced the Michigan Six, Judge Picard was back on the front pages of newspapers across the country. On March 12, 1956, the judge was sitting behind the raised bench of the Bay City courtroom presiding over a criminal jury trial and listening to the closing argument of Flint defense attorney Leon Seidell. Suddenly, Stanley Wloch, "a bespectacled, little man of 68,"[46] pointed the sawed-off barrel of a 16-gauge shotgun through the doors at the back of the courtroom and fired at the judge from 50 feet away. Shotgun pellets cratered the wall a dozen feet behind the judge, leaving a pattern 16 inches across, but missed his head by inches. Wloch hid the shotgun behind the courtroom's open outer door and began walking down the corridor toward the stairs. FBI agent Lewis Wright emerged from his office across the hallway from the courtroom, saw a short, elderly, well-dressed man in a brown overcoat and seized him. The people in the courtroom had not seen Wloch and were not sure what had happened. Some thought it was a bomb, while the judge thought it was a firecracker and joked to Seidell that his argument "went over with a bang." When he found out what had happened, Judge Picard went to Wright's office and confronted Wloch. He then returned to the courtroom, assured the jurors, six women and five men, that the shooting "wasn't too important," and resumed the trial. Because he had not been wounded, the judge assumed that Wloch had fired a blank cartridge, and only later, during the recess, did anybody notice the pellet-pocked wall.[47]

Judge Picard and his staff knew Stanley Wloch well. In 1947, Wloch filed a federal civil case alleging that lawyers and officials in Clare County, Michigan, had conspired to award his wife the family farm in their divorce. Judge Picard dismissed the case for lack of subject matter jurisdiction and told Wloch to go to a state court. Instead of taking the judge's advice, Wloch became determined to have his federal case revived. After he sent the judge 14 threatening postcards containing "libelous, scurrilous, and defamatory language," the judge reported him to the FBI, which arrested Wloch and brought him before Judge Levin in Detroit. A psychiatrist appointed by Judge Levin determined that Wloch was psychotic, and in 1950 a Wayne County probate judge committed him to the Ypsilanti State Mental Hospital. Security at the hospital was lax, and Wloch walked away in April 1952.

Four years later, in February 1956, Wloch returned to Bay City and hired a private detective, James McEvoy, to investigate the legality of his commitment to the hospital in Ypsilanti. A week or two before the shooting, McEvoy warned Judge Picard that Wloch was back in town and "had something on his mind other than what a normal man would have,"[48] but the judge shrugged it off and did not increase the court's casual security

measures. After the event, several jurors reported having seen Wloch skulk-
ing outside the court house holding what looked like a shotgun, and he
was able to walk into the building and upstairs to the court with the gun
hidden under his coat.

On March 13, Wloch was arraigned before commissioner (and resident
deputy clerk) Clarence Pettit on a charge of assaulting a federal officer while
in the performance of his duties. "Befuddled," grey haired, and frail, Wloch
explained in a thick accent that he was a good shot and was not trying to
kill the judge, but just wanted to get publicity for his case. He also described in chilling detail how easily he could have ambushed the judge at
his Saginaw home if he had wanted to kill him. Pettit set bail at $25,000
and returned Wloch to the Bay County jail. In June, after a sanity hearing,
Judge Thornton committed the prisoner to a federal mental institution at
Springfield, Missouri. In December 1957, a federal judge in Missouri found
Wloch competent to stand trial and ordered him returned to Bay City. The
Northern Division's grand jury indicted Wloch on a charge of attempted
murder, and, on January 30, 1958, Judge Thornton accepted his plea of
not guilty but also told him: "You appear to be mentally sick."[49] In May
1958, a Bay County probate judge committed Wloch once more to a state
mental hospital, still under indictment.[50] The pock-marked pattern remained on the wall behind the bench of the Bay City courtroom through
several renovations and was a fascinating sight for new law clerks, but it
finally disappeared during a 1990s courtroom makeover.

District Judge Clifford Patrick O'Sullivan

Born: December 8, 1897 (Chicago, Illinois), to Patrick Thomas and Mary
    Agnes Clifford O'Sullivan
Education: University of Notre Dame Law School (LL.B. 1920)
Military: U.S. Army (World War I)
Nominated/Confirmed: June 6/August 5, 1957 (Dwight D. Eisenhower)
Vacancy: Koscinski (Senior Status)
Left Court: August 4, 1960 (Appointed to Sixth Circuit)
Died: October 7, 1975 (Detroit, Michigan)

Clifford P. O'Sullivan, the tenth of 11 children, entered Notre Dame University in 1915, but left school in 1917 to enlist in the army. After returning
from Europe and earning a law degree, Judge O'Sullivan joined a law firm
in Port Huron where he remained for 37 years, with only a two-year hiatus,
until he was appointed to the district court. In 1928, Judge O'Sullivan married Theresa Kearney of Chicago; they had five children. During his years
in private practice, he was active in Republican politics, serving as St. Clair
County Republican chairman for eight years and as Republican national committeeman from Michigan during President Eisenhower's administration.

Fig. 62. Judge Clifford Patrick O'Sullivan. (Historical Society for the United States District Court for the Eastern District of Michigan)

Judge O'Sullivan remained a district judge for fewer than three years before President Eisenhower appointed him to the Sixth Circuit to fill the seat vacated by the retirement of Judge Simons.

District Judge Frederick William Kaess

Born: December 1, 1910 (Detroit, Michigan), to Frederick Charles, Jr. and Dorothy Koch Kaess
Education: University of Michigan, Wayne University, Detroit College of Law (LL.B. 1932; J.D. hon. 1961)
Nominated/Confirmed: June 10/July 2, 1960 (Dwight D. Eisenhower)
Vacancy: Lederle (Senior Status)
Senior Status: December 13, 1975
Left Court: March 30, 1979 (Died)

Frederick W. Kaess grew up in St. Clair Shores, Michigan. While in law school, he married Phyllis Marie Danckmeyer; they were the parents of one son, Frederick Charles Kaess, III. After admission to the bar, Kaess was elected municipal judge for St. Clair Shores. A year later, he joined the Michigan Mutual Liability Company in Lansing as an attorney and claims manager, serving in that position from 1933 until 1945. In 1945, he put his insurance experience to work in private practice, specializing in civil practice and personal injury cases. Kaess was active in politics, serving as chair of the Wayne County Republican Committee from 1938 to 1952. In 1953,

Fig. 63.   Judge Frederick William Kaess. (Historical Society for the United States District Court for the Eastern District of Michigan)

President Eisenhower appointed him U.S. attorney for the Eastern District, where he remained until appointed to the district court bench. He served as chief judge of the district court from 1972 until 1975.

Sentencing Councils

In November 1960, the judges of the district court adopted a proposal by Chief Judge Theodore Levin to create a revolutionary procedure under which criminal sentences imposed by each district judge would be reviewed and discussed by the rest of the bench. The reviewing judges would not have the power to change a colleague's sentence decision, but Levin hoped that a frank discussion would tend to generate a consistent philosophy of sentencing and to decrease the differences between sentences imposed on defendants in similar circumstances.[51] Sentencing had been a concern of Judge Levin since he joined the court in 1946 because of the differences in sentences and also because, with no background in criminal practice, he felt ill equipped to decide what a just and effective sentence should be. The options available to a federal judge had increased over the years, including the Probation Act in 1925, which allowed imposing a suspended sentence and probation, and the Parole Act of 1958, which introduced indeterminate and split sentencing. The district court's sentencing councils met periodically with a representative from the Probation Office to review several sentences. At first, all of the judges participated in each session, but when the court grew from six to eight judges, scheduling became difficult and they decided to meet in rotating groups of three. As time passed, the judges found that their sentences did become more consistent and that the ability to discuss sentences helped the individual judges to define their individual sentencing philosophies. The council system was adopted by many other district courts over the years and became the foundation for the system of federal sentencing guidelines enacted by Congress in 1984.

The Politics of A Failed Judicial Appointment

John Feikens is one of the very few people to have served as a U.S. district judge twice. His first go-around began on October 13, 1960, when President Eisenhower gave him a recess appointment to the district court seat vacated by Judge O'Sullivan's appointment to the Sixth Circuit. He was "sworn in by a person I came dearly to love later,"[52] Chief Judge Theodore Levin. A recess appointment, made when the Senate is not in session, is effective immediately without action by the Senate, but if the Senate does not confirm the appointment before the end of the next session of Congress, the position becomes vacant again. On January 10, 1961, before President John F. Kennedy took office, President Eisenhower nominated Judge Feikens again for the same seat, but that nomination was not confirmed by the Senate.

Feikens's problem was a political dispute that became personal. He was a highly regarded attorney, but he had also been the chairman of the Republican Party in Michigan. That, in and of itself, was not enough to quash his nomination. U.S. attorney general Robert Kennedy admired Feikens and had convinced his brother, the new president, to submit Feikens's nomination again. The roadblock was, instead, an implacable enemy in the Senate. Feikens had offended Michigan's Democratic senator Patrick V. McNamara by accusing him of accepting illegal union contributions in 1954.[53] Still smarting from this charge, McNamara warned the Kennedy brothers that Feikens would never be confirmed because Feikens was "personally repugnant," and he threatened to hold up appropriations for foreign aid if the nomination was not withdrawn. President Kennedy had no choice but to give in to McNamara, and Feikens's first experience as a federal judge ended on September 27, 1961.

Notes

1. For this chapter heading, I am indebted to Professor James T. Patterson's *Grand Expectations: The United States, 1945–1974* (New York: Oxford University Press, 1997).

2. It is instructive that the Andy Hardy image was exactly the America portrayed in countless television situation comedies over the next decades.

3. The district's other major growth spot from 1950 to 1960 was Genesee County, where the automobile industry fueled an increase of 103,360 residents between 1950 and 1960. The rest of the district grew slowly or lost population.

4. "Report of Special Committee on United States District Courts in Michigan," H. Rep. 1005, 83rd Cong., 1st Sess., 76–77.

5. In 1952, the Northern Division accounted for only 186 of the court's 2,001 new cases. "Report of the Special Committee on United States District Courts in Michigan," House Report 1005, 83rd Cong., 1st Sess., 76.

6. In 1956, there were 362 new personal injury cases, including 216 automobile cases and 53 under the Jones and Federal Employers' Liability Acts, but only 160 contract cases. The predominance of personal injury cases was a trend among most district courts.

7. *Detroit News*, March 2, 1951.

8. *Detroit Free Press*, November 23, 1959.

9. 54 Stat. 885, 890.

10. *Sullivan v. Milner Hotel Co.*, 66 F. Supp. 607 (E.D. Mich. 1946).

11. *Droste v. Nash-Kelvinator Corp.*, 64 F. Supp. 716 (E.D. Mich. 1946).

12. *Detroit Free Press*, July 3, 1946.

13. Patrick S. Nertney to Robert E. Hannegan, June 25, 1946, Official File 921, Truman Library.

14. Walter C. Averill, Jr. to Harry S. Truman, July 7, 1946; Clayton Fairfax to Harry S. Truman, August 5, 1946. Copies of both communications are in Box 170, File 170.12, Avern Cohn Papers.

15. Clara Van Auken to Harry S. Truman, July 4, 1946, Box 170, File 170.12, Avern Cohn Papers.

16. Telegram, allegedly Walter P. Reuther et alia to Harry S. Truman, July 3, 1946, Official File 921, Truman Library.

17. John Dingell, Sr. to Philip Slomovitz, August 14, 1935, Box 170, File 170.12, Avern Cohn Papers.

18. *Detroit Free Press*, July 7, 1946.

19. E. Cyril Bevan to Harry S. Truman, July 8, 1946. Box 170, File 170.12, Avern Cohn Papers.

20. *Detroit Free Press*, July 7, 1946.

21. *Detroit Free Press*, July 7, 1946. Hook alleged that his opposition to Starr, a justice of the Michigan Supreme Court, was based on the fact that Starr's vacancy on the Supreme Court would be filled by Michigan's Republican governor. However, there is evidence that he wanted to control the nomination himself. *Detroit Free Press*, July 4, 1946.

22. Frank Schwartz to Harry S. Truman, July 23, 1946, Box 170, File 170.12, Avern Cohn Papers.

23. David Halberstam, *The Fifties* (New York: Villard Books, 1993), 23.

24. The younger generation of Levins has also been very successful. Charles Levin was a Michigan Supreme Court justice, Joseph Levin was a candidate for a seat in the United States House of Representatives, Daniel Levin is a real estate developer in Chicago, and daughter Mimi Levin Lieber served on the New York State Board of Regents. Judge Levin's nephews Carl and Sander Levin are, respectively, a U.S. senator and a U.S. representative.

25. *Arrowsmith v. Voorhies*, 55 F.2d 310 (E.D. Mich. 1931). All three judges had strong ties to Michigan: Circuit Court of Appeals Judge Charles Simons, District Judge Arthur Denison of the Western District, and District Judge Ernest O'Brien of the Eastern District.

26. 62 Stat. 896, 897.

27. See 72 Stat. 497.

28. Russell R. Wheeler, *Origins of the Elements of Federal Court Governance* (Federal Judicial Center 1992), 11–12.

29. The title senior district judge resurfaced in legislation passed in 1957 to describe those judges who choose senior service, i.e., to leave active service but remain available for such judicial service "as he is willing and able to undertake." 71 Stat. 495.

30. 54 Stat. 670, codified at 18 U.S.C. sec. 10, 11, and 13. In 1948, Congress reworded and recodified the relevant parts of the Smith Act at 18 U.S.C. sec. 2385, but did not change its substance.

31. 86 Cong. Rec. 9036 (June 22, 1940).

32. *U.S. v. Dennis*, 183 F.2d 201 (2d Cir. 1950).

33. *U.S. v. Dennis*, 341 U.S. 494 (1951).

34. Saul Wellman had been a commissar in the International Brigades during the Spanish Civil War and a U.S. paratrooper at the siege of Bastogne. William Allan was a correspondent for the *Daily Worker* and the *Michigan Worker*. Thomas Dennis was the organizational secretary of the Communist Party of Michigan. Nat Ganley was the editor of the *Michigan Worker*; Philip Schatz organized the Communist Party at Ford Motor Company; and Helen Winter was a member of the Michigan State Committee of the Party.

35. Ernest Goodman was born in Hemlock, Michigan, in 1906, and graduated from what is now Wayne State University Law School in 1928. He defended sit-down strikers at the Ford Motor Company in the 1930s, served as associate general counsel for the United Automobile Workers union in the 1940s, and argued labor and civil rights cases before the U.S. Supreme Court.

36. Judge Picard was always popular with the mainstream press, perhaps because his own experience as a reporter taught him how to court them. He was always "good copy," enjoying a flair for the dramatic comment and a "renowned whimsey." One Detroit columnist described him as "a wondrously humorous, philosophical guy" whose motto was "Action, action, and still more action," who walked and talked quickly, and who "never lingered over decisions." Some litigants and attorneys have described him less positively. He was notoriously thin-skinned about criticism and a stickler for procedural detail. One current district judge who appeared before Judge Picard remembered that he could be brutally hard on young attorneys and their clients. Another remarked that: "Frank Picard was a wild man . . . I can tell you some stories about Frank Picard that would shock you." Certainly, the defendants in the Michigan Six case and their counsel would not have recognized the "wondrously humorous," twinkle-eyed Judge Picard.

37. *U.S. v. Wellman*, 227 F.2d 757 (6th Cir. 1955).

38. Rohr, Marc, "Communists and the First Amendment: The Shaping of Freedom of Advocacy in the Cold War Era," *San Diego Law Review*, 28:1 (1999), 5, 29.

39. *Mesarosh v. U.S.*, 352 U.S. 862 (1956).

40. *Wellman v. U.S.*, 354 U.S. 931 (1957).

41. *Wellman v. U.S.*, 253 F.2d 601 (6th Cir. 1958).

42. The Smith Act was not the only tool the United States used during the 1950s to attack the CPUSA. The government also made a concerted effort to revoke the citizenship of naturalized immigrants on the grounds that they had not revealed during their naturalization interview that they were or had been members of one or more Communist organizations. These were civil proceedings, but the possibility of criminal prosecution under the Smith Act placed the defendants in a dilemma. E.g., *Brown v. U.S.*, 234 F.2d 140 (6th Cir. 1956), *aff'd*, 356 U.S. 148 (1958); *U.S. v. Nowak*, 133 F. Supp. 191 (E.D. Mich. 1955), *aff'd*, 238 F.2d 282 (6th Cir. 1956), *rev'd sub nom. Nowak v. U.S.*, 356 U.S. 660 (1958) and *Maisenberg v. U.S.*, 356 U.S. 670 (1958).

43. 68 Stat., Part 1, 8. The law created 21 new permanent district judgeships and six new temporary district judgeships, while making permanent three existing temporary district judgeships. The same law ended a long-running statutory curiosity. Since 1911, Congress had listed Port Huron as a venue for the Northern Division, but also assigned St. Clair County, where Port Huron is located, to the Southern Division. The 1954 law returned Port Huron as a Southern Division venue, although the change was merely clerical because up to that time no judges had wanted to hold court there.

44. H. Rep. 1005, 83rd Cong., 1st Sess., 74.

45. John Feikens Oral History, 78.

46. *Bay City Times*, March 13, 1956.

47. *Bay City Times*, March 12, 1956, 1,4.

48. *Bay City Times*, March 12, 1956, 4.

49. *Bay City Times*, January 31, 1958, 4.

50. *Bay City Times*, May 20, 1958.

51. Levin, 499.

52. For Feikens' insights regarding this dispute, see Feikens Oral History, 68.

53. *Time*, August 25, 1961.

CHAPTER 12

District Judges Appointed 1961–1976

During the district court's first 122 years (1838–1960), only 17 persons (all men) were appointed to its bench and confirmed by the Senate. Then, during the next 16 years, another 14 judges joined the court, four to fill new judgeships, five to replace judges taking senior status, two to succeed judges who died in office, and two to replace judges appointed to the Sixth Circuit. Six of the new judges were appointed by Democratic presidents (Kennedy and Johnson) and eight by Republican presidents (Nixon and Ford), one (Judge McCree) was the first African American on the court, and another (Judge Kennedy) was the first woman. The result was two practically complete changes of the court's judges and of their party affiliations. In 1960, three of the court's six judges had been appointed by Democratic presidents and three by Republican presidents, but in 1968, six of the court's eight judges had been appointed by Democrats, while in 1974, eight of the court's ten judges had been appointed by Republicans.

Nomination By	District Judge	Confirmed
President Kennedy (4)	Thaddeus M. Machrowicz	1961
	Wade H. McCree, Jr.	1961
	Talbot Smith	1962
	Stephen J. Roth	1962
President Johnson (2)	Damon J. Keith	1967
	Lawrence Gubow	1968
President Nixon (6)	Cornelia G. Kennedy	1970
	John Feikens	1970
	Philip Pratt	1970
	Robert E. DeMascio	1971
	Charles W. Joiner	1972
	R. James Harvey	1973
President Ford (2)	James P. Churchill	1974
	Ralph B. Guy, Jr.	1976

Fig. 64.   Judges' meeting, 1960s. L–R: Chief Judge Levin; Judges Thornton, Kaess, Smith, Freeman, McCree. (Historical Society for the United States District Court for the Eastern District of Michigan)

Thaddeus Michael Machrowicz

Born: August 21, 1899 (Gostyn, Germany, now in Poland), to Boniface and
    Frances Werbel Machrowicz
Education: Detroit College of Law (LL.B. 1924)
Military: Polish "Blue Army," France and Poland (1917–1921)
Nominated/Confirmed: August 21/September 1, 1961
Vacancy: Judge Picard (Senior Status)
Left the Court: February 17, 1970 (Died)

Judge Machrowicz's family immigrated from what was then Germany and settled in Chicago and then Milwaukee. He graduated in 1916 from Alliance College in Pennsylvania, a school founded by the Polish National Alliance. During World War I, he, along with 23,000 other Polish Americans, joined the Polish "Blue Army" and fought in France and newly independent Poland. Machrowicz also acted as a war correspondent and served with the American Advisory Commission to the Polish government and the American Relief Mission to Poland. After he received his law degree, he opened a private practice in Hamtramck, Michigan. On June 5, 1935, he married Sophie Jara; they were the parents of two sons. In addition to his law practice, Machrowicz became involved in Democratic politics and served in a number of elected and appointed positions. In 1950, he was

Fig. 65.   Judge Thaddeus Michael Machrowicz. (Society for the United States District Court for the Eastern District of Michigan)

elected to the U.S. House of Representatives with an overwhelming major-ity. Over the next ten years, he won four more congressional elections, never with less than 80 percent of the vote. He was a leader in the creation of the St. Lawrence Seaway. In the 1960 election, Representative Machrowicz re-ceived more than 90 percent of the vote, but he decided to accept a seat on the district court rather than to complete his sixth term.

Wade Hampton McCree, Jr.

Born: July 3, 1920 (Des Moines, Iowa), to Wade Hampton and Lulu H.
    McCree
Education: Boston Latin School, Fisk University (A.B. 1941), Harvard Law
    School (LL.B. 1948)
Military: U.S. Army (Captain, Bronze Star for Valor)
Nominated/Confirmed: September 18/23, 1961
Vacancy: New Seat
Left the Court: September 7, 1966 (Appointed to Sixth Circuit)
Death: August 30, 1987

In the Omnibus Judgeship Act of 1961,[1] a new Democratic majority in Con-gress created 63 additional district court judgeships, two of which went to the Eastern District of Michigan. President Kennedy filled one of those positions with Wade H. McCree, Jr., the first African American appointed to the court, who would become one of the most honored and celebrated Michiganders of his era. In years to come, he would also be the first African American judge on the Sixth Circuit (1966–1977) and the second African

Fig. 66. Judge Wade Hampton
McCree, Jr. (Historical Society for
the United States District Court
for the Eastern District of
Michigan)

American, after Thurgood Marshall, to become solicitor general of the
United States (1977–1981).

Judge McCree's father, a pharmacist, was one of the first African Americans hired as a federal narcotics inspector, and the family followed his
postings to Hawaii, Chicago, and Boston. After graduating summa cum
laude from Fisk, Judge McCree enrolled at Harvard Law School, but he
interrupted his education during World War II.

On July 29, 1946, he married Dores M. McCree[2] and they moved to
Detroit ; they were the parents of three children. In Detroit, he began a
general practice with Harold E. Bledsoe, a mentor to young African American attorneys. In 1952, Michigan governor G. Mennen Williams appointed
McCree to the Workmen's Compensation Commission and two years later
appointed him a judge of Wayne County Circuit Court. At the next election, he became the first African American to be elected to that court, and
he continued in that position until he was appointed to the federal bench.
As solicitor general, he argued on behalf of the United States in the U.S.
Supreme Court in two of the most important cases of the generation, the
Nixon tapes and papers case and the Allan Bakke reverse discrimination
case. In 1981, Judge McCree returned to Michigan and taught as the Lewis
M. Times Professor of Law at the University of Michigan.

Judge McCree was a member and leader of numberless professional
and community organizations. He also received honorary LL.D. degrees
from Wayne State University, Tuskegee Institute, Detroit College of Law,
University of Detroit, Harvard University, Michigan State University, the University of Michigan, Oakland University, Lewis and Clark Law School, and
Northwestern School of Law.

Talbot Smith

Born: October 11, 1899 (Fayette, Missouri), to Franklin C. and Mary Major
    Smith
Education: United States Naval Academy (B.S. 1920, M.S. 1928); University
    of Michigan Law School (J.D. 1934)
Military: U.S. Navy (1917–1931)
Recess Appointment: October 5, 1961
Nominated/Confirmed: January 15/February 5, 1962
Vacancy: New Seat
Senior Status: October 31, 1971
Death: December 21, 1978

President Kennedy's appointment to the Eastern District's second new
seat went to Michigan Supreme Court justice Talbot Smith. After receiving
two degrees from the U.S. Naval Academy and serving 14 years in the
Navy, Judge Smith resigned his naval commission and entered private
practice in Detroit and Ann Arbor. He was a Professor of Law at both the
University of Missouri (1937–1941) and University of California at Berkeley
(1945). When the United States entered World War II, he was too old to
return to the Navy, and became an attorney for the Office of Price Administration. In 1946, he took up his law practice in Ann Arbor again and
in 1955, he was appointed to the Michigan Supreme Court by Governor
G. Mennen Williams. In 1921, Judge Smith married Lola Hamlen; they had
two children. One of Judge Smith's former law clerks, Wallace Riley, remembered that: "Talbot had the infinite patience of a great teacher. He

Fig. 67. Judge Talbot Smith.
(Historical Society for the United
States District Court for the
Eastern District of Michigan)

had the forgiveness of a minister. He had the sternness of a naval officer. And he had the inspiration of a saint."

Stephen John Roth

Born: April 21, 1908 (Sajószöged, Hungary) to Charles John and Johanna Zillai Roth
Educated: Flint Public Schools, University of Notre Dame (Ph.B. 1931), University of Michigan Law School (LL.B. 1935)
Military: U.S. Army (1942–1945)
Nominated/Confirmed: April 19/May 1, 1962
Vacancy: Judge Feikens (Not Confirmed)
Left the Court: July 11, 1974 (Died)

When Senator McNamara finally blocked the appointment of John Feikens, President Kennedy turned to Stephen J. Roth of Flint, a judge of the Genesee County Circuit Court (1952–1962) and a former Michigan attorney general (1949–1951). Judge Roth's nomination was supported by the Genesee County Bar Association, but, as was so often the case, rivalry among the northern cities led to opposition. The Saginaw County Bar Association, which preferred its own Vincent A. Scorsone, argued that four recent cases in which Judge Roth was over-ruled by the Michigan Supreme Court demonstrated that he lacked an adequate understanding of law and procedure.[3] The nominating committee, which included U.S. senators Philip A. Hart and Patrick V. McNamara, was not dissuaded.

Fig. 68. Judge Stephen John Roth. (Historical Society for the United States District Court for the Eastern District of Michigan)

Judge Roth's father immigrated to the United States in 1911 and found work at the Buick plant in Flint, Michigan, where, two years later, he was joined by his family. After law school, Judge Roth returned to Flint and began a private practice. Roth was married twice, to Francese Jane Bowerman on November 20, 1937, and, after her death, to Evelyn L. Gunner. He was the father of five children. Judge Roth was initially assigned to the Detroit courthouse. When the district court opened a court in Flint in October 1962, he assumed that docket while maintaining a full caseload in Detroit. This dual caseload led him to be assigned *Milliken v. Bradley*, the Detroit school desegregation case for which he is best remembered.

Appointments by President Lyndon B. Johnson

Damon Jerome Keith

Born: July 4, 1922 (Detroit, Michigan) to Perry and Anne Louise Williams Keith

Education: Detroit Northwestern High School (1939), West Virginia State College (B.A. 1943), Howard University School of Law (J.D. 1949), Wayne State University Law School (LL.M. 1956)

Military: U.S. Army (1943–1946)

Nominated/Confirmed: September 25/October 12, 1967

Vacancy: Judge Thornton (Senior Status)

Left the Court: October 20, 1977 (Appointed to Sixth Circuit)

Fig. 69.   Judge Damon Jerome Keith. (Historical Society for the United States District Court for the Eastern District of Michigan)

The first of President Lyndon Johnson's two appointments to the Eastern District was Detroit attorney and civil rights leader Damon J. Keith, the son of a foundry worker for Ford Motor Company and the second African American judge in the Eastern District. After Judge Keith graduated from law school, he returned to Detroit and opened a private law practice, which he continued until he became U.S. district judge. In 1964, Judge Keith was appointed co-chair with John Feikens of the Michigan Civil Rights Commission. In 1953, Judge Keith married Dr. Rachel Boone Keith, and they had three daughters. Dr. Keith died on January 4, 2007.

Judge Keith served as chief judge of the district court from 1975 to 1977. On September 28, 1977, President Jimmy Carter nominated him to a vacancy on the U.S. Court of Appeals for the Sixth Circuit created when Judge Wade H. McCree, Jr. was appointed Solicitor General of the United States. Judge Keith assumed senior status on the court of appeals on May 1, 1995. From 1979 to 1986, Judge Keith was very active in the work of the Judicial Conference of the United States. In 1985, he chaired the Committee on the Bicentennial of the Constitution of the Sixth Circuit, and in 1987, he served as National Chairman of the Judicial Conference Committee on the Bicentennial of the Constitution.

Judge Keith has been awarded more than 30 honorary doctorates in law, including degrees from the University of Michigan, Yale University, and Harvard University. In 2011, Wayne State University Law School inaugurated the Damon J. Keith Center for Civil Rights.

Lawrence Gubow

Born: January 10, 1919 (Detroit, Michigan) to Jacob and Dora Rubin Gubow
Education: Detroit Northern High School (1936), University of Michigan
      (A.B. 1940, LL.B. 1950)
Military: U.S. Army (Captain, 1941–1948)
Nominated/Confirmed: August 2/September 13, 1968
Vacancy: Judge McCree (Appointed to Sixth Circuit)
Left the Court: March 26, 1978 (Death)

President Johnson's appointment of Judge McCree to the Sixth Circuit created a vacancy on the district court to which the president appointed Lawrence Gubow, since 1961 the U.S. attorney for the Eastern District of Michigan. After leaving the army in 1948, Judge Gubow married Estelle Schmalberg; they were the parents of three children. Upon becoming a member of the Michigan bar, Judge Gubow conducted a private practice in Detroit until 1953, when Governor Williams appointed him to the Michigan Corporations and Securities Commission, where he rose to the position of commissioner. During that time, Governor Williams also named him to various other state commissions studying legal and governmental issues. As corporations and securities commissioner, he gained national attention because of regulations he introduced in 1960 to end discrimination by real estate brokers against home buyers and, specifically, to end the

Fig. 70. Judge Lawrence Gubow.
(Historical Society for the United
States District Court for the
Eastern District of Michigan)

screening system brokers used to make sure black buyers would not be shown homes in Grosse Pointe.[4] He left the commission a year later when President Kennedy named him U.S. attorney.

Judge Gubow was actively involved in the Jewish War Veterans organization, serving as commander of the Michigan chapter (1956–1957) and as a member of the national executive committee (1956–1976). He also served as president of the Jewish Community Council of Metropolitan Detroit and on many other religious and civic organizations. Judge Gubow continued to perform his duties as district judge even though he had been legally blind for the two years preceding his death.

Appointments by President Richard M. Nixon

Cornelia Groefsema Kennedy

Born: August 4, 1923 (Detroit, Michigan) to Elmer and Mary Groefsema
Education: University of Michigan (B.A. 1945, J.D. 1947)
Nominated/Confirmed: September 3/October 6, 1970
Vacancy: Judge Machrowicz (Died)
Left Court: September 25, 1979 (Appointed to Sixth Circuit)

Cornelia Groefsema Kennedy was the first woman appointed to the bench of the Eastern District of Michigan, the fourth woman appointed to any

Fig. 71. Judge Cornelia Groefsema Kennedy. (Historical Society
for the United States District
Court for the Eastern District of
Michigan)

U.S. district court, and the only woman among the 179 district court nominations made by President Nixon.[5] She was born Cornelia Groefsema into
a legal family—her father was a prominent attorney and her mother became a law student at the University of Michigan Law School, although
she died when Judge Kennedy was just nine years old. Elmer Groefsema
raised his daughters himself and "instilled in them a deep love of the law."[6]
Judge Kennedy's sister, Margaret Schaeffer, was the first woman to serve
as a law clerk on the Sixth Circuit Court of Appeals and also became a
judge. The third Grofesma sister, Christine, received her doctorate from
the University of Michigan in economics and was the president of Oakland
Community College, Auburn Hills Campus.

Judge Kennedy served a law clerkship with Judge Harold Stephens of
the U.S. Court of Appeals for the District of Columbia Circuit, and then, in
1948, returned to Detroit and private practice with her father and, later, for
13 years with Markle and Markle in Detroit. She married Charles Kennedy,
and in 1966, was elected a judge on the Wayne County Circuit Court, only
the third woman elected to a Michigan court of general jurisdiction.

Judge Kennedy served on the U.S. district court for nine years (1970–
1979), and was the court's chief judge from 1977 to 1979. Her performance
on the bench so impressed President Jimmy Carter that he nominated
her to a new seat on the Sixth Circuit, even though she was a Republican.
Although often mentioned for vacancies on the U.S. Supreme Court,
Judge Kennedy remained on the Sixth Circuit, taking senior status there
on March 1, 1999.[7]

John Feikens

Born: December 3, 1917 (Clifton, New Jersey) to Sipke and Corine Wisse
  Feikens
Education: Calvin College (B.A. 1939), University of Michigan Law School
  (J.D. 1941)
Nominated/Confirmed: October 7/November 25, 1970
Vacancy: New Seat
Senior Status: March 1, 1986
Left Court: May 15, 2011 (Died)

In June 1970, a Republican president and Democratic majority in both
Houses of Congress agreed to add 58 permanent and three temporary
district judgeships, of which the Eastern District again got two, raising its
total to ten.[8] The recipient of one of those seats was John Feikens, who
had been bumped from the court in 1961. Judge Feikens's grandparents
emigrated to the United States from the Zeeland and Friesland provinces
of the Netherlands. His parents ran a dairy farm in New Jersey, until his
father became a cattle dealer. During World War II, he supervised priorities and war allocations for Detroit's Detrex Corporation, a major supplier
of chemicals for the war effort. After the war, he entered private practice,
specializing in insurance defense, and also became involved in Republican
politics through his acquaintance with Michigan's senator Arthur H. Vandenberg. Feikens became a supporter of the presidential bid of General
Dwight D. Eisenhower, and in 1951, he was appointed chair of the Eisenhower Committee in Michigan and later the Republican State Central
Committee. As chief judge (1979–1986), Feikens won praise from the other
judges for his ability to lead by example and persuasion. He remained ac-

Fig. 72. Judge John Feikens.
(Historical Society for the United
States District Court for the
Eastern District of Michigan)

tively involved on the court and on the Historical Society until his death, although in 2010, he did finally give up 30-year stint supervising the Detroit Water Department.

Philip Pratt

Born: July 14, 1924 (Pontiac, Michigan) to Peter and Helen Statis Pratt
Education: Pontiac High School, University of Michigan Law School
  (LL.B. 1950)
Military: U.S. Army (1943–1946)
Nominated/Confirmed: October 7/November 25, 1970
Vacancy: New Seat
Left Court: February 7, 1989 (Died)

The district's other new seat, created in June 1970, went to Judge Philip Pratt of Oakland County Circuit Court. The son of Greek immigrants, Judge Pratt pursued Asian studies at the University of Michigan and the University of Chicago before joining the U.S. Army. He served in China as a sergeant with the Office of Strategic Services and was awarded the Bronze Star. After graduation from law school, he married Mary Charlotte Hill; they were the parents of three children. After time spent as a title examiner and an assistant prosecutor, Judge Pratt began a private practice in Pontiac, which he continued until 1963, when he was elected to the bench of the Oakland County Circuit Court. Judge Pratt served as chief judge of the district court from 1986 to 1989.

Fig. 73.   Judge Philip Pratt.
(Historical Society for the United
States District Court for the
Eastern District of Michigan)

Fig. 74.   Judge Robert Edward
DeMascio. (Historical Society for
the United States District Court
for the Eastern District of
Michigan)

Robert Edward DeMascio

Born: January 11, 1923 (Coraopolis, Pennsylvania) to Peter and Rosa Baretta
    DeMascio
Education: Wayne State University Law School (LL.B. 1951)
Military: U.S. Navy (1943–1946)
Nominated/Confirmed: June 14/July 22, 1971
Vacancy: Judge Theodore Levin (Died)
Senior Status: January 16, 1988
Left Court: March 23, 1999 (Died)

This son of Italian immigrants left Pittsburgh at the age of 13 to join his
brother who had found work in Detroit. After four years as a Navy seaman
in the Pacific, he worked full-time while attending law school and, upon
graduation, he began a private practice in Detroit. In 1954, he was appointed an assistant U.S. attorney for the Eastern District of Michigan, and
in 1955, he married Margaret Loftus; they were the parents of three children. He rose to become chief of the criminal division, but the office was
subject to the winds of politics, and he returned to private practice in 1961,
after the Democratic victory in the 1960 presidential election. In 1967, he
was elected judge of Recorders Court, at that time the criminal court for the
city of Detroit, where he served until his appointment by President Nixon.

Charles Wycliffe Joiner

Born: February 14, 1916 (Maquoketa, Iowa) to Melvin William and Mary von
    Schrader Joiner

Fig. 75. Judge Charles Wycliffe
Joiner. (Historical Society for the
United States District Court for
the Eastern District of Michigan)

Education: Maquoketa Junior College, University of Iowa (B.A. 1937,
     J.D. 1939)
Military: U.S. Army Air Corps (1943–1945)
Nominated/Confirmed: April 25, 1972/June 8, 1972
Vacancy: Judge Smith (Senior Status)
Senior Status: August 15, 1984

Charles W. Joiner is a rarity, a career academic who left academia to become a U.S. district judge at the age of 56. After law school, Judge Joiner
married Ann Helen Martin, with whom he had three children, and practiced law in Des Moines, Iowa, where he practiced until the United States
entered World War. In 1947, he was appointed to the faculty of the University of Michigan Law School, in 1960, associate dean, and in 1965–1966,
acting dean. He served as director of research and drafting for Michigan's
Constitutional Convention in 1961 and 1962. From 1967 to 1972, he was
dean and professor of law at Wayne State University Law School.

James Harvey

Born: July 4, 1922 (Iron Mountain, Michigan) to Martin and Agnes Thomas
     Harvey
Education: Iron Mountain High School, University of Michigan (J.D. 1948)
Military: U.S. Army Air Corps (1942–1945)
Nominated/Confirmed: December 5/13, 1973
Vacancy: Judge Freeman (Senior Status)
Senior Status: March 31, 1984
Left Court: June 29, 1992 (Retired)

Fig. 76. Judge James Harvey.
(Historical Society for the United
States District Court for the
Eastern District of Michigan)

James Harvey was the youngest of six children; his mother was born in
Cornwall as were his father's parents. His father was a lumberman and
handyman. Like many of the judges of this era he was poor but ambitious.
He arrived in Ann Arbor with just $100 in his pocket to pay his tuition and
supported himself by working, six hours a day, seven days a week, at the
Michigan Union.[9] Also, like many of his contemporaries, his education was
interrupted by the war, in which he served as a bomber navigator and in-
structor. He returned to Ann Arbor after the war and, although he did not
have an undergraduate degree, he was admitted to the law school.[10] While
a law student, in April 1948, he married June Elizabeth Collins; they had
two children. The Harveys moved to Saginaw, where he eventually joined
the firm of Smith and Brooker. After stints in a variety of local elected
and appointed positions, including mayor of Saginaw (1957–1959), in 1960,
he was elected to the U.S. House of Representatives and was re-elected
six times.

Judge Harvey began his judicial career in the Detroit court but, when
Judge Roth fell ill, he took over the Bay City court and moved his family
back to Saginaw. When Judge Roth died in July 1974, Judge Harvey took
over the Flint court as well. During his tenure in Flint and Bay City, Judge
Harvey presided over major renovations of the courtrooms and chambers
in both courthouses. After Judge Newblatt took over the Flint court, Judge
Harvey also reopened the Port Huron courtroom and chambers where he
held court each summer.

Appointments by President Gerald R. Ford

James Paul Churchill

Born: April 10, 1924 (Imlay City, Michigan), to Howard H. and Faye Shurte
    Churchill
Education: University of Michigan (B.B.A. 1947, LL.B. 1950)
Military: U.S. Army, France (1943–1946)
Nominated/Confirmed: December 2/18, 1974
Vacancy: Judge Stephen Roth (Died)
Senior Status: December 31, 1989

James Churchill's father was a bank cashier and later owned an insurance and real estate brokerage in Michigan's Thumb. After World War II, Judge Churchill completed his undergraduate degree and entered law school. There he joined a friend from his teenage years, future U.S. senator Robert Griffin, and met several future U.S. judges including Eastern District Judges Pratt, Harvey, Kennedy, and Joiner, as well as Albert Engel of the Western District. After law school, he married Ann Muir; they had three children. In 1951, he returned to the Thumb and opened a general private practice in Vassar, which he maintained until 1965, when he was elected the sole judge of Michigan's 40th Judicial Circuit Court, which then covered Lapeer and Tuscola Counties. He wanted to move up in the judicial world, and so accepted requests to try cases as a visiting judge around the state. After

Fig. 77. Judge James P. Churchill. (Historical Society for the United States District Court for the Eastern District of Michigan)

an unsuccessful campaign in 1974 for a seat on the Michigan Court of Appeals, he was contacted by Senator Griffin, who told him that President Ford was looking to fill a seat on the Eastern District and wanted a qualified appointee, even if he was not politically active. Judge Churchill accepted Griffin's invitation and began a career in the district court that has extended over 25 years. He spent his first decade on the federal court in Detroit, but in 1995, after Judge Harvey took senior status, he moved his chambers to Bay City. By nature and experience he is a populist, and has often expressed his belief that the job of a federal judge is to protect the people from the government the best he can. Judge Churchill was chief judge of the court in 1989, although he found it frustrating to try to keep watch over the court from Bay City.

Ralph B. Guy, Jr.

Born: August 20, 1929 (Dearborn, Michigan) to Ralph B. and Shirley Skladd Guy, Sr.
Education: Dearborn Fordson High School, University of Michigan (A.B. 1951, J.D. 1953)
Nominated/Confirmed: April 26/May 11, 1976
Vacancy: Judge Frederick Kaess (Senior Status)
Left Court: October 17, 1985 (Appointed to Sixth Circuit)

Judge Guy was born into a law-oriented family as his father was police chief in Dearborn, MI, and then a municipal judge. In 1955, after a short period in private practice, the younger Judge Guy became an assistant to the Dearborn corporation counsel (i.e., city attorney) and corporation

Fig. 78. Judge Ralph B. Guy, Jr.
(Historical Society for the United
States District Court for the
Eastern District of Michigan)

counsel (1958–1968). He then was hired by the U.S. attorney for the Eastern District, serving as chief assistant and then as U.S. attorney (1970–1976). Judge Guy was appointed to the Sixth Circuit by President Reagan and took senior status on that court on September 1, 1994.

Notes

1. 75 Stat. 80.

2. The couple had three children. Mrs. McCree was one of the founders of the Historical Society for the U.S. District Court for the Eastern District of Michigan.

3. *Detroit News*, July 18, 1961.

4. *New York Times*, July 5, 1960.

5. *Gatekeepers*, 288.

6. See Sarafa.

7. Thanks to Julie Titone for her unpublished essay, "Raised to Love the Law: A Conversation with Judge Cornelia Kennedy," a copy of which is in the archives of the U.S. Court of Appeals for the Sixth Circuit, Cincinnati, Ohio.

8. 84 Stat. 294.

9. Oral History, R. James Harvey, 9.

10. Idem., 15.

CHAPTER 13

The Protection of Civil Rights, 1961–1976

From 1961 to 1976, the United States experienced the longest uninterrupted period of economic expansion in its history and achieved unprecedented scientific and technological feats, including the establishment of a manned space program that evolved from nothing to landing 12 men on the moon in just 15 years. This was also a period of external and domestic conflict. The question of how to confront Communism brought the United States to a white-knuckle confrontation with the Soviet Union over Cuba and a war in southeast Asia. Frustration and anger among African Americans resulted in riots in Detroit and other cities, but also in the nation's most successful non-violent social movement. Drug use became a phenomenon of middle-class youth, causing Congress to increase the role of federal law, and of the federal courts, in attempts to control drug use.

The Eastern District, 1961–1976

Although few people noticed then, in retrospect it is clear that Detroit began to recede during the 1950s as it lost people and jobs. While the district's population grew by 31 percent between 1950 and 1970, despite losing four counties in 1954, Wayne County grew by only 10 percent and Detroit shrank by 18 percent. Also lost were hundreds of thousands of well-paid industrial jobs and the people who held them. At the same time, the population in the suburbs of Oakland and Macomb Counties grew by 164 percent. During the 1960s, the motivation for this exodus, which began in the 1940s to find fresh air and scarce housing, changed to race, "white flight," as the most racially segregated city in the northern United States became the nation's most racially segregated metropolitan area. Rather than live on an integrated street in Detroit, white families moved to the suburbs where black families were discouraged from following.[1]

294

Table 13.1   Average Annual Case Filings in the District Court, 1951–1976

Fiscal Year	Criminal	U.S. Civil	Private Civil	Total	Per Authorized Judgeship
1951–1960	686	602	612	1,900	336
1961–1970	743	634	956	2,333	300
1971–1976	1,484	622	1,631	3,737	374

The number of civil and criminal cases filed each year between 1960 and 1976 continued to increase relentlessly, and despite the addition of four judgeships (two in 1961 and two in 1971), the number of filings per judge in 1976 was 38 percent higher than in 1961. The increase in private civil cases from 1951 to 1970 was due largely to an increase in diversity cases, but from 1971 to 1976, civil rights cases and prisoner petitions increased from almost nothing to substantial numbers and continued to grow after this period. The growth of the criminal caseload from 1970 to 1976 was led by narcotics and selective service cases.

A Courtroom for Flint

On Wednesday, October 10, 1962, Chief District Judge Theodore Levin, joined by Circuit Judge Clifford O'Sullivan and District Judges Ralph Freeman, Frank Picard, and Stephen Roth, dedicated the new federal courtroom and judicial suite on the first story of the former main post office building at 600 Church Street in Flint, Michigan. That evening, Judge O'Sullivan was the speaker at a gala dinner at the Flint Golf Club celebrating the realization of a goal first imagined by Flint's civic leaders in 1927 and finally achieved despite a decade of fierce political infighting.

When Bay City won the contest to host federal court sessions in 1887, Bay County was the hub of a thriving lumber industry with a growing population that easily exceeded that of Flint's stagnant Genesee County. The race for a federal court was between Bay City and Saginaw, while Flint was not in the running. By the 1920s, though, Genesee County was the home of the Buick division of General Motors, had twice as many residents as Bay County, and was rapidly growing, while Bay County was not. When Congress offered Flint a new main post office building in 1927, city officials asked that it include a courtroom, but Congress was not interested in paying for what would have had to be a much bigger building. There matters remained, at least on the surface, until 1950 while Genesee County's population (270,953) ballooned, as did its advantage over Bay County which had only 88,461 residents in 1950. As the population difference grew, so did Flint's desire for the prestige and convenience of its own district court term. In 1952, Flint saw its chance in the scramble of local and

Fig. 79. The Flint Federal Building. (Historical Society for the United States District Court for the Eastern District of Michigan)

state officials to wheel and deal to get their needs or desires attached to the bill creating new judgeships across the country. By 1954, Flint had statewide backing for its quest for a court, and the final statute,[2] in addition to adding the Eastern District's sixth judge, also provided that: "Court for the Northern Division shall be held at Bay City and Flint ."[3]

The sole public objection to Flint hosting court terms came, not surprisingly, from Bay City. Officials there were only too aware of Flint's growing population and feared that authorizing a court in Flint, just 45 miles away, would sooner or later convince Congress to close "their" court. Bay County's freshman congressman, Elford Albin (Al) Cederberg, swore to do what was in his power to foil Flint's plans, but the coalition of eastern and western interests was too strong to stop the authority to hold court. Cederberg knew that, despite the mandatory "shall" of the statute, another federal law provided that: "Court shall be held only at places where Federal quarters and accommodations are available, or suitable quarters and accommodations are furnished without cost to the United States."[4] Because quarters that were suitable and free were rare, federal court sessions almost always required a federal courtroom, and Cederberg spent the rest of the 1950s opposing funding for a Flint court. In the summer of 1954, he managed (with the surprising assistance of Representative Kit Clardy of Flint) to block an appropriation of $179,400 for remodeling the Flint post office, but U.S. senator Homer Ferguson used his influence to restore the money.[5] An article in the *Bay City Times* on August 1, 1954, headlined "Flint Court Derided,"[6] suggested that the senator's purpose was to gather votes in Genesee County rather to fill any need for another court in the Northern District and declared that: "Those familiar with the activities of the federal court in Bay City, such as Deputy Clerk Clarence S. Pettit, call the proposed appropriation plain folly." According to the *Times*, Pettit pointed out that during the fiscal year ending June 30, 1954, the district court was in session in Bay City for only 49 days and that he had never, in his 30 years in office, heard a Flint attorney complain about having to travel to Bay City to attend court. Pettit asserted that Flint attorneys were involved in only 17 of 123 civil cases filed in Bay City, and that, although 50 percent of the division's criminal defendants were from Flint, "not more than two of the Flint defendants engaged attorneys," most of the rest pleading guilty without benefit of counsel. Pettit conceded that 80 percent of the division's 319 bankruptcy cases involved Flint residents, but he also noted that they were already serviced by a bankruptcy referee holding hearings one day each month in a Genesee County probate courtroom. The article concluded with the observation that the $179,400 was "just the beginning," and that with the cost of supplying Flint with a new law library and the salaries of a resident clerk, marshal, and U.S. attorney, "the upkeep would be greater than the original cost."

Even after the appropriation for a courtroom was restored, Cederberg persevered, knowing that the funds could not be spent so long as the post office occupied the Church Street building because the upper floor was too small and low to accommodate a court. Postmaster General Arthur Summerfield, a Flint booster, took notice and announced in February 1956 that a postal facility "of an entirely new character" would be built at a different location in Flint and that the present building would be used for other federal purposes—i.e., a court.[7] Cederberg was right that the 1954 appropriation was just the beginning. In January 1960, Flint's new post office was completed, and the federal government increased the amount available for the court suite to $633,000, almost as much as the building cost in 1927. Still Cederberg did not surrender, and on January 19, the *Flint Journal* reminded its readers that he remained a dangerous opponent: "As a member of the Appropriations Committee, he will have a powerful voice on the question. An easy way to deny the City a court would be to get the [money for the Flint project] deleted from the Federal court appropriation."[8] Indeed, a day later the *Bay City Times* reported that the Administrative Office of the United States Courts and the judges of the Eastern District had decided that the current caseload in the Northern Division did not justify a second court location and that only proceedings that did not require a courtroom, such as pretrial conferences and bankruptcy hearings, would be held in Flint. A week later, Mr. Airhart of the Administrative Office told the press that: "It is impossible to justify courts

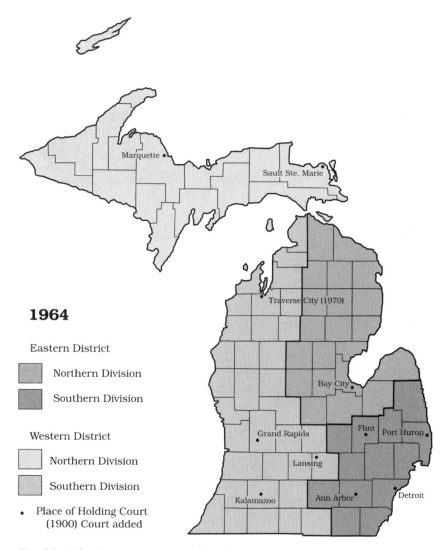

1964

Eastern District

Northern Division

Southern Division

Western District

Northern Division

Southern Division

• Place of Holding Court
   (1900) Court added

Fig. 80.   The Eastern District of Michigan, 1964. (Ellen White)

at both Bay City and Flint," although he went on to remark that even the Bay City court was "justified more by geography than by caseload."[9]

Nevertheless, in February 1960, Flint architects MacKenzie, Knuth, and Klein were picked to design the project to remove most of the postal functions and use 7,320 square feet on the first floor for two courtrooms (one for the district judge and one for a bankruptcy judge), chambers, law library, jury room, and offices for an assistant U.S. attorney, a probation officer, a court reporter, and a clerk. This contract set Cederberg off again.

He blasted the Flint court as a wasteful duplication of Bay City's court, which itself was not very busy: "To my knowledge, there hasn't been a case tried in federal court at Bay City for about three months. It's beyond my comprehension why we should build a federal court at Flint when the one at Bay City hasn't been used in that time."[10] In April, the Administrative Office admitted that the court projects in Flint, Kalamazoo, and Port Huron would go forward after all.[11] Airhart explained that construction contracts had already been let and that it was "easier to go ahead than to stop."[12] Airhart also remarked that a decision to build a federal courthouse or courtroom "is not really a judicial problem. It's a local political problem. First there's a designation on paper that a court may be held in a certain place. Then, on goes the pressure to put courtroom facilities in there. It's as simple as that."

After the courtroom dedication, Judge Roth, who was from Saginaw, was assigned to preside at Flint, although he also kept his full docket in Detroit on the assumption that there would not be much to do in Flint. The Flint court opened to the public for business on Monday, October 15, 1962,[13] and filings were indeed slow to start, with only three cases during what was left of calendar year 1962, but they did increase slowly (55 in 1963, 79 in 1964, 75 in 1965, and 67 in 1966).[14] When Judge Picard died in 1963, Judge Roth added the Bay City docket as well. Since Judge Roth's death, the Flint bench has been occupied by District Judges James Harvey, Stewart Newblatt, Paul Gadola, Jr., and Mark Goldsmith.

Al Cederberg was had one maneuver left. In October 1964, Congress moved Genesee and Shiawassee counties from the Northern to Southern Divisions and designated Flint as a Southern Division venue.[15] Once again, Bay City was the only Northern Division venue authorized for the district court in a shrunken Northern Division that then held only 12 percent of the Eastern District's population. Even this solution did not completely still Bay City's anxiety: when Judge Harvey, a resident and former mayor of Saginaw, was nominated to the district court in 1973, he had to make a public avowal that the seat of the Northern Division would not be moved to Saginaw.[16]

Port Huron Renovations

At the same time that it was planning the Flint remodeling, the Administrative Office was also proposing to remodel and update the courtroom and offices at Port Huron. The *Bay City Times* attacked that project as well, charging that it was merely a sop to Judge O'Sullivan's desire to work closer to his Port Huron home. After O'Sullivan was nominated for the Sixth Circuit in January 1960, the Administrative Office announced that the project was to be scaled down to a judge's office, a decision which the *Times* claimed was "an admission [that the courtroom] was being created for the convenience of Judge O'Sullivan."[17] When the judges and the Administrative Office reinstated Port Huron's full court renovation in April 1960, Airhart explained that the project was going forward "in anticipation of need" and predicted that, because of the recent opening of the St. Lawrence Seaway project: "In about five years it will get about as much use as the court at Bay City is getting now," although he did not mention how little that was. The *Times* offered its own prediction that the $330,000 to be spent in Port Huron "should cause Eastern District judges at Detroit to squirm on their benches for years to come" because the courtroom "will gather more cobwebs than it will legal business for years to come."[18] In the case of Port Huron, the *Times* proved to be the better prognosticator, as that courtroom remained unused until 1979, when Judge Harvey began hearing criminal cases there in the summers, has no resident clerk or magistrate judge, and has never been operated full time, although at this writing Senior District Judge Lawrence P. Zatkoff does have his chambers there.

One Voter, One Vote: *Marshall v. Hare*

The manner in which the citizens of a state elect their state legislators, judges, and other officials is at the heart of state sovereignty. Yet enforcement of federal constitutional principles can, at times, require the federal courts to inhibit and curtail that sovereignty. Such was the relief sought by the plaintiffs in *Marshall v. Hare*,[19] filed on June 23, 1963, the day after the Michigan Board of State Canvassers certified the ratification of Michigan's 1963 Constitution. Plaintiffs asked a three-judge federal panel to hold provisions in the new constitution dealing with the apportionment of seats in the state legislature unconstitutional. Specifically, to hold that they violated the Fourteenth Amendment to the U.S. Constitution on the grounds that they were irrational and "invidiously and purposefully discriminatory."

Plaintiffs, residents of three counties, Wayne, Oakland, and Muskegon, challenged Article IV, §§ 2–6 of the 1963 Constitution, which allocated the seats in the Michigan House of Representatives based on population, but with two provisos: that district boundaries were not to cross county lines and that every county with at least 0.7 percent of the state's population was guaranteed no less than one seat. According to the plaintiffs, this resulted in rural counties with smaller populations, most of which were in the northern third of the Lower Peninsula and in the Upper Peninsula, receiving greater per capita representation in the legislature than populous urban counties, most of which were in the southern half of the Lower Peninsula.[20] Michigan's secretary of state, the named defendant in the case, agreed with the plaintiffs and left the defense of the case to the Michigan Senate and the assistant attorney general.

Although the U.S. district courts were given, in 1875, the power to decide a claim that a state statute violates the U.S. Constitution,[21] since 1948 Congress has required that any such case be tried and determined by a panel of three federal judges, including at least one judge of the Court of Appeals.[22] In *Marshall v. Hare*, that panel consisted of Circuit Judge Clifford O'Sullivan of the U.S. Court of Appeals for the Sixth Circuit sitting with two district judges of the Eastern District, Judges Frederick W. Kaess and Stephen J. Roth. On March 16, 1964, the panel decided, 2 to 1, that the challenged provisions were constitutional. Judge Kaess, in an opinion with which Judge O'Sullivan concurred, noted that the U.S. Supreme Court had never mandated a strict one-person, one-vote standard of representation. He then posited that any apportionment plan should be subjected, instead, to three tests advanced by the U.S. solicitor general in similar cases: "(1) whether the basis for departure from the principle of equal population can be discerned, (2) whether it represents a legitimate objective in legislative apportionment, and (3) whether the principle of equal representation is subordinated to an excessive degree." Reviewing the mountains of evidence presented by the parties, Kaess found that the basis for departure was obvious: "a determination deliberately made to increase the representation of the people of Northern Michigan." He continued: "The second and third tests are also met. The assurance of adequate representation to a sparsely populated and impoverished region constitutes a proper objective, and the provisions of the new Constitution do not subordinate the principle of equal population to an excessive degree." On the second test, Judge Kaess found that advantaging northern Michigan was a legitimate objective: "The people of northern Michigan are placed at an economic disadvantage due to the depletion of their natural resources and the decline of some of their industries. They are far from the seat of government, far from the great concentrations of wealth and power. The difficult problems they face often are not those faced in other areas of the state." Moreover, the effect of the challenged provisions would be minimal: evidence showed that only two of the 110 seats in the House would be transferred from a more populous county to a less populous one.

Judge Roth dissented in a passionate defense of equality under the law, which he interpreted to mean that all legislative districts must have as close to the same population as practicable, a strict one-voter, one-vote rule: "The built-in, 'fair' advantage in the 1963 Constitution is completely at odds with our concept of the equality of man." He continued: "In our scheme of government, there is no provision for, nor room for, a caste system, even of the wise and the good. Nowhere is there to be found even an intimation that some of our citizens have greater or less political capacity or power than others." He even questioned the validity of the convention that drafted the 1963 Constitution because its delegates were not elected by one-voter, one-vote. In conclusion, he urged that the legislature should hold elections that ignored the 1963 Constitution and, "failing which, within a reasonable time, this Court should order elections for both Houses to be held at large."

In the end, Judge Roth's per se rule prevailed over the reliance of Judges O'Sullivan and Kaess on reasonableness. On June 15, 1964, three months after they announced their decision, the U.S. Supreme Court held, in *Reynolds v. Sims*,[23] that: "as a federal constitutional requisite both houses of a state legislature must be apportioned on a population basis." The Court explained that the equal protection clause of the 14th Amendment to the U.S. Constitution does not require a precise mathematical equality, but it does require "that a state make an honest and good faith effort to construct districts, in both houses of its legislature, as nearly of equal population as is practicable." Consequently, a week later, the Supreme Court reversed the *Marshall* panel's decision and remanded the case to the panel for further proceedings.[24] On remand, the three-judge panel held that the 1963 Constitution's weighted land area/population formulae violated equal protection under the U.S. Constitution.

The reaction of the state was curious in that the unconstitutional provisions were not amended and, indeed, they remain a part of the Michigan Constitution at this writing, a trap for an unwary reader. The Commission on Legislative Apportionment, also created by the 1963 Constitution, recommended reapportionment plans based on what it believed were the "constitutional requirements." Often those recommendations are attacked as the evil work of the political party in power, resulting in litigation. After the 1970 census, Judge Damon Keith found himself enmeshed in the dispute. In December 1971, a group of prominent Michigan Republicans sued Richard Austin, Michigan's secretary of state, challenging the existing congressional districts as out of compliance because of changes in population found by the 1970 census. Although most districts had gained population, the Upper Peninsula and parts of Wayne County had lost residents. Judge Keith later allowed a group of equally prominent Democrats as well as U.S. representative (and future U.S. district judge) James Harvey, a Republican from Saginaw, to join the case as plaintiffs. The parties stipulated that the districts had to be changed, but the impediment was the legislature, which could not agree on a plan. Finally, on May 12, 1972, fed up with the legislative dithering and with federal elections impending in November, Judge Keith announced that he had selected one of the plans submitted by the parties, and entered a final order on May 31.[25] In subsequent decades, the Michigan Supreme Court was left to sort out all out, if it could.[26] In 1996, the Michigan legislature finally codified the standards used by the Michigan Supreme Court in adopting state legislative redistricting plans in 1982 and 1992,[27] even though these standards did not prevent the filing of challenges in the district court. Following the 1992 reapportionment, for example, the

National Association for the Advancement of Colored People (NAACP) sued, alleging that the plan did not maximize the number of districts with an African American majority. A three-judge panel of Circuit Judge Martin and Eastern District Judges Avern Cohn and Bernard Friedman rejected that claim because "[s]tated concisely, the State is not obliged under the Act to provide for as many majority-minority districts as possible."[28]

The Court and Civil Rights Cases

Before 1972, there were not enough private civil rights cases filed in a year for federal judicial statistics to report for them as a separate category, despite the existence of a variety of constitutional and statutory remedies against discrimination since the post-Civil War era. In 1950, there were only 142 filed in all of the U.S. district courts and in 1960, only 280. This began to change, albeit slowly, when, in 1961, the U.S. Supreme Court, in *Monroe v. Pape*, held that the Civil Rights Act of 1971 (today known as Section 1983) could be used to sue employers of state and local employees for damages or an injunction because of "the deprivation of any rights, privileges, or immunities secured by the Constitution and laws."[29] Then, in 1964 and 1968, Congress passed new laws forbidding discrimination on the basis of race, color, gender, or religion in housing, employment, and public accommodations.[30] As a result, the number of civil rights cases filed nationwide increased to 3,985 in 1970 and 12,944 in 1980.[31] During the same period, the number in the Eastern District grew from nearly nothing before 1970 to 303 in 1975 and 405 in 1980. Two of the private civil rights cases that were most important to their communities and to the law were begun in 1969 and 1970. Both cases involved attempts to desegregate urban school systems in Michigan: *Davis v. Pontiac* in Pontiac and *Milliken v. Bradley* in Detroit. Although it is not as well remembered today as *Milliken v. Bradley*, Judge Damon Keith's February 1970 ruling in *Davis*, which ordered the integration of the public schools of Pontiac, and the resulting ferocious circus of public resistance to his ruling were fresh in the minds of the court and the parties when *Milliken* was filed six months later.

These cases, like other cases seeking to cure "structural" discrimination in state or local government, present district judges with difficult and dangerous problems. Such a judge "must perform one of the most difficult tasks in our system of government":

The judge must stand as an officer of the national government against a local majority represented by state and local officials. The trial judge facing such a task does not enjoy the rarified atmosphere of appellate courts. As one scholar has observed, trial judges must operate at the point where political and legal systems meet. And it is when a federal judge fashions a remedy following proof of a legal violation that the conflicts between law and politics and between federal courts and state and local officials become most intense. At that moment the difficulties that come in translating the principles involved in framing a government into the problems of running a government (such as the protection of individual rights against rule by the majority) are felt most keenly. It is the realm of hard judicial choices.[32]

Davis v. School District of the City of Pontiac

In 1869, just more than a century before African American parents of students in Pontiac and Detroit sued in the Eastern District to desegregate their respective school districts, the Michigan Supreme Court, in *People ex rel. Workman v. Detroit Board of Education*,[33] held that separate school systems for white and black students were inherently unequal and illegal under state law. That same court had also, however, upheld deed covenants and other devices used to separate neighborhoods by race.[34] The result, in many districts across Michigan, and the nation, was *de facto* segregation enhanced by decisions on the location of schools. In 1970, Pontiac was a factory city of 85,000 people, just 25 miles to the northwest of Detroit. Housing of the city's population was divided strictly along racial lines, with white neighborhoods in the north of the city and black neighborhoods in the south. Consequently, the city's neighborhood schools were also divided racially. On February 20, 1969, African American parents of children enrolled in Pontiac schools filed a class action in the district court against the school district, the school board, and the system's upper management, alleging intentional racial segregation of individual schools and discrimination in hiring and assigning African American employees, all in violation of the Fourteenth Amendment. The case was assigned to Judge Keith, who held a six-day trial and, on February 17, 1970, held that Pontiac's school district had deliberately created a segregated system by its choice of attendance regions, its location of new schools, and its assignment of faculty. He ordered the district to "integrate its school system at all levels, student body, faculties and administrators, before the beginning of the school year of September, 1970," and to submit a plan in that regard in 30 days.[35] On April 2, 1970, Keith approved a plan submitted by the defendants and ordered that the plan be implemented. Because housing in Pontiac was itself racially segregated, the plan necessarily required sending both black and white students by school bus to schools outside of their neighborhoods. The system's plan, which Judge Keith adopted, required 9,000 of the city's 24,000 school children to be bused to schools that were, on average, a 15-minute bus ride each way. As commentators noted, children in several school districts near Pontiac spent more time on a bus each day just to get to their nearest school, yet the school bus became the symbol around which resistance to the plan gelled.

The reaction by some white parents, vociferous but not initially violent, had many emotional roots. Racism was certainly the major factor; Michigan's own brand of racial tension was exacerbated by the fact that many of Pontiac's white residents, or their parents, were originally from the southern United States, and by the fact that Judge Keith was African American. In fact, it is possible to argue that all of the other reasons come back to race. Pontiac's white families were, for the most part, headed by automobile-factory workers whose high pay rates earned them a middle-class status that was both new and precarious. Consequently, they hated being ordered around by anybody, including the courts, and particularly a black judge, as if they were lower class. They also believed that they were inherently more intelligent, orderly, and law-abiding than black families, and that the presence of black children in their schools would "corrupt" their children. And they sincerely believed that they had worked hard in order to live near good schools. In their fervor to keep what they had, they rejected any suggestion that the black people who toiled beside them had worked just as hard and wanted the same things for their children.

The defendants appealed Judge Keith's order, and the Sixth Circuit stayed implementation of the plan for the 1970 to 1971 school year. On May 28, 1971, a three-judge panel of the Court of Appeals affirmed the order in an opinion by Circuit Judge McCree, also African American, who had left the district court three years earlier.[36] In his opinion, Judge McCree noted that: "We observe, as did the District Court, that school location and attendance boundary line decisions, for the past 15 years, more often than not tended to perpetuate segregation. Attempted justification of those decisions in terms of proximity of school buildings, their capacity, and safety of access routes requires inconsistent applications of these criteria. Although, as the District Court stated, each decision considered alone might not compel the conclusion that the Board of Education intended to foster segregation, taken together, they support the conclusion that a purposeful pattern of racial discrimination has existed in the Pontiac school system for at least 15 years."

On October 26, 1971, the Supreme Court denied defendants' petition for review,[37] leaving no legal barrier to enforcement of the integration plan. In the meantime, though, some Pontiac parents tried to impede implementation in other ways. Just days before the 1971 to 1972 school year was about to begin, Pontiac and its school system became national news when dynamite destroyed ten of the district's school buses and damaged three others. Six members of the Ku Klux Klan were arrested and five, including the former Grand Dragon of the Klan in Michigan, were indicted by a federal grand jury for criminal violations of the civil rights acts. They waived a jury and were tried by Judge Gubow. After three weeks of trial, highlighted by the testimony of an informant, Judge Gubow found all of the defendants guilty.[38]

A few days after the bombing, women chained themselves to the gate of the bus garage to keep the buses inside. A white boycott of the schools lasted only a few days, but the district lost 11 percent of its students permanently. An organization called the National Action Group (NAG), which claimed 20,000 members in 81 chapters, demonstrated in Pontiac and lobbied Congress for a law banning busing. Its founder, Irene McCabe, walked to Washington to meet with Michigan's congressional delegation and the White House, but all in vain. The boycott ended on September 23, 1971.[39]

The United States v. John Sinclair

Davis was not the only case involving a landmark issue of civil rights before Judge Keith in 1971. He was also involved in a case that raised issues of governmental limits and constitutional interpretation, and that led to what many lawyers and judges consider to be his greatest decision. One author characterizes Judge Keith's decision as "a prime example of an independent Federal judge interposing his authority between an executive action and the general citizenry."[40] *The United States v. John Sinclair*, which lawyers, judges, and constitutional scholars know simply as "the Keith case," began on September 29, 1968, when a dynamite bomb exploded in front of a recruitment office for the Central Intelligence Agency in Ann Arbor, Michigan. The bomb made a small crater in the sidewalk (12 by seven inches, and six inches deep), broke a lot of glass, and did not injure anyone. This bombing occurred just a month after the 1968 Democratic National Convention in Chicago and was one of eight recent blasts in the Detroit area. A year later, on October 7, 1969, a federal grand jury returned sealed indictments against three self-styled "visionary maniac white motherfucker country dope fiend rock and roll freaks [sic],"[41] John Sinclair, Laurence Robert "Pun" Plamondon, and John "Jack" Waterhouse, for conspiracy to destroy government property. All of the defendants were officers of an organization called the White Panther Party, later renamed the Rainbow Peoples Party, which was a fixture in Ann Arbor's counter-culture movement.

The case was assigned to Judge Talbot Smith, but he withdrew because his home in Ann Arbor was near the house used by the defendants and local officials advised that he might be in danger of reprisals.[42] The case was then reassigned to Judge Keith by having the judges draw sealed slips of paper. The government was represented by the Eastern District's U.S. attorney, Ralph B. Guy, Jr., while the defendants were represented by a pair of celebrity anti-war attorneys, William Kunstler and Leonard Weinglass, and by Detroit attorney Hugh "Buck" Davis. Defense counsel filed several pretrial motions, seeking to dismiss the charges as violations of the defendants' rights to free expression, or to exclude part of the government's case, most of which Judge Keith denied. In one such motion, filed on October 5, 1970, the defense sought disclosure of any electronic surveillance of the defendants. Nobody involved in the case, not the parties, the attorneys, or the judge was aware of any surveillance, and the government attorneys agreed to enter into a stipulation to that effect and to ask the Justice Department to confirm their belief. Instead, Attorney General John N. Mitchell filed an affidavit stating that there were, in fact, recordings of Plamondon resulting from wiretaps, apparently aimed at other individuals, entered into without a warrant. The government produced the relevant records and files for the judge to review *in camera* and moved to dismiss the disclosure request on a claim of national security.

After extensive oral arguments, Judge Keith, on January 26, 1971, granted the defendants' disclosure motion and denied the government's motion.[43] He noted that: "The position of the Government in this matter, simply stated, is that the electronic monitoring of defendant Plamondon's conversations was lawful in spite of the fact that the surveillance was initiated and conducted without a judicial warrant. In support of this position, the Government contends that the United States Attorney General, as agent of the President, has the constitutional power to authorize electronic surveillance without a court warrant in the interest of national security." Judge Keith rejected that interpretation of the Fourth Amendment: "An idea which seems to permeate much of the Government's argument is that a dissident domestic organization is akin to an unfriendly foreign power and must be dealt with in the same fashion. There is great danger in an argument of this nature for it strikes at the very constitutional privileges and immunities that are inherent in United States citizenship. It is to be remembered that in our democracy all men are to receive equal justice regardless of their political beliefs or persuasions. The executive branch of our government cannot be given the power or the opportunity to investigate and prosecute criminal violations under two different standards simply because certain accused persons espouse views which are inconsistent with our present form of government."

The United States filed a petition for mandamus, to force Judge Keith to return the surveillance tapes he had impounded. Thus, the caption of the case in the Sixth Circuit was not *U.S. v. Sinclair* but, rather, *U.S. v. U.S. District Court for the Eastern District of Michigan, Southern Division, and Honorable Damon J. Keith*. On April 8, 1971, the appellate court affirmed Judge Keith's decision and denied the mandamus petition.[44] In his opinion for the court, Circuit Judge George C. Edwards explained first that: "This case has importance far beyond its facts or the litigants concerned." He also noted, wryly, that: "It is strange, indeed, that in this case the traditional power of sovereigns like King George III should be invoked on behalf of an American President to defeat one of the fundamental freedoms for which the founders of this country overthrew King George's reign." Then he got to the point: "We hold that in dealing with the threat of domestic subversion, the Executive Branch of our government, including the Attorney General and the law enforcement agents of the United States, is subject to the limitations of the Fourth Amendment to the Constitution when undertaking searches and seizures for oral communications by wire." The stage was set for review by the Supreme Court which granted certiorari and then, on June 19, 1972, affirmed in an 8 to 0 unanimous decision.[45]

In March 1973, after the United States complied with the disclosure order, Sinclair, Plamondon, and Forrest filed, in the U.S. District Court for the District of Columbia, what is known as a Bivens action, a civil suit seeking damages from the United States, President Nixon, Richard Kleindienst, Patrick Gray, and John Mitchell for violation of their rights under the Fourth Amendment. Claims against all of those original defendants were dismissed, but, in January 1979, plaintiffs amended their complaint to add three new defendants, FBI agents who had been named during discovery as having been engaged in the surveillance of the White Panther Party. In June 1983, the U.S. Court of Appeals for the District of Columbia circuit ordered the district court to grant plaintiffs' motion to transfer the case to the Eastern District of Michigan.[46] There, the case was assigned to Judge La Plata who, six years later, in June 1989, granted the agents' motion for summary judgment, ruling that plaintiffs had not shown that they suffered any objective harm and that, because the law requiring a warrant was not clearly established when the wiretaps in this case occurred, the defendants were entitled to qualified immunity.[47] In October 1990, the U.S. Court of Appeals for the Sixth Circuit affirmed Judge La Plata's reasoning and the dismissal of plaintiffs' damage claims,[48] thus ending 20 years of litigation.

Strange Bedfellows: *Milliken v. Bradley*

On August 18, 1970, as residents of Pontiac were still contemplating the desegregation plan approved by Judge Keith and wondering what the Sixth Circuit would do, the parents of Ronald Bradley and other black and white students attending Detroit public schools filed a complaint in the district court against Michigan governor William Milliken, Attorney General Frank Kelley, State Superintendent of Public Instruction John Porter, the Michigan Board of Education, the Detroit School Board, and Detroit school superintendent Norman Drachler.[49] Plaintiffs asked the court to rule unconstitutional a state statute, Public Act 48 (PA 48), which broke the Detroit school district into autonomous districts. Plaintiffs alleged that it was intended to preserve Detroit's tradition of racially segregated schools. Their ultimate goal, though, was to end, once and for all, that tradition of segregation. *Milliken v. Bradley,* was not only a hugely controversial case in Michigan and across the country, it was also one of the most contentious

Table 13.2   Racial Composition of Detroit and Suburbs, 1910–1970

Year	Detroit Population			Suburban Population (approximate)		
	Total	Black	Percent	Total	Black	Percent
1910	465,766	5,741	1.23	148,000	1,000	0.68
1930	1,568,662	120,066	7.65	609,000	17,000	2.79
1950	1,849,568	300,506	16.25	1,167,000	61,000	5.23
1970	1,511,482	660,428	43.69	2,668,000	97,000	3.64

and, ultimately, one of the most frustrating cases as Detroit schools were more segregated at the end of the case than at the beginning and the district judges in charge of the case were left with little constructive to do except to make the schools better, more equal rather than less separate. The case also demonstrated U.S. district judges at their best, resisting intense public pressure in order to enforce the laws of the nation.

School segregation in Detroit has a long history. Detroit's first public schools, opened during the 1840s, were deliberately segregated, and even when the state legislature barred school segregation in 1867, the city refused to comply until two years after the state supreme court's 1869 *Workman* decision. Detroit's schools remained integrated until about 1922, when the Detroit School Board began to gerrymander school attendance boundaries and use other bureaucratic devices to create a segregated system. There were two reasons for this change: the presumption by a majority of white residents that blacks were naturally inferior and the intersection of two of the great migrations of the 20th century, hundreds of thousands of southern black families moving from the Old South to the industrial cities of the north and hundreds of thousands of white families moving from those same northern cities to the suburbs.

In general, relations between black and white Detroit residents have never been warm, but until World War I, the city's black population was so small that private animosities and prejudices rarely became public. The increase between 1910 and 1930, although no greater than for immigrants from various European countries, resulted in concerted efforts to confine blacks to certain rundown neighborhoods in the city, so that by the 1920s, the city's residential areas were strictly segregated and any attempt by a person of color to cross a "color line" was prevented by any number of devices (red-lining, steering, racial covenants) followed, if necessary, by anger, hostility, and occasional mob violence. Even so, the migration from the south did not stop or even slow, and neither did the migration to the suburbs which, although begun in search of better housing and lifestyle, had by 1970, become frankly about race.[50] Yet, even as the black population grew, Detroit's neighborhoods and public schools remained segregated.

When blacks began to move into a white neighborhood, whites protested, threatened, and then moved out.

Even as black students became a majority in Detroit's public schools in 1963, most individual schools were identifiably black or white. Those whites who had not left the city for the suburbs were concentrated in northwest and northeast enclaves, where the schools remained almost all white, while students in the schools in the rest of the city were almost all black. As neighborhoods changed from white to black, the Detroit School Board, a great majority of whose members were white, adjusted school attendance areas in ways that preserved segregation. Manipulation of school construction and of funding also guaranteed that black schools were older, more crowded, and underfunded.

Black leadership was divided as to the importance of integrating the schools. Integration had been the undisputed goal in southern states, and integration remained the goal of the NAACP and its Detroit chapter. However, other black leaders in Detroit, such as Michigan senator Coleman Young, saw school integration as a diversion from what really mattered, obtaining political power in places where blacks were a majority. In 1969, after watching decades of futile efforts to integrate Detroit's public schools, Young sponsored a bill in the state legislature which required "Class 1" cities (Detroit was the only one) to divide their school districts into between seven and 11 independent districts. The expectation was that the school board would divide Detroit along racial lines, thus satisfying both the proponents of segregation and those of black political power, but the board, where a liberal-black-labor coalition majority had recently taken over, had other ideas.

In April 1970, the board unveiled a decentralization plan which called for 9,000 students to change schools in order to increase integration of both black and white schools. The plan was not well accepted, to say the least. White parents promised resistance, violent incidents occurred in several schools, and coalition board members were recalled. Coleman Young went back to the legislature and emerged with PA 48, which superseded the board's plan and imposed its own: eight districts with students required to be assigned to neighborhood schools except that white students in changing neighborhoods could use "open enrollment" to transfer to white schools. As one black state legislator grieved, "Michigan voted officially to nullify the Bill of Rights and the Constitution and violate the basic laws of the United States Supreme Court."[51]

PA 48 and the recall of pro-integration board members convinced the local and national NAACP that they had no choice but to sue and that, paradoxically, PA 48 had strengthened their side. The case was assigned by the blind draw to Judge Roth who still maintained a Detroit docket as well as handling all Flint and Bay City cases. With the new school year approaching, plaintiffs sought a preliminary injunction to enjoin the board from implementing PA 48 and to reinstste the board's plan. At the injunction hearing on September 3, 1970, Judge Roth was openly skeptical that plaintiffs could prove their claims, and he refused to grant the injunction. holding that there was no convincing proof that the board had acted to maintain "a dual system of schools, either de jure or de facto," and that, to the contrary, the board had worked to desegregate the system. And there the case might have foundered were it not for Public Act 48, which opened the door to attack not just on the legislature's statutory "plan" but also white flight to the suburbs, which made integration of Detroit's schools impossible.

The "only feasible desegregation plan," the NAACP's lawyers came to realize, must include the suburban school districts in metropolitan Detroit, but they hesitated to push for it because it was so controversial in both camps. Instead, they appealed Judge Roth's order to the Sixth Circuit which, on October 13, 1970, reversed. The appellate court declared Public Act 48 unconstitutional because it interfered with a constitutionally mandated desegregation plan and remanded the case to the district court for a prompt trial on the merits.[52] Still skeptical, Judge Roth decided not to implement the board's April 1970 plan and instead ordered the board to submit alternative plans for his consideration. In December 1970, Roth accepted a plan involving magnet schools, and the Sixth Circuit refused to hear plaintiffs' interlocutory appeal, although the appeals court did chide the judge and the parties for delaying trial on the merits and directed them to get on with it.[53]

Judge Roth began trial on April 6, 1971, and ended it on July 22 after 41 days of testimony. Plaintiffs were represented by a team of veteran civil rights attorneys including Nathaniel Jones, Louis Lucas, Paul Dimond, Robert Pressman, and J. Harold (Nick) Flannery; the board by Detroit attorney George Bushnell, and the state by Frank Kelley's assistants. Also involved were counsel for two groups which Roth allowed to intervene as defendants, the Detroit Federation of Teachers, represented by Detroit labor attorney Theodore Sachs, and a group of white parents represented by Alexander Ritchie, also from Detroit.

With PA 48 out of the case, plaintiffs faced a difficult task. Although the U.S. Supreme Court's decision in *Brown v. Board of Education* established that segregation by law (de jure) violated the Constitution, the Sixth Circuit had held that segregation resulting solely from residential patterns did not.[54] Thus Jones and his colleagues had to convince Roth that the defendants caused or contributed to the school segregation. They began by presenting evidence of the reality and history of segregation in Detroit's housing and only then turned to proof of the defendants' culpability for the resulting school segregation. Through a series of fact and expert witnesses and the board's own documents, plaintiffs convinced the formerly skeptical Judge Roth that over the decades the board had used housing segregation and other means to maintain segregated schools.

Just as black leaders were split on integration versus control, white groups were divided on the value of an integration plan involving suburban school districts, known as a metropolitan plan. Suburban parents were, on the whole, vehemently opposed to sending their children to the schools that many suburbanites had moved to avoid instead of the schools their taxes had built. The white Detroit parents represented by Ritchie, though, had a different perspective. They came to understand that only a metropolitan plan would keep their children from being a tiny minority in overwhelmingly black Detroit schools. Whereas the plaintiffs' attorneys decided not to raise the possibility of such a plan, Ritchie repeatedly got witnesses to admit that a Detroit-only plan was futile and that only a metropolitan plan could achieve true integration. This testimony convinced Roth of the need for a remedy that would include at least some suburban school districts.

On September 27, 1971, Judge Roth ruled that the board had failed to fulfill its affirmative duty to do what was possible to integrate Detroit's schools and, to the contrary, had made decisions that preserved racial segregation. Therefore, the board was guilty of de jure segregation and the state responsible for assisting and failing to supervise the board's actions.[55] Until then, the trial had attracted very little publicity or interest, especially in the suburbs. That changed immediately on October 4 when Judge Roth, as part of the remedy, directed the school board and the state to develop and submit desegregation plans " designed to achieve the greatest possible degree of actual desegregation, taking into account the practicalities of the situation." The order specifically directed defendants to submit a Detroit-only plan but left open the possibility that a metropolitan plan might be necessary.

Although we might think of suburbs as homes of middle- or upper-income families, many of Detroit's suburbs, especially those in Wayne County, were better described as blue collar. Wealth seemed to make little difference, though, in the suburban reaction to the mere possibility of involving their school districts in a remedy. As one author noted, "outside observers might have thought that Judge Roth was guilty of murder or some other unspeakable crime."[56] Indeed, one of the many bumper stickers that quickly appeared read "Judge Roth is a child molester." The judge was hung in effigy and death threats resulted in around-the-clock protection for the judge and his family by U.S. marshals.

After Judge Roth received the proposed plans, he allowed another white citizens' group and some suburban school districts to intervene, most of the latter represented by William Saxton, who argued against involving other districts absent proof of their active culpability in segregating Detroit's schools. Then, on June 14, 1972, Roth announced that any Detroit-only plan would simply make every school identifiably black and thus accelerate white flight, so the remedy must go beyond school-district boundaries and would have to include cross-district busing. He designated a "deseg-regation area" that included Detroit and 53 suburban districts.[57]

Judge Roth's rulings came before a panel of the Sixth Circuit on August 24, 1972. On December 8, the panel affirmed two of Judge Roth's orders, reversed three others, and, most importantly, "affirmed in principle the ruling of the District Court on the propriety of a metropolitan remedy to accomplish desegregation." The judges of the court of appeals then granted rehearing en banc, by all of the active judges of the court, and, on June 12, 1973, issued a 41-page majority opinion that affirmed Judge Roth's con-clusion that both the board and the state had committed acts of de jure segregation.[58] Because of the state's involvement in those acts, and be-cause all Michigan school districts operate under the jurisdiction of the state, the en banc court affirmed Roth's decision to impose a multidistrict remedy, but the court also held that the suburban school districts had to be made parties to the litigation and given an opportunity to be heard on any proposed plan.

Defendants sought review from the U.S. Supreme Court, which granted their petition for certiorari, but only as to the remedy, leaving standing the holding of de jure segregation. The Court listened to arguments on Febru-ary 27, 1974, and, on July 25, in a 5 to 4 decision, rejected the use of a multidistrict remedy. The majority opinion by Chief Justice Warren Burger pointed to the lack of evidence that the suburban school districts had committed acts of segregation or that the acts of the Detroit School Board had any effect in other districts.[59] The dissenting opinions, by Justices Douglas, White, and Marshall, expressed their disappointment that the ma-jority had ignored the evidence and had ham-strung federal courts faced with school segregation that could not be remedied by an order limited to one district. Later, Sixth Circuit Judge George Edwards wrote of the denial of a multidistrict remedy, "I know of no decision made by the Supreme Court of the United States since the Dred Scott decision . . . which is so fraught with disaster for this country."[60]

Judge Roth did not live to learn of the Supreme Court's decision. He had suffered a series of heart attacks, which crippled his ability to perform his judicial duties, and on July 10, 1974, he suffered a third massive heart attack and died the next day. Those who knew Judge Roth had no doubt that the strain of controlling such a contentious, emotional case had shortened his life. One journalist wrote that "Judge Roth never publicly acknowledged the criticism and he seldom discussed it, even with his clos-est friends. But it bothered him deeply," although he remained certain that the metropolitan remedy "was the right thing to do."[61]

Although the Supreme Court rejected a multidistrict remedy based on the facts before the court, the opinion left open to the plaintiffs a chance to produce additional evidence to prove discrimination by the suburban districts. As Professor Baugh has noted, though, Nathaniel Jones feared that "the time and resources necessary to pursue inter-district relief in *Milliken* likely would have hampered his legal team's ability to handle future single-district cases that also needed to be litigated."[62] Meanwhile, Judge Roth's decision that the Detroit School Board and the state had engaged in deliberate segregation still stood, and somebody had to take over the case and formulate a Detroit-only plan. Chief Judge Damon Keith put the names of the judges in a hat; the first name pulled out was that of 76-year-old Senior District Judge Thomas Thornton. His ruddy face went pale, and he told Judge Keith that he could not do it. The next name pulled was that of Judge Robert DeMascio. At first, Judge DeMascio did not think he had been given a particularly difficult assignment because, as he later admitted, he did not know the demographics of the Detroit Public Schools. He changed his mind when he was informed that by then 74 percent of the students in the school district were black and that the percentage was increasing every year.

An intensely private person, Judge DeMascio was also unprepared for the publicity, the anger, and the threats to himself and to his family that followed his assignment to the case. As he later recalled, he could not go out in public, and he had to have the protection of U.S. marshals at his home. He regretted that this public scrutiny applied as well to his family, and particularly his young daughter. He also greatly regretted being limited to a Detroit-only remedy because he believed that it would have been far simpler and effective to mix Detroit students with those in contiguous districts, maximizing integration while minimizing costs and the hardship on students.

As Judge Roth had done, Judge DeMascio ordered the parties to present proposals for Detroit-only integration. He held nine weeks of hearings on the proposed plans and, in an opinion issued in August 1975,[63] he essentially rejected both plans and imposed his own, in the process involving the district court deeply in the operations of Detroit's schools. He held that, given the decision of the Supreme Court, desegregation in this case meant eliminating racially identifiable white schools. He also held that busing should be a last resort, that any plan must consider the financial condition and resources of the school district, and that, where necessary, the court should become involved in the quality of education in the district. Throughout his lengthy and highly detailed opinion, Judge DeMascio emphasized the "practicalities of the situation," which were taken to include the requirement for a Detroit-only plan, the percentages of black and white students in the district, and the resources available. As a first step toward whatever desegregation was possible, Judge DeMascio ordered a limited busing plan and directed the board to acquire, and the state to pay for, 150 new school buses.[64] After rejecting two plans, he approved the third on November 4, 1975.[65] Defendants appealed once more, but the Sixth Circuit affirmed most of Judge DeMascio's order, differing only on his exclusion from the busing plan of three regions in which the percentage of black students exceeded 90 percent.[66] The Supreme Court granted defendants' petition for certiorari, but, on June 27, 1977, affirmed the decision of the Sixth Circuit.[67] Thus, seven years after plaintiffs filed their complaint, the Detroit schools had a desegregation plan. Judge DeMascio also decided that if he could not end segregation in Detroit schools, he could at least improve the schools. Among other measures, he drafted a code for student conduct with Dean Wilbur Cohen of the University of Michigan, to improve security.

Judge DeMascio would not be allowed to steer his efforts through to completion, though. In 1976, plaintiffs filed a petition asking him to recuse himself because of allegedly improper ex parte contacts with court-appointed experts, community groups, and representatives of the board and the teachers' union. There was no question that Judge DeMascio did hold meetings, as a mediator, to try to avoid a teachers' strike, but the petition may have been more about the personal tension between Judge DeMascio, a self-described "no nonsense" judge who could be intimidating and abrupt, and plaintiffs' new attorney, Thomas I. Atkins, who had a similar temperament. In January 1977, Judge DeMascio filed a written denial of the charge of impropriety and referred the recusal motion to Chief Judge Keith,[68] who conducted a blind draw which assigned the motion to Judge Churchill. In April 1977, Judge Churchill absolved Judge DeMascio, finding that "there is no appearance of any partiality whatsoever on the part of Judge Robert E. DeMascio in this matter." In an opinion dated April 4, 1980, the court of appeals agreed with Judge Churchill's comment that: "It is my opinion that the manner in which Judge Robert E. DeMascio has presided in this case has been exemplary and should command the respect of the parties, counsel, the judiciary, and the public." Then, in language reminiscent of that directed to Judge O'Brien in 1935, the court pulled the rug from under DeMascio: "However, in view of the public interest in the instant school desegregation case, the challenge raised by the plaintiffs, and the bitter feelings that have developed, this court suggests that, on remand, the Chief Judge of the District Court for the Eastern District of Michigan reassign this case either to himself or to another appropriate judge."[69] Initially, Judge DeMascio, who felt "crushed" by this suggestion, refused to accept it, and the new chief judge, John Feikens supported him, but, eventually, Judge DeMascio decided to withdraw.

At the suggestion of Judge Churchill, Chief Judge Feikens established a three-judge panel to take over the case. Using a complicated blind draw, he reassigned the case to himself and to Judges Cohn and Boyle. By then the school district was 87 percent black, and integration was no longer an issue, but there remained the educational programs established by Judge DeMascio: "reading, in-service training, testing, counseling and guidance, the Student Code of Conduct, school community relations, vocational education, and bilingual education."[70] The panel decided to make the parties resolve those issues, to the extent possible, by the use of frequent in-chambers conferences and persuasion, backed by the threat of judicial action, and by forcing the school board to conduct open hearings so that the public had a voice in the outcome. Slowly but surely, the number of issues dwindled, although the panel remained in charge of the schools, with the court of appeals second-guessing their decisions.[71] As the issues were checked off, Judge Cohn took over the case alone. As he has noted, he was "the first judge to be assigned the case who was born and raised in Detroit and a graduate of the Detroit Public Schools. And to me that had some emotional significance or subliminal significance since I had my roots in Detroit. Indeed, my father had been born in Detroit and was a graduate of the Detroit Public Schools."

In 1988, the school board moved to end the case on the ground that the school district had "reached unitary status"–i.e., that it had eliminated all vestiges of de jure segregation in the district. Most of the other parties filed written objections, on which Judge Cohn held a hearing on December 8, 1988. On January 11, 1989, he granted the board's motion and, on February 24, 1989, he entered a final judgment closing the case. It is hard to say what good came out of the case. One black leader told Judge Cohn that the only benefit from 20 years of litigation was that the school district received a temporary influx of some extra money from the state.

Perhaps the two most telling and poignant comments on this case come from Judge DeMascio and plaintiffs' attorney Nick Flannery. In his oral history, the judge recalled seeing black children walking to Detroit schools on one side of Alter Road and white children walking to Grosse Pointe schools on the other side. He was struck by how easy it would have been to have all of them walk to integrated schools on both sides of the road.[72] Flannery, on the other hand, was all too prescient in 1970 when he warned that without an interdistrict plan, white flight would continue and Detroit's public schools would become "a segregated, under-financed school system."[73] Whatever the cause, it is indisputable that, 40 years after the case was filed, segregated and under-financed is the reality that the schools and the city must struggle against every day.

Abortion and Free Speech

Despite the Supreme Court's 1973 holding in *Roe v. Wade*,[74] that the right to privacy "is broad enough to encompass a woman's decision whether or not to terminate her pregnancy," state and local efforts to limit abortion in one way or another have resulted in a small but steady addition to the district court's caseload. By the luck of the blind draw, some of those cases are assigned to the more conservative judges. They and their more liberal colleagues, whatever their personal views on abortion, have consistently rejected those state and local laws.[75] One such case arose before *Roe* when abortion was illegal in Michigan. In *Mitchell Family Planning Inc. v. City of Royal Oak*,[76] District Judge Philip Pratt was faced with the related question of whether a city ordinance banning advertisements for any means by which an abortion could be procured violated the right of free speech guaranteed by the First Amendment. On January 5, 1972, Judge Pratt entered an injunction barring the city from enforcing its ordinance.

The advertisement at issue, on a billboard at Woodward Avenue and Thirteen Mile Road, in Royal Oak, provided the telephone number of an abortion clinic in New York, where certain abortions were legal. For Judge Pratt, the location of the clinic was key, but he first had to resolve a different issue, that of abstention. Although the attorneys for Royal Oak had not raised abstention, Judge Pratt noted that: "it is a matter which the Court must consider when it is requested to act in a manner which may affect the sensitive area of federal-state relations." The essence of abstention is a reluctance to interfere in matters of state criminal law except in those cases in which a prosecution has been threatened but has not yet begun. Finding this to be the facts here, the judge ruled: "Under these circumstances plaintiffs have passed between Scylla and Charybdis and this Court must not abstain." Passing to the speech issue, Judge Pratt held that the ordinance was too broad because it barred speech relating to both legal and illegal abortions and because objections to "immoral" advertising were just too vague to withstand scrutiny. He also held that the billboard did not present a "clear and present danger" of illegal conduct because there was no assurance that an illegal abortion would result from a telephone call. Quoting Justice Brandeis, he reminded the city that: "Among free men, the deterrents ordinarily to be applied to prevent crime are education and punishment for violations of the law, not abridgement of the rights of free speech."

Notes

1. For a thorough discussion of segregated housing in Detroit and its suburbs, see Joyce A. Baugh, *The Detroit School Busing Case:* Milliken v. Bradley *and the Controversy Over Desegregation* (Lawrence, KS: The University of Kansas Press, 2011), 19–42.

2. This transferred 387,067 residents (8.1 percent of the Eastern District's 1950 population) to the Western District.

3. 68 Stat., Part 1, 8.

4. 62 Stat. 898, codified at 28 U.S.C. 142 and since rescinded.

5. *Bay City Times*, August 1, 1954.

6. *Bay City Times*, August 1, 1954.

7. *Bay City Times*, February 17, 1956.

8. *Flint Journal*, January 19, 1960.

9. *Bay City Times*, January 20, 1960.

10. *Bay City Times*, February 25, 1960.

11. *Bay City Times*, January 28, 1960.

12. *Bay City Times*, April 3, 1960.

13. *Flint Journal*, October 11, 1962. Bankruptcy Judge Harold Bobier (alleged to be the last serving federal judge not to have attended a law school) had been holding court in Flint for a year.

14. Nedra Bennett to Mossing, March 5, 1986, Archives of the Historical Society for the U.S. District Court for the Eastern District of Michigan.

15. 78 Stat. 1003.

16. *Bay City Times*, August 18, 1973.

17. *Bay City Times*, January 28, 1960.

18. *Bay City Times*, April 3, 1960.

19. *Marshall v. Hare*, 227 F. Supp. 989 (E.D. Mich. 1964).

20. According to U.S. census records, in 1960 Michigan had a population of 7,823,194. Thus, any county with a population of at least 5,477 would have at least one representative. Of the 33 counties in the Eastern District, only three (Crawford, Montmorency, and Oscoda) were below that level.

21. 18 Stat. (Part3) 470.

22. 28 U.S.C. 2284.

23. *Reynolds v. Sims*, 377 U.S. 533 (1964).

24. *Marshall v. Hare*, 378 U.S. 561 (1964).

25. *Dunnell v. Austin*, 344 F. Supp. 210 (E.D. Mich. 1972).

26. See *In re Apportionment of State Legislature—1982*, 413 Mich. 96 (1982).

27. Mich. Comp. Laws, sec. 4.261.

28. *NAACP, Inc. v. Austin*, 857 F. Supp. 560 (E.D. Mich. 1994).

29. 17 Stat. 13, now codified at 42 U.S.C. 1983.

30. The broad Civil Rights Act of 1964, 78 Stat. 241, outlawed, *inter alia*, racial discrimination in public accommodations, such as hotels or theaters, in the use of governmental facilities, education, and employment. The Civil Rights Act of 1968, 82 Stat. 696, also known as the Fair Housing Act, provided private remedies against discrimination in housing.

31. Surrency, 109, citing the Annual Reports of the Administrative Office of the U.S. Courts.

32. Phillip J. Cooper, *Hard Judicial Choices: Federal District Court Judges and State and Local Officials* (New York: Oxford University Press, 1988), 3–4.

33. *People ex rel. Workman v. Detroit Board of Education*, 18 Mich. 400 (1869).

34. E.g., *Mrsa v. Reynolds*, 317 Mich. 632 (1947).

35. *Davis v. School Dist. of City of Pontiac, Inc.*, 309 F. Supp. 734 (E.D. Mich. 1970).

36. *Davis v. School Dist. of City of Pontiac, Inc.*, 443 F.2d 573 (6th Cir. 1971).

37. *School District of the City of Pontiac, Inc., v. Davis*, 404 U.S. 913 (1971).

38. *New York Times*, May 22, 1973. See *U.S. v. Fruit*, 507 F.2d 194 (6th Cir. 1974).

39. *Bay City Times*, October 1, 1971.

40. Joseph C. Goulden, *The Benchwarmers: the Private World of the Powerful Federal Judge* (New York: Ballantine, 1976), 351.

41. From John Sinclair's 1968 "White Panther Manifesto," quoted at Samuel C. Damren, "The Keith Case," *The Court Legacy* vol. xi, no. 4 (November 2003), 3.

42. Talbot Smith to Ralph M. Freeman, December 30, 1969; Orville H. Trotter to Ralph M. Freeman, December 3, 1969, Archives of the Historical Society.

43. *U.S. v. Sinclair*, 321 F. Supp. 1074 (E.D. Mich. 1971).

44. *U.S. v. U.S. Dist. Court for Eastern Dist. of Mich., Southern Div.*, 444 F.2d 651 (6th Cir. 1971).

45. *U.S. v. U.S. Dist. Court for Eastern Dist. of Mich., Southern Division*, 407 U.S. 297 (1972). Justice Rehnquist recused himself because he had been involved in discussions of a the legality of warrantless searches while working at the Justice Department.

46. *Sinclair v. Kleindienst*, 711 F.2d 291 (D.C. Cir. 1983).

47. *Detroit News*, June 23, 1989.

48. *Sinclair v. Schriber*, 916 F.2d 1109 (6th Cir. 1990).

49. In the district court, the caption of the case was *Bradley v. Milliken*, but it became nationally famous under its caption in the U.S. Supreme Court, *Milliken v. Bradley*. Except where otherwise noted, I have relied on Joyce A. Baugh, *The Detroit School Busing Case: Milliken v. Bradley and the Controversy Over Desegregation* (Lawrence, KS: The Kansas University Press, 2011) and four articles published in *The Court Legacy* in 2008 and 2009: Jennifer A. Huff, "'The Only Feasible Desegregation Plan,' *Milliken v. Bradley* and Judge Roth's Order for Cross-District Busing," vol. XV, no. 2 (May 2008); John R. Runyan, "*Milliken v. Bradley I*: The Struggle to Apply *Brown v. Board of Education* in the North," vol. XV, no. 3 (September 2008); Samuel C. Damren, "*Milliken v. Bradley I* On Remand: The Impossible Assignment," vol. XVI, no. 1 (February 2009); Avern Cohn and John P. Mayer, "Winding Up *Bradley v. Milliken*," vol. XVI, no. 2 (June 2009).

50. The percentage of African Americans in the state's population also grew from less than 1 percent in 1910 to 11 percent in 1970. Such was the degree of racial separation in the state that two-thirds of that 11 percent resided in Detroit.

51. State representative Jackie Vaughn, quoted in Baugh, 81.

52. *Bradley v. Milliken*, 433 F.2d 897 (6th Cir. 1970).

53. *Brown v. Board of Education*, 347 U.S. 483 (1954).

54. *Deal v. Cincinnati Board of Education*, 419 F.2d 1387 (6th Cir. 1969).

55. *Bradley v. Milliken*, 338 F. Supp. 582 (E.D. Mich. 1971).

56. Baugh, 118.

57. *Bradley v. Milliken*, 345 F. Supp. 914 (E.D. Mich. 1972).

58. *Bradley v. Milliken*, 484 F.2d 215 (6th Cir. 1973) (en banc).

59. *Milliken v. Bradley*, 418 U.S. 717 (1974).

60. *Bradley v. Milliken*, 519 F.2d 679 (6th Cir. 1975).

61. William Grant, *Detroit Free Press*, quoted at Baugh, 164.

62. Baugh, 180.

63. *Bradley v. Milliken*, 402 F. Supp. 1096 (E.D. Mich. 1975).

64. The state appealed, alleging the order violated the Eleventh Amendment, but the Sixth Circuit affirmed DeMascio, and the Supreme Court denied the state's petition for *certiorari*. *Bradley v. Milliken*, 519 F.2d 679 (6th Cir. 1975), *cert. den'd*, 423 U.S. 930 (1975).

65. *Bradley v. Milliken*, 411 F .Supp. 943 (E.D. Mich. 1975).

66. *Bradley v. Milliken*, 540 F.2d 229 (6th Cir. 1976).

67. *Milliken v. Bradley*, 433 U.S. 267 (1977).

68. *Bradley v. Milliken*, 426 F. Supp. 929 (E.D. Mich. 1977).

69. *Bradley v. Milliken*, 620 F.2d 1143 (6th Cir. 1980).

70. Cohn and Mayer, 3.

71. *E.g., Bradley v. Milliken*, 772 F.2d 266 (6th Cir. 1985).

72. DeMascio oral history, quoted in Baugh, 181.

73. J. Harold Flannery to Nathaniel R. Jones, September 4, 1970, Supplement to Part 23, Series C, Section II, NAACP Papers, Library of Congress.

74. *Roe v. Wade*, 410 U.S. 113 (1973).

75. *E.g., Abortion Control of Michigan, Inc. v. Michigan Department of Public Health*, 426 F. Supp. 471 (E.D. Mich. 1977) (Judge Kennedy); *Birth Control Centers, Inc. v. Reizen*, 508 F. Supp. 1366 (E.D. Mich. 1986) (Judge Feikens); *Evans v. Kelley*, 977 F. Supp. 1283 (E.D. Mich. 1997) (Judge Rosen); *Woman Care of Southfield, P.C. v. Granholm*, 143 F. Supp. 2d 827 (E.D. Mich. 2000) (Judge Tarnow).

76. *Mitchell Family Planning Inc. v. City of Royal Oak*, 335 F. Supp. 738 (E.D. Mich. 1972).

PART V
A Major Metropolitan Court, 1977–2010

If the court's first 33 years were notable for the longevity of a single judge, Ross Wilkins, the most recent 33 have been notable, in part, for the five additional judgeships and the 28 judges appointed, as well as for a decreasing number of trials, the activation of court rooms in Port Huron and Ann Arbor, and fluctuations in the court's docket between a preponderance of civil or criminal cases. Civil rights cases alleging discrimination against African-Americans continued to be an important component of the docket and were joined by a notorious prosecution alleging a homicide committed with anti-Asian animus and by two reverse-discrimination suits against the University of Michigan which may eventually be considered the most important cases of those decades.

CHAPTER 14

District Judges Appointed, 1977–1985

Rapid caseload increase is a national phenomenon not limited to the Eastern District. In 1960, the district courts received 89,112 new civil and criminal cases; in 1972, there were 145,227. In 1973, Henry J. Friendly, the influential chief judge of the U.S. Court of Appeals for the Second Circuit, warned that caseload increase threatened the entire federal court system.[1] He explained that although the number of civil cases filed each year in all of the district courts had increased between 1961 and 1968 by 23 percent (58,293 to 71,449), criminal filings had been almost stagnant (28,460 to 30,714), so that with the addition of 97 additional district judgeships during that period, "the situation seemed well under control." Then, during just the next four years, civil filings jumped to 96,173 and criminal filings to 47,043, straining district courts to their breaking point as the average caseload per district judge jumped from 316 in 1968 to 375 in 1972. Friendly predicted that caseloads would continue to grow, particularly in areas like civil rights and prisoner petitions, which had increased from 5 percent of the district courts' docket in 1961 to 22 percent in 1972.

Although Congress had authorized the appointment of another 61 new district judges in 1970, bringing the total to 389, Friendly was skeptical that the crisis could be cured by simply doubling the number of judges because, given the relatively low federal judicial salaries and the loss of prestige district judgeships would suffer if they were to become even more numerous, the quality of the judges and their efficiency would suffer. He preferred that Congress contract the jurisdiction of the federal district courts by abolishing diversity jurisdiction, except for cases involving aliens, by creating special trial courts for patent, tax, and antitrust cases, and by sweeping away federal criminal statutes that have no relationship to the federal government other than that the crime crossed a state line.

Congress has largely ignored Judge Friendly's suggestions and has periodically resorted to the more politically useful solution of adding district judgeships.[2] Nationally, the number of district judges has increased from 381 in 1972 to 678 in 2010. In the Eastern District, the number of judgeships, which had increased from eight to ten in 1970, grew again in 1978 to 13 and then in 1984 to 15. Those additions and other circumstances (judges dying, assuming senior status, or being appointed to the Sixth Circuit) allowed Presidents Carter and Reagan to appoint 17 judges to the bench of the Eastern District between 1977 and 1991.

President Reagan continued his predecessor's procedure of convening judicial review committees to recommend candidates for judicial appointments. "In Michigan, a twenty-five-member Judicial Review Committee appointed by the state Republican chairman included token representatives of diverse bar associations. Vacancies were advertised in the newspapers and bar publications. Candidates identified by these ads were sent questionnaires asking them to detail their relevant qualifications and experiences; moreover, their backgrounds were checked through bar grievance committees. Only after the Review Committee had reviewed each questionnaire and interviewed each candidate were the candidates rated, ranked, and their names forwarded to the Republican congressional delegation for final evaluation. . . . Michigan sent multiple names—usually three to five—to Washington without preference ordering. It did so, however, with the expectation that the White House *would* ask questions about 'ideological preferences' and the expectation that individual supporters, including some members of the Review Committee or congressional delegation, would lobby the White House on their preferred recruit."[3]

Appointments by President Jimmy Carter

Julian Abele Cook, Jr.

Born: June 22, 1930 (Washington, D.C.)
Education: Pennsylvania State University (B.A. 1952), Georgetown University
    Law Center (J.D. 1957)
Military: U.S. Army, Signal Corps (1952–1954)
Nominated/Confirmed: July 25/September 23, 1978
Vacancy: Judge Gubow (Died)
Chief Judge: 1989–1996
Senior Status: December 30, 1996

Fig. 81.   Judge Julian Abele
Cook, Jr. (Historical Society for
the United States District Court
for the Eastern District of
Michigan)

Patricia Jean Boyle

Born: March 31, 1937 (Detroit, Michigan)
Education: University of Michigan; Wayne State University (B.A. 1963, J.D.
1963)
Nominated/Confirmed: July 25/September 22, 1978

Fig. 82.   Judge Patricia Jean
Boyle. (Historical Society for the
United States District Court for
the Eastern District of Michigan)

Vacancy: Judge Damon Keith (Appointed to Sixth Circuit)
Left Court: April 20, 1983 (Appointed to Michigan Supreme Court)

Avern Levin Cohn

Born: July 23, 1924 (Detroit, Michigan)
Education: John Tarleton Agricultural College; Stanford University; Loyola
    School of Medicine; University of Michigan (B.A. 1943, J.D. 1949)
Military: U.S. Army (1943–1946)
Nominated/Confirmed: May 17/September 25, 1979
Vacancy: New Seat
Senior Status: October 9, 1999

Fig. 83. Judge Avern Levin
Cohn. (Historical Society for the
United States District Court for
the Eastern District of Michigan)

Stewart Albert Newblatt

Born: December 23, 1927 (Detroit, Michigan)
Educated: Millersburg (Kentucky) Military Institute; University of Michigan
    (B.A. 1950, J.D. 1952)
Military: U.S. Army, Criminal Investigation Division, Philippines (1946–1947)
Nominated/Confirmed: May 17/September 25, 1979
Vacancy: New Seat
Senior Status: December 23, 1993

Fig. 84. Judge Stewart Albert Newblatt. (Historical Society for the United States District Court for the Eastern District of Michigan)

Anna Diggs Taylor

Born: December 9, 1932 (Washington, D.C.)
Education: Barnard College (B.A. 1954); Yale Law School (LL.B. 1957)
Nominated/Confirmed: May 17/October 31, 1979
Vacancy: New Seat
Chief Judge: 1998–1996
Senior Status: December 31, 1998

Fig. 85. Judge Anna Diggs Taylor. (Historical Society for the United States District Court for the Eastern District of Michigan)

Fig. 86.   Judge Horace Weldon
Gilmore. (Historical Society for
the United States District Court
for the Eastern District of
Michigan)

Horace Weldon Gilmore

Born: April 4, 1918 (Columbus, Ohio)
Education: University of Michigan (B.A. 1939; J.D. 1942)
Military: U.S. Naval Reserve (1942–1945)
Nominated/Confirmed: May 22/June 18, 1980
Vacancy: Judge Kennedy (Appointed to Sixth Circuit)
Senior Status: May 1, 1991
Left Court: January 25, 2010 (Died)

Appointments by President Ronald W. Reagan

George Edward Woods, Jr.

Born: October 10, 1923 (Cleveland, Ohio)
Education: Ohio Northern University; Texas A&M.; Illinois Institute of
    Technology; Detroit College of Law (J.D. 1949)
Military: U.S. Army (1943–1946)
Nominated/Confirmed: November 1/15, 1983
Vacancy: Judge Patricia Boyle (Appointed to Michigan Supreme Court)
Senior Status: November 16, 1993.
Left Court: August 13, 2004 (Retired)
Death: October 9, 2007

Fig. 87.   Judge George Edward
Woods, Jr. (Historical Society for
the United States District Court
for the Eastern District of
Michigan)

Richard Fred Suhrheinrich

Born: 1936 (Lincoln City, Indiana)
Education: Wayne State University (B.S. 1960); Detroit College of Law (J.D.
  1963); University of Virginia School of Law (LL.M. 1990)

Fig. 88.   Judge Richard Fred
Suhrheinrich. (Historical Society
for the United States District
Court for the Eastern District of
Michigan)

Nominated/Confirmed: September 6/October 3, 1984
Vacancy: Judge James Harvey (Senior Status)
Left Court: July 10, 1990 (Appointed to Sixth Circuit)

_____

District Judge George La Plata

Born: October 17, 1924 (Detroit, Michigan)
Education: Wayne State University (A.B. 1951); Detroit College of Law (L.L.B. 1956)
Military: U.S. Marine Corps (World War II and Korean War); Colonel U.S. M.C. Reserve
Nominated/Confirmed: February 27/April 3, 1985
Vacancy: New Seat
Left Court: August 3, 1996 (Retired)
Died: November 14, 2010 (Naples, Florida)

Fig. 89. Judge George La Plata. (Historical Society for the United States District Court for the Eastern District of Michigan)

_____

Lawrence Paul Zatkoff

Born: 1939 (Detroit, MI)
Education: University of Detroit (B.S. 1962); Detroit College of Law (J.D. 1966)
Nominated/Confirmed: January 21/March 3, 1986
Vacancy: Judge Ralph Guy, Jr. (Appointed to Sixth Circuit)
Chief Judge: 1999–2004
Senior Status: June 16, 2004

Fig. 90.   Judge Lawrence Paul
Zatkoff. (Historical Society for the
United States District Court for
the Eastern District of Michigan)

Barbara Kloka Hackett

Born: 1928 (Detroit, Michigan)
Education: University of Detroit (Ph.B. 1948); University of Detroit School of
   Law (J.D. 1950)
Nominated/Confirmed: February 11/March 27, 1986
Vacancy: Judge Joiner (Senior Status)

Fig. 91.   Judge Barbara Kloka
Hackett. (Historical Society for
the United States District Court
for the Eastern District of
Michigan)

Senior Status: April 8, 1997
Left Court: March 1, 2000 (Retired)

Patrick James Duggan

Born: 1933 (Detroit, Michigan)
Education: Xavier University (B.S. 1955); University of Detroit School of Law
    (LL.B. 1958)
Nominated/Confirmed: September 11/October 8, 1986
Vacancy: New Seat
Senior Status: September 29, 2000

Fig. 92. Judge Patrick James
Duggan. (Historical Society for
the United States District Court
for the Eastern District of
Michigan)

Paul V. Gadola

Born: 1929 (Flint, Michigan)
Education: Michigan State University (A.B. 1951); University of Michigan Law
    School (J.D. 1953)
Military: U.S. Army (1953–1955)
Nominated/Confirmed: April 23, 1987/October 14, 1988
Vacancy: Judge John Feikens (Senior Status)
Senior Status: January 31, 2001

Fig. 93.   Judge Paul V. Gadola. (Historical Society for the United States District Court for the Eastern District of Michigan)

Bernard A. Friedman

Born: 1943 (Detroit, Michigan)
Education: Detroit Institute of Technology; Detroit College of Law (J.D. 1968)
Military: U.S. Army Reserve, Judge Advocate General's Corps (1967–1973)

Fig. 94.   Judge Bernard A. Friedman. (Historical Society for the United States District Court for the Eastern District of Michigan)

Nominated/Confirmed: February 2/April 19, 1988
Vacancy: Judge Robert DeMascio (Senior Status)
Chief Judge: 2004–2009
Senior Status: January 1, 2009

Appointments by President George H. W. Bush

Gerald Ellis Rosen

Born: October 26, 1951 (Chandler, Arizona)
Education: Kalamazoo College (B.A. 1973); George Washington University
    Law School (J.D. 1979)
Nominated/Confirmed: November 9, 1989/March 9, 1990
Vacancy: Judge Philip Pratt (Died)
Chief Judge: 2009–2011

Fig. 95. Judge Gerald Ellis
Rosen. (Historical Society for the
United States District Court for
the Eastern District of Michigan)

Robert Hardy Cleland

Born: 1947 (St. Clair, Michigan)
Education: Michigan State University (B.A. 1969); University of North
    Carolina School of Law (J.D. 1972)
Nominated/Confirmed: February 20/June 18, 1990
Vacancy: Judge James P. Churchill (Senior Status)

Fig. 96.   Judge Robert Hardy
Cleland. (Historical Society for the
United States District Court for
the Eastern District of Michigan)

Nancy Garlock Edmunds

Born: 1947 (Detroit, Michigan)
Education: Cornell University (B.A. 1969); University of Chicago (M.A.T.
    1971); Wayne State University Law School (J.D. 1976)
Nominated/Confirmed: September 11, 1991/February 6, 1992
Vacancy: Judge Richard F. Suhrheinrich (Appointed to Sixth Circuit)

Fig. 97.   Judge Nancy Garlock
Edmunds. (Historical Society for
the United States District Court
for the Eastern District of
Michigan)

Notes

1. Henry J. Friendly, *Federal Jurisdiction: A General View* (New York: Columbia University Press, 1973). Friendly blamed the explosive increases in their caseloads on several factors, including decisions of the federal courts opening the jurisdictional doors wider or creating new causes of action, the attitude of litigants that federal courts are the reformers and remedy-makers of choice, and Congress' creation of many new statutes (civil rights, environmental, criminal, welfare), which direct public and private plaintiffs to the federal courts.

2. Between 1973 and 2010, Congress increased the number of district judgeships by 66 percent. During that same period, the number of active senior district judges increased even faster, a development that Judge Friendly had not taken into account. In his concern for quality, Friendly also failed to take notice of the untapped reservoir of qualified female and minority attorneys who rarely were nominated for a federal judgeship in those days.

3. C. K. Rowland and Robert A. Carp, *Politics and Judgments in Federal District Courts* (Lawrence: University Press of Kansas, 1996), 105.

CHAPTER 15

Growth Pains, 1977–1990

The Eastern District, 1977–1990

The period covered in this chapter is notable for several trends. One is the continuing flight of population from Wayne County, particularly from Detroit. The population of the district grew by only 94,539 residents between 1970 and 1980 and then decreased by 118,173 during the next decade. During those two decades, Wayne County lost more than a half million residents, although it remained the most populous county in the district, with twice as many residents in 1990 (2,111,687) as the next largest, Oakland (1,083,592). Oakland and other suburban counties surrounding Wayne (Macomb, Washtenaw, Livingston, Monroe, and Washtenaw) were the major beneficiaries of what had become a middle-class flight from the city that included all races, but the counties of the Northern Division and the Thumb also increased in population. Another trend was the tremendous increase in the district court's overall caseload from 1961 to 1990, although each component told a different tale.

The Criminal Balloon Busted

The *Court Compendium*, a publication produced by the Eastern District clerk's office in 1977, was well justified in concluding that there was a caseload crisis and that, "[a]s with so many other United States District Courts, Michigan East has turned into primarily a criminal Court." As noted in Chapter 14, a boom in criminal filings during the past few years and the mandates of the Speedy Trial Act forced the court's judges to spend most of their time on their criminal dockets. Looking forward, the authors of the publication projected, not unreasonably, that the district court would receive 1,600 new criminal cases in fiscal year 1977.[1] In fact, though, the boom in criminal cases was over. The actual number of criminal filings in 1977 was only 1,178; in 1978 it was 773. The average number of filings for 1979–1983 was only 483. This decrease was not a temporary

Table 15.1   Average Annual Case Filings in the District Court, 1961–1990

Fiscal Years	Criminal	U.S. Civil	Private Civil	Total	Per Authorized Judgeship
1961–1970	743	634	956	2,333	300
1971–1980	1,185	1,050	2,024	4,259	390
1981–1990	622	2,269	4,188	7,079	502

aberration. The average number of criminal filings from 1984 to 2010 was 635, and from 1999 to 2010 only 550. The latter figure amounts to 37.5 for each of the 15 district judges assigned to the court during those years, compared to 172 per judge in 1965. The 487 criminal cases filed in 2010 is the second least since 1920, even though the population of the Eastern District more than doubled between 1920 and 2010.The ups and downs of criminal case filings does not mean that residents of the Eastern District suddenly became less law-abiding in 1971 or more law-abiding in 1978. As Rowland F. Kirks, director of the Administrative Office of the United States Courts from 1970 until his death in 1977, explained, the number of criminal cases filed in a district does not reflect the number of federal crimes committed: "The Federal criminal caseload is to a large extent a reflection of the priorities of the Justice Department in regards to active prosecution. The number and types of defendants proceeded against are not necessarily a realistic index of the occurrence of Federal crimes. The Federal caseload is rather an indication of the amount of investigative and prosecution resources that can be committed, enforcement agency priorities, changes in the criminal law, and lastly, the extent to which certain criminal cases can be diverted to state or local criminal systems."[2] The simple explanation for the decrease after 1976 is that, beginning in 1977, President Carter redirected federal resources and priorities away from buy/bust narcotics cases and toward "higher level conspiracy and substantive investigations aimed towards immobilization of the most important violators and their organizations."[3]

The court's criminal balloon did leave one lingering effect after it burst. In October 1978, Congress authorized three additional judgeships for the Eastern District, bringing the total to 13, an increase of seven since 1960. The additional judges and the precipitous drop in criminal filings decreased the caseload per judge from 457 in 1977 to 324 in 1978, but the average then surged to levels not seen since Prohibition (averaging 491 between 1979 and 1990) because of increases in both U.S. and private civil cases.

Debt Collection and Social Security

Even as the number of criminal cases decreased during the period 1977–1990, most U.S. district courts saw tremendous increases in U.S. civil cases, principally because of two types of cases, social security cases (including appeals of benefit claim denials, suits to recover overpayments, and suits to enforce judgments) and what the Administrative Office of the United States Courts characterized as contract cases, almost all of which brought to collect overpayment of veterans' benefits or defaulted federal or federally-guaranteed student loans.[4] The Eastern District was no exception to this trend. To the contrary, between 1983 and 1987, the court received 8,230 social security cases, the highest number filed in any U.S. district court in each of those years.[5] In 1984, for example, when the court had a record 4,331 U.S. cases filed, 63 percent (2,707) were social security cases, while another 23 percent (990) were contract cases. In contrast, just 120 social security cases were begun during 1974 and only 271 in 1990, while there were only 45 contract cases filed in 1974 and 419 in 1990.

The social security case bubble began with the Social Security Amendments Act of 1972,[6] which resulted in a flood of applications to the Social Security Administration for disability benefits, most of which were denied. Appeals of those denials began to be felt in the district court in 1976 and were a substantial portion of the court's docket until 1990. However they arrived, it is hard to tell how much these appeals added to the burden of the district judges because the court responded by hiring staff attorneys to screen the appeals and used the magistrate judges for much of the work. Fluctuations in the number of collection cases on the court's docket had a different cause: waxing and waning in the Justice Department's emphasis on such cases rather than the actual number of loan defaults. Thus, the average number of contract cases filed in the Eastern District each year from 1970 to 1976 was 70, from 1980 to 1986 was 1,016, and from 1987 to 1991 was 628. Then, in 1992 alone, the U.S. attorney filed 3,122 such cases, while just two years later, in 1995, there were only 430.

A Private Civil Explosion

With the exception of 1939,[7] the Eastern District had never had as many as 1,000 new private civil cases in a single year until 1964, but from 1969 to 1975, the filings exceeded 1,000 each year and from 1977 to 1990, the average was 3,738 with a range between 2,328 in 1977 and 4,769 in 1988. Congress did manage to decrease the number of diversity cases filed by raising the minimum jurisdictional amount in controversy from $10,000 to $50,000 in 1988 (effective May 18, 1989),[8] resulting in a 28 percent decrease nationally from 1988 to 1992, but the total number of private cases declined only 3 percent because of increases in federal question cases such as state-prisoner petitions, civil rights, and labor law cases.[9] In the Eastern District, the increase in the jurisdictional amount had a greater effect on private civil case filings, a 23 percent decrease between 1988 and 1992. Diversity case filings did not consistently recover to 1980s levels until 2005, while federal question cases remained fairly constant.[10]

The Vincent Chin Case

Not long after the national media lost interest in *Milliken v. Bradley*, another case with racial overtones returned the spotlight to Detroit. *United States v. Ronald Ebens and Michael Nitz*, known as the Vincent Chin case, began in a seedy strip club in Highland Park, Michigan, called the Fancy Pants Lounge.[11] Among those drinking and enjoying the show on the night of June 12, 1982, were four young men, friends celebrating the impending marriage of one of their number, Vincent Chin, a 26-year-old industrial draftsman. Chin was a native of China and a U.S. citizen who had been adopted by his Chinese-American parents as a child. He and his parents were among the 56,000 persons of Asian origin living in Michigan in 1980, less than 1 percent of the total population. His father had died seven months before, and he lived with his mother. On the other side of the stage were two white men, Ronald Ebens, a supervisor at a nearby Chrysler plant, and his stepson Michael Nitz, 23 years old and a part-time student who also worked in a furniture store.

As the evening progressed, alcohol flowed and tempers shortened. Some kind of taunting went on between the groups, a scuffle broke out, a chair was thrown, Nitz was bloodied, and the club's bouncer ejected both groups. After another round of taunts in the parking lot, they separated. Still angry, Ebens and Nitz went looking for Chin and found him, about half-an-hour later and two blocks away. Ebens took a baseball bat from his car and beat Chin brutally, hitting him repeatedly in the body and on the head. Chin was rushed to Henry Ford Hospital, but he never regained consciousness and died on June 23, 1982, his mother's birthday. That much of the story is undisputed, but many questions remained. Who started the fight? What was Nitz doing while Ebens beat Chin? Did Ebens and/or Nitz kill Chin because he was Asian?

The possibility of a racial motive was irrelevant under state law and so was never considered by the Highland Park police who arrested Ebens and Nitz, by the arraigning judge, Thomas Bayles of Highland Park's 30th Judicial District Court, or by the Wayne County prosecutor who charged both defendants with second-degree murder, meaning murder with malice but no premeditation. A few months later, Ebens agreed to plead guilty to manslaughter, deliberate killing without malice, while Nitz pleaded *nolo contendere* to manslaughter, which had the same effect as a guilty plea but could not be used against him in a civil proceeding. On March 16, 1983, they appeared before Wayne County Circuit Judge Charles Kaufman, who accepted the pleas. As was then common, no prosecutor attended the hearing, nor was Chin's family given notice and a chance to be heard. Thus, there was nobody to contradict the defense attorneys when they characterized Chin's death as the result of an ordinary barroom brawl that went too far and emphasized their clients' otherwise clean records. Judge Kaufman, considered to be a liberal and well-respected judge, sentenced each defendant to three years' probation, a $3,000 fine, and $780 in court costs.

Until the sentencing, the case had generated little public interest, but news of what seemed insanely lenient sentences for an admittedly deliberate homicide caused an uproar in the local press and among Asian Americans. The latter were convinced that Ebens and Nitz had acted out of a hatred of Asians, fueled not just by alcohol but also by Detroit's pervading resentment of Japanese auto makers who, in 1982, were increasing their share of the American market. Many auto workers blamed the Japanese for the closing of American auto plants and the lay-offs of auto workers such as Nitz and many of Ebens's friends. The initial statements taken by the police did not mention any racial animosity, but Chin's friends subsequently charged that Ebens and Nitz used racial epithets and yelled that: "Because of you little motherfuckers that we're out of work," either assuming Chin was Japanese or not caring to make any distinction.

An organization named the American Citizens for Justice (ACJ) urged the prosecutors to appeal the sentences and, with other Asian organizations, mobilized a campaign against the sentences which was supported by Detroit's newspapers, television channels, and radio stations. National media, public rallies, and members of Congress increased the pressure. However, Michigan law did not allow the prosecution to appeal seeking to increase a legal sentence, so the ACJ turned to the federal government for relief. As a media storm gathered, Mrs. Chin and representatives of the ACJ met with Assistant United States Attorney General William Bradford Reynolds, while thousands of letters and petitions descended on the Justice Department and the U.S. attorney for the Eastern District, Leonard Gilman. Although unsure of the strength of the case, Gilman convened a grand jury which heard evidence from witnesses and in November 1983, indicted both Ebens and Nitz on charges of violating and conspiring to violate Chin's constitutional and federal statutory rights on the basis of his race.[12] Thus, the question of racial animus, unimportant in the state court, became the single-most important issue in the federal case.

The district court's blind draw system assigned the case to Judge Anna Diggs Taylor who, after more than four years on the bench, was a seasoned veteran, although this was her first high-profile case. The trial attorneys were also well qualified. Ebens was represented by Frank Eaman, vice president of the Legal Aid and Defender Association, and by future District Court Judge David Lawson, then in private practice. Nitz was represented by two attorneys from the Federal Defender Office, Chief Deputy Miriam Siefer and Kenneth Sasse. The prosecution was led by Ross Conneally from the Civil Rights Division of the Department of Justice in Washington.

After seven months of pretrial maneuvering and more than 50 motions including defendants' motion for a change of venue, which the judge denied, trial began on June 5, 1984. Judge Taylor devised a careful system to voir dire each of the 150 prospective jurors and managed to seat a jury that swore it was able to give the defendants a fair trial. The trial lasted three weeks, with dozens of witnesses, issues, motions, and arguments. One issue proved to be key: the defense moved to admit into evidence audio tapes made by an officer of the ACJ as she interviewed prosecution witnesses and tried to harmonize their memories prior to their grand jury testimony. Defense counsel argued that the tapes were evidence of witness coaching which brought into question the trial testimony of those witnesses. Judge Taylor sustained the prosecution's hearsay objections as to statements by the ACJ officer although she did allow defense counsel to confront the prosecution witnesses with their own statements.

Overall, the government was aggressive, either righteously forceful or overly zealous depending on which side you were on. As Ross Parker, then chief of the local U.S. attorney's criminal division, later noted, "the Civil Rights Division attorneys' aggressive presentation was clearly aimed more at a favorable verdict than an appeal-proof record."[13] The jury deliberated for several days before finding Nitz not guilty on both counts and Ebens guilty of the civil rights charge, but not guilty of conspiracy. This verdict was a great disappointment for the defendants, the ACJ, and Mrs. Chin.

On September 18, 1984, Judge Taylor sentenced Ebens to 25 years in prison, and Ebens appealed. On September 11, 1986, two years after the verdict and nine months after oral argument in Cincinnati, the Sixth Circuit reversed Ebens's conviction.[14] The court did affirm Judge Taylor's decision not to change venue, noting that "the process for selecting the jury was carried out with exceptional care and sensitivity," thus minimizing any prejudice. The court also affirmed her denial of Ebens's motion for directed verdict because the evidence, taken in a light most favorable to the government, supported the conviction. But the court held that the exclusion of the interview tapes was reversible error. At oral argument, the prosecutors admitted that statements by the ACJ officer were not hearsay and argued instead that any error was harmless because there was sufficient other evidence to support the conviction. The court of appeals rejected that argument and also held that Judge Taylor should have excluded testimony about a 1974 incident of the use of racial epithets that involved a man named "Ron" whose description generally matched Ebens. The court reserved its strongest statements for the prosecutor: "[W]e deem it necessary to register most strongly our disapproval of the inflammatory language employed by government counsel."

With the case back before her, Judge Taylor determined that the reversal itself had created another wave of publicity that now did require a change of venue of Ebens's retrial to the Southern District of Ohio's district courthouse, also in Cincinnati. During the retrial, prosecutors struggled with the burden of unfavorable evidentiary rulings mandated by the Sixth Circuit and the fading of witnesses' memories. After listening to the evidence, the jury in Cincinnati acquitted Ebens, ending the Vincent Chin case as a legal matter, although, for the families of those involved, and for the Asian American community in Michigan, it can neither end nor be forgotten.

Hard Time and Hard Remedies

Many prisoner petitions are frivolous, filed by inmates with nothing to lose and too much time on their hands. Others, though, do raise serious issues about constitutional issues. Dealing with those petitions raises difficult questions for federal judges, particularly petitions by prisoners in state or local custody who challenge the conditions of their treatment as cruel and unusual punishment or as violations of their rights to due process.[15] Until the 1970s, almost all federal courts refused to interfere in the operation of state and local prisons out of respect for the separation of powers between state and federal governments and between executive and judicial branches, as well as a sense of the difficulties involved in achieving a lasting remedy. It was easy enough for a district judge to hold a state law unconstitutional and to award damages, then close the case. As the school desegregation cases proved, though, fashioning, supervising, and enforcing what is known as a structural injunction, one that undertakes to change in detail the way organizations such as schools, jails, water and sewage systems, or police and fire departments operate, is an exhausting and thankless task. In 1974, however, the U.S. Supreme Court, in *Procunier v. Martinez*,[16] made it clear that federal courts had a duty to protect the constitutional rights of prisoners whether they were in federal, state, or local institutions.

The Supreme Court's imprimatur did not reduce the difficulties involved in such cases or their length, as two cases filed in 1977 and assigned to Judge John Feikens demonstrate. One, a suit by the female inmates of the Detroit House of Correction, challenged the inequality in treatment and rehabilitation facilities available to male and female inmates.[17] After expanding the case to include female prisoners in other state facilities, Judge Feikens found that defendants had violated the plaintiffs' constitutional rights. Although he entered an order in 1979 directing the establishment of a comprehensive rehabilitative and educational program for women,[18] enforcement and supervising kept the case open until 1981.[19] The other case involved living conditions at the sprawling and aging State Prison of Southern Michigan at Jackson, in the far western part of the district. After nine years of litigation and negotiation, the suit was resolved by a consent decree entered in 1986, but enforcement of the decree required keeping the case open until 2001.[20]

Cases involving the operations of state or local government can raise uncomfortable issues of federal-state relations for federal judges on a personal level as well as constitutional. Because they are required to be both lawyers and residents of the districts in which they serve, most district judges have had professional and personal contact with the state and local governments before them. For example, before joining the federal bench in 1973, Judge James Harvey was mayor of the city of Saginaw and then for 12 years represented the Saginaw area in Congress and still lived there as a judge.[21] In 1975, inmates of the Saginaw county jail filed a class action against Saginaw County and its officers alleging that a variety of practices and procedures at the three-year-old jail violated their constitutional rights.[22] The case was assigned automatically to Judge Harvey, the sole district judge for the Northern Division at that time. The defendants may have been happy with the assignment, but if so they erred in their estimation of Judge Harvey. After an evidentiary hearing and a visit to the jail, Judge Harvey ruled in favor of the inmates on practically every claim, finding that there were numerous deficiencies including the jail's safety procedures, the system for discipline, the lack of access to religious services, medical treatment, recreation, books and magazines, the visitation system, and the failure to segregate convicted criminals from those awaiting trial or sentencing. On September 14, 1977, he entered an injunction mandating reforms as simple as providing each inmate with a toothbrush, toothpaste, and clean socks and bedding and as complex as a set of detailed rules and procedures for imposing discipline and the contents of an inmate guide to be distributed to all inmates.

Like the defendants in Judge Feikens's cases and in most jail cases, Saginaw County argued that it simply lacked the money to comply with Harvey's order. Meanwhile improving conditions for people arrested for or convicted of crimes was not popular among the county's voters. The desire to keep as many of the accused and the convicted in jail as long as possible conflicted, as it did across the nation, with an equally strong aversion to paying the bill.[23] Judge Harvey joked that: "The sheriff of Saginaw ran against me twice." Nevertheless, except for a provision regarding contact visitation, which the judge later dropped, the reforms were implemented.

Magistrates and Magistrate Judges

As the court's docket pressures began to ease after World War II, the district judges of the Eastern District acted on their nagging concerns about the deficiencies of the U.S. commissioner system, at least as it operated in Detroit. They worried that their commissioners had become too friendly with the bail bondsmen, gave lower bonds to clients of crony lawyers, and hiked bail astronomically in response to public outcries over particular cases.[24] When highly respected U.S. commissioner Stanley Hurd retired in 1947, Judge Lederle convinced the other judges that they should not fill Hurd's position and that the judges should take over the commissioner's duties themselves in Detroit, while the resident deputy clerks in Flint and

Bay City could act as commissioners as needed.[25] Each week, one judge served a term as the miscellaneous judge who did what the commissioners had done before: issue warrants, hold arraignments, try minor criminal cases, and set bail. The result was one of the lowest case backlogs of any large U.S. district court.[26]

By 1966, judges of other district courts, as well as members of Congress, had become convinced that the U.S. commissioners were not providing the help that district judges needed. Of the 701 U.S. commissioners, 180 were not practicing attorneys, 17 were clerks or deputy clerks, and only 16 were full-time or listed no other profession. Most were underworked, so that only 72 of them had earned more than $3,000 in fees in each of the three previous years. On the other hand, because Congress had capped their annual fee income at $10,500, in some busy districts the U.S. commissioners were overworked and underpaid.[27] There were no set criteria or procedures for their appointment, and their restricted authority limited their ability to reduce district judges' caseloads. Committees in both houses of Congress began to investigate how best to resolve those problems. One proposed solution was the creation of a new quasi-judicial position whose members would be attorneys, salaried, and full-time, with more extensive duties and greater authority than given to U.S. commissioners. Others, including most of the judges of the Eastern District, preferred a different solution, more district judges.

On February 12, 1966, Judge Levin, at that time the district court's chief judge, appeared before a U.S. Senate subcommittee on improvements in the federal judiciary to explain how his court had all but abolished commissioners.[28] He explained that, by keeping the grand jury in session, the Eastern District was able to begin most criminal cases by indictment, avoiding the need for preliminary hearings. He added that the presiding judge easily handled the rest of a commissioner's duties in two daily sessions. Instead of creating a new position to perform the commissioner's duties, he asked, "Why not appoint another judge?" Chief Judge Levin did not speak for all of the district's judges, though. After Levin completed his testimony, Judge Talbot Smith addressed the committee. Noting the large number of duties that commissioners were authorized to perform, he said that: "It has been suggested that the time involved in performance of these functions is not extensive. I have difficulty accepting this suggestion." He urged the senators to provide the district courts with more assistance of the type provided by the commissioners, not less.[29]

Judge Smith's view was that held by the majority of district judges across the country, and it turned out to be the remedy adopted by Congress in October 1968 when it enacted the Federal Magistrates Act.[30] This statute replaced U.S. commissioners with a new position, called U.S. magistrates, to be appointed by a majority vote of each district's judges to serve a fixed term of office (eight years for full-time magistrates, four years for part-time magistrates). U.S. magistrates were required to be attorneys licensed by the state in which they served, were to be paid a salary, and were given broader powers in order to lessen the burden on district judges. In 1990, Congress changed their title from U.S. magistrate to U.S. magistrate judge.[31]

Although the 1968 law provided U.S. magistrates were to be appointed by district judges, it also left it to the Judicial Conference of the United States to decide how many U.S. magistrate positions each district would be allocated, based on studies performed by the AOUSC. The program began cautiously with a pilot project in five districts in May 1969.[32] The results were positive and, by March 1970, the Judicial Conference had authorized 546 U.S. magistrate positions, with appointments made between November 1970 and June 1971.[33] The Eastern District was allocated two magistrate positions for Detroit and one to serve both Flint and Bay City, but the Judicial Council of the Sixth Circuit ordered the court to fill only one of the Detroit positions to see if the second position was necessary.[34] On February 12, 1971, the district judges filled Flint/Bay City position by appointing Warren Krapohl, who had been the U.S. commissioner in Flint. For the Detroit position, they named former Assistant United States Attorney Paul J. Komives. Several months later, a majority of the district's judges were sufficiently pleased with the new system to vote to ask the Sixth Circuit to authorize a second magistrate for Detroit,[35] although Chief Judge Ralph Freeman felt one was enough.[36] The Sixth Circuit delayed, and it was not until March 1, 1973, that Barbara K. Hackett (now a senior district judge) was appointed to join magistrate Komives in Detroit. Over the years, the number authorized has increased to eight, five assigned to Detroit and one each to Flint, Bay City, and Ann Arbor.

The Eastern District's judges came to appreciate the assistance of magistrates in holding arraignments and preliminary hearings, conducting settlement conferences, hearing pretrial motions, and making recommendations regarding prisoner and social security cases, they were leery of the portion of the 1968 act allowing a majority of the district judges to vote to allow assignment of magistrates to "additional duties as are not inconsistent with the Constitution and laws of the United States." Part of their concern was that, like many other district courts, they were not sure about the meaning of that language or the constitutional limits of such assignments to non-Article III judicial officers. In 1976[37] and in 1979,[38] Congress amended the 1968 act to specify that, with the consent of the parties, a district court could designate U.S. magistrates to adjudicate civil cases in the same manner as a district judge, including presiding over jury or nonjury trials and entering judgments. For a majority of the Eastern District's judges, that was a step too far because the Constitution vests the power to decide cases within the judicial power of the United States in Article III judges. They argued that allowing magistrates to perform that function, even with the consent of the parties, was both unconstitutional and an intrusion on the powers of Article III judges. Consequently, a majority voted not to allow U.S. magistrates to preside over civil cases.

That decision did not please the district's U.S. magistrates who knew that other district courts had given magistrates broad authority, including hearing dispositive motions and trying admiralty cases.[39] In February 1983, the Eastern District's six magistrates[40] submitted a memorandum to then Chief Judge Ralph Freeman asking the district judges to consider designating them to try civil cases on consent.[41] They pointed out that 88 percent of full-time magistrates in all districts were certified to try civil cases, of which 75 percent had been designated to do so, that only two of 31 metropolitan districts did not certify magistrates, that 24 of those metropolitan districts designated magistrates to try civil cases, and that the District of Oregon, for all intents and purposes, treated its magistrate as another district judge. The judges of the Eastern District were not convinced, however, and did not agree to change their decision. In September 1983, magistrate Barbara Hackett notified Chief Judge Freeman that she would be leaving the court. Although she was not specific as to why she felt that it was "time to move ahead,"[42] it was known in the courthouse that the court's decision not to let magistrates try civil cases convinced her to go.

Congress's decision in 1990 to change the title of magistrates to magistrate judge[43] may have been meant to boost morale of the magistrates, but it also boosted the level of tension in the Eastern District of Michigan's courthouses. Judge Cook remembered that some district judges felt that the magistrate judges were "taking over their turf." In order to preserve their position, those judges did not want the magistrates to be addressed as judge, did not want them to use the judges' elevator, and did not want the rooms where they did their paperwork to be called chambers or where they held hearings to be called courtrooms.[44] If the magistrates needed further proof that they were subordinates, the judges required them to keep time records and to advise the court when they left their "offices." During his term as chief judge (1989–1996), Judge Cook again asked the judges to consider allowing the magistrate judges to try civil cases, but that attempt "went over like the proverbial lead balloon,"[45] even though, by that time, only one other district court, the District of Montana, did not designate magistrate judges to try civil cases. Finally, in September 1998, the district judges, by a one-vote majority, enacted Local Rule 73.1, which allowed magistrate judges "to conduct all proceedings in a civil case and order entry of judgment in the case" but only with the consent of the parties and "approval of the district judge to whom the case is assigned."[46] Nevertheless, as Judge Zatkoff recalled, when he became chief judge in 1999, many of the district judges would not let magistrate judges try civil cases and complained that the magistrate judges were behaving like the district judges' equals.[47] A decade later, although a few of the district judges are willing to designate magistrate judges to adjudicate civil cases, most are not, both because they have lingering doubts of designation's legality and because their dockets are so current that they see no need for the help.[48] Thus, in 2009 when magistrate judges nationwide terminated 11,402 civil cases assigned to them with the consent of the parties, the Eastern District of Michigan joined the districts of Alaska, Guam, and the Virgin Islands in having none.[49] Not that the Eastern District's magistrate judges were idle. During the same year, they conducted 3,878 felony preliminary hearings, 2,581 civil pretrial conferences, and 320 criminal pretrial conferences while also issuing 773 reports and recommendations on social security appeals, prisoner petitions, and other matters.[50]

Changes in the Clerk's Office

After Frank Dingell resigned as clerk of the district court in 1958, the position was held for relatively short periods by John J. Ginther (1959–1963) and Julius L. Kabatsky (1963–1964). Frederick W. Johnson was clerk for ten years (1964–1973), followed by Henry R. Hanssen (1973–1978). In 1979, John P. Mayer began his long term as clerk and as district court executive, a new position created at the behest of U.S. Supreme Court Chief Justice Warren Burger. When John Winder undertook to become clerk of the district court for the District of Michigan, his duties were simple: keep the records, schedule trials and hearings, draft orders and writs, and do whatever else had to be done to keep the court working. Even a century later, when George Read took over the clerk's office, it was run like a medium-sized law firm in which the clerk was the office manager and the judges were the partners who made all of the final decisions. With more cases and more than one judge to serve, the clerk had to hire and administer a staff of deputies and stenographers, and, in the Eastern District, the clerk also assigned the cases among the judges, according to instructions from the "senior judge." The bulk of the chief clerk's day, though, was still directed towards the records, accepting or rejecting pleadings presented for filing, assessing fees, and other clerical duties. By the 1970s, the job had become much more complicated. "[D]istrict court clerks were, in fact, spending more and more time managing personnel and attending to other business that did not relate to their traditional document-screening and record-keeping functions."[51]

Convinced that the administration of the district courts needed a change, Chief Justice Burger directed the Judicial Conference of the United States to include in its budget request for 1981 funds to provide a district court executive in each of the 15 district courts with ten or more judges.[52] The executive was to be separate from the clerk's office and was to be responsible for certain administrative duties previously handled by the clerk, although exactly which duties was not made clear. Because both clerk and executive reported directly to the district judges, there was obvious potential for turf battles. Both district judges and district clerks generally opposed the creation of a new level of bureaucracy, but in 1981, Congress did approve funds to establish, as a pilot program, an office of the court executive in five districts, including the Eastern District of Michigan. John Mayer was appointed to the new position and Robert A. Mossing became clerk of the district court. Overall, the court executive experiment was not a success, and within a decade all of the districts with pilot programs had reverted to a system with one head. In the eastern district, John Mayer was given the title district court administrator/clerk of the court in 1990 and was placed in charge of all of the operations of the office of the clerk. He was succeeded in 1999 by David J. Weaver.

Trouble in the Bankruptcy Court

The roles of magistrates and court executives were not the only internal issues roiling the waters of the district court in the early 1980s. Revelations of misfeasance, malfeasance, and corruption in the district's U.S. bankruptcy court brought very public embarrassment to the district and its judges. Two court employees and a prominent local attorney were indicted, a bankruptcy judge resigned, and lascivious tales of drinking and sexual escapades in the bankruptcy court were spread across the country by newspapers, radio, and television.

In a sense, this story began on November 6, 1978, when Congress passed a bankruptcy reform act,[53] effective October 1, 1979, which revised the structure of bankruptcy administration by creating a new federal court devoted solely to bankruptcy cases. Each of the previous four U.S. bankruptcy statutes enacted since 1800 provided for non-judicial officers of the court to carry out many routine and ministerial duties under the supervision of the district judges, but the cases were considered to be part of the district judge's docket, and administrative matters in bankruptcy cases were the responsibility of the clerk of the district court. Besides creating a new court, the 1978 act also created a new category of judge, U.S. bankruptcy judges, who, although appointed by the president, were not Article III judges. President Carter appointed the Eastern District's first bankruptcy judges, nominating the three referees then serving in the Eastern District, Harry G. Hackett, George Brody, and David H. Patton. They then appointed William L. Harper, an experienced employee of the district clerk's office, to be clerk of their bankruptcy court. This proved to be an unfortunate choice.

Less than two years later, on April 21, 1981, Harper was indicted on charges that he had, in 1976, purchased items from a bankrupt's estate, a clear conflict of interest and a violation of federal law. The district judges removed Harper pending resolution of the charges, but that was just the beginning of a nightmare. Rumors were circulating in the courthouse of on-the-job drunkenness, sexual misconduct, and low morale in the bankruptcy clerk's office. Even worse, there were allegations that the bankruptcy court's blind-draw system for allocating cases among the judges had been compromised by one of the deputy bankruptcy clerks to keep certain attorneys' cases from being heard by Judge Brody.

When they took office, the bankruptcy judges decided that Judge Patton would be assigned all of the reorganization cases for individuals filed under Chapter 13 of the act. The intake clerks were to assign 30 percent of the other cases to Patton and 35 percent each to Hackett and Brody, using sets of index cards. Each card had a judge's name on it, and the names on the cards in each pack were distributed in proportion to each judge's allocation. When a new case was filed, the intake clerk took the top card from the pack and turned it over to reveal the judge's name. This system worked fine if the intake clerks did their job, but one of them did not. Kathleen Bogoff had become involved romantically with a busy and successful bankruptcy attorney, Irving August, whose firm initiated about half of the business reorganization cases filed in the Eastern District. In addition to their sexual relationship, August gave Bogoff thousands of dollars in cash. It appears that August found Judge Brody to be too stingy in awarding attorney fees in his cases, and, beginning in October 1979, he conspired with Bogoff to fix the blind draw. When an August employee showed up at the intake desk to file a case, Bogoff would manipulate the cards so that the case was assigned to Hackett or Patton.

Eventually, other employees of the court noticed that August's cases rarely went to Judge Brody, and rumors started flying both in the courthouse and in the press. Chief Judge Feikens had the authorities begin an investigation which confirmed the rumors and, to make things worse, also revealed that Judge Harry Hackett and a female companion often socialized with August and Bogoff, and that Hackett had accepted favors from August at the same time that he had been granting August suspiciously generous attorney fees. On May 6, 1981, after consulting with the district judges, the Judicial Council of the Sixth Circuit entered an order placing the bankruptcy court "under the supervision of the United States District Court for the Eastern District of Michigan. Such supervision should include the oversight of the general operation of the Bankruptcy Court Clerk's Office, the appointment of an Acting Clerk of the Bankruptcy Court and the approval of all personnel actions affecting employees of the Bankruptcy Court."[54] On May 18, 1981, the district judges directed Chief Judge Feikens to assume supervisory responsibility for the bankruptcy court. Judge Hackett resigned on June 24, 1981, after he was advised that he would not be re-appointed. Harper and Bogoff also resigned. August and Bogoff were indicted on multiple counts of fraud, conspiracy, and bribery.

On June 28, 1983, August was convicted on three counts and Bogoff on two counts, and both were sentenced to prison. On October 29, 1984, the Sixth Circuit affirmed the convictions and sentences.[55] In 1982, the Judicial Conference of the United States published a rule that placed the district courts back in control of bankruptcy by limiting the power of the bankruptcy judges to issue final, binding orders. In 1984, Congress amended the bankruptcy code to do much the same thing.

The Ann Arbor Federal Building

The district judges have treated the district court for the Eastern District, from its inception, as a Detroit court, and that attitude continues to prevail. Even though by 1977 the court had active court facilities in Bay City and Flint and an unused but functional facility in Port Huron, the district court continued to concentrate its judicial resources in Detroit, including eight of the court's nine sitting district judges (there was one vacancy), all of its four senior district judges, and 73 of the 85 employees of the clerk's office, leaving Judge Harvey to preside in Flint and Bay City with eight members of the clerk's office in Flint and four in Bay City.[56] When Congress approved three additional district judgeships for the district in 1978, all three were initially assigned to chambers in the Detroit courthouse, although one of the appointees, Judge Stewart Newblatt, asked to be assigned to Flint.

Despite this centralizing tendency, during the 1960s and 1970s pressure grew to situate another federal court facility outside Detroit, in this case in Ann Arbor, just 45 miles west of Detroit and 55 miles south of Flint. On March 11, 1982, the district court did dedicate a new U.S. courtroom in that city's strikingly post-modern federal building. As a growing community anchored on the University of Michigan, Ann Arbor had been seeking a new post office and federal building since the 1940s in order to ease crowding at its 1909 post office on Main Street and to consolidate other federal agencies in the area. In 1968, the General Services Administration (GSA) sent to the House and Senate Public Works Committees a proposal for a new federal building in downtown Ann Arbor, near the offices of the city and county governments, at a cost of $3,776,000, including $1,308,000 for acquisition, design, and engineering.[57] However, that plan ran into a long Congressional moratorium on funding federal construction, and it was not until 1972 that Congress came up with the means to finance the project.

The Public Building Amendments Act of 1972[58] authorized the administrator of general services to enter into a contract under which a private developer would design, finance, and build a federal building which the GSA would lease for up to 30 years, whereupon title would pass to the federal government.[59] The GSA and the Ann Arbor city government began to explore a likely site for such a building, and in January 1973 Ann Arbor Congressman Marvin Esch announced that the GSA had selected the city's third proposal, half of a city block on the south side of East Liberty Street between South Fourth and South Fifth Avenues.[60] The original plan was to begin demolition of the buildings on the site in early 1974 and to complete construction in late 1975 or early 1976, but, by March 1974, no work had been done on the site, and GSA announced there would be another year's delay.[61] The official reason for the delay was problems acquiring all the necessary property and relocating persons living on the site,[62] but that was the least of GSA's problems. In fact, the federal building had stirred opposition on several fronts. First, the project was initiated and funded during the Vietnam War when a substantial number of the city's residents were hostile to the federal government and suspicious of anything it did. Second, although the city's government envisioned the federal building as a key element in its plans to revitalize downtown Ann Arbor, the addition of a main post office among two-lane streets in the middle of an already cramped downtown was bound to exacerbate the area's traffic jams and lack of parking. Third, the site plan called for the demolition of a number of buildings, including Ann Arbor's striking, five-story, art deco Masonic Temple.

The Masonic Temple was inaugurated in 1925 to house the city's active masonic organizations. By 1972, though, the Temple was financially rocky and in danger of foreclosure. Nevertheless, when the GSA announced that the Temple would have to be demolished and replaced by a ground-level parking lot in order to obtain the 90 parking spaces required by federal specifications, Masons, the city council, and the citizenry at large were appalled. The Masons, of course, did not want to lose their gem, which had been built with the proceeds from bake sales and pancake suppers. The city's residents, who, despite their progressive politics, disliked change when it came to the city's buildings, inundated the city council with complaints, and the council did what it could. In truth, the GSA held all of the cards, because it did not need the approval of anybody in Ann Arbor. Besides the Temple dispute, the GSA also had a problem with the Postal Service, which could not make up its mind whether it wanted to relocate from Main Street to the new building. All of this took time, and bidding for the demolition and construction contract did not take place until 1975.

In late 1974, while the questions of the Temple and traffic were being argued, the architects, TMP Associates of Bloomfield Hills, Michigan, unveiled a design which the company boasted was unlike any other governmental building, at least in the Eastern District.[63] TMP explained that it would have a "light, airy, inviting quality,"[64] and would "avoid the standard authoritarian concept of government offices."[65] The design included four stories, each stepped back about 40 feet from the story below so as to minimize the contrast with the neighboring one and two story buildings.

Fig. 98.   The Ann Arbor Federal Building. (Historical Society for the United States District Court for the Eastern District of Michigan)

The front, facing East Liberty Street, was to have ribbons of reflective, insulated windows and skylights along its front on East Liberty Street, but there were to be no windows at all on the other three sides in order to conserve energy. Inside, the design emphasized an "open office" concept, again to counter any authoritarian impulses.[66] The design won honors from the Federal Design Council and the Michigan Society of Architects and the American Institute of Architects for its "low profile, human scale," although some private citizens decried it as bleak and as "the ugliest building in Ann Arbor" for its massive, windowless side walls.

Construction bids from four contractors were opened in June 1975, but federal regulations disqualified the three lowest bidders leaving only the $3,862,035 bid of Barton-Malow Construction[67] which was awarded the contract and ownership of the building for 20 years.[68] By now, the total cost total of the project had spiraled to $7.3 million, of which $1 million was spent for land acquisition. The Masonic Temple and other obstructions were cleared in August and September 1975,[69] and the groundbreaking ceremony took place on October 6, accompanied by protesters including a group of mimes from "Fear Breeds Idiocy" and opponents of the proposed Criminal Justice Reform Act.[70] Construction took about a year-and-a-half. The Postal Service moved in on July 9, 1978, and other agencies followed over the next few months, but not the district court.

Bringing the district court to Ann Arbor required a separate campaign which began in 1960 with the desire of Judge Talbot Smith, an Ann Arbor resident, to hold court nearer to home. In October 1964, as part of the politics of the resolution of the Flint/Bay City dispute, Congress added

Ann Arbor to the list of cities where "[c]ourt for the Southern Division shall be held,"[71] but, as in Flint, lack of suitable facilities thwarted the congressional "shall" for many years.[72] The decision to build a new federal building seemed to solve that problem, and the building's design made provisions for court facilities, but a GSA report in 1974 determined that there would not be enough federal cases "in the near future" to warrant the cost of maintaining a court in Ann Arbor,[73] an opinion with which the Sixth Circuit agreed. In 1980, however, Judges Joiner and Feikens, both of whom wanted to hold court in Ann Arbor, pressed the point again with the support of Judge Newblatt (who wanted their support to take over the Flint court) and Judge Harvey (who wanted to drop Flint and add summer-time sessions in Port Huron). The result was an agreement to open a courtroom in Ann Arbor to handle cases arising in Washtenaw, Monroe, Lenawee, and Jackson counties. Judge Joiner, an Ann Arbor resident, was assigned to be Ann Arbor's first resident district judge.

Moving in the district court necessitated moving out the Internal Revenue Service, which was occupying the spaces designated for the court in the original design, as well as making substantial modifications to the completed building which eventually cost about $500,000. On May 1, 1981, construction began on the court facilities, including, on the first floor, a 1,800 square foot courtroom, offices for the deputy clerk and deputy marshal, and a small lock-up. The district judge's chambers were placed on the fourth floor, requiring the construction of a private elevator. No assistant U.S. attorney has been assigned to Ann Arbor, but space for those who attend the court when required was provided on the second floor.

The court opened for business on February 16, 1982, although Judge Joiner was stuck in Detroit trying a case and not all of the furniture had arrived. The courtroom was dedicated on March 11, 1982, at which time the court was presented with a portrait of Judge Smith. In 1983, Judge Joiner welcomed U.S. magistrate Steven D. Pepe, and a second courtroom was built for his use. Judge Joiner continued presiding in Ann Arbor after he took senior status in 1984, and Judge La Plata moved his chambers to Ann Arbor in 1987. In 1996, Judge La Plata retired, and Judge Barbara Hackett replaced him in Ann Arbor. In 1999 Judge Steeh joined her, to be replaced by Judge Battani in 2000. In 2011, Senior Judge John Corbett O'Meara presides at Ann Arbor, but as a further sign of consolidation, the Ann Arbor clerk's office has been closed.

Liuzzo v. United States

It did not take long for the Ann Arbor courtroom to host its first historically significant trial. In 1983, Judge Joiner presided over the suit brought against the United States by the family of civil-rights martyr Viola Liuzzo. The family sought damages under the Federal Tort Claims Act for what they alleged was the FBI's responsibility for Mrs. Liuzzo's murder by members of the Ku Klux Klan while she was in Alabama in 1965 for the civil rights march from Selma to Montgomery. One of the four men in the vehicle from which the fatal shots came, Gary Thomas Rowe, was an undercover informant for the FBI. He notified his FBI contact of the shooting, and local police arrested the other three men the next day. Later, Rowe testified against the men before state and federal grand juries and in two state murder trials and a federal trial for violations of the civil rights laws.[74] During their trials, two of the other men, Collie Leroy Wilkins and Eugene Thomas, claimed that Rowe had fired the shot that killed Liuzzo. Although the FBI and Rowe denied that claim, it became known that in his undercover role Rowe had participated in other acts of violence against African Americans. The Liuzzo family charged that "the agents of the F.B.I. directing Rowe did not act as ordinary reasonably prudent agents in carrying out the duties to which they had been assigned." Judge Joiner presided over an eight-day bench trial in Ann Arbor, after which, on May 27, 1983, he ruled in favor of the United States. Joiner rejected the testimony of Wilkins and Thomas that Rowe pulled the trigger as not credible, stating that "The evidence indicates that Collie Leroy Wilkins shot her and that he was encouraged to do so by Eugene Thomas. The court believes that Rowe did not encourage Collie Leroy Wilkins to shoot." Joiner also found no evidence that the U.S. conspired to do harm to Mrs. Liuzzo. Rather, he found, her death was the result of "mindless egos [of the three men in the car with Rowe] feeding each other, gradually working themselves up until violence erupted." Finally, Joiner found that Rowe was present in the car as part of his undercover assignment and that his FBI handlers had acted reasonably in using Rowe as an informant in a highly volatile situation requiring intelligence on the plans of the Klan that could be obtained only by informants. In dismissing the complaint, Judge Joiner assessed costs against the plaintiffs in the amount of $79,873, later reduced to $3,645.[75]

The Port Huron Courtroom

After decades of little or no use, the Port Huron court was activated in 1979 to allow Judge Harvey to hear cases during the summer until he retired in 1992. The courtroom and chambers had been ignored since Judge O'Sullivan was appointed to the Sixth Circuit in 1957. Attorney Patrick Dreisig, a law clerk for Judge Harvey in 1979, remembers that when he and the judge first went to Port Huron, it looked as if people had just run out of the courtroom 20 years before and then never went back, leaving books, papers, and water glasses on the tables.[76] In 1986, the GSA performed a comprehensive restoration and modernization of the Port Huron Federal Building. Exterior improvements included stone steps at the north and east entrances, new sidewalks and curbing, removal of the six obsolete chimneys, and landscaping. One highly appreciated change looked backward: the dome received new copper to restore its original shine—the galvanized copper plating had never been a success. Inside, GSA added a new lobby and returned to view eight columns which had been covered over during earlier remodeling. The first and third floors were brought up to current standards for office space, and the second floor underwent major changes to the courtroom, judge's chambers, and offices for court staff. As a state-of-the-art touch, GSA installed ultrasonic devices to chase away the pigeons that had taken to flocking around the building's entrances. After Judge Harvey's retirement, the Port Huron court was unused until Judge Zatkoff took senior status in June 2004 and agreed to move his chambers there.

Challenges to the U.S. Census

The 1964 decision of the U.S. Supreme Court in *Marshall v. Hare* established that Michigan's legislative districts had to be apportioned according to population, which meant according to the decennial census conducted by the U.S. Census Bureau. That decision did not, however, address the accuracy of the census, an issue raised in two cases filed in 1980 and 1990. In the former case, Coleman Young, mayor of Detroit, sued the U.S. secretary of commerce, Philip M. Klutznick, and the director of the U.S. Bureau of the Census, seeking a recount or an upward adjustment of the 1980 census count of African Americans in Michigan, citing as authority the apportionment clause of the U.S. Constitution.[77] Young argued that the census was inaccurate because it found and counted a smaller percentage of the members of some racial and social groups than the percentage of white persons. The result, according to Young, was that districts in which those groups had a large presence actually had more residents than shown by the census, destroying the equality of representation. The case was first assigned to Judge Guy who refused to dismiss the case for lack of standing. When Guy was elevated to the Sixth Circuit, the case went to Judge Gilmore who presided over trial of the case in August and September 1980. On September 25, he found that the 1980 census did indeed have an undercount that the defendants had a constitutional duty to correct. He ordered them "to adjust population figures for the 1980 census at the national, state, and sub-state level to reflect the undercount, and to adjust the differential undercount to prevent the known undercount of Blacks and Hispanics, as well as whites,"[78] an order, in effect, to revise the entire 1980 census.

The defendants appealed, and, on June 15, 1981, the Sixth Circuit reversed, 2 to 1. The majority opinion held that the Michigan legislature was not required by the U.S. Constitution to accept the census figures and that, until it decided whether to adjust the census figures, the issue was not ripe for adjudication and plaintiffs lacked standing. The majority also found that any undercount affected all poor people, not just those of one race.[79] Judge Damon Keith drafted a long and detailed dissent in which he characterized the majority opinion as "myopic" and remarked that it: "presents an amusing sociological analysis. It would be nice if the court's views had some support in the record. Unfortunately, they do not." Judge Keith then presented his detailed refutation of the majority's argument as to standing, ripeness, the existence of a racial undercount, and the duty of the defendants to cure it.

Ten years later, Mayor Young tried again, suing the federal government demanding either a recount of the 1990 census throughout Michigan or a statistical adjustment. This time, the government did not contest that, despite their best efforts, the 1990 census takers undercounted the population or that the undercount rate for African Americans nationally (4.8 percent) was almost three times that of whites (1.7 percent). Nevertheless, Judge Zatkoff granted defendants' motion for summary judgment holding that plaintiffs lacked standing because neither state nor federal legislatures were compelled to use unadjusted census figures. Thus, "the conduct of intervening third parties, not the actions of the defendants, are directly responsible for plaintiffs' claimed injuries."[80] He also held that plaintiffs had failed to state a constitutional violation of a cognizable right or to show any lack of good faith by defendants. On appeal, the Sixth Circuit held that plaintiffs did have standing to argue that an undercount would decrease federal funding calculated based on population but that the appropriation clause did not authorize suits to challenge the bureau's methodology. The appellate court also declined to "take sides in a dispute among statisticians, demographers, and census officials concerning the desirability of making a statistical adjustment to a census headcount."[81]

The District Court and the Media

Relations between most courts and most journalists are strained except where the press has become too friendly with the court to do its business well. Some judges view the media as a distraction or as a threat to due process, while reporters become convinced that judges are making mistakes or are trying to hide the truth. This mutual suspicion is always present if not always evident, and when a court tries to restrain the media, judges usually lose, at least in the court of public opinion. One of the great public donnybrooks during Michigan's territorial period occurred when the *Detroit Gazette* published an article highly critical of the manner in which the supreme court of the territory handled a case involving the theft of a watch. Judges William Woodbridge and Henry Chipman, both Whigs and the article's principal targets, took umbrage and voted to fine owner John Sheldon, a Democrat, for contempt of court. When he refused to pay, the court tossed him into the Wayne County jail, where his friends held a gala banquet in his honor.[82] A century later, Judge Tuttle, who cultivated the air of a man whom no criticism could affect, revealed that he too had a thin skin. Edwin R. Cornish was a Socialist and the editor of a small newspaper, *The Worker's Voice*, which ran an article criticizing a ruling by Tuttle in a case involving a workers' strike against the Pere Marquette Railroad. In September 1922, Tuttle had Cornish hauled before him and found him in criminal contempt. Cornish appealed, and the Sixth Circuit not only reversed the contempt order, it implied that Tuttle had over-reacted and chastised him for presiding over the contempt hearing himself.[83]

Even Judge Theodore Levin managed to run afoul of the press. In 1959, a Detroit architecture firm sued a former partner in the district court alleging embezzlement. At the firm's request, and in order to avoid public embarrassment for the parties, Judge Levin suppressed the record, holding that the court had the "inherent right" to suppress any case.[84] Detroit police investigated and arrested not the partner, but the firm's bookkeeper who had managed to siphon off nearly $1,000,000 of the firm's receipts.[85] Detroit's newspapers published the story and dared the court to hold them in contempt. Congressmen chimed in, Judge Levin was summoned to testify before a Congressional committee,[86] and even Judge Lederle roared from his hospital bed: "The court's business is the public business." Polite and conciliatory as ever, Judge Levin pointed out that the newspapers could not be held to be in contempt because they had not obtained or published any information from the suppressed record. This satisfied the *Free Press* and *Times*, but the *News* promised to breach the suppression order and to challenge the court's alleged "inherent right."

Twenty years later, the tension between the court and the media crystallized during the so-called Vista trials, in which close associates of Detroit mayor Coleman Young were charged with bribery and corruption in the letting of contracts by the city's water and sewer department. After information from the U.S. attorney's investigation and testimony before the grand jury was leaked to the media in 1983, Chief Judge John Feikens appointed a law and media committee, chaired by Judge Cohn, to investigate the effect of the leaks on the rights of parties in court to a fair trial. After the defendants' conviction in December 1983, a group of criminal defense attorneys (including future District Judge Paul Borman) expressed to the court their concerns that the behavior of media members in and around the courthouse during high-profile criminal trials, including contacting and "harassing" jurors, had affected the fairness and perceived fairness of the trials. In August 1984, after study, internal discussions, and meetings with media representatives, the committee issued a draft set of guidelines. As the committee reported, "Media reaction to the Guidelines was immediate, hostile, and hyperbolic," even though, in the committee's opinion the guidelines merely proposed "limited time, place and manner standards."[87] More meetings and revisions to the guidelines were followed by two days of public hearings in May 1985, attended mostly by the media and by attorneys on both sides of the issue. Throughout, the committee and the media seem to have been able to operate in a cooperative and dignified manner, although the media made it clear that no negotiation or give-and-take was possible. In September 1985, the committee issued its report to the court in which it recommended that "the adoption of the Guidelines at this time would not be a productive step."[88] The court agreed, and, on October 17, 1985, a news release announced the end of the guideline initiative.

Notes

1. *Court Compendium*, "Description of the Court" (U.S. District Court for the Eastern District of Michigan, 2007), 2.

2. *Annual Report of the Director of the Administrative Office of the United States Courts (1972)*, 132–133.

3. *Annual Report of the U.S. Attorney General (1978)*, 49.

4. *Annual Report of the Director of the Administrative Office of the United States Courts (1988)*, 9.

5. The disproportionate number of such cases filed in the Eastern District was rumored to have been the result of local personal-injury attorneys who used the promise to file a social security disability claim as part of their marketing strategy.

6. 86 Stat. 1329.

7. 1939, at the height of the collection cases brought by federal bank receivers.

8. 106 Stat. 4646.

9. *Annual Report of the Director of the Administrative Office of the United States Courts (1992)*, 62–63.

10. Civil rights cases during this period included claims of reverse discrimination, such as *Marsh v. Flint Board of Education*, 581 F. Supp. 614 (E.D. Mich. 1984), aff'd, 762 F.2d 1009 (6th Cir. 1985), vacated and remanded, 476 U.S. 1137 (1986), on remand, 708 F. Supp. 821 (E.D. Mich. 1989), and claims of violations of the right to free speech under the First Amendment, such as *Doe v. University of Michigan*, 721 F. Supp. 852 (E.D. Mich. 1989).

11. I am indebted to Ross Parker's detailed and balanced discussion of this case, "'It's not fair . . . ,' Vincent Chin's Last Words," *The Court Legacy*, vol. XIV, no. 4 (November 2007), 1–10.

12. The indictments charged violations of 18 U.S.C. 245 and 18 U.S.C. 241.

13. Parker, *supra*, 6.

14. *U.S. v. Ebens*, 800 F.2d 1422 (6th Cir. 1986).

15. For a short history of prisoner litigation nationally, see Phillip J. Cooper, *Hard Judicial Choices: Federal District Court Judges and State and Local Officials* (New York: Oxford University Press, 1988), 205–270.

16. *Procunier v. Martinez*, 416 U.S. 396 (1974).

17. *Mary Glover v. Perry Johnson*, Eastern District of Michigan Civil Action No. 77-1229.

18. *Glover v. Johnson*, 478 F.Supp. 1075 (E.D. Mich. 1979).

19. *Glover v. Johnson*, 510 F.Supp. 1019 (E.D. Mich. 1981).

20. *Hadix v. Johnson*, 2001 WL 812217 (E.D. Mich. 2001).

21. A more amusing issue related to Harvey's congressional service arose in 1975 when a local motel owner sued in the district court because the Bay County treasurer refused to let him pay $4,300 in property taxes with gold and silver coins valued at the current market rate for their metal. The plaintiff moved to disqualify Harvey because, as a congressman, he had voted to remove the silver from dimes and quarters. Harvey denied the motion and dismissed the suit. *Bay City Times*, August 16, 1975.

22. *O'Bryan v. Saginaw County*, 437 F. Supp. 582 (E.D. Mich. 1977).

23. See Cooper, supra, 261–266.

24. Until the mid-20th century, it was customary for court clerks to be appointed also as magistrates and later as U.S. magistrates. This was particularly true for a court facility with no resident district judge, such as Bay City. When the Flint court opened in 1963, the court decided instead to hire an experienced attorney, Warren F. Krapohl, as U.S. commissioner for Flint and Bay City.

25. Remarks of Chief Judge Ralph Freeman at the induction ceremony for Magistrate Komives.

26. *Time*, June 3, 1966.

27. *Annual Report of the Director, Administrative Office of the U.S. Courts* (1967), 151.

28. *Detroit News*, February 13, 1966.

29. *Idem.*

30. 82 Stat. 1107.

31. Sec. 321, 104 Stat. 5089, 5117.

32. *Annual Report of the Director, Administrative Office of the U.S. Courts* (1969), 97. The commissioners in each district remained in office until replaced by magistrates.

33. *Annual Report of the Director, Administrative Office of the U.S. Courts* (1971), 93.

34. *Idem.*, 94.

35. Ralph Freeman to Harry Phillips, October 7, 1971, Topical–2d Magistrate File, Box 2, Ralph Freeman Papers.

36. Ralph Freeman to Harry Phillips, February 28, 1972, Topical–2d Magistrate File, Box 2, Ralph Freeman Papers.

37. 90 Stat. 2729.

38. 93 Stat. 643.

39. Oral Histories, Paul J. Komives.

40. Magistrates Komives, Hackett, Carlson, Hooe, Rhodes, and Walker.

41. Magistrates to Ralph Freeman, February 1, 1983, Topical–Magistrates 1983 Folder, Box 2, Ralph Freeman Papers.

42. Barbara Hackett to Ralph Freeman, September 8, 1983, Topical–Magistrates 1983 Folder, Box 2, Ralph Freeman Papers.

43. Sec. 321, 104 Stat. 5089, 5117.

44. Oral histories, Julian A. Cook, 95.

45. Oral histories, Julian A. Cook, 96.

46. Eastern District of Michigan Local Rule 73.1(a).

47. Oral histories, Lawrence P. Zatkoff, 151–153.

48. This attitude is in stark contrast to that of the Central District of California, which has announced a civil consent pilot project under which, as of January 2, 2009, "magistrate judges will be included in the pool of judicial officers for random selection as the assigned judge for all civil cases except class actions, death penalty habeas petitions, bankruptcy appeals or bankruptcy withdrawal of reference cases, cases referred to a magistrate judge for a Report and Recommendation under General Order 05-07 or any successor General Order, and cases in which a request for a temporary restraining order or motion for preliminary injunction is presented when the action is initiated." The parties to a case assigned to a magistrate judge may, nevertheless, withhold consent and require reassignment of the case to a district judge.

49. *Judicial Business of the U.S. Courts (2009)*, Table M5, 381.

50. Id., Tables M1—M4.

51. I. Scott Messinger, *Order in the Courts: A History of the Federal Clerk's Office* (Federal Judicial Center, 2002), 6.

52. Id., 68.

53. 92 Stat. 2549.

54. The judicial council's order and the subsequent order of the district court directing Chief Judge Feikens to assume responsibility for the bankruptcy court are quoted in *Guercio v. Brody*, 911 F.2d 1179 (6th Cir. 1990).

55. *U.S. v. August*, 745 F.2d 400 (6th Cir. 1984).

56. *Court Compendium*, 2.

57. *Ann Arbor News*, March 29, 1968.

58. 86 Stat. 216, 219.

59. *Ann Arbor News*, June 8, 1972.

60. *Ann Arbor News*, January 12, 1973.

61. *Ann Arbor News*, March 8, 1974.

62. *Ann Arbor News*, July 23, 1975.

63. *Ann Arbor News*, December 11, 1974.

64. *Ann Arbor News*, August 14, 1974.

65. *Ann Arbor News*, June 10, 1976.

66. *Ann Arbor News*, December 26, 1975; *Idem.*, June 10, 1976.

67. *Ann Arbor News*, June 13. 1975.

68. *Ann Arbor News*, July 23, 1975.

69. *Ann Arbor News*, September 4, 1975.

70. *Ann Arbor News*, October 6, 1975.

71. 78 Stat. 1003.

72. 28 U.S.C. 142.

73. *Ann Arbor News*, March 8, 1974.

74. The first murder trial resulted in a mistrial and the second in an acquittal, but the defendants were indicted and convicted for violating Mrs. Liuzzo's civil rights under the "Ku Klux Klan Act," 42 U.S.C. 1983.

75. Quotations in this paragraph are from Judge Joiner's opinion, *Liuzzo v. U.S.*, 565 F. Supp. 640 (E.D. Mich. 1983). For a more complete discussion of the murder of Mrs. Liuzzo, see John H. Dise Jr., "She Didn't Accept the Evil System: From Selma to Ann Arbor, 1965 to 1983," *The Court Legacy*, vol. X, no. 2 (November

2002). Despite Judge Joiner's ruling, conspiracy theorists remain convinced that Rowe killed Mrs. Liuzzo and that the FBI was involved in the conspiracy. The U.S. district court for the middle district of Alabama found that Rowe had been guaranteed immunity by both the U.S. and the State of Alabama in return for his testimony and so enjoined the state from prosecuting him in 1980, and the U.S. court of appeals affirmed. *Rowe v. Griffin*, 497 F. Supp. 610 (M.D. Ala. 1980), aff'd, 676 F.2d 524 (11th Cir. 1982).

76. Interview by the author with Patrick Dreisig.

77. U.S. Const., art. I, § 2, cl. 3.

78. *Young v. Klutznick*, 497 F. Supp. 1318 (E.D. Mich., 1980).

79. *Young v. Klutznick*, 652 F.2d 617 (6th Cir., 1981), *cert. denied*, 455 U.S. 939 (1982).

80. *City of Detroit v. Franklin*, 800 F. Supp. 539 (E.D. Mich., 1992).

81. *City of Detroit v. Franklin*, 4 F.3d 1367 (6th Cir., 1993).

82. The contempt case, *U.S. v. John P. Sheldon*, Case no. 1315, William W. Blume, *Transactions of the Supreme Court of Michigan, 1805–1836*, 6 vols. (Ann Arbor, MI: University of Michigan Press, 1935–1940), vol. V, 107–108, is discussed at Kermit L. Hall, *The Politics of Justice: Lower Federal Judicial Selection and the Second Party System, 1829–61* (Lincoln, NE: University of Nebraska Press, 1979), 3–4. For information on the underlying criminal case, see *U.S. v. John Reed*, Case no. 1307, Blume, vol. V, 105–106.

83. *Cornish v. U.S*, 299 F. 283 (6th Cir. 1924). Cornish was represented by recently retired U.S. district attorney John E. Kinnane.

84. *Time*, January 4, 1960.

85. *Time*, December 21, 1959.

86. *Detroit News*, December 17, 1959.

87. Recommendations and Report of the Law and Media Committee on Proposed Guidelines for Conduct of Attorneys, Court Personnel, and the Media (September 1985), 8.

88. Recommendations and Report, 2–3.

CHAPTER 16

At the Millennium 1990–2010

The Eastern District, 1990–2010

After falling between 1980 and 1990, the population of the Eastern District rebounded by 2000, increasing by 341,000 to an all-time high of 6,624,331, but during the next decade it declined again by 157,111 to 6,467,220. Wayne County's population, although easily still the highest of any county in the district and the state, decreased by 291,103 between 1990 and 2010, with most of that loss occurring in Detroit, which lost 314,197 residents during the period to a population of 713,777, the city's lowest since 1910. The Detroit metropolitan area as a whole remained the engine of population growth. Oakland and Macomb Counties grew by a combined 242,348, while other nearby counties also grew as commuters kept moving further west and north from the city. The counties of the Northern Division did experience growth, although very limited and spotty, during these two decades, adding 37,760 residents. Isabella County (the city of Mt. Pleasant and Central Michigan University) had the greatest increase in the north (6,960), while Bay and Saginaw Counties lost a combined 12,256 residents.

After the frantic growth of court dockets of the previous decades, the number of civil and criminal cases filed reached its zenith in 1984 and began a moderate decrease in 2000. As has been the case since 1977, criminal filings remain the smallest component with only 487 such cases filed in 2010, the fourth lowest number since 1919. The major change in the makeup of the docket during this period has been a 48 percent drop in U.S. civil cases in 2001–2010 resulting in a 19 percent overall decrease.

Congress has not added to the district court's judgeships since 1984, yet the frequency of judicial appointments has barely slowed from prior periods, largely due to judges taking senior status. Between 1992 and 2010, 12 judges were appointed to the Eastern District bench by Presidents Bill Clinton (8), George W. Bush (3), and Barack Obama (1), resulting in

363

Table 16.1   Average Annual Case Filings in the District Court, 1971–2010

Fiscal Year	Criminal	U.S. Civil	Private Civil	Total	Per Authorized Judge	Weighted Rank
1971–1980	1,185	1,050	2,024	4,259	390	53
1981–1990	622	2,269	4,188	7,079	502	28
1991–2000	692	2,225	4,104	7,021	468	40
2001–2010	542	1,146	4,002	5,690	379	60

another complete turnover of the 15 judgeships since 1990. Although there remained a vacancy in 2010, there were also eight active senior district judges to take their share of the caseload.

One striking aspect of these appointments reflects the politicization of the process. As we have seen, the process by which the president appoints and the Senate confirms judicial candidates has always had, by its nature, a hefty political component. Disputes, however, were, with rare exceptions, intra-party, among the president and the senators or senior congressmen of the president's party. By custom, other parties usually recognized the president's right to choose judges, and confirmations rarely occurred more than a few weeks after an appointment.[1] That peaceful comity changed in the 1990s. During the early 1970s, the usual interval between nomination and appointment in the Eastern District was six weeks, although Judge Harvey waited only eight days, Judge Guy only two weeks. Later that decade, the average interval increased to two months, likely because there were a larger number of judges to process and because confirmation hearings, unusual when Judge Levin was nominated, became the norm, with members of the Senate Judiciary Committee questioning nominees at length and listening to citizen comments for and against nominees. During the 1980s, the interval returned to a median of six weeks, but confirmation of the three nominations of President George H. W. Bush (Judges Rosen, Cleland, and Edmunds) stretched from four to five months after nomination. The first few nominations of President Clinton were similar, but the last five took eight months to a year, and two of the three nominations by President George W. Bush took more than a year.

The reason for the increased delays in confirmations is not a secret: both Republicans and Democrats have come to believe in the value of using the nomination/confirmation process to make political hay. The story of the third nomination by President George W. Bush is a pertinent example. In June 2006, Stephen Joseph Murphy III was the well-regarded U.S. attorney for the Eastern District when President Bush nominated him and Raymond M. Kethledge to what had traditionally been two "Michigan seats" on

Table 16.2   Judicial Appointments, 1992–2010

Name	Nominated/ Confirmed	Nominated By	Education
Denise Page Hood	March 9/ June 15, 1994	Clinton	Yale (B.A. 1974), Columbia (J.D. 1977)
Paul D. Borman	March 24/ August 9, 1994	Clinton	Michigan (B.A. 1959, J.D. 1962), Yale (LL.M. 1964)
John C. O'Meara*	April 26/ September 4, 1994	Clinton	Notre Dame (A.B. 1955), Harvard (LL.B. 1962)
Victoria A. Roberts	July 31, 1997/ June 26, 1998	Clinton	Michigan (B.A. 1973), Northeastern University (J.D. 1977)
George C. Steeh, III	Sept. 24, 1997/ May 13, 1998	Clinton	Michigan (B.A. 1969, J.D. 1973)
Arthur J. Tarnow	Sept. 24, 1997/ May 13, 1998	Clinton	Wayne State University (B.A. 1963, J.D. 1965)
Marianne O. Battani	Aug. 5, 1999/ May 24, 2000	Clinton	University of Detroit (B.A. 1966), Detroit College of Law (J.D. 1972)
David M. Lawson	Aug. 5, 1999/ May 24, 2000	Clinton	Notre Dame (B.A. 1973), Wayne State University (J.D. 1976)
Sean Francis Cox	Feb. 14, 2005/ June 8, 2006	G. W. Bush	Michigan (B.G.S. 1979), Detroit College of Law (J.D. 1983)
Thomas L. Ludington	Feb. 14, 2005/ June 8, 2006	G. W. Bush	Albion College (B.A. 1976), University of San Diego (J.D. 1979)
Stephen J. Murphy, III	April 15/ June 24, 2008	G.W. Bush	Marquette University (B.S. 1984) St. Louis University (J.D. 1987)
Mark A. Goldsmith	Feb. 24/ June 21, 2010	Obama	Michigan (B.A. 1974), Harvard (J.D. 1977)

* Senior Status, January 1, 2007.

the Sixth Circuit. In November 2006, the Democrats regained control of the Senate and Michigan's two Democratic senators refused to confirm any Bush nominees to the Sixth Circuit, noting that a Republican majority had rejected the confirmation of President Clinton's nominations to that court including Judge Helene White of the Michigan Court of Appeals. Eighteen months later, in April 2008, the parties resolved their impasse: President Bush renominated Judge White to the Sixth Circuit, while the senators agreed to confirm Kethledge's nomination to that court. The senators also agreed not to oppose the nomination of Murphy to the Eastern District, where he filled the vacancy open since Judge Duggan took senior status in 2000, 8 years earlier.[2]

The Theodore Levin United States Courthouse

On November 2, 1994, both houses of Congress and President Clinton signed into law an act to designate Detroit's 1934 federal building as the Theodore Levin United States Courthouse. The act was co-sponsored by Representative John C. Dingell, Jr., who had been one of Judge Levin's law clerks, and Representative Barbara Rose Collins. This designation was a project dear to the heart of Senior District Judge John Feikens, for whom Judge Levin had been a mentor, a great friend, and a constant support.[3] The official naming ceremony took place on May 1, 1995, Law Day, in front of the courthouse.

Intellectual Property and the Automobile Industry

Since the beginning of the American automobile industry, patents have been crucial to the success of many companies. Because it sits in the heart of that industry, the Eastern District has been the site of a great deal of patent litigation, and Judge Tuttle, for one, always argued that there could have been more had not plaintiffs been scared away by the court's over-stuffed caseload. Many of the court's patent cases never reached the law reporters, either because the case was settled or because it was not con-sidered worthy of publication by the presiding judge.[4] One reason for the large number of patent cases involving the automobile industry in the first half of the 20th century was the attitude of the manufacturers toward pat-ent claims, which Judge Tuttle described in an opinion in 1928: "The record shows, too, that Mr. Henry Ford, who dominates the defendant corpora-tion, is absolutely opposed to the operation of the present patent system and to the payment of royalties to any one. This is clearly expressed by a statement made by Mr. Davis, defendant's patent attorney stationed at the plant: 'There is no power on earth, this side of the Supreme Court of the United States, which would make Henry Ford sign a license agreement or pay a royalty.'"[5] Mr. Davis's opinion notwithstanding, after a forty-day bench trial, Judge Tuttle made Mr. Ford pay a royalty of $367,174.36, plus interest and costs. However, Ford's attitude was, and is, common among automobile manufacturers who see most patents as roadblocks set up by people who are trying to cash in on a product that was merely a slight improvement based on prior work by many other people or, in the lan-guage of patent attorneys, not non-obvious.

Intellectual property litigation (patents, copyrights, trademarks) remains an integral but numerically modest part of the Eastern District's docket, averaging 178 cases per year from 1991 to 2010, about 4 percent of the private civil cases filed during that period, which places the Eastern District among the top 15 districts in the number of intellectual property cases filed. Although few, such cases, particularly patent cases, impose a disproportionate burden on trial judges, both in time and complexity. Although a few district judges relish the challenge of such cases, many others would prefer to duck them. Not only are they complicated, the attorneys chosen to try them are too often patent attorneys with little or no litigation experience, so that pretrial and trial rarely go smoothly. For many years, whenever a new district judge joined the bench of the Eastern District, the other judges selected cases to transfer to the newcomer.[6] Human nature being what it is, the cases transferred tended to be what the judges called "dog cases," the most difficult, annoying, or intractable cases on the transferor's docket. As many judges have noted, patent cases figured prominently in their batch of dog cases, and they spent their early years on the bench trying little else. Eventually, judges who had been the recipients of such doubtful largesse from their colleagues recognized the unfairness of the process, and, beginning with the arrival of Judge Edmunds in 1991, transfers have been made by the clerk of the court based on a blind draw system.

Judge Cohn is one of the select few on the bench who enjoy the challenge of patent cases, and he has been known to volunteer to take them over from other judges. However, even he probably tired of the saga of one particular patent case, that of the intermittent windshield wiper, which spanned twenty years and became famous nationally through the book and motion picture *A Stroke of Genius*. Judge Cohn might also agree that having a patent attorney unskilled in litigation may well be better for all concerned than no attorney at all.

In 1978 and 1979, Dr. Robert W. Kearns, an engineering professor at Wayne State University, filed patent suits against the Ford Motor Company, Wood Motors, Inc., Mercedes-Benz (Daimler-Benz Aktiengesellschaft), and Porsche (Dr. Ing. h.c.F. Porsche, A.G). A German components manufacturer, SWF (SWF Speziakfabik fur Autozubehor Gustav Rau, G.m.b.H.) filed a declaratory action in federal court in Maryland against Kearns, which was eventually transferred to the Eastern District of Michigan, where all of the cases were consolidated for pre-trial purposes. Kearns alleged the defendants had infringed a series of patents to circuitry integral to his invention of an electronically-operated intermittent windshield wiper. Kearns had created the device in the early 1960s in his home and offered it to Ford, which turned him down. He persevered and obtained his first patent on the wiper system in 1967 and two others a few years later. In 1969, Ford introduced intermittent wipers using the same principles as Kearns's patent, and other vehicle manufacturers followed Ford's lead. By the 1990s, more than 30 million intermittent wipers were being sold around the world each year.[7]

Robert Kearns was a small man physically (one author described him as "a few inches taller than elfin"), with hunched shoulders, a high voice, and white hair. He was also an intelligent, well-educated engineer, a World War II veteran of the Office of Strategic Services, possessed of a tenacity and determination that could spill over into obsession. He also lacked experience in the business world, so that what the defendants treated as a commercial dispute, ultimately about money, he saw as a morality play, a test of good versus evil. These characteristics led him to riches but also to some dark places.

The consolidated cases were assigned to Judge Pratt, who remarked that the litigation "had proved to be a fertile ground for problems."[8] One problem was the slow pace of the pretrial process and of the defendants' production of relevant documents. As Kearns's wife complained, "We'd gear ourselves up for a hearing in ninety days, and then, on the eighty-ninth day, the phone would ring and I would hear Bob screaming and yelling, and it would turn out that Ford had dumped a bunch of new documents on us and the hearing would be postponed."[9] Many experienced attorneys representing defendants in civil cases operate on a philosophy that time is on the side of the defense. In this case, Fabian discovery tactics, although apparently legal, frustrated Kearns into becoming involved in what Judge Pratt characterized as "outrageous and unethical conduct, . . . the stuff of detective novels."[10] In August 1983, Kearns's attorneys filed a motion for summary judgment based on various documents attached to the motion papers. Defense counsel expressed outrage because Ford considered the documents to be highly confidential and privileged and had, consequently, withheld them from discovery. Eventually, Judge Pratt determined the documents were, indeed, exempt from discovery and ordered Kearns to return them to Ford. In the meantime, Ford tried to get Kearns to reveal how he had obtained them. Now it was Kearns's turn to stall, because the truth was that his son, a private investigator, had obtained the documents, which the son knew to be confidential, by seducing and lying to a paralegal employed by defendants' attorneys. Following extensive discovery and a long evidentiary hearing, Judge Pratt assessed Kearns $10,000 in court costs as well as the defendants' fees and expenses on this matter (over $100,000), and allowed Kearns's attorneys to withdraw, his second or third set of attorneys to leave the case.[11]

Finally, the trial of *Kearns v. Ford* began on January 3, 1990, before Judge Cohn, to whom the cases had been reassigned after Judge Pratt died in 1989. The liability portion of the trial testimony lasted three weeks, during which Ford tried to convince the jury that the Kearns patents were invalid because they violated the doctrine of non-obviousness—that they were mere extensions of existing devices, obvious to a person of ordinary skill in the art when the invention was made. Ford argued that the components Kearns used—a transistor, capacitor, and variable resistor—were an obvious way to cause the wipers to pause. The jury deliberated for a week before returning a verdict in Kearns's favor on validity and infringement. Before the damages portion of the trial began, in April 1990, Ford offered Kearns $30 million, which he rejected. The first jury could not reach a decision, so a second trial was held in July 1990, in which the jury awarded Kearns $5.2 million, plus interest from 1978 to 1988, when the patent expired. Kearns had left the court a week earlier to protest a ruling, and Judge Cohn had to force him to come back and accept the verdict. Eventually, the parties settled for $10 million.

Kearns now turned to Chrysler, which had agreed in 1982 to be bound on the issue of the validity of the patents by the result in the Ford case. Kearns had decided to try the case himself, without counsel, and was successful; in December 1991, the jury found Chrysler had infringed the patents. After a damage trial, it returned a verdict, in June 1992, awarding Kearns $0.90 per unit sold, resulting in a judgment of $18,740,465.43, including interests and costs. Kearns was now a very rich man, but he was crushed that the jury found that Chrysler had not willfully infringed the patents. The new U.S. Court of Appeals for the Federal Circuit, which was created to hear all appeals in patent cases, rejected both sides' arguments and affirmed the judgment.[12]

General Motors, which Kearns sued in 1985, was next, but Kearns, who again represented himself, reached the end of Judge Cohn's patience. The problem was that GM had used 32 different circuit boards, and Kearns claimed that each board violated every one of what were now his 23 patents. Unless the case were simplified, the jury would have to make decisions on 4,424 different "claim chart interpretations," a nearly impossible task. So Judge Cohn ordered the parties to simplify the case by limiting the issues to representative circuit boards and patents. GM agreed to focus on five of its circuit boards, but Kearns insisted on trying all of his patents against all of the boards. When Kearns allowed several deadlines to pass and still refused to choose which patents to try, GM moved to dismiss the case with prejudice. In July 1993, after a hearing, Judge Cohn granted GM's motion, based on "[t]he confusion exhibited by plaintiff's papers, his inability to focus his case, his complete failure to comply with the Court's order requiring that the claims-in-suit be designated . . . and offering no good reason for such failure."

He explained that: "There is a vast difference between a pro se plaintiff with a meritorious case unable to afford counsel and a pro se plaintiff with a meritorious case declining to employ counsel because of a misplaced lack of trust in lawyers or an inflated opinion notion of his ability to prosecute his own case. Here, we certainly have the latter. . . . The civil justice system can absorb just so much abuse from a pro se litigant. Plaintiff clearly exceeded the limit of abuse and for that reason this case is no longer in court." The US. Court of Appeals for the Federal Circuit, which hears patent appeals from all district courts, affirmed Judge Cohn's decision.[13]

If Kearns's obstinance likely cost him $20 million against GM, his subsequent inability or unwillingness to follow the court's orders cost him the rest of his pending cases. Kearns had not paid the sanctions imposed by Judge Pratt in 1983, and refused or delayed discovery, refusing to retain counsel. After another hearing, in January 1994, at which Kearns again refused to retain counsel, Judge Cohn dismissed the consolidated cases, because of "the confusion exhibited in his papers and in his oral presentations to the Court, his inability to focus, his inability to understand the rules of law, his failure to follow the Court's orders, his failure to comply with discovery orders, such that in the Court's view this case will never get to trial, and if it did, plaintiff would be unable to present a case; all of which prejudices defendants by subjecting them to inordinate expense in attempting to secure discovery, by depriving them of discovery to which they are entitled, and by making it impossible for them to prepare for trial." In February, he dismissed the remaining cases on the court's docket, against Japanese and European car manufacturers. The Federal Circuit once more affirmed Judge Cohn's decisions as well as his order that the sanctions, now up to almost $200,000 be paid from the funds paid into the court by losing defendants in Kearns's other cases.[14] Dr. Kearns died on February 9, 2005.

Naturalization

Unlike immigration, which was virtually unregulated until passage of the Chinese Exclusion Acts, the naturalization of new citizens has always been controlled and limited by Congress. The Naturalization Act of 1795[15] limited citizenship to "free, white persons" who had resided in the United States. The Naturalization Act of 1870[16] acknowledged that the Fourteenth Amendment extended citizenship to "aliens of African nativity and to persons of African descent," while the Supreme Court held in 1898 that the amendment applied to Asians born in the United States to parents who were permanent residents.[17] Most other Asians, however, were excluded from becoming citizens until 1952.

The first Naturalization Act, passed in 1790, allowed persons seeking to become citizens to apply to "any common law court of record,"[18] and applicants tended to use the court most convenient to them, usually a state court, whereas people living near federal courts tended to petition there. As we have seen in the district court's first session in 1837, decrees of naturalization have always been part of the court's repertoire, and they became a major part of its business during the immigration waves of the late 19th century and, even more so, during the 20th century. In 1934, Judge Tuttle remarked that the court naturalized about 200 new citizens each week at sessions held in the Detroit courthouse on Monday afternoons.[19] Seventy-five years later, the pace continued as the district naturalized approximately 12,000 new citizens during 2008 and 10,500 in 2009. In his 2009 report on the state of the court, Chief Judge Gerald Rosen explained that: "Bi-weekly naturalization ceremonies continue to take place in the Court's multi-purpose room. In addition to those ceremonies, judicial officers presided over several large off-site ceremonies throughout the Eastern District including venues such as Cobo Hall and Comerica Park."[20]

Troubled Waters

By the turn of the 21st century, the interval between the filing of a suit and its resolution had decreased substantially from what had been the case during the 1970s, often two to three years for routine civil cases, but there were still cases that threatened to become permanent fixtures on the court's docket. As we have seen with the jail cases, complex judicial remedies may call for supervision over a period of years. The record setter for longevity in the Eastern District goes to *U.S. v. City of Detroit*, which the United States Environmental Protection Agency (EPA) began in May 1977 to stop violations of federal water pollution standards by the Detroit Water and Sewage Department, an agency of the city of Detroit, which operates a water system serving most of southeastern Michigan. Despite a consent judgment entered in September 1977, the case remains open and very active in 2011 and has spawned many related civil and criminal cases. From 1977 until he retired in 2010 at the age of 93, Judge John Feikens found himself metropolitan Detroit's water czar, involved in virtually every decision necessary to keep the system working.[21]

For some other cases, their long life was the result of particularly persistent parties and uncertain law, as happened in the civil and criminal cases brought by the United States against John Rapanos. In 1988, Rapanos, a real estate developer, decided to clear trees and wet areas from a 175-acre tract of land his companies owned in Bay County, in the Northern Division. Despite warnings from the Michigan Department of Natural Resources and the EPA that his actions violated the Clean Water Act (CWA),[22] Rapanos filled the wet areas with earth and sand without filing for or receiving a permit under the CWA. In 1993, a grand jury returned an indictment against Rapanos in the Northern Division of the Eastern District, charging that he had knowingly discharged pollutants into waters of the United States, in violation of the CWA.[23] After Judge Cleland, then the presiding in the Northern Division, recused himself, the case was reassigned to the Flint court and to Judge Newblatt. When he also recused himself, the case was reassigned to Judge Zatkoff, but remained assigned for trial in Flint. A first jury trial ended in a mistrial on July 12, 1994. In the second trial, held in February and March 1995 in Flint, the jury convicted Rapanos of a knowing violation of the CWA, but acquitted him of intimidating a witness. However, in August 1995, Judge Zatkoff granted Rapanos's motion for a new trial on the basis that he had been prejudiced by questions asked by the prosecutor regarding defendant's refusal to allow the government access to the property.[24] The new trial was delayed while the United States appealed, and it was not until May 1997 that the Sixth Circuit reversed Judge Zatkoff, reinstated the conviction under the CWA, and remanded the case for sentencing.[25] In December 1998, Judge Zatkoff, now Chief Judge, denied Rapanos's renewed motion for a new trial and sentenced him to three years' probation and a fine of $185,000. Both sides appealed, and, in December 2000, the Sixth Circuit affirmed the conviction but also held that the sentence was too light under the Sentencing Guidelines and remanded the case to Judge Zatkoff once more for re-sentencing.[26] In June 2001, before Judge Zatkoff could comply, the U.S. Supreme Court granted Rapanos's petition for certiorari, summarily vacated his convictions, and remanded the case to the Sixth Circuit[27] for reconsideration in light of a recent Supreme Court decision[28] that limited the scope of water and wetlands covered by the CWA. The Sixth Circuit, in turn, remanded the case to Judge Zatkoff,[29] who, in February 2002, vacated the convictions because, he found, the wetlands in question were not covered by the CWA because they were not adjacent to navigable waters.[30] The government appealed again, and, in August 2003, the Sixth Circuit reinstated the convictions.[31]

When the Supreme Court denied Rapanos's second petition for certiorari in his criminal case in April 2004,[32] that seemed to be the end of the criminal case, ten years after the first trial, but the parallel civil-enforcement suit filed by the EPA in February 1994[33] was on its way to the Supreme Court. The civil case was reassigned to Judge Friedman after Judge Cleland recused himself again. After years of pretrial motions and maneuvering, Judge Friedman held a 13-day bench trial from March 31 to April 20, 1999, and a year later he issued his findings of fact as to liability in which he found defendants liable under the CWA and, specifically, that the CWA applied to the wetlands in question because they were adjacent to "waters of the United States." Following a further trial on damages, Judge Friedman ordered Rapanos to submit a mitigation plan and to deposit $3,000,000 in escrow to fund the execution of the plan. He deferred consideration of possible civil penalties. In February 2003, after further proceedings, Judge Friedman entered a partial final judgment which the Sixth Circuit affirmed in July 2004, holding that there was federal jurisdiction based on the sites' hydrological connections to the nearby ditches or drains, or to more remote navigable waters.[34]

The Supreme Court granted Rapanos's petition for certiorari in the civil case,[35] and then, on June 19, 2006, reversed the decisions of the lower courts and remanded the case for further fact finding.[36] The justices voted 5 to 4 to remand, but as Justice Roberts commented, "It is unfortunate that no opinion commands a majority of the Court on precisely how to read Congress' limits on the reach of the Clean Water Act."[37] An opinion written by Justice Scalia and joined in by three other justices adopted a restrictive interpretation: a wetland may not be considered "adjacent to" remote "waters of the United States" unless it has a continuous surface connection to bodies that are "waters of the United States" in their own right. For Scalia, the United States had to prove, for each wetland in question, that the adjacent channel contains a relatively permanent "wate[r] of the United States," and that each wetland has a continuous surface connection to that water, making it difficult to determine where the water ends and the wetland begins. A dissenting opinion by Justice Stevens, also joined by three other justices, would affirm the judgments and give greater weight to the EPA's determination that the CWA applies to wetlands adjacent to tributaries of navigable waters. Justice Kennedy supplied the fifth vote to remand, but he proposed a third test: "When the Corps seeks to regulate wetlands adjacent to navigable-in-fact waters, it may rely on adjacency to establish its jurisdiction. Absent more specific regulations, however, the Corps must establish a significant nexus on a case-by-case basis when it seeks to regulate wetlands based on adjacency to nonnavigable tributaries."[38]

After remand to the district court, the parties engaged in protracted settlement discussions. On December 29, 2008, the EPA announced that: "John A. Rapanos and related defendants have agreed to pay a civil penalty and recreate approximately 100 acres of wetlands and buffer areas to resolve violations of the Clean Water Act . . . Rapanos has agreed to pay a $150,000 civil penalty and will spend an estimated $750,000 to mitigate for 54 acres of wetlands that were filled without authorization under the Clean Water Act. Rapanos has also agreed to preserve an additional 134 acres of wetlands that were unaffected by the unauthorized activity. Under the agreement, the preservation of these areas will be enforced via a conservation easement held by the State of Michigan."[39] On March 10, 2009, Rapanos voluntarily dismissed his appeal of the criminal case, and, on March 18, 2009, Judge Friedman signed a consent order in the civil case under which defendants agreed to pay a collective fine of $150,000 and to complete the restoration of the properties. More than 20 years after John Rapanos decided to ignore the state's warnings and rearrange the landscape, the resulting litigation was, at long last, over.

Court Technology

When John Winder opened the district court clerk's office in 1837, his equipment consisted of pens, paper, blank record books, and ink. Forms followed a few years later, but there was not much more technological development until the appearance of the typewriter. The *1977 Court Compendium* could boast, though, that: "The Clerk's Office, Michigan East, is probably the most modern Clerk's Office in the United States."[40] Indeed, the mechanical devices used by the court in 1977 were a great improvement in court administration, although some of the automation wonders of the 1970s have become obsolete curiosities 30 years later. According to the *Compendium*, "The modernization started with the installation of automated filing equipment named Lektrievers" to replace conventional filing cabinets for storing 12,000 pending and closed case files. Each Lektriever consisted of a large cabinet holding shelves, which revolved vertically, using electricity, to present a clerk quickly, and at a convenient height, the shelf containing any selected file. The *Compendium* also noted that the court had acquired a machine which automatically inserted notices into envelopes for the 750,000 letters mailed by the court annually and an electronic cash register which, "at the press of a button, . . . will print out the postings of some 30 different accounts—an operation that formerly required from 2 to 3 hours manual effort."[41] The clerk's office was also beginning its computerization, including the process for the selection of a pool of prospective jurors. The court was one of six district courts selected for a pilot project to computerize the criminal docket with plans to computerize the other dockets in the future. This transition of the clerk's office to computers did not, of course, involve personal computers. Even though 1977 saw the introduction of the Apple II, the world's first mass-produced personal computer, the court's computers were bulky, stand-alone devices which could perform only a small number of functions.

By 2010, the clerk's office had been transformed, particularly with regard to intake. In the past, all papers filed in pending cases were presented to the appropriate clerk's office (in Detroit, Flint, Bay City, or Ann Arbor), either in person or by mail. Those documents were accepted, reviewed, recorded by typing information on the case's paper docket sheet, and placed in the official file in the clerk's office, after which a copy (supplied by the party filing it) was sent to the judge's file kept in chambers, all by employees of the clerk's office for whom intake was their principal function. That all changed in 2002, when the Administrative Office of the United States Courts selected the Eastern District to implement an electronic case filing (ECF) system. After some delays, the district court enacted a local rule[42] requiring that all papers filed after November 30, 2005, be filed electronically in PDF format. In March 2008, the court took another step and allowed attorneys to commence new cases electronically. The court also keeps its official record of filings for each case, its case docket, electronically, so that the parties and the court can access the docket, as well as the filings themselves, in real time. Although individual judges are allowed to require that parties send them paper copies of filings for their chambers file, the clerk's office no longer maintains a paper file for cases.

The ECF system is a tremendous convenience for attorneys because they can file papers at any time of the day, without having to travel to the courthouse to meet deadlines, and they can monitor other parties' filings and the overall docket from their own computers. The general public can access the filings (except for social security and immigration matters) by logging on to the federal courts' PACER website. ECF has also increased the efficiency of the clerk's operations greatly by eliminating most of the physical tasks involved in case intake and freeing up the office space used for paper files. The system has another advantage, at least in principle: it makes tampering with the blind draw even more difficult. Cases are assigned to judges and magistrate judges based on a random-number generator programmed to assign an equal load to each judge and to take into consideration the partial caseload undertaken by each senior judge.[43] A repeat of the Hackett/August incident, although presumably not impossible, would require much more effort and sophistication than just suborning an intake clerk.

Computers are also integrated into the judges' chambers. In 1977, in most judges' chambers legal research still meant cracking the books and usually was performed by law clerks. The Detroit court (but neither Flint nor Bay City) did have one "legal research terminal," located in the court's library and connected by a dedicated telephone line to Lexis, but most judges preferred research performed the old way. Reliance on books also meant that one of the most important, if tedious, functions of law clerks was inserting new pocket parts in the books in their judge's chambers. In 2010, most legal research by judges and by law clerks is performed online, and each chamber has several personal computers available, usually portable laptops, with access to the Internet.

The Rise and Fall of Administrative Court Units

The assignment of newly-filed civil cases among the various places of holding court and the various judges is determined first by the place in which the case arises or is related to. Civil cases arising in or related to the counties of the Northern Division are assigned to the Bay City court while those arising in the counties of the Southern Division are assigned to Detroit, Ann Arbor, Flint, or Port Huron, the specific location depending on the location of the chambers of the judge to whom the case is allocated by the blind draw system. Criminal cases are assigned under similar rules except that the determining factor is where the offense is alleged to have been committed. Offenses allegedly occurring in the counties of the Northern Division are assigned there. In the Southern Division, cases involving offenses allegedly occurring in Genesee, Lapeer, Livingston, or Shiawassee counties are assigned to Flint, while cases of offenses allegedly occurring in the Southern Division's other counties may be assigned to Detroit, Ann

Arbor, or Port Huron, again according to the location of the chambers of the judge receiving the case by blind draw. Thus, a civil case involving parties in Flint, or a criminal case allegedly occurring in Port Huron, might be assigned to the Ann Arbor court. However, as only four of the 22 district judges and active senior judges do not have their chambers in Detroit, civil cases arising in Flint or criminal cases arising in Ann Arbor are far more likely to be assigned to Detroit than to any other court.

This was not always the court's system. For its first 50 years, all cases were assigned to Detroit. In 1887, Congress required the court to hold terms in Bay City, and in 1894 required that all cases arising in the new Northern Division be assigned to Bay City and that a deputy clerk and marshal be assigned there. When the Flint courthouse opened in 1962, the judges decided to create a separate administrative unit by assigning to Flint a deputy clerk and all civil and criminal cases arising in Genesee, Lapeer, Shiawassee, and Livingston counties. Twenty years later, in 1982, the judges created another administrative unit for the Ann Arbor court, with its own deputy clerk and all cases arising in Washtenaw, Jackson, Monroe, and Lenawee counties.

This system was convenient for parties, jurors, and witnesses who would not have to travel too far to attend court for cases arising locally. It was also popular with attorneys practicing in or near Ann Arbor, Bay City, and Flint who were more likely to be hired to litigate cases assigned locally than if those cases were assigned to a distant venue. For the judges, though, the system had its drawbacks. One problem was that there was no way to make sure that judges in Bay City, Flint, or Ann Arbor would carry the same caseload as the judges assigned to Detroit. In fact, the Flint and Bay City courts usually received far fewer new cases, so until 1975 the judges assigned to those locations also presided over cases assigned to the Detroit court as well. Another concern of some judges was the types of cases assigned to the Northern Division or to the Flint and Ann Arbor units. Those judges believed that cases arising in Detroit were more likely to be significant, interesting, and professionally satisfying than those arising elsewhere. Some judges refused to move their chambers to Flint or Bay City court for this reason, and those venues came to be assigned to the judges with the least seniority. Judge shopping was also a grave concern. A case assigned to Detroit might be assigned to any one of 18 judges of different backgrounds and political philosophies. Cases assigned to Bay City, Flint, or Ann Arbor, on the other hand, had to be heard by the sole district judge resident in that court whose tendencies and beliefs attorneys at least thought they knew. Some attorneys began raising intricate arguments as to why a particular case just happened to "arise" in the division or unit where they believed the judge would be more favorable than not to their client's position. Successive clerks of the court also disliked the decentralization of their functions. Particularly in the days before computerization, the deputy clerks were to a large extent autonomous, operating their offices without daily oversight. They also had a tendency to look to the judge resident in their court as their boss instead of to the clerk of the court.

The present unified centralized system in the Southern Division, adopted in 1993, resolved most of the judges' concerns, and the judges reduced any travel burden centralization might have imposed on persons summoned for jury in the Southern Division by creating a separate jury division for each of the division's courts. The clerks of the court also benefitted from the ECF system under which all case filings must be filed via the internet. This reduced the need for separate clerks offices, so that the Flint and Bay City offices have been reduced and the Ann Arbor office was closed in September 2011. Most recently, there has been a proposal to petition Congress to delete the separate divisions in order to unify case assignment throughout the entire court and to remove the last possibility for judge shopping for civil cases.

Grutter v. Bollinger and Gratz v. Bollinger

In 1997, two "reverse discrimination" cases were filed in the Eastern District against the University of Michigan that are generally recognized to be the most important civil litigation in the court since *Milliken v. Bradley*. The University of Michigan is one of the great public universities of the world, and its undergraduate colleges, including its School of Literature, Science, and the Arts (LSA), receive nearly 30,000 applications each year from highly-qualified students to fill a freshman class of fewer than 6,000. Consequently, many Michigan residents with excellent high school records and test scores are turned away. The Law School is even more elite, usually ranked as one of the top half dozen law schools of all descriptions, and it is even more selective, receiving about 6,000 applications for a first-year class of 360.

In October 1997, Jennifer Gratz and Patrick Hamacher, both white, unsuccessful applicants for admission as undergraduates to LSA, brought a class action suit against university president Lee Bollinger, former president James Duderstadt, and the university in a case that came to be known as *Gratz v. Bollinger*.[44] In December, Barbara Grutter, a white woman denied admission to the University of Michigan Law School, filed a similar suit directed specifically to the policies of the law school, a suit known as *Grutter v. Bollinger*.[45] In both cases, the plaintiffs alleged that the admissions policies of LSA or the Law School gave special consideration to "under-represented racial or ethnic minority groups." Although LSA and the Law School had separate admissions selection systems, the suits alleged that each system illegally discriminated against them on account of their race, in violation of the Fourteenth Amendment to the U.S. Constitution and of Title VI of the Civil Rights Act of 1964,[46] which prohibits discrimination on the basis of race, color, and national origin in programs and activities receiving federal financial assistance.

The "special consideration" that plaintiffs complained of was the consequence both of the difficult road followed by African Americans in America in general and of the university's own uneasy history with regard to admitting black students. The university, which opened in 1817 in Detroit and moved to Ann Arbor in 1837, began admitting African American undergraduates in 1868, when two black men from Detroit became students. In 1878, the first black woman was admitted (just eight years after the first woman of any description), and there have been African Americans in most graduating classes since then. The problem, made apparent in the 1960s, was that there have never been very many black students, and the number did not increase with the increasing percentage of African Americans in the state's population (from no more than 1 percent until 1920, to 6.9 percent in 1950, to 11.2 percent in 1970, and to 14.2 percent in 2008).

In April 1968, following the assassination of Dr. Martin Luther King, the university promised to increase black enrollment and teaching staff, but when nothing much happened, in March 1970 a student organization called the Black Action Movement (BAM) organized strikes and picket lines to try to get a firm commitment to reach BAM's goal of 10 percent black enrollment by 1973. The university waffled, finally accepted a goal of 10 percent, but then seemed to forget it. In 1975, another strike (BAM II) led to reinstatement of the 10 percent goal, but again progress towards it was slow. Despite repeated campaigns by the university, particularly by President Duderstadt, by 1997 "minorities" were 25 percent of the student body, but only 8 percent was black (against 14 percent of the state's population), while 10 percent were Asian (one percent of the state's population) and 6 percent Hispanic (3 percent of Michigan's population).[47]

Both 1997 lawsuits were sponsored and financed by the Center for Individual Rights (CIR), a conservative/libertarian public-interest law firm, which had targeted affirmative-action programs at prominent state universities, such as the University of Texas, where in 1996, the U.S. Court of Appeals for the Fifth Circuit had invalidated a special preference program for minorities.[48] CIR selected the lead plaintiffs in both cases carefully to emphasize its argument that this was not just about the exclusion of well-to-do, suburban males. Jennifer Gratz, from blue-collar Southgate, Michigan, is the daughter of a police officer and a secretary, neither of them college graduates. Despite a 3.9 GPA and a 25 on the ACT, she was rejected by LSA for the 1995 freshman class. Patrick Hamacher, who had slightly higher test scores and slightly lower GPA, was rejected for the 1996 LSA class. Barbara Grutter, who was rejected by the Law School for admission in 1997, was a 43-year-old mother of two.

The suits drew national attention both because of the university's stature and because the U.S. Supreme Court, since its landmark decision 20 years earlier in *Regents of the University of California v. Bakke*,[49] had not given a clear explanation as to what steps a public university can legally take to admit a higher number of minority applicants whose grades and scores are lower than those of rejected non-minority applicants. More importantly for observers across the nation, these "reverse discrimination" suits, like *Milliken* and busing more than two decades earlier, struck at the most sensitive nerves of the community and of the nation, evoking heated rhetoric and fervent emotions, punctuated only occasionally by thoughtful discussion. Although the legal and ethical bases for integrated education were no longer controversial, the validity of, and the necessity for, affirmative action had become an emotional flash point to which both sides brought their fears and aspirations. For supporters of the university's affirmative action programs, discrimination and its effects were still alive and affecting minority students so that, without special treatment, progress for them and for their children was doomed. And many of those supporters believed that this was exactly what opponents of affirmative action also understood. For opponents of affirmative action, discrimination and its effects were mainly in the past, and the only effect of the affirmative action programs was to perpetuate race as an invidious basis for characterizing people (instead of, say, wealth or class or environment) which would in itself delay racial harmony. To white parents, affirmative action had a more practical objection, the denial to them and their children of a prize for which they had, by hard work and talent, proven themselves better qualified. And many of those opponents believed that this was exactly what supporters of affirmative action also understood.

As the cases progressed, it became clear that this was another "case of the century" in which the facts were not greatly in dispute; what divided the parties was what the law and the facts meant. The university admitted that it had, for many years, given special consideration to applicants who were members of an "under-represented racial or ethnic minority group" (defined as African American, Hispanic, or Native American), that LSA and the Law School used different methods, and that LSA's methods had changed over the years. In 1995 and 1996, the admissions officers responsible for LSA used tables which combined grade-point, national test scores, and other factors to determine admission; but there were different tables for minority and non-minority applicants who were, thus, considered separately. The tables made it clear that both Gratz and Hamacher would have been admitted if they had been African American. In 1998, after *Gratz* was filed, LSA changed to a point system under which all applicants would be considered based on the same number of points, but applicants received enough points just for being "under-represented" that almost all who met the university's minimum standards were admitted. In

1999 and 2000, LSA added a "flagging' component under which applicants with characteristics which LSA deems important to the composition of a class, including membership in an under-represented minority, could be kept in the review pool for further consideration.

The Law School used a more sophisticated system which had a stated goal of attaining diversity in its student body for the benefit of the Law School and the entire student body. In his concurring opinion in *Bakke*, Justice Lewis F. Powell, Jr., suggested or held (depending on how you read his opinion) that "the State has a substantial interest that legitimately may be served by a properly devised admissions program involving the competitive consideration of race and ethnic origin."[50] a constitutionally legal basis for affirmative action, if the remedy were carefully tailored. Admission to the Law School was based on "hard" factors (grade-point and LSAT scores) and "soft" factors, including what each applicant could contribute to the school's community, including diversity.[51]

Gratz and *Grutter* were assigned to different district judges by the court's blind draw, so that Judge Patrick Duggan received *Gratz* while Judge Bernard Friedman was assigned *Grutter*. In both cases, African American and Hispanic individuals who intended to apply for admission and an organization "with the mission of preserving higher educational opportunities for African American and Latino students in the State of Michigan" petitioned to intervene as defendants to protect "their interests as the preservation of race as a factor in the admissions policy of the University," arguing that, for political reasons, it was unlikely that the university itself would present a strong defense. In July 1998, both judges denied the petitions to intervene because the interveners had shown neither an interest separate from that of the university nor evidence that the university would not pursue the case diligently.[52] The interveners appealed in both cases, and, on August 10, 1999, the Sixth Circuit reversed the denials of their motions and ordered both judges to enter orders permitting intervention.[53] The appellate court found that the interveners had an interest in continuing affirmative action and that it was not likely that the university would raise its own past or present discrimination as a defense.

While the interveners' appeals were pending, there ensued an internal court dispute, which, in the heated environment of these cases, became grist for the publicity mill. A week after the rulings denying intervention, the university asked Chief Judge Anna Diggs Taylor to transfer *Grutter* to Judge Duggan in order to promote judicial efficiency.[54] Alternatively, the university asked Judge Friedman to give up the Law School case because *Gratz* and *Grutter* were companion cases and *Gratz* had been filed first.[55] Because Chief Judge Taylor's husband was a Regent of the University, and thus a defendant, she assigned "the motion" to Judges John Feikens and Julian A. Cook, Jr. On August 6, 1998, following a hearing, they issued their written opinion that the cases were companions, but they did not enforce that opinion by an order. On August 17, Judge Friedman issued his own opinion and order striking the Feikens/Cook opinion, on the basis that Judge Taylor's assignment of the motion to them was illegal.[56] Judge Friedman noted first that the "companion" issue was addressed to him, and not to Chief Judge Taylor, and he proceeded to hold that the cases were not companions. As for the "efficiency" issue, Judge Friedman held that, although Chief Judge Taylor was right to disqualify herself, she had no authority to choose the judges who would hear it, and, besides, there was no federal authority for a two-judge panel to hear any motion. He noted that her sole legal alternatives were to pass the motion to the judge next senior to her[57] or to assign it by blind draw.[58] In the end, *Grutter* remained assigned to Judge Friedman.

In *Gratz*, Judge Duggan entered an order, on December 23, 1998, bifurcating the case into liability and remedy segments. Both plaintiffs and defendants moved for summary judgment, motions argued on November 16, 2000. As proof of the intense state and national interest in these cases, the court received a dozen briefs from *amici curiae* (friends of the court), including the State of Michigan, General Motors and many other corporations, civil rights organizations, and academic and scholarly associations representing hundreds of universities and professors. On December 13, 2000, Judge Duggan held that the LSA admissions criteria and systems in place from 1995 through 1998 were illegal, but he also validated the systems that LSA used in 1999 and 2000.[59] Applying the Powell opinion in *Bakke*, Judge Duggan accepted that diversity could be a compelling governmental interest allowing the consideration of race in admissions, and he held that LSA's admissions systems in place in 1999 and 2000 used race as only one factor among many in a single point-based system and thus were narrowly tailored to minimize the effect of race. He also held that the systems in place when Gratz and Hamacher were rejected had not been narrowly tailored and constituted, essentially, two separate systems based on race.

The parties in *Grutter* also moved for summary judgment, but instead of ruling on those motions Judge Friedman took them under advisement and advanced the case for a bench trial, which took place on fifteen days between January 16 to February 16, 2001. On March 27, 2001, Judge Friedman issued an opinion in which he conceded that the individual defendants had a qualified immunity from suit, and should be dismissed, but that he was required to enter judgment in favor of plaintiffs on all other respects.[60] Judge Friedman held that achieving a diverse student body was not a compelling governmental interest sufficient to validate the Law School's affirmative action program and that, even if it had been, the system in place was not narrowly tailored to achieve that end. Therefore, Judge Friedman enjoined the Law School from using an applicant's race as a factor in admissions decisions. On April 3, Judge Friedman denied defendants' motion for a stay of the injunction,[61] but two days later the Sixth Circuit granted plaintiffs a stay in order to allow the Law School to use its existing admissions criteria in selecting its incoming 2001 first-year class.[62] The appellate court expedited oral argument on defendants' appeal to October 23, before a three-judge panel, but, on October 19, that hearing was cancelled and, instead, the appeals in both cases were argued *en banc, i.e.,* before all nine non-senior judges of the Sixth Circuit, on December 6, 2001.[63] Five months later, on May 14, 2002, the court, voting five to four, reversed Judge Friedman's decision in *Grutter* and upheld the Law School's admission policy.[64] The majority, in a lengthy opinion by Chief Circuit Judge Boyce F. Martin, Jr., cited *Bakke* to hold that diversity was indeed a compelling governmental interest of the Law School and that its admissions policy was narrowly tailored to meet that interest. In an equally lengthy dissenting opinion, Circuit Judge Danny J. Boggs went back to the adoption of the Fourteenth Amendment to argue that the purpose of the amendment was precisely to outlaw governmental decisions based, in any way, on race that could not survive "strict scrutiny" based on a documented history of past discrimination by the defendant. In a "procedural appendix," Judge Boggs also criticized what he characterized as Judge Martin's manipulation of the court's scheduling and *en banc* rules to prevent a decision by a three-judge panel that might have included a senior judge likely to rule for plaintiffs.[65]

Inevitably, Ms. Grutter petitioned the Supreme Court for review, and, when, five months after the Sixth Circuit's decision that court had still done nothing in *Gratz,* Ms. Gratz asked the Supreme Court to review Judge Duggan's decision directly along with *Grutter.* On December 2, 2002, the Supreme Court agreed to hear both cases. In anticipation of the hearing, more than seventy *amicus curiae* briefs were filed, most of them in support of the university but others, including one from the U.S. Department of Justice and one from an association of Asian American students, supported the plaintiffs.

The Supreme Court heard argument on both cases on April 1, 2003, and, on June 23, 2003, in separate opinions, held that the Law School's program was legal but that none of LSA's programs were. In *Gratz,* the Court, voting six to three, held that LSA's 2000 admissions policy violated the Equal Protection Clause, Title VI, and 42 U.S.C. 1981 because, although student diversity could be a compelling state interest, LSA's blanket grant of 20 points to every applicant from an "under-represented minority," rather than an individualized investigation of the circumstances of each such applicant, was not narrowly tailored to achieve diversity. As the Court noted, the twenty points was enough to assure almost all of minority applicants would be accepted.[66] In *Grutter,* the voting was complicated because six of the justices filed separate opinions. Justices Ginsburg and Breyer concurred totally with the opinion of Justice O'Connor, although

Justice Ginsburg wrote her own concurring opinion with which Justice Breyer joined. Justices Scalia and Thomas concurred in part with the O'Connor opinion. Justices Scalia and Thomas also wrote opinions in which they concurred in part and dissented in part with Justice O'Connor. Justice Thomas joined in Justice Scalia's opinion, but Justice Scalia joined only in part with Justice Thomas's opinion. Chief Justice Rehnquist dissented totally in an opinion joined by Justices Scalia, Kennedy, and Thomas, while Justice Kennedy also wrote a separate dissenting opinion. Despite this surfeit of opinions, it was possible to discern a majority holding that the Fourteenth Amendment "does not prohibit the Law School's narrowly tailored use of race in admissions decisions to further a compelling interest in obtaining the educational benefits that flow from a diverse student body." The majority determined that the system was narrowly tailored because applicants from under-represented groups were not isolated from competition for admission with other applicants.[67]

Although the decisions of the Supreme Court in *Gratz* and *Grutter* answered the question of the validity of the LSA and Law School admission systems, they did not end the involvement of the federal courts with the general issue of the status of affirmative action in Michigan. In July 2004, Ms. Gratz and an organization known as Michigan Civil Rights Initiative (MCRI) began a signature drive to place on the November 2006 state ballot an amendment of Michigan's constitution, known as Proposal 2, which would bar the state, and specifically its public colleges and universities, from discriminating against or granting preferential treatment to any person on the basis of race, sex, color, ethnicity, or national origin "in the operation of public employment, public education, or public contracting." The initiative succeeded in gathering the required signatures, but an organization named Operation King's Dream asked the Board of Canvassers to refuse to certify the initiative because, the organization alleged, MCRI, both actively and by the wording of the petition, had fraudulently convinced some signers that the initiative was in favor of affirmative action. When the Board did not act to certify or reject the petition, MCRI sought mandamus in the Michigan Court of Appeals which held that the Board had no authority to pursue the claims of fraud.[68] In December 2005, the Board held a meeting which was disrupted by protesters opposing the petition. Again, the Board did not act on the petition, and the court of appeals directed the state to place the petition on the November 2006 ballot.

Shortly thereafter, Operation King's Dream, two locals of the American Federation of State, County, and Municipal Employees, and several individuals, including Detroit mayor Kwame M. Kilpatrick, filed suit in the district court against Gratz, MCRI, the Michigan secretary of state, the Board of Canvassers, and the state director of elections, seeking to keep the initiative off the ballot because the alleged fraud violated the U.S. Voting Rights Act. The case was assigned to Judge Arthur J. Tarnow who, after an evidentiary hearing, entered an opinion, on August 29, 2006, in which he found that MCRI had, indeed, committed fraud as alleged, but also ruling that such fraud did not violate the Voting Rights Act because MCRI's fraudulent acts did not prevent minority voters from having equal access to the voting process.[69]

On election day, November 7, 2006, Proposal 2 passed by 58 percent to 42 percent. Immediately, a new suit was filed in the district court by the Coalition to Defend Affirmative Action, Integration and Immigration Rights and Fight for Equality by Any Means Necessary (BAMN), other organizations, and several individuals against the state of Michigan and the governing boards of the state's universities, colleges, community colleges, and public school districts, seeking a declaration that Proposal 2, now Article 1, section 26 of the Michigan Constitution of 1963, violated the U.S. Constitution. The case, known as *Coalition to Defend Affirmative Action v. Granholm*, was assigned to District Judge David M. Lawson. On December 19, 2006, he entered an injunction, agreed to by the parties, staying the application of Section 26 so that the state's three largest universities could complete their admissions for the class entering in August 2007 under their existing programs.[70] However, another organization which was not a party to the suit and a prospective applicant sought to intervene to overturn the injunction. When Judge Lawson did not rule on their motion to intervene by December 21, two days before Section 26's effective date, they sought relief in the Sixth Circuit, but, on December 27, while briefing was still going on in the Sixth Circuit, the district court denied the motion to intervene. On December 29, the appellate court overturned the stay because, given the precedents, plaintiffs had little chance of success on the merits,[71] and the Supreme Court refused to reinstate the stay.[72] On March 18, 2008, Judge Lawson granted the state summary judgment and ruled that Section 26 did not violate the U.S. Constitution because it prohibited preferential treatment, which was not guaranteed by the Constitution, and did not prohibit equal protection, which was.[73] On December 11, 2008, Judge Lawson refused to reverse himself.[74] Plaintiffs appealed to the Sixth Circuit and defendants cross-appealed; on July 1, 2011, a three-judge panel held Section 26 unconstitutional; and on September 9, 2011, a majority of the court's judges voted to vacate the panel's decision and order rehearing by all of the judges.

All of this unhappiness and litigation begs the question: if in *Milliken* the Supreme Court had trusted the judgment of Judges Roth and DeMascio that inter-district integration was appropriate, instead of leaving most of the state's African American students in underfunded and poorly run school districts, would the University of Michigan have thought 20 years later, to adopt the policies challenged in *Grutter* and *Gratz*, in order to admit qualified minority students?

United States v. John Bass

On August 1, 2003, in the courtroom of Judge Arthur Tarnow, testimony began in the murder and drug trial of John Bass, leader of a Detroit criminal gang known as the Dog Pound.[75] Bass's case was one of the hundreds filed in the Eastern District every year, but it is notable because it produced the first capital murder trial in the Eastern District since Max Stephan's in 1942, because the defendant challenged the Justice Department's selection of cases in which to seek death by arguing racial discrimination and selective prosecution, and because the jury, in the end, rejected the death penalty.

The case began in August 1997, when the grand jury indicted Bass and 17 other alleged members of the gang with conspiring to distribute cocaine base in Michigan and Ohio. Six months later, in February 1998, the Sixth Circuit invalidated the Eastern District's jury plan,[76] which forced the government to seek new indictments in many cases, including Bass's case, by a properly constituted grand jury. Bass and 14 co-defendants were indicted again on the cocaine charges in May 1998, and then, in December 1998, the grand jury returned another indictment against Bass, this time charging him with four counts of murder carrying the death penalty. This second superseding indictment charged John Bass with ordering the murders of his half-brother Patrick Webb and of Armenty Shelton, whom Bass had hired to kill Webb, and with murdering two other gang members, Darius Hawthorne and Derrick Poole.[77] The prosecution then filed notice that it would seek the death penalty on three homicide charges.

Bass's attorneys filed a flurry of motions, including one to dismiss the notice, alleging selective prosecution because the United States sought the death penalty against black defendants, like Bass, at a statistically higher rate than against white defendants. In the alternative the defense sought discovery of documents relating to how the attorney general decides to seek the death penalty. Under federal law, the decision to seek the death penalty in federal court was the sole responsibility of the U.S. attorney general, who was at that time John Ashcroft. In June 2001, Ashcroft had announced that he was dropping a policy adopted by Janet Reno of not seeking the death penalty in states which did not have capital punishment. Instead, he began to pursue the death penalty aggressively in such states, although with little success. When Bass's trial began, the United States had obtained only one death sentence in 17 cases tried in states without capital punishment.[78]

Following a hearing in October 2000, Judge Tarnow denied Bass's motion to dismiss, but he did grant the defendant's discovery request. On January 10, 2001, after the United States refused to comply, citing the work-product and deliberative-process privileges against discovery, he dismissed the death-penalty notice, holding that any such privileges were outweighed by the constitutional questions raised by the defense in the context of race and the death penalty. The government appealed, but the Sixth Circuit affirmed Judge Tarnow,[79] based largely on a survey conducted for the U.S. Justice Department,[80] which did, in fact, find significant statistical differences between white and black defendants charged with crimes eligible for the death penalty, differences principally caused by the decision by local U.S. attorneys as to which federal crime to ask the grand jury to charge defendants. The U.S. sought review by the Supreme Court, which, on June 28, 2002, summarily reversed the lower courts, holding that Bass had failed to present any evidence that white defendants similarly situated to him had been charged with non-capital crimes.[81]

During Bass's trial on the cocaine charges and the murders of Webb and Shelton, the principal testimony against the defendant was provided by former members of the Dog Pound. On August 11, the jury acquitted Bass of the murder of Webb but found him guilty of the other charges.[82] During the penalty phase of the trial, the defense presented evidence of Bass's horrific upbringing, amid poverty and violence, and argued that, even if spared the death penalty, Bass would die in jail. The prosecution pointed out the extreme brutality and callousness of Bass's crimes, but assistant U.S. attorney Michael Leibson did not directly call for the death penalty and did not attempt to contradict the evidence of Bass's upbringing. Instead, he told the jurors that, if they followed the judge's instructions, "any verdict that you reach will be the right one."[83] On August 14, the jury agreed unanimously that Bass should be sentenced to life in prison without the possibility of release.[84] Judge Tarnow imposed that sentence in November 2003, and Bass appealed unsuccessfully to the Sixth Circuit. The Supreme Court refused to consider his case.[85]

At the time of the penalty verdict, Judge Tarnow expressed his belief that this was a case that should have been tried in a state court. In fact, Bass had been convicted of state crimes before he was indicted in 1997, and he spent the intervening years in state custody. It can be argued that, but for the Ashcroft policy of pursuing the death penalty in non-death penalty states, Bass would have been tried for murder in Wayne County Circuit Court, would have been convicted, and would have received the same sentence meted out by the jury in federal court. It is also possible, though, that the county and state could not have invested the time and money that the federal government did to gather the evidence of the conspiracy and murders. As with most "what if" questions in history, the answer is unknowable. What is clear is that, although Mr. Ashcroft's death-penalty policy may have been useful in inducing guilty pleas, it ultimately produced very few death verdicts nationwide, none in the Eastern District of Michigan, and only one in the Western District.[86]

Notes

1. Judge Feikens's experience in 1961 was an exception of sorts, although technically Senator McNamara blocked President Kennedy's nomination of Feikens.

2. Similarly, three years passed between Judge O'Meara's assuming senior status and his replacement by Judge Goldsmith. At that, both Murphy and Goldsmith were fortunate—many nominees have given up waiting for confirmation in this politically charged era.

3. John Feikens oral history, 76.

4. Sadowski, Jeffrey A. "Patents, Automobiles, and the Eastern District of Michigan," *The Court Legacy*, no. 4 (December 1994), 1–4.

5. *Parker Rust Proof Co. v. Ford Motor Co*, 23 F.2d 502 (E.D. Mich. 1928).

6. E.g., Letter, Freeman to judges, regarding transfer of cases to Judge Gubow based on the "same formula," 14–20 percent from each, no cases pending more than three years; also no criminal cases or U.S. contract cases because Gubow had been U.S. attorney. Freeman Papers, September 23, 1968.

7. Seabrook, 19.

8. *Kearns v. Ford Motor Co.*, 114 F.R.D. 57 (E.D. Mich. 1987).

9. Seabrook, 24.

10. *Kearns v. Ford Motor Co.*, 114 F.R.D. 57 (E.D. Mich. 1987).

11. *Kearns v. Ford Motor Co.*, 114 F.R.D. 57, 68 (E.D. Mich. 1987).

12. *Kearns v. Chrysler Motors Corp.*, 32 F.3d 1541 (Fed. Cir. 1994), cert den'd, 514 U.S. 1032 (1995).

13. *Kearns v. General Motors Corp*, 31 F.3d 1178 (Fed. Cir. 1994).

14. *Kearns v. Wood Motors, Inc.*, 106 F.3d 427 (Fed. Cir. 1997); *Kearns v. Toyota*, 53 F.3d 345 (Fed. Cir. 1995).

15. 1 Stat. 414.

16. 16 Stat. 254.

17. *U.S. v. Wong Kim Ark*, 169 U.S. 649 (1898).

18. 1 Stat. 103.

19. Arthur J. Tuttle to Charles R. Dickerson, April 14, 1934, Topical Office Files, Aug. 1933–July 1937, Box 33, Tuttle Papers.

20. Chief Judge Gerald Rosen, *2009 State of the Court Message* (September 15, 2009), http://www.fbamich.org/Documents/stateofcourt2009.pdf. (Accessed 9/6/11).

21. Although this is a very notable case, I have chosen not to discuss it at length for a number of reasons. It is still an open case, for many years my former law firm represented parties to the case, one of my former partners was appointed and served until recently as the court's special master in the case, and the case has generated so much controversy and spawned so many related matters, both civil and criminal, that I simply cannot cover it in the space available here. This case deserves a book of its own.

22. 86 Stat. 816, as amended, 33 U.S.C. § 1251 et seq.

23. *U.S. v. John A. Rapanos*, Case No. 1:93-cr-20023-LPZ-1.

24. *U.S. v. Rapanos*, 895 F. Supp. 165 (E.D. Mich. 1995).

25. *U.S. v. Rapanos*, 115 F.3d 367 (6th Cir. 1997).

26. *U.S. v. Rapanos*, 235 F.3d 256 (6th Cir. 2000).

27. *Rapanos v. United States*, 533 U.S. 913 (2001).

28. *Solid Waste Agency of Northern Cook County v. U.S. Army Corps of Engineers*, 531 U.S. 159 (2001).

29. *U.S. v. Rapanos*, 16 Fed. Appx. 345 (6th Cir. 2001).

30. *U.S. v. Rapanos*, 190 F. Supp. 2d 1011 (E.D. Mich. 2002).

31. *U.S. v. Rapanos*, 339 F.3d 447 (6th Cir. 2003).

32. *Rapanos v. U.S.*, 541 U.S. 972 (2004).

33. *U.S. v. John A. Rapanos et al.*, Case No. 1:94-cv-10058 BC, renumbered 2:94-cv-70788-BAF-PJK after transfer to Judge Friedman.

34. *U.S. v. Rapanos*, 376 F.3d 629 (6th Cir. 2004).

35. *Rapanos v. U.S.*, 546 U.S. 932 (2005).

36. *Rapanos v. U.S.*, 547 U.S. 715 (2006).

37. Idem., 758.

38. Idem., 782.

39. "John Rapanos agrees to pay for Clean Water Act violations," Environmental Protection Agency press release, December 29, 2008, http://yosemite.epa.gov/opa/admpress.nsf/0/B029AB82BF92CD5F8525752E0072FC60. (Accessed 10/7/11)

40. *Court Compendium* (1977), Paper 8, 2.

41. Idem., 3.

42. Local Rule of the U.S. District Court for the Eastern District of Michigan 51.1.

43. Judge Rosen reported in his 2009 State of the Court presentation that, as of September 2009, "eight senior judges continue to contribute substantially to the work of the Court. Judges Cohn, Zatkoff, Duggan, Friedman and O'Meara receive cases at the same rate as district judges in active service. Senior Judges Feikens, Cook and Taylor are assigned cases between 50% and 75% of that of a district judge in active service." Rosen, *2009 State of the Court Message*, 1.

44. *Jennifer Gratz, et al. v. Lee Bollinger*, Case No. 2:97-cv-75231-PJD. The caption remained the same although the named defendants changed over the years. For example, plaintiffs initially named the university and LSA as defendants, but later amended their complaints to replace them with the legally correct defendant, the Board of Regents of the University of Michigan.

45. *Barbara Grutter v. Lee Bollinger, et al.*, Case No. 2:97-cv-75928-BAF.

46. 42 U.S.C. 2000d *et seq.*

47. Perry, 51–55.

48. *Hopwood v. Texas*, 84 F.3d 750 (5th Cir. 1996).

49. *Regents of the University of California v. Bakke*, 438 U.S. 265 (1978).

50. *Bakke*, 438 U.S. at 320, 98 S. Ct. 2733.

51. Perry, 56–61.

52. *Gratz v. Bollinger*, 183 F.R.D. 209 (E.D. Mich. 1998); Judge Friedman's opinion in *Grutter* was not published.

53. *Grutter v. Bollinger*, 188 F.3d 394 (6th Cir. 1999).

54. Local Rule 83.11(b)(2): "To promote docket efficiency, or to conform to the requirement of any case management plan adopted by the Court, or upon consent of the parties, or after notice and hearing, or in the interests of justice, the Chief Judge may order a civil case to be reassigned, but only with the consent of the Judge to whom the case was originally assigned and with the consent of the Judge to whom it is to be reassigned."

55. Local Rule 83.11(b)(7)(A): "Companion cases are those cases in which it appears that: (i) substantially similar evidence will be offered at trial, or (ii) the same or related parties are present, and the cases arise out of the same transaction or occurrence."

56. *Grutter v. Bollinger*, 16 F. Supp. 2d 797 (E.D. Mich. 1998).

57. 28 U.S.C. 136(e).

58. Local Rule 83.11(d)(1).

59. *Grutter v. Bollinger*, 122 F. Supp. 2d 811 (E.D. Mich. 2000).

60. *Grutter v. Bollinger*, 137 F. Supp. 2d 821 (E.D. Mich. 2001).

61. *Grutter v. Bollinger*, 137 F. Supp. 2d 874 (E.D. Mich. 2001).

62. *Grutter v. Bollinger*, 247 F.3d 631 (6th Cir. 2001).

63. *Gratz v. Bollinger*, 277 F.3d 803 (6th Cir. 2001).

64. *Grutter v. Bollinger*, 288 F.3d 732 (6th Cir. 2002).

65. *Id.*, at 810.

66. *Gratz v. Bollinger*, 539 U.S. 244 (2003). On January 31, 2007, Judge Duggan entered an order approving a settlement under which the university paid Ms. Gratz and Mr. Hamacher $10,000 each in return for a release of all liability and decertification of the class.

67. *Grutter v. Bollinger*, 539 U.S. 306 (2003). *Grutter* was closed by court order on March 22, 2004.

68. *Michigan Civil Rights Initiative v. Board of State Canvassers*, 268 Mich. App. 506 (2005).

69. *Operation King's Dream v. Connerly*, 2006 WL 2514115 (E.D. Mich. 2006). Plaintiffs appealed, but the Sixth Circuit dismissed the appeal in August 2007 because the election rendered their claims moot and because the court would not consider whether the new section of the Michigan constitution violated the U.S. constitution as the issue had not been raised before Judge Tarnow. *Operation King's Dream v. Connerly*, 501 F.3d 584 (6th Cir. 2007).

70. *Coalition To Defend Affirmative Action v. Granholm*, 2006 WL 3953321 (E.D. Mich. 2006).

71. *Coalition to Defend Affirmative Action v. Granholm*, 473 F.3d 237 (6th Cir. 2006).

72. *Coalition to Defend Affirmative Action v. Granholm*, 549 U.S. 1176 (2007).

73. *Coalition to Defend Affirmative Action v. Regents of University of Mich.*, 539 F. Supp. 2d 924 (E.D. Mich. 2008).

74. *Coalition to Defend Affirmative Action, Integration and Immigration Rights v. Regents of University of Michigan*, 592 F. Supp. 2d 948 (E.D. Mich. 2008).

75. *Detroit News*, August 2, 2003.

76. *United States v. Ovalle*, 136 F.3d 1092, 1109 (6th Cir.1998). Concerned that its jury panels contained insufficient African Americans, and after trying other remedies, the court constructed a jury selection plan under which one in five non-African Americans were removed randomly from the jury wheel. The Sixth Circuit found this method a violation of the Jury Selection and Service Act.

77. *U.S. v. Bass*, 460 F.3d 830 (6th Cir. 2006); *Detroit Free Press*, August 1, 2003.

78. *Detroit News*, August 15, 2003.

79. *U.S. v. Bass*, 266 F.3d 532 (6th Cir. 2001).

80. Department of Justice, "The Federal Death Penalty System: A Statistical Survey" (September 12, 2000).

81. *U.S. v. Bass*, 536 U.S. 862 (2002).

82. *Detroit News*, August 12, 2003.

83. *Detroit News*, August 14, 2003.

84. *Detroit News*, August 15, 2003.

85. *U.S. v. Bass*, 460 F.3d 830 (6th Cir. 2006), cert. den'd, 551 U.S. 1124 (2007).

86. See *United States v. Gabrion*, 517 F.3d 839 (6th Cir. 2008), cert. den'd, 129 S. Ct. 1905 (2009).

CHAPTER 17

Into the Future

As the district court for the Eastern District of Michigan moves into the second decade of the 21st century, it faces several challenges and concerns, some of which the court has addressed successfully, and others that are more difficult to deal with because the solutions are, to a large degree, out of the court's control. Computers and related technologies have transformed the ways in which the court performs its tasks, conducts legal research, and communicates with the public. However, the court is housed in a set of beautiful yet aging buildings that require constant maintenance, are cramped, and cannot easily meet increased security requirements for federal buildings. In 2002 and 2008, the court formally requested a new Detroit courthouse, or, at least, a new building annex to house active district court judges to meet design guide security requirements to conduct criminal trials. Because of budget restrictions, those requests have not been considered at this writing.

Caseloads, Trials, and Courtroom Usage

The numbers of cases filed in the court have, as we have seen, increased during the court's lifetime, to a degree that Judge Wilkins could likely never imagine. As recently as 1948, there were only 1,375 new civil and criminal cases filed, while 60 years later, in 2008, there were 5,930 cases. On the other hand, by one measure, cases filed per authorized district judge, the caseload of the district court barely changed during that period. The number of new civil and criminal cases filed, per authorized district judge, from 2001 to 2008 (383) is only slightly less than the average for all years since 1950 (394). As we have seen, though, those averages mask considerable year-to-year variation and do not reflect the profound changes in the subject matter and complexity of the cases that come before the district court.[1]

391

Congress has tried several times to stem the number of diversity cases, the traditional first target in any discussion of how to decrease caseloads, by raising the minimum amount in controversy required for such cases. In 1958, it was raised from $3,000 to $10,000 and in 1988, to $50,000. Although the sponsors of the latter increase predicted that Congress would not have to revisit the issue for three decades or more, in 1996, the amount was raised to $75,000 and in 2005, Congress imposed a separate requirement that damages sought in any diversity class action must aggregate more than $5,000,000.[2] The effectiveness of these changes has been questionable, as each increase has brought a temporary decrease in diversity filings that disappeared within a few years: nationally, 68,224 diversity cases were filed in 1988 and 102,585 in 2010.

One aspect of the court's business, though, has changed drastically, possibly forever: trials conducted. In 1919, even before Prohibition caused his docket to explode, Judge Tuttle complained, loudly and often, that he was engaged in trying cases six days per week, from early morning until late at night.[3] His papers reflect that the federal courthouse was teeming with humanity, bustling with attorneys and litigants, throughout every workday. In 1925, it appears from the records, that he and Judge Simons terminated 356 cases by trial.[4] From 1971 to 1980, the court averaged 45.5 completed trials per authorized judge, per year. In 1976 alone, the court's ten district judges conducted 580 civil and criminal trials and each spent, on average, 146 days in trial and another 41 days in court on matters related to pending cases.[5] By contrast, the Administrative Office of the United States Courts reported that between 2000 and 2010 the court averaged, each year, only 12 "trials completed" for each of the 15 authorized district judgeships. Actually, the true averages per judicial officer were lower because, although there was one vacant district judgeship during some of that period, the court also benefitted from five senior judges who volunteered to take on a full caseload and three others who carried between 50 percent and 75 percent of a full caseload. Consequently, a visitor to the courtrooms of today finds little teeming or bustling, and very few litigants or even attorneys.

It is undeniable that almost all U.S. district courts have experienced a decrease in trials in recent years. In 1925, there were more than 18,000 trials in district courts, but after Prohibition, trials declined along with filings. In 1965, there were 11,600 trials in district courts (38 per authorized judge). Increases in criminal and civil rights cases doubled the number of trials to 19,550 in 1976 (49 per authorized judge) in the 1970s. By 1990, the number of trials nationwide increased slightly to 20,700, but, because of the addition of hundreds of district judgeships, there were only 36 completed trials per judge in 1990. By 2005, the number of trials completed nationally again receded to 12,882, an average of 19 per authorized judge. But, even in this national decline in trials, between 1999 and 2008, the

Eastern District was consistently among the ten to 20 districts with the fewest number of completed trials. The court's annual average of trials completed per judge during that period (36) ranked it 41st of 95 districts, but on such a downward trend the Eastern District slipped to an average ranking in that category of 77 from 1988 to 1990. As we shall see, this trend has continued relentlessly so that the court had an average ranking of 81 from 1991 to 2000 and 79 from 2001 to 2010.

As with any statistic, these numbers need close attention. Part of the reason for the court's low ranking in trials is its low ranking in criminal case filings per authorized judge. Criminal cases are very unevenly distributed among district courts. In 2009, a third of the 74,108 criminal cases begun in district courts were filed in just five districts along the border with Mexico and principally involve immigration and, to a lesser degree, drugs.[6] From 1998 to 2009, the Eastern District ranked in the middle among all district courts in total case filings and weighted case filings, but was never higher than 77th in criminal felony cases filed and averaged 83rd, very close to the court's ranking for trials. In the Sixth Circuit in 2008, the Eastern District was sixth of nine districts in total criminal filings, ninth in felony filings per judge, and ninth in trials (civil and criminal) per judge. Apparently, fewer felony cases resulted in fewer trials. Furthermore, the number of filings and trials does not indicate how complicated the felony cases are or how long the trials. If the cases tried involve multiple defendants and complex claims, they likely required longer trials and more motions than trials of simple immigration cases.[7] This is particularly true when the U.S. attorney is trying major drug gangs on conspiracy and charges brought under the Racketeer Influenced and Corrupt Organizations Act.

Of course, courtrooms are used for more than just trials. In 2008, the Eastern District's courtrooms were the scene of 699 guilty pleas, although that is still only 46 for each of the 15 district judgeships, which means that, on average, each district judge accepted just one guilty plea per week, even without adjusting for the senior judges and magistrate judges who are involved in the plea process. The court was busier on the civil side, but not bustling. Of the total number of civil cases terminated in 2008, almost half, 1,933 cases, were terminated during or after pretrial, presumably by settlement or by a dispositive motion. However, if even half of those cases were terminated by motion (a very generous assumption), that still comes down to just over five cases per judge terminated each month. Visitors to the court buildings can sense the lack of public activity by the silence in public spaces. Because of its size, this is particularly evident in the Theodore Levin Courthouse. Although part of this silence and lack of people in the corridors can be attributed to the building's security measures, which discourage casual sightseers or court watchers, and to the absence of other federal agencies such as the Internal Revenue Service or Customs, which

Table 17.1   The Growth in the Number of Senior
District Judges

Year	All District Courts	Eastern District
1960	45	1
1990	224	5
2010	367	8

might attract larger numbers of citizens, there is also a sense that the facilities, and the judges, are not being used fully.

Like the dearth of trials, low overall courtroom usage is also common in district courts across the nation. A study conducted in 2007 by the Federal Judicial Center to determine courtroom use in a sample of 26 U.S. district courts (not including the Eastern District) found that, during the study period of 63 workdays, courtrooms assigned to a single district judge were used for trial on an average of 11 workdays, those assigned to a single senior judge on four workdays, and those assigned to a single magistrate judge on one workday. Over the survey period, the average amount of time in each workday courtrooms were used for case proceedings was 1.86 hours for courtrooms assigned to a single district judge, 0.77 hours for courtrooms assigned to a single senior judge, and 1.12 hours for courtrooms assigned to a single magistrate judge.[8]

The lack of trials and low courtroom usage are not a reflection on the work ethic of federal district judges. One of the hard truths of the judge business is that there are no rain-maker judges, nobody out glad-handing prospective litigants or taking them to lunch hoping to solicit more work. Judges can only work with the business that the U.S. attorney and private parties decide to bring to each court.[9] Likewise, judges cannot force parties to go to trial, and many believe strongly that, in civil cases at least, justice is often best served by settlements. In reality, though, the real caseload and trial statistics are even lower because they do not take into consideration the work done by senior district judges who comprise a substantial portion of the district court judiciary, although not all of them are active. Those who are classified as active might have as little as a half of a district judge's caseload.

All of this analysis does not change the fact, however, that in many districts, the outstanding legal skills of district judges are not fully utilized. Some critics have argued that it may be time to allow some judgeships to lapse, but it can also be argued that the court is in a temporary lull in the growth of its caseload and that it would be unwise to give up judgeships that a district might have to fight to get back. In any case, the value of judicial appointments as political tools (both as patronage and as support for the appointers' political policy) makes a decrease in judgeships very unlikely. Likewise, given the district courts' caseloads, the frequent call for Congress to withdraw their jurisdiction over diversity cases seems almost perverse.

Judicial Diversity

Diversity has been an important social and political concern since the beginning of the 20th century, although diversity, like justice, is a moving target, subject to a multitude of meanings and subjective analyses. When all district judge candidates were white men, diversity was measured by religion and national origin: the first Jewish judge (Simons, 1923), the first Catholic (O'Brien, 1931), the first Polish Catholic (Koscinski, 1945), the first Italian Catholic (DeMascio, 1971), and the first Hispanic Catholic (La Plata, 1985). The appointments of Judge McCree (1961) and Judge Kennedy (1970) showed that diversity had expanded to include race and gender, even as religion and national origin became less of a political factor. Of the district court's 61 judges, six have been African American (McCree, Keith, Cook, Taylor, Hood, and Roberts), and eight have been women (Kennedy, Boyle, Taylor, Hackett, Edmunds, Hood, Roberts and Battani). Although the presence of any women and African American judges at all is undeniable evidence of progress in diversity, only 11 of 43 appointments since 1961 have been to women and African Americans. At this writing, of the 14 judges filling the court's 15 authorized district judgeships (there is one vacancy), ten are white men, two are white women, two are African American women, and there are no African American men (indeed, the court has never had more than one male African American judge on the court at one time). Judicial appointments are, of course, out of the control of the court and the other judges and are, instead in the gift (as the English say) of politicians, the president and the Senate. As it happens, all of this court's African American judges were nominated by Democratic presidents, as were five of the women, but on the other hand, Judge Kennedy, the district's first woman judge, was nominated by President Nixon to the district court and by President Carter to the Sixth Circuit.

Conclusion

So, in the end, what can we say about the courts of the District and Eastern District of Michigan? They have certainly accomplished the role envisioned for them by the first Congress. They have provided, and continue to provide, a forum in which the United States can enforce its criminal and revenue laws, seek to recover moneys owed to it, and provide a unified body of admiralty law. The courts have also been a haven for out-of-state parties seeking to avoid local prejudice, although the existence of such prejudice may have become less likely. And, as Congress intended in 1789, the courts' judges have been the face of the federal government, first in Michigan as a whole and then in the Eastern District, for much of this period. However, those first congressmen would have been astounded at the scope of civil and criminal cases adjudicated in the district courts. That the federal government would pass laws criminalizing drug use and sale, requiring permits to drain private land, or setting the minimum wages of private employees, would have had them scratching their wigs, while the possibility that an individual might sue his or her state government in an inferior federal court would have caused outraged anti-federalists to shout "I told you so!"

It was the decision of Congress in 1875 to grant the circuit courts (and, later, the district courts) general federal-question jurisdiction (jurisdiction authorized by Article III, but lost in the horse trading of 1789) that began the courts' transformation from tribunals of rather narrow scope, concerned mainly with relatively few federal crimes, with admiralty libels, and with mundane commercial cases under their diversity jurisdiction, to what is the district court's most important role today, the first line of enforcement and protection of the Constitution and of federal statutes, even if those cases are a minority among the thousands filed in the Eastern District each year. In particular, as cases like *Marshall v. Hare, Milliken v. Bradley, Gratz v. Bollinger,* and *Grutter v. Bollinger* have shown, the district court has become the principal forum in which the constitutional and statutory civil rights of individuals, in suits against employers, landlords, state and local governments, and even against other branches of the federal government, are tested. Despite the fears of the anti-federalists, it is those cases that best justify the existence of inferior federal courts, including the U.S. District Court for the Eastern District of Michigan. Without the independent and talented judges of the court, with time to ponder the issues, it is unlikely that those cases could have been litigated and decided without suspicion of secret political motives and deals. Certainly the state courts made it very clear that they had no stomach for the issues involved in *Gratz* and *Grutter,* and it is highly unlikely that even the most sincere and courageous judges of Wayne County Circuit Court, if assigned *Milliken,* could have found the time, withstood the calumny, and remained in office long enough to make the best of the poor choices left to Judge DeMascio by the Supreme Court. Likewise, cases requiring long supervision of governmental operations or a large allocation of assets, such as in the prosecution of drug gangs and of governmental corruption, might well never have been attempted but for the assets and continuity provided by a federal court. That is the crucial role that the district court has played for a century and is likely to play for another century.

Notes

1. The bare numbers do not take into consideration the complexity of the cases or the amount of time the assigned judge allocated to each of them. A more sophisticated measure, weighted case filings per judge, was introduced by the Administrative Office of the U.S. Courts (AOUSC) in 1947. The AOUSC assigns a weight to different types of cases based on the amount of judicial time usually required, but weights have changed several times over the years, making year-to-year comparisons of less use than comparisons among district courts in any given year. Weighted filings are published in the AOUSC's annual publication, known first as *Management Statistics for United States Courts* and later titled *Federal Court Management Statistics*.

2. 72 Stat. 415 (1958), 102 Stat. 4606 (1988), 110 Stat. 3850 (1996), 119 Stat. 9 (2005).

3. e.g., Arthur J. Tuttle to John W. Warrington, March 31, 1919, Box 20, "Judge, Additional 1" file, Tuttle Papers.

4. According to the annual report of the attorney general in 1925, they closed 158 criminal cases by trial, and entered judgments in 198 civil trials (cases terminated otherwise than by dismissal or discontinuance, presumably most of them as the result of a trial).

5. *Court Compendium* (1977).

6. The Southern and Western Districts of Texas, the Southern District of California, and the Districts of Arizona and New Mexico.

7. Another variable, the number of defendants in each felony case, has only a minor effect, varying only between 1.9 and 1.5 over the last decade.

8. *Use of Courtrooms in U.S. District Courts*, Table 3, 19.

9. The U.S. attorney, in particular, is limited by budgets and priorities set elsewhere, and the amount of time and effort that office invests in a case may never show up in the court's statistics. A two-year investigation by a dozen FBI agents might result in a dozen indictments, but if the defendants are grouped in one or two cases and they all plead guilty, the record shows two cases begun and terminated, and no trials.

APPENDIX A

Chief Judges of the U.S. District Court for the Eastern District of Michigan

Arthur F. Lederle	1948–1959
Frank A. Picard	1959
Theodore Levin	1959–1967
Ralph M. Freeman	1967–1972
Frederick W. Kaess	1972–1975
Damon J. Keith	1975–1977
Cornelia G. Kennedy	1977–1979
John Feikens	1979–1986
Philip Pratt	1986–1989
James P. Churchill	1989
Julian A. Cook, Jr.	1989–1996
Anna D. Taylor	1996–1998
Lawrence P. Zatkoff	1999–2004
Bernard A. Friedman	2004–2009
Gerald E. Rosen	2009–

APPENDIX B

Succession of the Judges of the District and Eastern District of Michigan

I	I(A)	II	III	IV	V	VI
Wilkins	Simons	Moinet	O'Brien	Lederle	Picard	Freeman
Longyear		Levin	Thornton	Machrowicz	Kaess	Harvey
Brown		DeMascio	Keith	Kennedy	Guy	Suhrheinrich
Swan		Friedman	Boyle	Gilmore	Zatkoff	Edmunds
Angell			Woods	O'Meara	Cox	
Tuttle			Hood	Goldsmith		
Koscinski						
O'Sullivan						
Feikens						
Roth						
Churchill						
Cleland						

VII	VIII	IX	X	XI	XII	XIII	XIV	XV
McCree	Smith	Feikens	Pratt	Cohn	Newblatt	Taylor	LaPlata	Duggan
Gubow	Joiner	Gadola	Rosen	Lawson	Borman	Battani	Roberts	Murphy
Cook	Hackett	Ludington						
Tarnow	Steeh							

APPENDIX C

Clerks of the Courts of the District and Eastern District of Michigan

District of Michigan			
U.S. District Court		*U.S. Circuit Court*	
John Winder	1837–1848	John Winder	1837–1857
William D. Wilkins	1848–1857	William D. Wilkins	1857–1863
John Winder	1857–1863		

Eastern District of Michigan			
U.S. District Court		*U.S. Circuit Court*	
John Winder	1863–1870	William D. Wilkins	1863–1870
Darius J. Davison	1870–1904	Addison Mandell	1870–1882
Carrie Davison	1904–1911	Walter S. Harsha	1882–1909
Elmer W. Voorheis	1912–1937	Martin J. Cavanaugh	1909–1911
George M. Read	1937–1951		
Frank J. Dingell	1951–1959		
John J. Ginther	1959–1963		
Julius L. Kabatsky	1963–1964		
Frederick W. Johnson	1964–1973		
Henry R. Hanssen	1973–1978		
John P. Mayer	1979–1981		
Robert A. Mossing	1981–1989		
David Sherwood	1989–1990		

District Court Executive		*Chief of Court Operations*	
John P. Mayer	1981–1990	David Sherwood	1993–1997

District Court Administrator/ Clerk of the Court		*Deputy District Court Administrator*	
John P. Mayer	1990–1999	David J. Weaver	1998–1999
David J. Weaver	1999–	Mary E. Miers	1999–2006
		Libby Smith	2006–

Magistrates and Magistrate Judges of the Eastern District of Michigan

Name	Years of Service	Assigned Courthouse
Warren F. Krapohl	1971–1979	Flint/Bay City
Paul J. Komives*	1971–1997	Detroit
	1998–	Detroit
Barbara K. Hackett	1973–1984	Detroit
Chris E. Stith	1976–1980	Detroit
Irwin F. Hauffe, II**	1976–1977	Bay City
Harvey D. Walker**	1977–1983	Bay City
Thomas A. Carlson	1979–2003	Detroit
Lynn V. Hooe, Jr.	1981–1993	Detroit
	1994–1998	Detroit
Howard R. Grossman**	1981–1984	Detroit
Steven W. Rhodes	1981–1985	Detroit
Marc L. Goldman	1983–2001	Flint
Steven D. Pepe*	1983–2009	Detroit/Ann Arbor
Charles E. Binder	1984–	Bay City
Marcia G. Cooke	1984–1992	Detroit
Virginia M. Morgan	1985–2011	Detroit/Ann Arbor
Donald A. Scheer	1994–2010	Detroit
Wallace J. Capel, Jr.	1999–2006	Flint
R. Steven Whalen	2002–	Detroit
Mona K. Majzoub	2004–	Detroit
Michael Hluchaniuk	2008–	Flint
Mark A. Randon	2009–	Detroit
Laurie Michelson	2011–	Detroit
David R. Grand	2011–	Ann Arbor

* Continues Serving on Recall Status
** Part-time

United States Marshals in the District and Eastern District of Michigan

Territory of Michigan

Name	Dates of Service
Thomas Rowland	1815–1830
John L. Leib	1830
Peter Desnoyers	1831–1836

District of Michigan

Name	Dates of Service
Conrad Ten Eyck	1836–1841
Joshua Howard	1841–1844
Levi S. Humphrey	1844–1846
Austin E. Wing	1846–1850
Charles H. Knox	1850–1852
Hiram Becker	1852–1853
George W. Rice	1853–1857
Robert W. Davis	1857–1858
John S. Bagg	1858–1861
Charles Dickey	1861–1863

Eastern District of Michigan

Name	Dates of Service
Charles Dickey	1866–1867
Norman S. Andrews	1867–1869
Joseph R. Bennett	1869–1877
Salmon S. Matthews	1877–1882
Galusha Pennell	1882–1886
William Van Buren	1886–1893

Name	Dates of Service
Henry G. Blanchard	1893–1894
Eugene D. Winney	1894–1898
William R. Bates	1898–1906
Milo D. Campbell	1906–1914
Henry Behrendt	1914–1918
Frank T. Newton	1922–1931
John H. Grogan	1931–1934
John J. Barc	1934–1949
Joseph L. Wisniewski	1949–1954
Austin J. Connor	1954
Williams A.Nowicki	1954–1957
Clark W. Gregory	1957–1961
Orville H. Trotter	1961–1969
Anthony E. Rozman	1969–1977
Fred H. Paramore	1977–1978
Anthony Bertoni	1978–1990
James Stewart	1990–1994
James Douglas, Jr.	1994–2002
Robert M. Grubbs	2002–

District and Circuit Court Case Filings, 1837–2010

Year	Criminal	U.S. Civil	Private Civil	Total
1837	12	37	24	73
1838	26	41	285	352
1839	6	45	389	440
1840	16	49	278	343
1841	11	48	231	290
1842	7	39	185	231
1843	8	72	159	239
1844	30	34	127	191
1845	5	15	156	176
1846	9	24	142	175
1847	14	10	178	202
1848	10	12	148	170
1849	23	28	220	271
1850	19	74	161	254
1851	39	19	131	189
1852	2	1	156	159
1853	111	10	154	275
1854	17	13	185	215
1855	9	16	369	394
1856	14	7	316	337
1857	7	9	422	438
1858	3	2	504	509
1859	16	3	296	315
1860	60	10	267	337
1861	32	9	240	281
1862	25	47	168	240
1863	152	25	118	295
1864	115	47	115	277
1865	189	63	80	332

Year	Criminal	U.S. Civil	Private Civil	Total
1866	298	44	140	482
1867	480	84	126	690
1868	492	41	168	701
1869	316	54	163	533
1870	216	12	234	462
1871	221	24	259	504
1872	105	19	302	426
1873	135	15	390	540
1874	133	11	459	603
1875	91	4	558	653
1876	111	13	522	646
1877	175	5	482	662
1878	26	12	254	292
1879	45	13	249	307
1880	53	33	179	265
1881	103	10	356	469
1882	148	4	211	363
1883	81	6	397	484
1884	101	5	515	621
1885	81	49	422	552
1886	70	7	673	750
1887	99	97	433	629
1888	69	2	403	474
1889	121	16	221	358
1890	27	16	297	340
1891	86	2	418	506
1892	59	16	303	378
1893	74	6	312	392
1894	72	17	590	679
1895	166	28	327	521
1896	47	34	294	375
1897	40	53	280	373
1898	30	0	183	213
1899	30	9	181	220
1900	50	15	219	284
1901	50	50	188	288
1902	69	12	137	218
1903	80	14	205	299
1904	66	9	131	206
1905	86	6	137	229
1906	145	6	162	313
1907	33	5	134	172
1908	46	18	142	206
1909	73	58	125	256
1910	64	30	118	212
1911	47	21	29	97

Year	Criminal	U.S. Civil	Private Civil	Total
1912	75	29	170	274
1913	162	38	117	317
1914	125	60	161	346
1915	114	13	131	258
1916	118	16	141	275
1917	152	25	133	310
1918	334	8	107	449
1919	384	53	109	546
1920	556	30	109	695
1921	585	162	187	934
1922	651	104	211	966
1923	644	174	155	973
1924	945	274	159	1378
1925	1447	633	170	2250
1926	1361	688	149	2198
1927	1706	800	252	2758
1928	266	949	392	1607
1929	1831	1241	304	3376
1930	2386	1349	381	4116
1931	1463	1113	313	2889
1932	1610	1291	450	3351
1933	1415	1092	465	2972
1934	614	202	820	1636
1935	272	90	491	853
1936	678	313	807	1798
1937	591	188	890	1669
1938	575	162	925	1662
1939	554	200	1552	2306
1940	507	211	600	1318
1941	362	206	743	1311
1942	574	139	705	1418
1943	567	251	253	1071
1944	664	264	195	1123
1945	722	743	206	1671
1946	496	607	276	1379
1947	529	563	506	1598
1948	615	303	457	1375
1949	1027	413	485	1925
1950	738	907	503	2148
1951	751	724	526	2001
1952	631	810	560	2001
1953	709	445	535	1689
1954	622	357	611	1590
1955	659	496	651	1806
1956	584	659	686	1929
1957	674	519	639	1832

Year	Criminal	U.S. Civil	Private Civil	Total
1958	823	866	685	2374
1959	693	556	607	1856
1960	717	587	619	1923
1961	631	523	719	1873
1962	857	593	842	2292
1963	976	585	901	2462
1964	769	607	1100	2476
1965	622	677	958	2257
1966	625	753	901	2279
1967	725	586	984	2295
1968	717	412	986	2115
1969	633	637	1017	2287
1970	876	970	1154	3000
1971	1021	507	1333	2861
1972	1439	580	1352	3371
1973	1661	590	1431	3682
1974	1621	597	1601	3819
1975	1718	651	1890	4259
1976	1442	809	2181	4432
1977	1178	1064	2328	4570
1978	773	1018	2423	4214
1979	567	2242	2688	5497
1980	429	2442	3017	5888
1981	426	2016	3433	5875
1982	471	2160	4062	6693
1983	523	2494	4334	7351
1984	635	4331	4260	9226
1985	521	2529	4509	7559
1986	574	2129	4449	7152
1987	1283	1803	4506	7592
1988	605	2044	4769	7418
1989	555	1874	4040	6469
1990	626	1308	3516	5450
1991	952	1602	3508	6062
1992	740	3730	3457	7927
1993	793	2300	3580	6673
1994	708	2129	4449	7286
1995	622	1285	3553	5460
1996	688	1036	5123	6847
1997	587	1885	3635	6107
1998	648	2559	6556	9763
1999	575	3213	3650	7438
2000	602	2514	3526	6642
2001	525	1602	3440	5567
2002	576	1186	3791	5553
2003	697	877	3787	5361

Appendix F

Year	Criminal	U.S. Civil	Private Civil	Total
2004	619	826	3818	5263
2005	488	1228	4644	6360
2006	554	1014	4358	5926
2007	488	1406	4209	6103
2008	496	1057	4377	5930
2009	470	1002	4007	5479
2010	545	1080	3996	5621

Bibliographical Notes

The greatest part of writer's time is spent in reading, in order to
write; a man will turn over half a library to make one book.
                                                    —*Dr. Samuel Johnson.*

Case Statistics

Throughout this book, I refer to, and draw conclusions from, the number
of cases of various types commenced, terminated, and pending each year
from 1837 to the present—i.e., the caseload of the district and circuit
courts. Unless I note otherwise, my sources for those statistics are:

1837–1912 Docket books (also known as "calendars"), journals, and case
   files of the district and circuit courts of the District and Eastern District
   of Michigan;
1871–1944 Annual reports of the attorney general of the United States;
1939–1992 Annual reports of the director of the Administrative Office of
   the United States Courts (AOUSC), contained in the reports of the Proceedings of the Judicial Conference of the United States;
From 1995 Statistical tables for the federal judiciary;
From 1994 Federal judicial caseload statistics;
From 1983 Federal court management statistics.

When statistics of the U.S. courts are presented by year, I mean:

1837–1871 Calendar year
1872–present Fiscal year, ending on June 30, so that 1995 means the
   year July 1, 1994–June 30, 1995.

The primary source materials, the courts' original records, are maintained at the Great Lakes Division of the National Archives and Records
Administration, 7358 South Pulaski Road, Chicago, IL 60629-5898. The
two sets of annual reports are available at law libraries (usually in incomplete sets) and online at websites such as the University of Michigan's

MIRLYN (http://www.lib.umich.edu/) or the Law Library Microform Consortium (LLMC) (http://llmc.com/). The more recent compilations of the statistical tables for the federal judiciary, federal judicial caseload statistics, and federal court management statistics are published online at the United States' courts website (http://www.uscourts.gov/Statistics.aspx). Compilations for most earlier years are available in hard copy and on LLMC.

Finding the numbers, though, is not the end of the hunt. Unfortunately, both primary and secondary source materials must be approached with caution, especially those from the 19th century. As to the primary sources, in his 1886 annual report, U.S. attorney general Augustus H. Garland warned about the appalling condition of records kept by the U.S. courts: "The condition of the records of several United States courts makes it as difficult to know what the records are as, in some instances, it would be to restore a lost record by substitution of other records, files, and papers relating to the subject-matter of the records, from the fact that the records and files of certain courts, [over] the accumulation of years, have been thrown into disorder and cast heedlessly into heaps in rooms for storage in such a confused way that the papers are to all intents and purposes lost, their availability being impossible because of their condition."[1] Thanks to the efforts of 180 years of clerks in Michigan, and to the careful stewardship of the staff of the Great Lakes Division, most of the primary sources of caseload information for Michigan's federal courts have survived. These consist of original case files, journals (day-to-day records of sessions of the court), calendar and docket books (a record, organized chronologically, of each case commenced in the court and of papers filed and orders entered therein), and a variety of other records such as order books, judgment books, and attorney rolls. Using them is complicated, though, by the number of different record sets and by differences in how succeeding clerks kept them. From 1789 through 1911, each federal judicial district had two trial courts, circuit and district, which, for most of that time, had separate clerks who each kept their own records. Moreover, Congress did not tell either set of clerks how to keep track of the papers in their charge.[2] For the district court for the District of Michigan, clerk John Winder opened a calendar book in 1837, entitled *U.S. Cases*, but in which he recorded all of the court's civil and criminal cases from 1837 to 1846 and the criminal and U.S. civil cases until 1857, numbered from 1 to 409. In 1846, he opened a second calendar, entitled *Admiralty*, in which he recorded the district court's private civil cases, not all of which involved admiralty and maritime law, again starting with "case 1." In 1851, William D. Wilkins, the son of District Judge Ross Wilkins, who had taken over the district clerkship in 1848, opened a criminal calendar for the district court, starting with "case 1." In 1857, after Winder and Wilkins switched jobs, Winder closed the district court's *U.S. Cases* calendar and began recording U.S. civil cases in the *Admiralty* calendar. When Congress divided the district into Eastern and Western Districts in 1863, Winder opened a new criminal docket for the Eastern District, again starting with "case 1," but he did not open a new *Admiralty* docket, rather the one opened in 1846 remained in use until 1907, when the Justice Department ordered it merged into a general civil docket.

For the circuit court for the District of Michigan, Winder opened three separate calendars in 1838, divided into criminal cases, cases in chancery (including cases filed by both the United States and private parties), and cases at law (all of which were private cases). These dockets continued open until the circuit court was abolished at the end of 1911, but there were also other calendars in which the clerks recorded bits and pieces. There is a habeas corpus calendar book that was apparently used for that purpose a few times from 1890 to 1902 and that also contains a mystery written in John Winder's elegant early-19th century hand: docket sheets for private civil cases, numbered 1 through 17, apparently commenced in February through May, 1837, but which do not appear in the main calendars. There are also a few other specialized calendars, including one for cases filed under the short-lived Bankruptcy Act of 1841. The usefulness of the calendars is further compromised by clerks who went back in a book to use up blank spaces rather than start a new book (which they would have had to pay for), by clerks who did not count correctly, and by clerks who failed to provide standard information.

Annual reports to Congress by the attorney general and the director of the AOUSC are based on data supplied by the clerks and district/U.S. attorneys in each district, but during the 19th and the first decades of the 20th centuries there was no system to verify the numbers. As District Judge Arthur J. Tuttle of the Eastern District pointed out in 1940, the director of the new AOUSC, as compiler of the data, and senior judges as users, had to trust in the good faith of clerks and deputy clerks: "1. All the Senior Circuit Judges know about the statistics for the Northern division is what you tell them. 2. All you know about that subject is what Judge Read, the Clerk of the Court at Detroit, tells you and reports to you. 3. All that Judge Read knows about that is what Clarence Pettit, the Deputy Clerk at Bay City, reports to him."[3]

In the Eastern District, reliance on the clerks may have been seriously misplaced during the last decades of the 19th century because a comparison of the numbers reported with the dockets suggests that somebody, perhaps District Court Clerk Darius Davison, was not operating in good faith. For example, the number of private non-U.S. cases reported as pending at the end of the year rose from an already unlikely 1,049 in 1876 to 4,478 in 1895, a figure almost 14 times the number of new cases of that type filed, and more than 22 times the number terminated, in 1895. The primary sources began to explain what had happened. First, clerks of both courts had, since before the Civil War, failed to enter orders formally closing hundreds of inactive and abandoned cases, which were then reported as pending. These recording errors were not cured until 1913, after Judge Arthur Tuttle and Clerk Elmer Voorheis assumed responsibility for the court and entered orders entered closing thousands of cases.

Another example of suspect numbers is found in the reports of the number of admiralty cases commenced and terminated. The attorney general reported that from 1876 to 1879, the Eastern District was second only to the Southern District of New York in the number of admiralty cases filed and disposed of. According to those reports, District Judge Henry Billings Brown was buried under an avalanche of 2,725 new admiralty cases, of which he heroically closed 2,083. Now, Judge Brown was a nationally acknowledged expert on admiralty, and admiralty litigators may have been attracted to his court, but he was also lazy and chronically ill, so it seems unlikely that he could have endured such a caseload. In fact, the district court's *Admiralty* calendar recorded only 560 civil cases of all kinds commenced during those three years, including at least 25 U.S. civil cases. Just as troubling is the fact that, from 1877 to 1886, the Eastern District did not report the total number of private civil cases pending, only the subset of admiralty cases, and even those numbers are not consistent with each other. The calendar reveals that instead of the 400, or 600, or 800 new admiralty cases reported to (and by) the attorney general, after 1876 there were never more than 200 filed in a year, and after 1900 there were never more than 100. Until another calendar surfaces in which, for some reason, the clerks recorded the missing admiralty cases, I will rely instead on a manual count of cases from the *Admiralty* docket.

All references to population are based on the decennial censuses of the U.S. Census Bureau. Those censuses did not include Native Americans until 1860.

Legal Citations

For legal citations (laws and cases), I have followed the accepted citation practices familiar to attorneys. Opinions in a case are referred to in the endnotes either by the case's court number (e.g., Civil No. 23456) and the date of decision, or, if published, by the place of publication, with the volume number preceding an abbreviation of the series name, followed by the first page and then, in parentheses, by the name of the court and the year of the opinion. For example, 234 F. Supp. 2d 1245 (E.D. Mich. 2005) means the opinion can be found at page 1245 of volume 234 of the *Federal Supplement*, Second Series, and that it is a decision of the district court for the Eastern District of Michigan, issued in 2005. Other series cited include the *U.S. Supreme Court Reports* (U.S.); the *Federal Reporter*, First, Second, and Third Series (F., F.2d and F.3d, respectively); *Federal Cases* (F. Cas.) and the *Federal Rules Decisions* (F.R.D.). Decisions by the old circuit courts, designated C.C. and the abbreviation for the district (as in C.C. E.D. Mich.), should not be confused with decisions by the U.S. Circuit Courts of Appeals, which are designated by the circuit number alone (e.g., 6th Cir.) or, for the Federal Circuit, by Fed. Cir.

Specific lawsuits, or cases, are referred to by the names of the first named plaintiff versus the first-named defendant, so that a case brought by plaintiffs Steve Smith and Emily Smythe against John Jones and Jane Ghones is referred to as *Smith v. Jones*, or, sometimes, just *Smith.*

Statutes, laws passed by Congress, also called Acts of Congress, are identified by their popular names (e.g., the Fugitive Slave Acts, the Evarts Act), and by the volume and page of the *U.S. Statutes at Large* in which they first appeared. For example, 24 Stat. 2356 means that the text of the statute begins at page 2356 of volume 24. Since the 19th century, those laws have, from time to time, been organized and reorganized, by subject matter, into codes. I have avoided referring to those codifications because they do not contain the original text of the laws but only as they were in effect at a particular time. The rare exception is for laws as they appear in the current codification, known as the United States Code (U.S.C.), using the volume and page system.

Finally, the U.S. Constitution, our true national treasure, I cite by article (art.), section (§) and clause (cl.).

Sources

Primary Sources

Bentley Historical Library, Ann Arbor, Michigan
Longyear, John W., Papers
Tuttle, Arthur J., Papers

Clarence M. Burton Historical Collection, Detroit, Michigan, Public Library
Cass, Lewis, Papers
Catlin, George B., Papers
Howard, Jacob M., Papers
Wilkins, Ross, Papers

National Archives and Records Administration, College Park, Maryland
Records Group 59, State Department Records

National Archives and Records Administration, Great Lakes Region, Chicago, Illinois
Records Group 21, Records of the District Courts of the United States
District of Michigan
Eastern District of Michigan

Papers of the Historical Society for the U.S. District Court for the Eastern District of Michigan

Archives of the Genesee Historical Collections at the University of Michigan-Flint, Flint, Michigan
Freeman, Ralph M., Papers

Books

Allen, W. B., and Gordon Lloyd. *The Essential Antifederalist*. Lanham, MD: University Press of America, 1985.
Bald, F. Clever. *Michigan in Four Centuries*. New York: Harper and Row, 1961.
Barnett, Leroy, and Roger Rosentreter. *Michigan's Early Military Forces: A Roster and History of Troops Activated Prior to the American Civil War*. Detroit, MI: Wayne State University Press, 2003.
Baugh, Joyce A. *The Detroit School Busing Case:* Milliken v. Bradley *and the Controversy over Desegregation*. Lawrence: University of Kansas Press, 2011.
Bay City Board of Trade. *Bay City Illustrated*. Gregory Printing, 1898.
Bennett, James V. *I Chose Prison*. New York: Alfred A. Knopf, 1970.
Bicentennial Committee of the Judicial Conference of the United States. *History of the Sixth Circuit: A Bicentennial Project*. Washington, D.C., 1977.
Bierce, Lucius Verus. *Historical Reminiscences of Summit County*. Akron, OH: T. and H. G. Canfield, 1854.
Bingay, Malcolm. *Detroit is my Home Town*. Indianapolis, IN: Bobbs-Merrill, 1946.
Blume, William W. *Transactions of the Supreme Court of Michigan, 1805–1836*. 6 vols. Ann Arbor: University of Michigan Press, 1935–1940.
Boardman, Fon W. *America and the Progressive Era: 1900–1917*. New York: Henry Z. Walck, 1970.
Brown, Henry Billings. *Cases on the Law of Admiralty*. St. Paul, MN: West Publishing, 1896.
———. *Reports of Admiralty and Revenue Cases Argued and Determined in the Circuit and District Courts of the United States for the Western Lake and River Districts [1856-1875]*. New York: Baker, Voorhis, 1876.
Burton, Clarence M. *1819–72 Court and Other Records Copied from Original Files*. Detroit, MI: Burton Historical Collection, 1910–1911.
———. *Detroit Free Press Digest, 1858*. Detroit, MI: Burton Historical Collection, n.d.
Catlin, George B. *The Story of Detroit*. 2nd and rev. ed. Detroit, MI: The Detroit News, 1926.
Chandler, Alfred D., Jr. *The Visible Hand: The Managerial Revolution in American Business*. Cambridge, MA: Belknap Press, 1977.
Charlesworth, Hector Willoughby. *The Canadian Scene, Sketches: Political and Historical*. Toronto, ON: Macmillan, 1927.
Common Council of Detroit. *Journal of the Proceedings of the Common Council of the City of Detroit: From the Time of its First Organization, September 21, A.D. 1824*. n.p., n.d., ca. 1843.
Conkling, Alfred. *Treatise on the Organization, Jurisdiction and Practice of the Courts of the United States*. Albany, NY: William A. Gould, 1831.

Cooper, Phillip J. *Hard Judicial Choices: Federal District Court Judges and State and Local Officials*. New York: Oxford University Press, 1988.

Daniels, Roger. *Coming to America: A History of Immigration and Ethnicity in American Life*. 2nd ed. New York: Harper Perennial, 2002.

Douglas, R. Alan. *Uppermost Canada: The Western District and the Detroit Frontier*. Detroi, MI: Wayne State University Press, 2001.

Dunbar, Willis F., and George S. May. *Michigan: A History of the Wolverine State*. rev. ed. Grand Rapids, MI: Eerdmans Publishing, 1980.

Faber, Don. *The Toledo War: The First Michigan-Ohio Rivalry*. Ann Arbor: University of Michigan Press, 2008.

Farmer, Silas. *History of Detroit and Wayne County and Early Michigan*. 3rd ed. Detroit, MI: Silas Farmer, 1890.

Farrell, Margaret G. *Special Masters*. Federal Judicial Center, Washington, D.C., n.d., http://ftp.resource.org/courts.gov/fjc/sciam.4.spec_mast.pdf.Federal Judicial Center. *The Use of Courtrooms in U.S. District Courts: A Report to the Judicial Conference on Court Administration & Case Management*. Washington, D.C., July 18, 2008.

Ferguson, Niall. *The Ascent of Money: A Financial History of the World*. New York: Penguin Press, 2008.

Ferry, W. Hawkins. *The Buildings of Detroit: A History*. Detroit, MI: Wayne State University Press, 1968.

Fine, Sidney. *Frank Murphy: The Detroit Years*. Ann Arbor: University of Michigan Press, 1975.

———. *Frank Murphy: The New Deal Years*. Chicago: University of Chicago Press, 1979.

Fish, Peter Graham. *The Politics of Federal Judicial Administration*. Princeton, NJ: Princeton University Press, 1973.

Fitzpatrick, Doyle. *The King Strang Story: The Vindication of James J. Strang, the Beaver Island Mormon King*. Lansing, MI: National Heritage, 1970.

Flippin, William S. *Reports of Cases Argued and Determined in the Circuit and District courts of the United States for the Sixth Judicial Circuit*. Chicago, IL: Callahan, 1881–1882.

Frankfurter, Felix, and James M. Landis. *The Business of the Supreme Court: A Study in the Federal Judicial System*. New York: MacMillan, 1928.

Friedman, Lawrence M. *A History of American Law*. 3rd ed. New York: Simon and Schuster, 2005.

Friendly, Henry J. *Federal Jurisdiction: A General View*. New York: Columbia University Press, 1973.

Gage, Beverly. *The Day Wall Street Exploded: A Story of America in Its First Age of Terror*. New York: Oxford University Press, 2009.

Geib, George W., and Donald B. Kite, Sr. *Federal Justice in Indiana: The History of the United States District Court of the Southern District of Indiana*. Indianapolis, IN: Indiana Historical Society, 2007.

George, Sister Mary Carl. *The Rise and Fall of Toledo, Michigan: The Toledo War!* Lansing, MI: Michigan Historical Commission, 1971.

Glazer, Lawrence M. *Wounded Warrior: the Rise and Fall of Michigan Governor John Swainson*. East Lansing: Michigan State University Press, 2010.

Goulden, Joseph C. *The Benchwarmers: the Private World of the Powerful Federal Judge*. New York: Ballantine, 1976.

Halberstam, David. *The Fifties*. New York: Villard Books, 1993.

Hale, Matthew. *Hale's History of Pleas of the Crown*. London, 1800.

Hall, Kermit L. *The Politics of Justice: Lower Federal Judicial Selection and the Second Party System, 1829–61*. Lincoln: University of Nebraska Press, 1979.

Hall, Kermit L., and Peter Karsten. *The Magic Mirror: Law in American History*. 2nd ed. New York: Oxford University Press, 2008.

Harsha, Walter S. *Rules of the United States Courts for the Districts of Michigan; Rules of the United States Supreme Court and of the United States Circuit Court of Appeals for the Sixth Circuit*. Detroit, MI: n.p., 1891.

Hershock, Martin J. *The Paradox of Progress: Economic Change, Individual Enterprise, and Political Culture in Michigan, 1837–1878*. Athens: Ohio University Press, 2003.

Hoffmann, Charles. *The Depression of the Nineties: An Economic History*. Santa Barbara, CA: Greenwood Press, 1970.

Johnson, Christopher H. *Maurice Sugar: Law, Labor, and the Left in Detroit, 1912–1950*. Detroit, MI: Wayne State University Press, 1988.

Johnston, James Dale. *Johnston's Detroit City Directory and Advertising Gazetteer of Michigan*. Detroit, MI, 1859.

———. *Johnston's Detroit City Directory and Advertising Gazetteer of Michigan for 1856–57*. Detroit, MI, 1856.

———. *Johnston's Detroit City Directory and Advertising Gazetteer of Michigan, With an Appendix Carefully Revised*. Detroit, MI, 1861.

Kavieff, Paul R. *The Violent Years: Prohibition and the Detroit Mobs*. Fort Lee, NJ: Barricade Books, 2001.

Kent, Charles A. *Memoir of Henry Billings Brown: Late Justice of the Supreme Court of the United States*. New York: Duffield and Co., 1915.

Kilar, Jeremy W. *Michigan's Lumbertowns: Lumbermen and Laborers in Saginaw, Bay City, and Muskegon, 1870–1905*. Detroit, MI: Wayne State University Press, 1990.

La Plata, George. *From the Barrio to the Bench*. New York: Vantage Press, 2008.

Leake, Paul. *History of Detroit*. Chicago: Lewis Publishing, 1912.

Lee, Antoinette J. *Architects to the Nation: The Rise and Decline of the Supervising Architect's Office*. New York: Oxford University Press, 2000.

Ludecke, Kurt G. W. *I Knew Hitler: The Story of a Nazi Who Escaped the Blood Purge*. New York: Charles Scribner's Sons, 1937.

Lumley, Darwyn H. *Breaking the Banks in Motor City: The Auto Industry, the 1933 Detroit Banking Crisis and the Start of the New Deal*. Jefferson, NC: McFarland, 2009.

Lyles, Kevin L. *The Gatekeepers: Federal District Courts in the Political Process*. Westport, CN: Praeger, 1997.

McLean, John. *Reports of Cases Argued and Decided in the Circuit Court of the United States for the Seventh Circuit*. 6 vols. Cincinnati, OH: H. W. Darby, 1840–1856.

Mason, Philip P. *Rum Running and the Roaring Twenties: Prohibition on the Michigan-Ontario Waterway*. Detroit, MI: Wayne State University Press, 1995.

Meints, Graydon M. *Michigan Railroads and Railroad Companies*. East Lansing, MI: Michigan State University Press, 1992.

Messinger, I. Scott. *Order in the Courts: A History of the Federal Clerk's Office.* Washington, D.C.: Federal Judicial Center: 2002.

Mills, James Cooke. *History of Saginaw County, Michigan.* Saginaw, MI: Seeman and Peters, 1918.

Moore, John Bassett. *A Treatise on Extradition and Interstate Rendition.* 2 vols. Boston, MA: The Boston Book Company, 1891.

Nevins, Allan. *War for the Union: The Organized War, 1863–1864.* New York: Charles Scribner's Sons, 1971.

Newberry, John Stoughton. *Reports of Admiralty Cases, argued and adjudged in the District Courts of the United States.* Albany, NY: Banks, Gould and Co., 1857.

Okrent, Daniel. *Last Call: The Rise and Fall of Prohibition.* New York: Scribner, 2010.

Palmer, Friend. *Early Days in Detroit.* Detroit, MI: Hunt and June, 1906.

Parker, Ross. *Carving Out the Rule of Law: The History of the United States Attorney's Office in Eastern Michigan, 1815–2008.* Bloomington, IN: Author House, 2009.

Parks, Robert J. *Democracy's Railroads: Public Enterprise in Jacksonian Michigan.* Port Washington, NY: Kennicat Press, 1972.

Patterson, James T. *Grand Expectations: The United States, 1945–1974.* New York: Oxford University Press, 1997.

Perry, Barbara A. *The Michigan Affirmative Action Cases.* Lawrence: University of Kansas Press, 2007.

Pienkos, Donald E. *PNA: A Centennial History of the Polish National Alliance of the United States of North America.* Boulder, CO: East European Monographs, 1984.

Purcell, Edward A., Jr. *Litigation and Inequality: Federal Diversity Jurisdiction in Industrial America, 1870–1958.* New York: Oxford University Press, 1992.

Read, Anthony. *The World on Fire: 1919 and the Battle with Bolshevism.* New York: W. W. Norton, 2008.

Read, George M. *A Monograph of the United States Courts in Michigan Compiled by the Office of the Clerk.* n.p., 1941.

Reed, George I. *Bench and Bar of Michigan: A Volume of History and Biography.* Chicago, IL: Century Publishing and Engraving, 1897.

Rogers, Howard S. *History of Cass County.* Cassopolis, MI: H. W. Mansfield, 1875.

Ross, Robert Budd. *Early Bench and Bar of Detroit: From 1805 to the End of 1850.* Detroit, MI: Richard M. Joy and Clarence M. Burton, 1907.

———. *The Patriot War.* Detroit, MI: The Detroit News, 1890.

Ross, Robert Budd, and George Catlin. *Landmarks of Wayne County and Detroit.* Detroit, MI: Evening News Association, 1898.

Rowland, C. K., and Robert A. Carp. *Politics and Judgment in the Federal District Courts.* Lawrence: University of Kansas Press, 1996.

Seabrook, John. *Flash of Genius: And Other True Stories of Invention.* New York: St. Martin's Griffin, 2008.

Shove, J. *Shove's Business Advertiser and Detroit Directory for 1852–53.* Detroit, MI: Free Press Book and Job Office, 1852.

Smith, Michael O. "The First Michigan Colored Infantry: A Black Regiment in the Civil War." Master's thesis, Wayne State University, 1987.

Smith, R. Grant. *From Saginaw Valley to Tin-Pan Alley: Saginaw's Contribution to American Popular Music, 1890–1955.* Detroit, MI: Wayne State University Press, 1998.

Speek, Vickie Cleverley. *"God Has Made Us a Kingdom": James Strang and the Midwest Mormons.* Salt Lake City, UT: Signature Books, 2006.

Stanton, Mary. *From Selma to Sorrow: The Life and Death of Viola Liuzzo.* Athens: University of Georgia Press, 1998.

Stevens, Kenneth R. *Border Diplomacy: The Caroline and McLeod Affairs in Anglo-American-Canadian Relations, 1837–1842.* Tuscaloosa: University of Alabama Press, 1989.

Surrency, Erwin C. *History of the Federal Courts.* New York: Oceana Publications, 1987.

Taylor, Paul. *Orlando M. Poe: Civil War General and Great Lakes Engineer.* Kent, OH: Kent State University Press, 2009.

Theller, Edward A. *Canada in 1837–38: by Historical Facts, the Causes of the Late Attempted Revolution and Its Failure; the Present Condition of the People, Their Future Prospects, Together with the Personal Adventures of the Author.* 2 vols. Philadelphia, PA: Henry F. Anners, 1841.

Twain, Mark, and Charles Dudley Warner. *The Gilded Age: A Tale of Today.* New York: American Publishing Co., 1873.

United States Department of Justice. *The Federal Death Penalty System: A Statistical Survey.* September 12, 2000.

United States District Court for the Eastern District of Michigan. *Court Compendium.* 1977.

Van Noord, Roger. *Assassination of a Michigan King: The Life of James Jesse Strang.* Ann Arbor, MI: University of Michigan Press, 2000.

Western Historical Company. *History of St. Clair County, Michigan.* 1883.

Wheeler, Russell R. *Origins of the Elements of Federal Court Governance.* Washington, D.C.: Federal Judicial Center, 1992.

Wheeler, Russell R., and Cynthia Harrison. *Creating the Federal Judicial System.* 2nd ed. Federal Judicial Center, 1994.

Wickham, Chris. *The Inheritance of Rome: A History of Europe from 400 to 1000.* New York: Viking Penguin, 2009.

Widmer, Ted. *Martin Van Buren.* New York: Henry Holt, 2005.

Williams, Alpheus S. *The Civil War Letters of General Alpheus S. Williams: From the Cannon's Mouth.* Milo Quaife, ed. Detroit, MI: Wayne University Press and Detroit Historical Society, 1959.

Wilson, James R. *No Ordinary Crime: An Authentic Tale of Justice Influenced by War Hysteria.* Swartz Creek, MI: Broadblade Press, 1989.

Wolicki, Dale Patrick. *The Historic Architecture of Bay City, Michigan.* Bay City, MI: Bay County Historical Society, 1998.

Woodford, Frank B. *Father Abraham's Children: Michigan Episodes in the Civil War.* 2nd ed. Detroit, MI: Wayne State University Press, 1999.

Wynbrandt, James. *The Excruciating History of Dentistry: Toothsome Tales & Oral Oddities from Babylon to Braces.* New York: St. Martin's Press, 1998.

Zelden, Charles L. *Justice Lies in the District: The U.S. District Court, Southern District of Texas.* College Station, TX: Texas A&M Press, 1993.

Zunz, Olivier. *The Changing Face of Inequality.* Chicago, IL: University of Chicago Press, 1982.

Articles

Brazer, Marjorie Cahn. "Feudalism on the Frontier." *Michigan History* 69, no. 3 (May/June 1985): 32.

Broad, Trevor. "Forgotten Man in a Tumultuous Time: The Gilded Age as Seen by United States Supreme Court Associate Justice Henry Billings Brown." *Michigan Journal of History* (Winter 2005).

Chardavoyne, David G. "The Northwest Ordinance and Michigan's Territorial Heritage." *The History of Michigan Law.* Paul Finkelman and Martin J. Hershock, eds. Athens: Ohio University Press, 2006.

———. "The *U.S.S. Michigan:* The U.S. Navy's First Iron Warship." *The Court Legacy* 11, no. 3 (September 2003).

———. "The Federal Trial of James Jesse Strang." *The Court Legacy* 11, no. 2 (June 2003).

———. "Intemperate Habits and Appetites: Temperance Laws in Early Michigan." *The Court Legacy* 13, no. 2 (September 2005): 8.

Christie, Judy. "Bay City and Its Courthouses." *The Court Legacy* 13, no. 1 (February 2005): 1.

Cohn, Avern L., and John P. Mayer. "Winding Up *Bradley v. Milliken.*" *The Court Legacy* 16, no. 2 (June 2009).

Collins, Michael G. "Before *Lochner*–Diversity Jurisdiction and the Development of General Constitutional Law." *Tulane Law Review* 74 (March 2000): 1263.

Damren, Samuel C., "*Milliken v. Bradley I* On Remand: The Impossible Assignment." *The Court Legacy* 16, no. 1 (February 2009).

———. "The Keith Case." *The Court Legacy* 11, no. 4 (November 2003).

Dawe, Alison M. "The Eastern District Courthouse, circa 1897, and the 'Million Dollar Courtroom.'" *The Court Legacy* 9, no. 1 (September 2001).

Dise, John H., Jr. "The First Session and First Local Rules." *The Court Legacy* 11, no. 1 (February 2003).

———. "She Didn't Accept the Evil System: From Selma to Ann Arbor, 1965 to 1983." *The Court Legacy* 10, no. 2 (November 2002).

Engelmann, Larry D. "A Separate Peace: The Politics of Prohibition Enforcement in Detroit, 1920–1930." *Detroit in Perspective: A Journal of Regional History* 1, no. 1 (Autumn 1972).

Foschio, Leslie G. "A History of the Development of the Office of United States Commissioner and Magistrate Judge System." *Federal Courts Law Review*, no.4 (December 1999).

Fox, Cynthia G. "Income Tax Records of the Civil War Years." *Prologue Magazine* (Winter 1986), http://www.archives.gov/publications/prologue/1986/winter/civil-war-tax-records.html.

Graham, Mary C., and Marian J. Martyn. "Millard Fillmore, George C. Bates, and James Jesse Strang: Why Michigan's Only King Was Tried in Federal Court." *The Court Legacy* 11, no. 2 (June 2003).

Grams, Grant W. "Karl Respa and German Espionage in Canada During World War One." *Journal of Military and Strategic Studies* 8, no. 1 (Fall 2005).

Hall, Kermit L. "Andrew Jackson and the Judiciary: The Michigan Territorial Judiciary as a Test Case, 1828–1832." *Michigan History* 59 (Fall 1975).

———. "Judicial Power and Independence in Early Michigan." *The Court Legacy* 5, no. 1 (Spring 1997).

Huff, Jennifer A. "'The Only Feasible Desegregation Plan,' *Milliken v. Bradley* and Judge Roth's Order for Cross-District Busing." *The Court Legacy* 15, no. 2 (May 2008).

Heron, Matthew, and Matthew Dawson. "Port Huron Federal Building." Parts 1 and 2. *The Court Legacy* 12, no. 2 (June 2004): 9; 13, no. 1 (February 2005): 10.

Jones, Alan. "Thomas M. Cooley and the Michigan Supreme Court: 1865–1885." *American Journal of Legal History* 10 (1966): 98–99.

Keve, Paul W. "The House of Correction That Detroit Built." *The Court Legacy* 7, no. 1 (April 1999).

Kiern, Lawrence I. "War and the Law in Detroit, 1917-1919." (Ph.D. diss.. University of Connecticut, 1996), http://digitalcommons.uconn.edu/dissertations/AAI9717516.

Kundinger, Matthew. " Racial Rhetoric: The *Detroit Free Press* and Its Part in the Detroit Race Riot of 1863." *Michigan Journal of History* (Winter 2006).

Leaming, Margaret A. "An Occurrence at Milan–Michigan's Last Execution," *The Court Legacy*. no. 3 (April 1994): 1.

Lindquist, Charles A. "The Origin and Development of the United States Commissioner System." *American Journal of Legal History* 14 (January 1970).

McCabe, Peter G. "The Federal Magistrate Act of 1979." *Harvard Journal on Legislation* 16 (1979): 343.

Marty, Debian. "The Kentucky Raid: Lessons from Practical Abolitionism." Paper presented at the Borderlands III Underground Railroad Conference, September 16–18, 2004.

Mendenhall, T. C. and A. A. Graham. "Boundary Line Between Ohio and Indiana, and Between Ohio and Michigan." *Ohio Archaeological and Historical Quarterly* 4 (1896): 147.

Miller, Peggy. "Truth, Justice, and the Military Way." *The Court Legacy*, no. 2 (October 1993).

Morey, Charles R. "The Fine Arts in Higher Education." *A University Between Two Centuries: Proceedings of the 1937 Celebration of the University of Michigan*, Wilfrid B. Shaw ed. Ann Arbor: University of Michigan Press, 1937.

O'Neill, Stephen C. "Why Are Judges' Robes Black?" *The Court Legacy* 11, no. 1 (February 2003): 5.

Parker, Ross. "'It's not fair . . . ,' Vincent Chin's Last Words." *The Court Legacy* 14, no. 4 (November 2007).

Purcell, Edward A., Jr. "Reconsidering the Frankfurtian Paradigm: Reflections on Histories of Lower Federal Courts." *Law & Social Inquiry* 24 (Summer, 1999): 679.

Rohr, Marc. "Communists and the First Amendment: The Shaping of Freedom of Advocacy in the Cold War Era." *San Diego Law Review* 28 (1999): 1.

Runyan, John R. "*Milliken v. Bradley I*: The Struggle to Apply *Brown v. Board of Education* in the North." *The Court Legacy* 15, no. 3 (September 2008).

Sadowski, Jeffrey A. "Patents, Automobiles, and the Eastern District of Michigan," *The Court Legacy*, no. 4 (December 1994).

Sarafa, Derek J. "Michigan Lawyers in History–Judge Cornelia G. Kennedy: First Lady of the Michigan Judiciary." *Michigan Bar Journal* (July 2000): 850.

Shepherd, Frederick J. "The Johnson's Island Plot." *Publications of the Buffalo Historical Society* 9 (1906): 1–52.

Sherwood, John C. "One Flame in the Inferno: The Legend of Marshall's 'Crosswhite Affair.'" *Michigan History* 73 (March/April 1989): 40.

Smith, Arthur L., Jr. "Kurt Lüdecke: The Man Who Knew Hitler." *German Studies Review* 26, no. 3 (October 2003): 597.

Titone, Julie. "Raised to Love the Law: A Conversation with Judge Cornelia Kennedy." Unpublished essay, copy located in Sixth Circuit Archives, Cincinnati, Ohio.

Veselenak, Aaron J. "Arthur J. Tuttle: 'Dean of the Federal Bench.'" *The Court Legacy* 7, no. 2 (September 1999): 6–11.

———. "Making Legal History–The Execution of Anthony Chebatoris." *The Court Legacy* 6, no. 2 (Fall 1998): 7.

Wilson, Benjamin C. "Kentucky Kidnappers, Fugitives, and Abolitionists in Antebellum Cass County, Michigan." *Michigan History* 60, no. 4 (Winter 1976).Woeste, Victoria Saker. "Detroit's Trial of the Century: *Sapiro v. Ford*, 1927." *The Court Legacy* 8, no. 2 (September 1999).

———. "Insecure Equality: Louis Marshall, Henry Ford, and the Problem of Defamatory Antisemitism, 1920–1929," *The Journal of American History* 91, no. 3 (December 2004).

Yzenbaard, John H. "The Crosswhite Case." *Michigan History* 53, no. 2 (Summer 1969): 131.

Chief Judge Gerald Rosen, *2009 State of the Court Message* (September 15, 2009), http://www.fbamich.org/Documents/stateofcourt2009.pdf.

Newspapers, Magazines, and Journals

Ann Arbor News
Bay City Daily Tribune
Bay City Sunday Times
Bay City Times
Bay City Times and Tribune
Bay City Times Press
Buffalo Daily Courier (New York)
Chicago Daily Tribune
Covington Journal (Kentucky)
Detroit Daily Advertiser
Detroiter
Detroit Evening Journal
Detroit Free Press
Detroit Journal
Detroit Post
Detroit Tribune
Detroit News
Evening Press (Bay City)
Evening Independent (St. Petersburg Florida)
Flint Journal
Ludington Daily News (Michigan)
Manchester Enterprise (Michigan)
Marshall Statesman (Michigan)
Michigan Socialist

Midland Daily News (Michigan)
Time
Wage Earner (Detroit)

Notes

1. Annual report of the attorney general of the United States (1886), p. 17.

2. The Process Act of 1789, 1 Stat. 93, directed clerks to copy state law for the form of the papers the court issued, but Congress said nothing about how the clerks were to organize and index those papers.

3. Arthur J. Tuttle to Will Shafroth, October 21, 1940, AOUSC file, Box 35, Tuttle Papers.

Index

425